Alexander Roberts, James Sir Donaldson

The writings of Clement of Alexandria

Ante-Nicene Christian Library, Volume 4

Alexander Roberts, James Sir Donaldson

The writings of Clement of Alexandria
Ante-Nicene Christian Library, Volume 4

ISBN/EAN: 9783742854506

Manufactured in Europe, USA, Canada, Australia, Japa

Cover: Foto ©ninafisch / pixelio.de

Manufactured and distributed by brebook publishing software (www.brebook.com)

Alexander Roberts, James Sir Donaldson

The writings of Clement of Alexandria

Works Published by T. & T. Clark, Edinburgh.

Ante-Nicene Christian Library.

A COLLECTION OF ALL THE WORKS OF THE FATHERS OF THE CHRISTIAN CHURCH, PRIOR TO THE COUNCIL OF NICÆA,

EDITED BY THE

REV. ALEXANDER ROBERTS, D.D.,
AUTHOR OF 'DISCUSSIONS ON THE GOSPELS,' ETC.;

AND

JAMES DONALDSON, LL.D.,
AUTHOR OF 'A CRITICAL HISTORY OF CHRISTIAN LITERATURE AND DOCTRINE, FROM THE DEATH OF THE APOSTLES TO THE NICENE COUNCIL,' AND RECTOR OF THE ROYAL HIGH SCHOOL, EDINBURGH.

The First Four Volumes:—THE APOSTOLIC FATHERS, in One Volume; JUSTIN MARTYR and ATHENAGORAS, in One Volume; TATIAN, THEOPHILUS, and the CLEMENTINE RECOGNITIONS, in One Volume; and CLEMENT OF ALEXANDRIA, Volume First, are now ready.

Full Prospectuses on Application.

The Subscription to the Series is at the rate of 21s. for Four Volumes when paid in advance (or 24s. when not so paid), and 10s. 6d. each Volume to Non-Subscribers.

'We give this series every recommendation in our power. The translation, so far as we have tested it, and that is pretty widely, appears to be thoroughly faithful and honest; the books are handsomely printed on good paper, and wonderfully cheap. . . . . . The work being done so well, can any one wonder at our hoping that the Messrs. Clark will find a large body of supporters?'—*Literary Churchman.*

'The work of the different translators has been done with skill and spirit. To all students of Church history and of theology these books will be of great value. . . . . . . We must add, also, that good print and good paper help to make these fit volumes for the library.'—*Church and State Review.*

'We promise our readers, those hitherto unaccustomed to the task, a most healthy exercise for mind and heart, if they procure these volumes and study them.'—*Clerical Journal.*

'For the critical care with which the translations have been prepared, the fulness of the introductory notices, the completeness of the collection, the beauty and clearness of the type, the accuracy of the indexes, they are incomparably the most satisfactory English edition of the Fathers we know.'—*Freeman.*

'It will be a reproach to the age if this scheme should break down for want of encouragement from the public.'—*Watchman.*

'The translations in these two volumes, as far as we have had opportunity of judging, are fairly executed.'—*Westminster Review.*

Works Published by T. & T. Clark,

'There is everything about these volumes to recommend them, and we hope they will find a place in the libraries of all our ministers and students.'—*English Independent.*

'The translation is at once good and faithful.'—*Ecclesiastic.*

'The translations are, in our opinion, and in respect of all places that we have carefully examined, thoroughly satisfactory for exact truth and happy expressiveness; and the whole business of the editing has been done to perfection.'—*Nonconformist.*

'The entire undertaking, as revealed in this instalment, is nobly conceived. .... We can most heartily congratulate the editors on this noble commencement of their voluminous responsible undertaking, and on the highly attractive appearance of these volumes; and we most heartily commend them to the notice of all theological students who have neither time nor opportunity to consult the original authorities.'—*British Quarterly Review.*

'The whole getting up of the work deserves warm commendation, and we conclude by again recommending it to notice, and expressing the hope that it will attain the wide circulation that it well deserves.'—*Record.*

'This series ought to have a place in every ministerial and in every congregational library, as well as in the collections of those laymen, happily an increasing number, interested in theological studies.'—*Christian Spectator.*

'If the succeeding volumes are executed in the same manner as the two now before us, the series will be one of the most useful and valuable that can adorn the library of the theological student, whether lay or cleric.'—*Scotsman.*

'The editing is all that it should be. The translation is well executed, perspicuously and faithfully, so far as we have examined. . . . . . There is nothing in English to compete with it. Not only all ministers, but all intelligent laymen who take an interest in theological subjects, should enrich their libraries with this series of volumes.'—*Daily Review.*

MESSRS. CLARK have the honour to include in the Subscription List, amongst other distinguished names, both of Clergy and Laity—

> His Grace the Archbishop of Canterbury.
> His Grace the Archbishop of York.
> His Grace the Archbishop of Armagh.
> The Right Rev. the Bishop of Winchester.
> The Right Rev. the Bishop of London.
> The Right Rev. the Bishop of Oxford.
> The Right Rev. the Bishop of Gloucester and Bristol.
> The Right Rev. the Bishop of Ely.
> The Right Rev. the Bishop of St. David's.
> The Right Rev. the Bishop of Kilmore.
> The Right Rev. the Bishop of Meath.
> The Right Rev. the Bishop of Barbadoes.
> The Right Rev. Bishop Eden of Moray.
> The Right Rev. Bishop Wordsworth of St. Andrews.
> The Rev. Principal, Cuddesdon College.
> The Rev. President, Trinity College, Oxford.
> The Rev. Canon Mansel, Christ Church.
> The Rev. Canon Robinson, Bolton Abbey.
> His Grace the Duke of Argyll.
> His Grace the Duke of Buccleuch.
> The Right Hon. the Marquis of Bute.
> The Right Hon. the Earl of Strathmore.
> The Right Hon. the Lord Justice Clerk.

38, George Street, Edinburgh.

Books for the Library of Clergymen and Educated Laymen.

Clark's Foreign Theological Library.

ANNUAL SUBSCRIPTION, ONE GUINEA (PAYABLE IN ADVANCE), FOR FOUR VOLUMES, DEMY 8VO.

*** *When not paid in advance, the retail bookseller is entitled to charge 24s.*

THE following are the Contents of each of the Series. Each Work may be had separately at the price within parentheses.

*** A SELECTION of Twelve Volumes from First Series will be supplied at the Subscription Price of Three Guineas; or Twenty Volumes from First and Second Series at the Subscription Price of Five Guineas; or of Thirty-two Volumes from First, Second, and Third Series for Eight Guineas (or a larger number at same ratio).

The following may be added to, or substituted for the same number of Volumes in, such a selection:—

    Macdonald's Introduction to the Pentateuch. 2 Volumes.
    Hengstenberg's Egypt and the Books of Moses. 1 Volume.
    Ackerman on the Christian Element in Plato. 1 Volume.
    Robinson's Greek Lexicon of the New Testament. 1 Volume.

FIRST SERIES.
Twenty-nine Volumes. Subscription Price, £7, 12s. 6d.

Hengstenberg's Commentary on the Psalms. 3 Volumes. (£1, 13s.)
Shedd's History of Christian Doctrine. 2 Volumes. (£1, 1s.)
Gieseler's Compendium of Ecclesiastical History. 5 Volumes. (£2, 12s. 6d.)
Neander's General Church History. 9 Volumes. (£2, 11s. 6d.)
Olshausen on the Gospels and Acts. 4 Volumes. (£2, 2s.)
Olshausen on the Romans. (10s. 6d.)
Olshausen on the Corinthians. (9s.)
Olshausen on the Galatians, Ephesians, Colossians, and Thessalonians. (10s. 6d.)
Olshausen on Philippians, Titus, and Timothy. (10s. 6d.)
Olshausen and Ebrard on the Hebrews. (10s. 6d.)
Havernick's General Introduction to the Old Testament. (10s. 6d.)

SECOND SERIES.
Twenty Volumes. Subscription Price, £5, 5s.

Stier on the Words of the Lord Jesus. 8 Volumes. (£4, 4s.)
Hengstenberg's Christology of the Old Testament. 4 Volumes. (£2, 2s.)
Ullmann's Reformers before the Reformation. 2 Volumes. (£1, 1s.)
Gerlach's Commentary on the Pentateuch. 1 Volume. (10s. 6d.)
Keil on Kings and Chronicles. 2 Volumes. (£1, 1s.)
Baumgarten's Apostolic History. 3 Volumes. (£1, 7s.)

[*Over.*

Works Published by T. & T. Clark, Edinburgh.

Foreign Theological Library—*continued.*

THIRD SERIES.

Twenty Volumes (1859-60-61-62-63). Subscription Price, £5, 5s.

N.B.—A single Year's Books (except in the case of the current Year) cannot be supplied separately. Non-subscribers, price 10s. 6d. each Volume, with exceptions marked.

⁂ The following is the order of Publication, but any Two Years or more can be had at Subscription Price :—

1st Year (1859).

Kurtz on Old Covenant Dispensation. 3 Volumes.
Stier on the Words of the Risen Saviour, and on the Epistle of St. James. 1 Vol.

2d Year (1860).

Hengstenberg on Ecclesiastes. 1 Volume. (9s.)
Tholuck on St John. 1 Volume. (9s.)
Tholuck on the Sermon on the Mount. 1 Volume.
Ebrard on Epistles of John. 1 Volume.

3d Year (1861).

Lange on St. Matthew's Gospel. Volumes I. and II.
Dorner on Person of Christ. Division I., Vol. I.; and Division II., Vol. I.

4th Year (1862).

Dorner on Person of Christ. Division I., Volume II.
Dorner on Person of Christ. Division II., Volume II.
Lange on Matthew and Mark. Volume III.
Oosterzee on St. Luke. Edited by Dr Lange. Volume I. (9s.)

5th Year (1863).

Oosterzee on St. Luke. Edited by Dr Lange. Vol. II. (Completion.) (9s.)
Dorner on Person of Christ. Division II., Volume III.
Kurtz on the Old Testament Sacrifices.
Ebrard on the Gospel History.

FOURTH SERIES.

1st Year (1864).

Lange, Commentary on the Acts of the Apostles. 2 Volumes.
Keil and Delitzsch, Commentary on the Pentateuch. Volumes I. and II.

2d Year (1865).

Hengstenberg on the Gospel of St. John. 2 Volumes.
Keil and Delitzsch on the Pentateuch. Volume III.
Keil and Delitzsch on Joshua, Judges, and Ruth.

3d Year (1866).

Keil and Delitzsch on Samuel. 1 Volume.
Keil and Delitzsch on Job. 2 Volumes.
Martensen's System of Christian Doctrine. 1 Volume.

4th Year (1867).

First Issue, now ready—
Delitzsch's System of Biblical Psychology.
Delitzsch's Commentary on Isaiah. Volume I.

The remaining Volumes for this Year will be—
Delitzsch on Isaiah, Volume II.; and probably
Auberlen on Divine Revelation.

Subscribers' Names received by all Booksellers.

EDINBURGH: T. AND T. CLARK.
LONDON (for Non-subscribers only): HAMILTON, ADAMS, AND CO.

Works Published by T. & T. Clark, Edinburgh.

Works Recently Published.

In demy 8vo, price 10s. 6d.,
THE DOCTRINE OF JUSTIFICATION.

An Outline of its History in the Church, and of its Exposition from Scripture, with Special Reference to Recent Attacks on the Theology of the Reformation.

By JAMES BUCHANAN, D.D.,
Professor of Divinity, New College, Edinburgh; Author of 'Analogy as a Guide to Truth and an Aid to Faith.'

In demy 8vo, price 9s.,
AN EXPOSITION OF THE EPISTLE OF JAMES,
In a Series of Discourses.
By the Rev. JOHN ADAM, Aberdeen.

In demy 8vo, price 10s. 6d.,
ECCE DEUS:
Essays on the Life and Doctrine of Jesus Christ.

'The production of a clever, sincere, religious mind. . . . . . The style is decidedly scholarlike, forcible, and pithy.'—*London Review.*

'Finer sentences than those we have quoted, we make bold to say, are not found even in Jeremy Taylor.'—*Daily Review.*

In crown 8vo, price 4s.,
REPRESENTATIVE RESPONSIBILITY:
A Law of the Divine Procedure in Providence and Redemption.
By Rev. HENRY WALLACE, Londonderry.

'The author shows a mind practised in philosophical analysis, and is fully abreast of all our recent literature on both sides of this difficult question.'—*Daily Review.*

In crown 8vo, price 5s.,
THE CHURCH:
Its Origin, its History, its Present Position.
From the German of Drs. LUTHARDT, KAHNIS, and BRÜCKNER, Professors of Theology, Leipsic.

'A finer theme for popular and instructive discourse it is not easy to have; and in the illustration of this theme there is much in this volume of suggestive truth, finely and impressively described.'—*Freeman.*

In crown 8vo, price 4s.,
THE ROMISH DOCTRINE OF THE IMMACULATE CONCEPTION.
Traced from its Source.
By Dr. E. PREUSS, Principal of Friedrich-Wilhelm's Gymnasium at Berlin.
Translated by GEORGE GLADSTONE.

In crown 8vo, price 5s. 6d.,
THE FATHERHOOD OF GOD,
And its Relation to the Person and Work of Christ, and the Operations of the Holy Spirit.

By the Rev. CHARLES H. H. WRIGHT, British Chaplain at Dresden.

ANTE-NICENE

CHRISTIAN LIBRARY:

TRANSLATIONS OF
THE WRITINGS OF THE FATHERS

DOWN TO A.D. 325.

EDITED BY THE

REV. ALEXANDER ROBERTS, D.D.,

AND

JAMES DONALDSON, LL.D.

VOL. IV.

CLEMENT OF ALEXANDRIA.

VOL. I.

EDINBURGH:
T. AND T. CLARK, 38, GEORGE STREET.

MDCCCLXVII.

MURRAY AND GIBB, EDINBURGH,
PRINTERS TO HER MAJESTY'S STATIONERY OFFICE.

THE WRITINGS

OF

CLEMENT OF ALEXANDRIA.

TRANSLATED BY

THE REV. WILLIAM WILSON, M.A.,
MUSSELBURGH.

EDINBURGH:
T. & T. CLARK, 38, GEORGE STREET.
LONDON: HAMILTON & CO.   DUBLIN: JOHN ROBERTSON & CO.
MDCCCLXVII.

CONTENTS.

	PAGE
INTRODUCTORY NOTICE,	11

EXHORTATION TO THE HEATHEN.

CHAP.
I. Exhortation to abandon the Impious Mysteries of Idolatry for the Adoration of the Divine Word and God the Father, ... 17
II. The Absurdity and Impiety of the Heathen Mysteries and Fables about the Birth and Death of their Gods, . 26
III. The Cruelty of the Sacrifices to the Gods, . . 48
IV. The Absurdity and Shamefulness of the Images by which the Gods are worshipped, ... 52
V. The Opinions of the Philosophers respecting God, . 66
VI. By Divine Inspiration Philosophers sometimes hit on the Truth, ... 69
VII. The Poets also bear Testimony to the Truth, . . 73
VIII. The True Doctrine is to be sought in the Prophets, . 76
IX. That those grievously sin who despise or neglect God's gracious Calling, ... 80
X. Answer to the Objection of the Heathen, that it was not right to abandon the Customs of their Fathers, . 85
XI. How great are the Benefits conferred on Man through the Advent of Christ, ... 100
XII. Exhortation to abandon their Old Errors and listen to the Instructions of Christ, ... 106

THE INSTRUCTOR.

BOOK I.

I. The Office of the Instructor, ... 113
II. Our Instructor's Treatment of our Sins, . . . 115
III. The Philanthropy of the Instructor, . . . 118

CHAP.		PAGE
IV.	Men and Women alike under the Instructor's Charge,	121
V.	All who walk according to Truth are Children of God,	122
VI.	The name "Children" does not imply Instruction in Elementary Principles,	131
VII.	Who the Instructor is, and respecting His Instruction,	149
VIII.	Against those who think that what is just is not good,	155
IX.	That it is the Prerogative of the same Power to be beneficent and to punish justly; also, the Manner of the Instruction of the Logos,	164
X.	That the same God, by the same Word, restrains from Sin by threatening, and saves Humanity by exhorting,	174
XI.	That the Word instructed by the Law and the Prophets,	179
XII.	The Instructor characterized by the severity and benignity of Paternal Affection,	181
XIII.	Virtue rational, Sin irrational,	184

BOOK II.

I.	On Eating,	186
II.	On Drinking,	200
III.	On Costly Vessels,	211
IV.	How to conduct ourselves at Feasts,	215
V.	On Laughter,	219
VI.	On Filthy Speaking,	222
VII.	Directions for those who live together,	225
VIII.	On the use of Ointments and Crowns,	230
IX.	On Sleep,	240
X.	Quænam de procreatione liberorum tractanda sint,	244
XI.	On Clothes,	255
XII.	On Shoes,	264
XIII.	Against excessive Fondness for Jewels and Gold Ornaments,	266

BOOK III.

I.	On the True Beauty,	273
II.	Against Embellishing the Body,	276
III.	Against Men who Embellish themselves,	284
IV.	With whom we are to Associate,	292
V.	Behaviour in the Baths,	296
VI.	The Christian alone Rich,	298
VII.	Frugality a good Provision for the Christian,	301
VIII.	Similitudes and Examples a most important part of right Instruction,	304

CHAP.	PAGE
IX. Why we are to use the Bath,	308
X. The Exercises suited to a good Life,	310
XI. A Compendious View of the Christian Life,	313
Clothes,	313
Ear-rings,	315
Finger-rings,	315
The Hair,	317
Painting the Face,	319
Walking,	324
The Model Maiden,	325
Amusements and Associates,	325
Public Spectacles,	326
Religion in Ordinary Life,	327
Going to Church,	328
Out of Church,	329
Love, and the Kiss of Charity,	329
The Government of the Eyes,	330
XII. Continuation, with Texts from Scripture,	332
Prayer to the Pædagogus,	342
A Hymn to Christ the Saviour,	343
To the Pædagogus,	346

THE MISCELLANIES; OR, STROMATA.

BOOK I.

I. Preface—The Author's Object—The Utility of Written Compositions,	349
II. Objections to the Number of Extracts from Philosophical Writings in these Books, Anticipated and Answered,	360
III. Against the Sophists,	362
IV. Human Arts, as well as Divine Knowledge, proceed from God,	364
V. Philosophy the Handmaid of Theology,	366
VI. The Benefit of Culture,	371
VII. The Eclectic Philosophy paves the way for Divine Virtue,	374
VIII. The Sophistical Arts useless,	376
IX. Human Knowledge necessary for the Understanding of the Scriptures,	379
X. To Act well of greater consequence than to Speak well,	381

CHAP.		PAGE
XI.	What is the Philosophy which the Apostle bids us shun?	384
XII.	The Mysteries of the Faith not to be divulged to All,	388
XIII.	All Sects of Philosophy contain a Germ of Truth,	389
XIV.	Succession of Philosophers in Greece,	391
XV.	The Greek Philosophy in great part derived from the Barbarians,	395
XVI.	That the Inventors of other Arts were mostly Barbarians,	401
XVII.	On the saying of the Saviour, "All that came before Me were thieves and robbers,"	406
XVIII.	He illustrates the Apostle's saying, "I will destroy the wisdom of the wise,"	410
XIX.	That the Philosophers have attained to some portion of Truth,	413
XX.	In what respect Philosophy contributes to the comprehension of Divine Truth,	418
XXI.	The Jewish Institutions and Laws of far higher Antiquity than the Philosophy of the Greeks,	421
XXII.	On the Greek Translation of the Old Testament,	448
XXIII.	The Age, Birth, and Life of Moses,	450
XXIV.	How Moses discharged the Part of a Military Leader,	455
XXV.	Plato an Imitator of Moses in Framing Laws,	459
XXVI.	Moses rightly called a Divine Legislator, and, though inferior to Christ, far superior to the great Legislators of the Greeks, Minos and Lycurgus,	461
XXVII.	The Law, even in Correcting and Punishing, aims at the Good of Men,	464
XXVIII.	The Fourfold Division of the Mosaic Law,	467
XXIX.	The Greeks but Children compared with the Hebrews,	469

INTRODUCTORY NOTICE.

TITUS FLAVIUS CLEMENS, the illustrious head of the Catechetical School at Alexandria at the close of the second century, was originally a pagan philosopher. The date of his birth is unknown. It is also uncertain whether Alexandria or Athens was his birthplace.[1]

On embracing Christianity, he eagerly sought the instructions of its most eminent teachers; for this purpose travelling extensively over Greece, Italy, Egypt, Palestine, and other regions of the East.

Only one of these teachers (who, from a reference in the *Stromata*, all appear to have been alive when he wrote[2]) can be with certainty identified, viz. Pantænus, of whom he speaks in terms of profound reverence, and whom he describes as the greatest of them all. Returning to Alexandria, he succeeded his master Pantænus in the catechetical school, probably on the latter departing on his missionary tour to the East, somewhere about A.D. 189.[3] He was also made a presbyter of the church, either then or somewhat later.[4] He continued to teach with great distinction till A.D. 202, when the persecution under Severus compelled him to retire from Alexandria. In the beginning of the reign of Caracalla we find him at Jerusalem, even then a great resort of Christian, and especially clerical, pilgrims. We also hear of him travelling to Antioch, furnished with a letter of recommendation by Alexander bishop of Jerusalem. The close of his career

[1] Epiph. *Hær.* xxxii. 6.   [2] *Strom.* lib. i. c. v.
[3] Eusebius, *Hist. Eccl.* vi. 6.
[4] Hieron. *Lib. de Viris illustribus*, c. 38; Ph. *Bibl.* 111.

is covered with obscurity. He is supposed to have died about A.D. 220.

Among his pupils were his distinguished successor in the Alexandrian school, Origen, Alexander bishop of Jerusalem, and, according to Baronius, Combefisius, and Bull, also Hippolytus.

The above is positively the sum of what we know of Clement's history.

His three great works, *The Exhortation to the Heathen* (λόγος προτρεπτικὸς πρὸς "Ελληνας), *The Instructor*, or *Pædagogus* (παιδαγωγός), *The Miscellanies*, or *Stromata* (Στρωματεῖς), are among the most valuable remains of Christian antiquity, and the largest that belong to that early period.

The Exhortation, the object of which is to win pagans to the Christian faith, contains a complete and withering exposure of the abominable licentiousness, the gross imposture and sordidness of paganism. With clearness and cogency of argument, great earnestness and eloquence, Clement sets forth in contrast the truth as taught in the inspired Scriptures, the true God, and especially the personal Christ, the living Word of God, the Saviour of men. It is an elaborate and masterly work, rich in felicitous classical allusion and quotation, breathing throughout the spirit of philosophy and of the gospel, and abounding in passages of power and beauty.

The *Pædagogus*, or *Instructor*, is addressed to those who have been rescued from the darkness and pollutions of heathenism, and is an exhibition of Christian morals and manners,—a guide for the formation and development of Christian character, and for living a Christian life. It consists of three books. It is the grand aim of the whole work to set before the converts Christ as the only Instructor, and to expound and enforce His precepts. In the first book Clement exhibits the person, the function, the means, methods, and ends of the Instructor, who is the Word and Son of God; and lovingly dwells on His benignity and philanthropy, His wisdom, faithfulness, and righteousness.

The second and third books lay down rules for the regulation of the Christian, in all the relations, circumstances, and actions of life, entering most minutely into the details of dress, eating, drinking, bathing, sleeping, etc. The delineation of a life in all respects agreeable to the Word, a truly Christian life, attempted here, may, now that the gospel has transformed social and private life to the extent it has, appear unnecessary, or a proof of the influence of ascetic tendencies. But a code of Christian morals and manners (a sort of "whole duty of man" and manual of good breeding combined) was eminently needed by those whose habits and characters had been moulded under the debasing and polluting influences of heathenism; and who were bound, and were aiming, to shape their lives according to the principles of the gospel, in the midst of the all but incredible licentiousness and luxury by which society around was incurably tainted. The disclosures which Clement, with solemn sternness, and often with caustic wit, makes of the prevalent voluptuousness and vice, form a very valuable contribution to our knowledge of that period.

The full title of the *Stromata*, according to Eusebius and Photius, was Τίτου Φλαυίου Κλήμεντος τῶν κατὰ τὴν ἀληθῆ φιλοσοφίαν γνωστικῶν ὑπομνημάτων στρωματεῖς[1] — Titus Flavius Clement's miscellaneous collections of speculative (gnostic) notes bearing upon the true philosophy. The aim of the work, in accordance with this title, is, in opposition to gnosticism, to furnish the materials for the construction of a true gnosis, a Christian philosophy, on the basis of faith, and to lead on to this higher knowledge those who, by the discipline of the Pædagogus, had been trained for it. The work consisted originally of eight books. The eighth book is lost; that which appears under this name has plainly no connection with the rest of the *Stromata*. Various accounts have been given of the meaning of the distinctive word in the title (Στρωματεύς); but all agree in regarding it as indicating the miscellaneous character of its contents. And they are very miscellaneous. They consist of the speculations of Greek philosophers, of heretics, and of those who cultivated the true Christian gnosis, and of quotations from sacred Scripture. The latter he affirms to be the source from which the

[1] Eusebius, *Hist. Eccl.* vi. 13, Phot. *Bibl.* 111.

higher Christian knowledge is to be drawn; as it was that from which the germs of truth in Plato and the Hellenic philosophy were derived. He describes philosophy as a divinely ordered preparation of the Greeks for faith in Christ, as the law was for the Hebrews; and shows the necessity and value of literature and philosophic culture for the attainment of true Christian knowledge, in opposition to the numerous body among Christians who regarded learning as useless and dangerous. He proclaims himself an eclectic, believing in the existence of fragments of truth in all systems, which may be separated from error; but declaring that the truth can be found in unity and completeness only in Christ, as it was from Him that all its scattered germs originally proceeded. The *Stromata* are written carelessly, and even confusedly; but the work is one of prodigious learning, and supplies materials of the greatest value for understanding the various conflicting systems which Christianity had to combat.

It was regarded so much as the author's great work, that, on the testimony of Theodoret, Cassiodorus, and others, we learn that Clement received the appellation of Στρωματεύς (the Stromatist). In all probability, the first part of it was given to the world about A.D. 194. The latest date to which he brings down his chronology in the first book is the death of Commodus, which happened in A.D. 192; from which Eusebius[1] concludes that he wrote this work during the reign of Severus, who ascended the imperial throne in A.D. 193, and reigned till A.D. 211. It is likely that the whole was composed ere Clement quitted Alexandria in A.D. 202. The publication of the *Pædagogus* preceded by a short time that of the *Stromata*; and the *Cohortatio* was written a short time before the *Pædagogus*, as is clear from statements made by Clement himself.

So multifarious is the erudition, so multitudinous are the quotations and the references to authors in all departments, and of all countries, the most of whose works have perished, that the works in question could only have been composed

[1] *Hist. Eccl.* vi. 6.

near an extensive library—hardly anywhere but in the vicinity of the famous library of Alexandria. They are a storehouse of curious ancient lore,—a museum of the fossil remains of the beauties and monstrosities of the world of pagan antiquity, during all the epochs and phases of its history. The three compositions are really parts of one whole. The central connecting idea is that of the Logos—the Word —the Son of God; whom in the first work he exhibits drawing men from the superstitions and corruptions of heathenism to faith; in the second, as training them by precepts and discipline; and in the last, as conducting them to that higher knowledge of the things of God, to which those only who devote themselves assiduously to spiritual, moral, and intellectual culture can attain. Ever before his eye is the grand form of the living personal Christ,—the Word, who "was with God, and who was God, but who became man, and dwelt among us."

Of course there is throughout plenty of false science, and frivolous and fanciful speculation.

Who is the rich man that shall be saved? (τίς ὁ σωζόμενος πλούσιος) is the title of a practical treatise, in which Clement shows, in opposition to those who interpreted our Lord's words to the young ruler as requiring the renunciation of worldly goods, that the disposition of the soul is the great essential. Of other numerous works of Clement, of which only a few stray fragments have been preserved, the chief are the eight books of *The Hypotyposes*, which consisted of expositions of all the books of Scripture. Of these we have a few undoubted fragments. *The Adumbrations*, or *Commentaries on some of the Catholic Epistles*, and *The Selections from the Prophetic Scriptures*, are compositions of the same character, as far as we can judge, as the *Hypotyposes*, and are supposed by some to have formed part of that work.

Other lost works of Clement are:

The Treatise of Clement, the Stromatist, on the
    Prophet Amos.
On Providence.
Treatise on Easter.

On Evil-speaking.
Discussion on Fasting.
Exhortation to Patience; or, To the newly baptized.
Ecclesiastical Canon; or, Against the Judaizers.
Different Terms.

The following are the names of treatises which Clement refers to as written or about to be written by him, but of which otherwise we have no trace or mention:—*On First Principles; On Prophecy; On the Allegorical Interpretation of Members and Affections when ascribed to God; On Angels; On the Devil; On the Origin of the Universe; On the Unity and Excellence of the Church; On the Offices of Bishops, Presbyters, Deacons, and Widows; On the Soul; On the Resurrection; On Marriage; On Continence; Against Heresies.*

Preserved among Clement's works is a fragment called *Epitomes of the Writings of Theodotus, and of the Eastern Doctrine*, most likely abridged extracts made by Clement for his own use, and giving considerable insight into Gnosticism.

Clement's quotations from Scripture are made from the Septuagint version, often inaccurately from memory, sometimes from a different text from what we possess, often with verbal adaptations; and not rarely different texts are blended together.

The works of Clement present considerable difficulties to the translator; and one of the chief is the state of the text, which greatly needs to be expurgated and amended. For this there are abundant materials, in the copious annotations and disquisitions, by various hands, collected together in Migne's edition; where, however, corruptions the most obvious have been allowed to remain in the text.

The publishers are indebted to Dr. W. L. ALEXANDER for the poetical translations of the Hymns of Clement.

EXHORTATION TO THE HEATHEN.

CHAPTER I.

EXHORTATION TO ABANDON THE IMPIOUS MYSTERIES OF IDOLATRY FOR THE ADORATION OF THE DIVINE WORD AND GOD THE FATHER.

AMPHION of Thebes and Arion of Methymna were both minstrels, and both were renowned in story. They are celebrated in song to this day in the chorus of the Greeks; the one for having allured the fishes, and the other for having surrounded Thebes with walls by the power of music. Another, a Thracian, a cunning master of his art (he also is the subject of a Hellenic legend), tamed the wild beasts by the mere might of song; and transplanted trees—oaks—by music. I might tell you also the story of another, a brother to these—the subject of a myth, and a minstrel—Eunomos the Locrian and the Pythic grasshopper. A solemn Hellenic assembly had met at Pytho, to celebrate the death of the Pythic serpent, when Eunomos sang the reptile's epitaph. Whether his ode was a hymn in praise of the serpent, or a dirge, I am not able to say. But there was a contest, and Eunomos was playing the lyre in the summer time: it was when the grasshoppers, warmed by the sun, were chirping beneath the leaves along the hills; but they were singing not to that dead dragon, but to God All-wise,—a lay unfettered by rule, better than the numbers of Eunomos. The Locrian breaks a string. The grasshopper sprang on the neck of the instrument, and sang on it as on a branch; and the minstrel, adapting his strain to the grasshopper's song, made up for the want of the missing string. The grasshopper then was attracted by the song of Eunomos, as the fable represents, according to which also a brazen statue of Eunomos with his lyre, and the Locrian's ally in the contest, was erected at Pytho. But of its own accord it flew to the lyre, and of its own accord sang, and was regarded by the Greeks as a musical performer.

How, let me ask, have you believed vain fables, and supposed animals to be charmed by music; while Truth's shining face alone, as would seem, appears to you disguised, and is looked on with incredulous eyes? And so Cithæron, and Helicon, and the mountains of the Odrysi, and the initiatory rites of the Thracians, mysteries of deceit, are hallowed and celebrated in hymns. For me, I am pained at such calamities as form the subjects of tragedy, though but myths; but by you the records of miseries are turned into dramatic compositions.

But the dramas and the raving poets, now quite intoxicated, let us crown with ivy; and distracted outright as they are, in Bacchic fashion, with the satyrs, and the frenzied rabble, and the rest of the demon crew, let us confine to Cithæron and Helicon, now antiquated.

But let us bring from above out of heaven, Truth, with Wisdom in all its brightness, and the sacred prophetic choir, down to the holy mount of God; and let Truth, darting her light to the most distant points, cast her rays all around on those that are involved in darkness, and deliver men from delusion, stretching out her very strong[1] right hand, which is wisdom, for their salvation. And raising their eyes, and looking above, let them abandon Helicon and Cithæron, and take up their abode in Sion. "For out of Sion shall go forth the law, and the word of the Lord from Jerusalem,"[2]—the celestial Word, the true athlete crowned in the theatre of the whole

---

[1] The Greek is ὑπερτάτην, lit. highest. Potter appeals to the use of ὑπέρτερος in Sophocles, *Electr.* 455, in the sense of *stronger*, as giving a clue to the meaning here. The scholiast in Klotz takes the words to mean that the hand is held over them.

[2] Isa. ii. 3.

universe. What my Eunomos sings is not the measure of Terpander, nor that of Capito, nor the Phrygian, nor Lydian, nor Dorian, but the immortal measure of the new harmony which bears God's name—the new, the Levitical song.[1] "Soother of pain, calmer of wrath, producing forgetfulness of all ills."[2] Sweet and true is the charm of persuasion which blends with this strain.

To me, therefore, that Thracian Orpheus, that Theban, and that Methymnæan,—men, and yet unworthy of the name,—seem to have been deceivers, who, under the pretence of poetry corrupting human life, possessed by a spirit of artful sorcery for purposes of destruction, celebrating crimes in their orgies, and making human woes the materials of religious worship, were the first to entice men to idols; nay, to build up the stupidity of the nations with blocks of wood and stone,—that is, statues and images,—subjecting to the yoke of extremest bondage the truly noble freedom of those who lived as free citizens under heaven, by their songs and incantations. But not such is my song, which has come to loose, and that speedily, the bitter bondage of tyrannizing demons; and leading us back to the mild and loving yoke of piety, recalls to heaven those that had been cast prostrate to the earth. It alone has tamed men, the most intractable of animals; the frivolous among them answering to the fowls of the air, deceivers to reptiles, the irascible to lions, the voluptuous to swine, the rapacious to wolves. The silly are stocks and stones, and still more senseless than stones is a man who is steeped in ignorance. As our witness, let us adduce the voice of prophecy accordant with truth, and bewailing those who are crushed in ignorance and folly: "For God is able of these stones to raise up children to Abraham;"[3] and He, commiserating their great ignorance and hardness of heart who are petrified against the truth, has raised up a seed of piety, sensitive to virtue, of those stones—of the nations, that is, who trusted in stones. Again, therefore, some venomous and false hypocrites, who plotted against righteousness, He once called "a brood of vipers."[4]

[1] Ps. xcvi. 1, xcviii. 1.   [2] *Odyssey*, v. 220.
[3] Matt. iii. 9; Luke iii. 8.   [4] Matt. iii. 7; Luke iii. 7.

But if one of those serpents even is willing to repent, and follows the Word, he becomes a man of God.

Others he figuratively calls wolves, clothed in sheep-skins, meaning thereby monsters of rapacity in human form. And so all such most savage beasts, and all such blocks of stone, the celestial song has transformed into tractable men. "For even we ourselves were sometime foolish, disobedient, deceived, serving divers lusts and pleasures, living in malice and envy, hateful, hating one another." Thus speaks the apostolic scripture: "But after that the kindness and love of God our Saviour to man appeared, not by works of righteousness which we have done, but according to His mercy, He saved us."[1] Behold the might of the new song! It has made men out of stones, men out of beasts. Those, moreover, that were as dead, not being partakers of the true life, have come to life again, simply by becoming listeners to this song. It also composed the universe into melodious order, and tuned the discord of the elements to harmonious arrangement, so that the whole world might become harmony. It let loose the fluid ocean, and yet has prevented it from encroaching on the land. The earth, again, which had been in a state of commotion, it has established, and fixed the sea as its boundary. The violence of fire it has softened by the atmosphere, as the Dorian is blended with the Lydian strain; and the harsh cold of the air it has moderated by the embrace of fire, harmoniously arranging these the extreme tones of the universe. And this deathless strain,—the support of the whole and the harmony of all,—reaching from the centre to the circumference, and from the extremities to the central part, has harmonized this universal frame of things, not according to the Thracian music, which is like that invented by Jubal, but according to the paternal counsel of God, which fired the zeal of David. And He who is of David, and yet before him, the Word of God, despising the lyre and harp, which are but lifeless instruments, and having tuned by the Holy Spirit the universe, and especially man,—who, composed of body and soul, is a universe in miniature,—makes melody to God on this

[1] Tit. iii. 3-5.

instrument of many tones; and to this instrument—I mean man—he sings accordant: "For thou art my harp, and pipe, and temple,"[1]—a harp for harmony—a pipe by reason of the Spirit—a temple by reason of the word; so that the first may sound, the second breathe, the third contain the Lord. And David the king, the harper whom we mentioned a little above, who exhorted to the truth and dissuaded from idols, was so far from celebrating demons in song, that in reality they were driven away by his music. Thus, when Saul was plagued with a demon, he cured him by merely playing. A beautiful breathing instrument of music the Lord made man, after His own image. And He Himself also, surely, who is the supramundane Wisdom, the celestial Word, is the all-harmonious, melodious, holy instrument of God. What, then, does this instrument—the Word of God, the Lord, the New Song—desire? To open the eyes of the blind, and unstop the ears of the deaf, and to lead the lame or the erring to righteousness, to exhibit God to the foolish, to put a stop to corruption, to conquer death, to reconcile disobedient children to their father. The instrument of God loves mankind. The Lord pities, instructs, exhorts, admonishes, saves, shields, and of His bounty promises us the kingdom of heaven as a reward for learning; and the only advantage He reaps is, that we are saved. For wickedness feeds on men's destruction; but truth, like the bee, harming nothing, delights only in the salvation of men.

You have, then, God's promise; you have His love: become partaker of His grace. And do not suppose the song of salvation to be new, as a vessel or a house is new. For "before the morning star it was;"[2] and "in the beginning was the Word, and the Word was with God, and the Word was God."[3] Error seems old, but truth seems a new thing.

Whether, then, the Phrygians are shown to be the most ancient people by the goats of the fable; or, on the other hand, the Arcadians by the poets, who describe them as older than

---

[1] Probably a quotation from a hymn.
[2] Ps. cx. 3. Septuagint has, "before the morning star."
[3] John i. 1.

the moon; or, finally, the Egyptians by those who dream that this land first gave birth to gods and men: yet none of these at least existed before the world. But before the foundation of the world were we, who, because destined to be in Him, pre-existed in the eye of God before,—we the rational creatures of the Word of God, on whose account we date from the beginning; for "in the beginning was the Word." Well, inasmuch as the Word was from the first, He was and is the divine source of all things; but inasmuch as He has now assumed the name Christ, consecrated of old, and worthy of power, he has been called by me the New Song. This Word, then, the Christ, the cause of both our being at first (for He was in God) and of our well-being, this very Word has now appeared as man, He alone being both, both God and man— the Author of all blessings to us; by whom we, being taught to live well, are sent on our way to life eternal. For, according to that inspired apostle of the Lord, "the grace of God which bringeth salvation hath appeared to all men, teaching us, that, denying ungodliness and worldly lusts, we should live soberly, righteously, and godly, in this present world; looking for the blessed hope, and appearing of the glory of the great God and our Saviour Jesus Christ."[1]

This is the New Song, the manifestation of the Word that was in the beginning, and before the beginning. The Saviour, who existed before, has in recent days appeared. He, who is in Him that truly is, has appeared; for the Word, who "was with God," and by whom all things were created, has appeared as our Teacher. The Word, who in the beginning bestowed on us life as Creator when He formed us, taught us to live well when He appeared as our Teacher; that as God He might afterwards conduct us to the life which never ends. He did not now for the first time pity us for our error; but He pitied us from the first, from the beginning. But now, at His appearance, lost as we already were, He accomplished our salvation. For that wicked reptile monster, by his enchantments, enslaves and plagues men even till now; inflicting, as seems to me, such barbarous vengeance on them as those who are

[1] Tit. ii. 11-13.

said to bind captives to corpses till they rot together. This wicked tyrant and serpent, accordingly, binding fast with the miserable chain of superstition whomsoever he can draw to his side from their birth, to stones, and stocks, and images, and such like idols, may with truth be said to have taken and buried living men with those dead idols, till both suffer corruption together.

Therefore (for the seducer is one and the same) he that at the beginning brought Eve down to death, now brings thither the rest of mankind. Our ally and helper, too, is one and the same—the Lord, who from the beginning gave revelations by prophecy, but now plainly calls to salvation. In obedience to the apostolic injunction, therefore, let us flee from "the prince of the power of the air, the spirit that now worketh in the children of disobedience,"[1] and let us run to the Lord the Saviour, who now exhorts to salvation, as He has ever done, as He did by signs and wonders in Egypt and the desert, both by the bush and the cloud, which, through the favour of divine love, attended the Hebrews like an handmaid. By the fear which these inspired He addressed the hard-hearted; while by Moses, learned in all wisdom, and Isaiah, lover of truth, and the whole prophetic choir, in a way appealing more to reason, He turns to the Word those who have ears to hear. Sometimes He upbraids, and sometimes He threatens. Some men He mourns over, others He addresses with the voice of song, just as a good physician treats some of his patients with cataplasms, some with rubbing, some with fomentations; in one case cuts open with the lancet, in another cauterizes, in another amputates, in order if possible to cure the patient's diseased part or member. The Saviour has many tones of voice, and many methods for the salvation of men; by threatening He admonishes, by upbraiding He converts, by bewailing He pities, by the voice of song He cheers. He spake by the burning bush, for the men of that day needed signs and wonders.

He awed men by the fire when He made flame to burst from the pillar of cloud—a token at once of grace and

[1] Eph. ii. 2.

fear: if you obey, there is the light; if you disobey, there is the fire; but, since humanity is nobler than the pillar or the bush, after them the prophets uttered their voice,—the Lord Himself speaking in Isaiah, in Elias,—speaking Himself by the mouth of the prophets. But if thou dost not believe the prophets, but supposest both the men and the fire a myth, the Lord Himself shall speak to thee, "who, being in the form of God, thought it not robbery to be equal with God, but humbled Himself,"[1]—He, the merciful God, exerting Himself to save man. And now the Word Himself clearly speaks to thee, shaming thy unbelief; yea, I say, the Word of God became man, that thou mayest learn from man how man may become God. Is it not then monstrous, my friends, that while God is ceaselessly exhorting us to virtue, we should spurn His kindness and reject salvation?

Does not John also invite to salvation, and is he not entirely a voice of exhortation? Let us then ask him, "Who of men art thou, and whence?" He will not say Elias. He will deny that he is Christ, but will profess himself to be " a voice crying in the wilderness." Who, then, is John?[2] In a word, we may say, "The beseeching voice of the Word crying in the wilderness." What criest thou, O voice? Tell us also. "Make straight the paths of the Lord."[3] John is the forerunner, and that voice the precursor of the Word; an inviting voice, preparing for salvation,—a voice urging men on to the inheritance of the heavens, and through which the barren and the desolate is childless no more. This fecundity the angel's voice foretold; and this voice was also the precursor of the Lord preaching glad tidings to the barren woman, as John did to the wilderness. By reason of this voice of the Word, therefore, the barren woman bears children, and the desert becomes fruitful. The two voices which heralded the Lord's —that of the angel and that of John—intimate, as I think, the salvation in store for us to be, that on the appearance of this Word we should reap, as the fruit of this productiveness, eternal life. The Scripture makes all this clear, by referring both the voices to the same thing: "Let her hear who has

[1] Phil. ii. 6, 7.   [2] John i. 23.   [3] Isa. xl. 3.

not brought forth, and let her who has not had the pangs of childbirth utter her voice : for more are the children of the desolate, than of her who hath an husband."[1]

The angel announced to us the glad tidings of a husband. John entreated us to recognise the husbandman, to seek the husband. For this husband of the barren woman, and this husbandman of the desert—who filled with divine power the barren woman and the desert—is one and the same. For because many were the children of the mother of noble race, yet the Hebrew woman, once blessed with many children, was made childless because of unbelief : the barren woman receives the husband, and the desert the husbandman ; then both become mothers through the word, the one of fruits, the other of believers. But to the unbelieving the barren and the desert are still reserved. For this reason John, the herald of the Word, besought men to make themselves ready against the coming of the Christ of God.[2] And it was this which was signified by the dumbness of Zacharias, which waited for fruit in the person of the harbinger of Christ, that the Word, the light of truth, by becoming the gospel, might break the mystic silence of the prophetic enigmas. But if thou desirest truly to see God, take to thyself means of purification worthy of Him, not leaves of laurel fillets interwoven with wool and purple ; but wreathing thy brows with righteousness, and encircling them with the leaves of temperance, set thyself earnestly to find Christ. " For I am," He says, " the door,"[3] which we who desire to understand God must discover, that He may throw heaven's gates wide open to us. For the gates of the Word being intellectual, are opened by the key of faith. No one knows God but the Son, and he to whom the Son shall reveal Him.[4] And I know well that He who has opened the door hitherto shut, will afterwards reveal what is within ; and will show what we could not have known before, had we not entered in by Christ, through whom alone God is beheld.

[1] Isa. liv. 1.   [2] This may be translated, "of God the Christ."
[3] John x. 9.   [4] Matt. xi. 27.

CHAPTER II.

THE ABSURDITY AND IMPIETY OF THE HEATHEN MYSTERIES AND FABLES ABOUT THE BIRTH AND DEATH OF THEIR GODS.

EXPLORE not then too curiously the shrines of impiety, or the mouths of caverns full of monstrosity, or the Thesprotian caldron, or the Cirrhæan tripod, or the Dodonian copper. The Gerandryon,[1] once regarded sacred in the midst of desert sands, and the oracle there gone to decay with the oak itself, consign to the region of antiquated fables. The fountain of Castalia is silent, and the other fountain of Colophon; and, in like manner, all the rest of the springs of divination are dead, and stripped of their vainglory, although at a late date, are shown with their fabulous legends to have run dry. Recount to us also the useless[2] oracles of that other kind of divination, or rather madness, the Clarian, the Pythian, the Didymæan, that of Amphiaraus, of Apollo, of Amphilochus; and if you will, couple[3] with them the expounders of prodigies, the augurs, and the interpreters of dreams. And bring and place beside the Pythian those that divine by flour, and those that divine by barley, and the ventriloquists still held in honour by many. Let the secret shrines of the Egyptians and the necromancies

---

[1] What this is, is not known; but it is likely that the word is a corruption of *ἱερὰς δρῦν*, the sacred oath.

[2] *ἄχρηστα χρηστήρια.*

[3] The text has *ἀνιέρου*, the imperative of *ἀνιερόω*, which in classical Greek means "to hallow;" but the verb here must be derived from the adjective *ἀνίερος*, and be taken in the sense "deprive of their holiness," "no longer count holy." Eusebius reads *ἀνιέρους*: "unholy interpreters."

of the Etruscans be consigned to darkness. Insane devices truly are they all of unbelieving men. Goats, too, have been confederates in this art of soothsaying, trained to divination; and crows taught by men to give oracular responses to men.

And what if I go over the mysteries? I will not divulge them in mockery, as they say Alcibiades did, but I will expose right well by the word of truth the sorcery hidden in them; and those so-called gods of yours, whose are the mystic rites, I shall display, as it were, on the stage of life, to the spectators of truth. The bacchanals hold their orgies in honour of the frenzied Dionysus, celebrating their sacred frenzy by the eating of raw flesh, and go through the distribution of the parts of butchered victims, crowned with snakes, shrieking out the name of that Eva by whom error came into the world. The symbol of the Bacchic orgies is a consecrated serpent. Moreover, according to the strict interpretation of the Hebrew term, the name Hevia, aspirated, signifies a female serpent.

Demeter and Proserpine have become the heroines of a mystic drama; and their wanderings, and seizure, and grief, Eleusis celebrates by torchlight processions. I think that the derivation of orgies and mysteries ought to be traced, the former to the wrath ($\mathrm{\mathit{\dot{o}}}\rho\gamma\dot{\eta}$) of Demeter against Zeus, the latter to the nefarious wickedness ($\mu\dot{\upsilon}\sigma\mathrm{o}\varsigma$) relating to Dionysus; but if from Myus of Attica, who Pollodorus says was killed in hunting—no matter, I don't grudge your mysteries the glory of funeral honours. You may understand mysteria in another way, as mytheria (hunting fables), the letters of the two words being interchanged; for certainly fables of this sort hunt after the most barbarous of the Thracians, the most senseless of the Phrygians, and the superstitious among the Greeks.

Perish, then, the man who was the author of this imposture among men, be he Dardanus, who taught the mysteries of the mother of the gods, or Eetion, who instituted the orgies and mysteries of the Samothracians, or that Phrygian Midas who, having learned the cunning imposture from Odrysus, communicated it to his subjects. For I will never be persuaded by that Cyprian Islander Cinyras, who dared to bring forth from night to the light of day the lewd orgies of Aphrodite in his eagerness to deify a strumpet of his own country. Others say that Melampus the son of Amythaon imported the festivals of Ceres from Egypt into Greece, celebrating her grief in song.

These I would instance as the prime authors of evil, the parents of impious fables and of deadly superstition, who sowed in human life that seed of evil and ruin—the mysteries.

And now, for it is time, I will prove their orgies to be full of imposture and quackery. And if you have been initiated, you will laugh all the more at these fables of yours which have been held in honour. I publish without reserve what has been involved in secrecy, not ashamed to tell what you are not ashamed to worship.

There is then the foam-born and Cyprus-born, the darling of Cinyras,—I mean Aphrodite, lover of the virilia, because sprung from them, even from those of Uranus, that were cut off,—those lustful members, that, after being cut off, offered violence to the waves. Of members so lewd a worthy fruit—Aphrodite—is born. In the rites which celebrate this enjoyment of the sea, as a symbol of her birth a lump of salt and the phallus are handed to those who are initiated into the art of uncleanness. And those initiated bring a piece of money to her, as a courtesan's paramours do to her.

Then there are the mysteries of Demeter, and Zeus's wanton embraces of his mother, and the wrath of Demeter; I know not what for the future I shall call her, mother or wife, on which account it is that she is called Brimo, as is said; also the entreaties of Zeus, and the drink of gall, the plucking out of the hearts of sacrifices, and deeds that we dare not name. Such rites the Phrygians perform in honour of Attis and Cybele and the Corybantes. And the story goes, that Zeus, having torn away the testicles of a ram, brought them out and cast them at the breasts of Demeter, paying thus a fraudulent penalty for his violent embrace, pretending to have cut out his own. The symbols of initiation into these rites, when set before you in a vacant hour,

I know will excite your laughter, although on account of the exposure by no means inclined to laugh. I have eaten out of the drum, I have drunk out of the cymbal, I have carried the Cernos,[1] I have slipped into the bedroom. Are not these signs a disgrace? Are not the mysteries absurdity?

What if I add the rest? Demeter becomes a mother, Kore[1] is reared up to womanhood. And, in course of time, he who begot her,—this same Zeus has intercourse with his own daughter Pherephatta,—after Ceres, the mother,—forgetting his former abominable wickedness. Zeus is both the father and the seducer of Kore, and has intercourse with her in the shape of a dragon; his identity, however, was discovered. The token of the Sabazian mysteries to the initiated is "the deity gliding over the breast,"—the deity being this serpent crawling over the breasts of the initiated. Proof surely this of the unbridled lust of Zeus. Pherephatta has a child, though, to be sure, in the form of a bull, as an idolatrous poet says:

"The bull
The dragon's father, and the father of the bull the dragon,
On a hill the herdsman's hidden ox-goad,"—

alluding, as I believe, under the name of the herdsman's ox-goad, to the reed wielded by the bacchanals. Do you wish me to go into the story of Pherephatta's gathering of flowers, her basket, and her seizure by Pluto (Aidoneus), and the rent in the earth, and the swine of Eubouleus that were swallowed up with the two goddesses; for which reason, in the Thesmophoria, speaking the Megaric tongue, they thrust out swine? This mythological story the women celebrate variously in different cities in the festivals called Thesmophoria and Scirophoria; dramatizing in many forms the rape of Pherephatta (Proserpine).

The mysteries of Dionysus are wholly inhuman; for while still a child, and the Curetes danced around [his cradle] clashing their weapons, and the Titans having come upon them by stealth, and having beguiled him with childish toys,

---

[1] The cernos some take to be a vessel containing poppy, etc., carried in sacrificial processions. The scholiast says that it is a fan.

[2] Proserpine or Pherephatta.

these very Titans tore him limb from limb when but a child, as the bard of this mystery, the Thracian Orpheus, says:

"Cone, and spinning-top, and limb-moving rattles,
And fair golden apples from the clear-toned Hesperides."

And the useless symbols of this mystic rite it will not be useless to exhibit for condemnation. These are dice, ball, hoop, apples, top,[1] looking-glass, tuft of wool.

Athene (Minerva), to resume our account, having abstracted the heart of Dionysus, was called Pallas, from the vibrating of the heart; and the Titans who had torn him limb from limb, setting a caldron on a tripod, and throwing into it the members of Dionysus, first boiled them down, and then fixing them on spits, "held them over the fire." But Zeus having appeared, since he was a god, having speedily perceived the savour of the pieces of flesh that were being cooked, —that savour which your gods agree to have assigned to them as their perquisite,—assails the Titans with his thunderbolt, and consigns the members of Dionysus to his son Apollo to be interred. And he—for he did not disobey Zeus—bore the dismembered corpse to Parnassus, and there deposited it.

If you wish to inspect the orgies of the Corybantes, then know that, having killed their third brother, they covered the head of the dead body with a purple cloth, crowned it, and carrying it on the point of a spear, buried it under the roots of Olympus. These mysteries are, in short, murders and funerals. And the priests of these rites, who are called kings of the sacred rites by those whose business it is to name them, give additional strangeness to the tragic occurrence, by forbidding parsley with the roots from being placed on the table, for they think that parsley grew from the Corybantic blood that flowed forth; just as the women, in celebrating the Thesmophoria, abstain from eating the seeds of the pomegranate which have fallen on the ground, from the idea that pomegranates sprang from the drops of the blood of Dionysus. Those Corybantes also they call Cabiri; and the ceremony itself they announce as the Cabiric mystery.

[1] The scholiast takes the ῥόμβος to mean a piece of wood attached to a cord, and swung round so as to cause a whistling noise.

For those two identical fratricides, having abstracted the box in which the penis of Bacchus was deposited, took it to Etruria—dealers in honourable wares truly. They lived there as exiles, employing themselves in communicating the precious teaching of their superstition, and presenting the genitals and the box for the Tyrrhenians to worship. And some will have it, not improbably, that for this reason Dionysus was called Attis, because he was castrated. And what is surprising at the Tyrrhenians, who were barbarians, being thus initiated into these foul indignities, when among the Athenians, and in the whole of Greece—I blush to say it—the shameful legend about Demeter holds its ground? For Demeter, wandering in quest of her daughter Core, broke down with fatigue near Eleusis, a place in Attica, and sat down on a well overwhelmed with grief. This is even now prohibited to those who are initiated, lest they should appear to mimic the weeping goddess. The indigenous inhabitants then occupied Eleusis: their names were Baubo, and Dusaules, and Triptolemus; and besides, Eumolpus and Eubouleus. Triptolemus was a herdsman, Eumolpus a shepherd, and Eubouleus a swineherd; from whom came the race of the Eumolpidæ and that of the Heralds—a race of Hierophants—who flourished at Athens.

Well, then (for I shall not refrain from the recital), Baubo having received Demeter hospitably, reaches to her a refreshing draught; and on her refusing it, not having any inclination to drink (for she was very sad), and Baubo having become annoyed, thinking herself slighted, uncovered her secret parts, and exhibited them to the goddess. Demeter is delighted at the sight, and takes, though with difficulty, the draught—pleased, I repeat, at the spectacle. These are the secret mysteries of the Athenians; these Orpheus records. I shall produce the very words of Orpheus, that you may have the great authority on the mysteries himself, as evidence for this piece of turpitude:

"Having thus spoken, she drew aside her garments,
And showed all that shape of the body which it is improper to name,
  the growth of puberty;
And with her own hand Baubo stripped herself under the breasts.

Blandly then the goddess laughed and laughed in her mind,
And received the glancing cup in which was the draught."

And the following is the token of the Eleusinian mysteries: *I have fasted, I have drunk the cup; I have received from the box; having done, I put it into the basket, and out of the basket. into the chest.* Fine sights truly, and becoming a goddess; mysteries worthy of the night, and flame, and the magnanimous or rather silly people of the Erechthidæ, and the other Greeks besides, "whom a fate they hope not for awaits after death." And in truth against these Heraclitus the Ephesian prophesies, as "the night-walkers, the magi, the bacchanals, the Lenæan revellers, the initiated." These he threatens with what will follow death, and predicts for them fire. For what are regarded among men as mysteries, they celebrate sacrilegiously. Law, then, and opinion, are nugatory. And the mysteries of the dragon are an imposture, which celebrates religiously mysteries that are no mysteries at all, and observes with a spurious piety profane rites. What are these mystic chests?—for I must expose their sacred things, and divulge things not fit for speech. Are they not sesame cakes, and pyramidal cakes, and globular and flat cakes, embossed all over, and lumps of salt, and a serpent the symbol of Dionysus Bassareus? And besides these, are there not pomegranates, and branches, and rods, and ivy leaves? and besides, round cakes and poppy seeds? And further, there are the unmentionable symbols of Themis, marjoram, a lamp, a sword, a woman's comb, which is a euphemism and mystic expression for a woman's secret parts.

O unblushing shamelessness! Once on a time night was silent, a veil for the pleasure of temperate men; but now for the initiated, the holy night is the tell-tale of the rites of licentiousness; and the glare of torches reveals vicious indulgences. Quench the flame, O Hierophant; reverence, O Torch-bearer, the torches. That light exposes Iacchus; let thy mysteries be honoured, and command the orgies to be hidden in night and darkness.[1]

[1] This sentence is read variously in various editions.

The fire dissembles not; it exposes and punishes what it is bidden.

Such are the mysteries of the Atheists. And with reason I call those Atheists who know not the true God, and pay shameless worship to a boy torn in pieces by the Titans, and a woman in distress, and to parts of the body that in truth cannot be mentioned for shame, held fast as they are in the double impiety, first in that they know not God, not acknowledging as God Him who truly is; the other and second is the error of regarding those who exist not, as existing and calling those gods that have no real existence, or rather no existence at all, who have nothing but a name. Wherefore the apostle reproves us, saying, "And ye were strangers to the covenants of promise, having no hope, and without God in the world."[1]

All honour to that king of the Scythians, whoever Anacharsis was, who shot with an arrow one of his subjects who imitated among the Scythians the mystery of the Mother of the gods, as practised by the inhabitants of Cyzicus, beating a drum and sounding a cymbal strung from his neck like a priest of Cybele, condemning him as having become effeminate among the Greeks, and a teacher of the disease of effeminacy to the rest of the Scythians.

Wherefore (for I must by no means conceal it) I cannot help wondering how Euhemerus of Agrigentum, and Nicanor of Cyprus, and Diagoras, and Hippo of Melos, and besides these, that Cyrenian of the name of Theodorus, and numbers of others, who lived a sober life, and had a clearer insight than the rest of the world into the prevailing error respecting those gods, were called Atheists; for if they did not arrive at the knowledge of the truth, they certainly suspected the error of the common opinion; which suspicion is no insignificant seed, and becomes the germ of true wisdom. One of these charges the Egyptians thus: "If you believe them to be gods, do not mourn or bewail them; and if you mourn and bewail them, do not any more regard them as gods." And another, taking an image of Hercules made of wood (for he happened most likely to be cooking something at home), said, "Come now,

[1] Eph. ii. 12.

Hercules; now is the time to undergo for us this thirteenth labour, as you did the twelve for Eurystheus, and make this ready for Diagoras," and so cast it into the fire as a log of wood. For the extremes of ignorance are atheism and superstition, from which we must endeavour to keep. And do you not see Moses, the hierophant of the truth, enjoining that no eunuch, or emasculated man, or son of a harlot, should enter the congregation? By the two first he alludes to the impious custom by which men were deprived both of divine energy and of their virility; and by the third, to him who, in place of the only real God, assumes many gods falsely so called,—as the son of a harlot, in ignorance of his true father, may claim many putative fathers.

There was an innate original communion between men and heaven, obscured through ignorance, but which now at length has leapt forth instantaneously from the darkness, and shines resplendent; as has been expressed by one[1] in the following lines:

"See'st thou this lofty, this boundless ether,
Holding the earth in the embrace of its humid arms."

And in these:

"O Thou, who makest the earth Thy chariot, and in the earth hast Thy seat,
Whoever Thou be, baffling our efforts to behold Thee."

And whatever else the sons of the poets sing.

But sentiments erroneous, and deviating from what is right, and certainly pernicious, have turned man, a creature of heavenly origin, away from the heavenly life, and stretched him on the earth, by inducing him to cleave to earthly objects. For some, beguiled by the contemplation of the heavens, and trusting to their sight alone, while they looked on the motions of the stars, straightway were seized with admiration, and deified them, calling the stars gods from their motion ($\theta\epsilon\grave{o}\varsigma$ from $\theta\epsilon\hat{\iota}\nu$); and worshipped the sun,—as, for example, the Indians; and the moon, as the Phrygians. Others, plucking the benignant fruits of earth-born plants, called grain Demeter, as the Athenians, and the vine Dionysus, as the

[1] Euripides.

Thebans. Others, considering the penalties of wickedness, deified them, worshipping various forms of retribution and calamity. Hence the Erinnyes, and the Eumenides, and the piacular deities, and the judges and avengers of crime, are the creations of the tragic poets.

And some even of the philosophers, after the poets, make idols of forms of the affections in your breasts,—such as fear, and love, and joy, and hope; as, to be sure, Epimenides of old, who raised at Athens the altars of Insult and Impudence. Other objects deified by men take their rise from events, and are fashioned in bodily shape, such as a Dike, a Clotho, and Lachesis, and Atropos, and Heimarmene, and Auxo, and Thallo, which are Attic goddesses. There is a sixth mode of introducing error and of manufacturing gods, according to which they number the twelve gods, whose birth is the theme of which Hesiod sings in his Theogony, and of whom Homer speaks in all that he says of the gods. The last mode remains (for there are seven in all)—that which takes its rise from the divine beneficence towards men. For, not understanding that it is God that does us good, they have invented saviours in the persons of the Dioscuri, and Hercules the averter of evil, and Asclepius the healer. These are the slippery and hurtful deviations from the truth which draw man down from heaven, and cast him into the abyss. I wish to show thoroughly what like these gods of yours are, that now at length you may abandon your delusion, and speed your flight back to heaven. "For we also were once children of wrath, even as others; but God, being rich in mercy, for the great love wherewith He loved us, when we were now dead in trespasses, quickened us together with Christ."[1] For the Word is living, and having been buried with Christ, is exalted with God. But those who are still unbelieving are called children of wrath, reared for wrath. We who have been rescued from error, and restored to the truth, are no longer the nurslings of wrath. Thus, therefore, we who were once the children of lawlessness, have through the philanthropy of the Word now become the sons of God.

[1] Eph. ii. 3-5.

But to you a poet of your own, Empedocles of Agrigentum, comes and says:

> "Wherefore, distracted with grievous evils,
> You will never ease your soul of its miserable woes."

The most of what is told of your gods is fabled and invented; and those things which are supposed to have taken place, are recorded of vile men who lived licentious lives:

> "You walk in pride and madness,
> And leaving the right and straight path, you have gone away
> Through thorns and briars. Why do ye wander?
> Cease, foolish men, from mortals;
> Leave the darkness of night, and lay hold on the light."

These counsels the Sybil, who is at once prophetic and poetic, enjoins on us; and truth enjoins them on us too, stripping the crowd of deities of those terrifying and threatening masks of theirs, disproving the rash opinions formed of them by showing the similarity of names. For there are those who reckon three Jupiters: him of Æther in Arcadia, and the other two sons of Kronos; and of these, one in Crete, and the others again in Arcadia. And there are those that reckon five Athenes: the Athenian, the daughter of Hephæstus; the second, the Egyptian, the daughter of Nilus; the third the inventor of war, the daughter of Kronos; the fourth, the daughter of Zeus, whom the Messenians have named Coryphasia, from her mother; above all, the daughter of Pallas and Titanis, the daughter of Oceanus, who, having wickedly killed her father, adorned herself with her father's skin, as if it had been the fleece of a sheep. Further, Aristotle calls the first Apollo, the son of Hephæstus and Athene (consequently Athene is no more a virgin); the second, that in Crete, the son of Corybas; the third, the son of Zeus; the fourth, the Arcadian, the son of Silenus (this one is called by the Arcadians Nomius); and in addition to these, he specifies the Libyan Apollo, the son of Ammon; and to these Didymus the grammarian adds a sixth, the son of Magnes. And now how many Apollos are there? They are numberless, mortal men, all helpers of their fellow-men, who similarly with those already mentioned have been so called. And what were

I to mention the many Asclepiuses, or all the Mercuries that are reckoned up, or the Vulcans of fable? Shall I not appear extravagant, deluging your ears with these numerous names? At any rate, the native countries of your gods, and their arts and lives, and besides especially their sepulchres, demonstrate them to have been men. Mars, accordingly, who by the poets is held in the highest possible honour:

"Mars, Mars, bane of men, blood-stained stormer of walls,"[1]—

this deity, always changing sides, and implacable, as Epicharmus says, was a Spartan; Sophocles knew him for a Thracian; others say he was an Arcadian. This god, Homer says, was bound thirteen months:

"Mars had his sufferings; by Alöeus' sons,
Otus and Ephialtes, strongly bound,
He thirteen months in brazen fetters lay."[2]

Good luck attend the Carians, who sacrifice dogs to him! And may the Scythians never leave off sacrificing asses, as Apollodorus and Callimachus relate:

"Phœbus rises propitious to the Hyperboreans,
When they offer sacrifices of asses to him."

And the same in another place:

"Fat sacrifices of asses' flesh delight Phœbus."

Hephæstus, whom Jupiter cast from Olympus, from its divine threshold, having fallen on Lemnos, practised the art of working in brass, maimed in his feet:

"His tottering knees were bowed beneath his weight."[3]

You have also a doctor, and not only a brass-worker among the gods. And the doctor was greedy of gold; Asclepius was his name. I shall produce as a witness your own poet, the Bœotian Pindar:

"Him even the gold glittering in his hands,
Amounting to a splendid fee, persuaded
To rescue a man, already death's capture, from his grasp;
But Saturnian Jove, having shot his bolt through both,
Quickly took the breath from their breasts,
And his flaming thunderbolt sealed their doom."

---

[1] *Iliad*, v. 31.   [2] *Iliad*, v. 385.   [3] *Iliad*, xviii. 410.

And Euripides:

"For Zeus was guilty of the murder of my son
Asclepius, by casting the lightning flame at his breast."

He therefore lies struck with lightning in the regions of Cynosuris. Philochorus also says, that Poseidon was worshipped as a physician in Tenos; and that Kronos settled in Sicily, and there was buried. Patroclus the Thurian, and Sophocles the younger, in three tragedies, have told the story of the Dioscuri; and these Dioscuri were only two mortals, if Homer is worthy of credit:

". . . . . but they beneath the teeming earth,
In Lacedæmon lay, their native land."[1]

And, in addition, he who wrote the Cyprian poems says Castor was mortal, and death was decreed to him by fate; but Pollux was immortal, being the progeny of Mars. This he has poetically fabled. But Homer is more worthy of credit, who spoke as above of both the Dioscuri; and, besides, proved Hercules to be a mere phantom:

"The man Hercules, expert in mighty deeds."

Hercules, therefore, was known by Homer himself as only a mortal man. And Hieronymus the philosopher describes the make of his body, as tall,[2] bristling-haired, robust; and Dicæarchus says that he was square-built, muscular, dark, hook-nosed, with greyish eyes and long hair. This Hercules, accordingly, after living fifty-two years, came to his end, and was burned in a funeral pyre in Œta.

As for the Muses, whom Alcander calls the daughters of Zeus and Mnemosyne, and the rest of the poets and authors deify and worship,—those Muses, in honour of whom whole states have already erected museums, being handmaids, were hired by Megaclo, the daughter of Makar. This Makar reigned over the Lesbians, and was always quarrelling with his wife; and Megaclo was vexed for her mother's sake. What would she not do on her account? Accordingly she hires those handmaids, being so many in number, and calls

---

[1] *Iliad*, iii. 243. Lord Derby's translation is used in extracts from the *Iliad*.

[2] The MSS. read "*small*," but the true reading is doubtless "*tall*."

them Mysæ, according to the dialect of the Æolians. These she taught to sing deeds of the olden time, and play melodiously on the lyre. And they, by assiduously playing the lyre, and singing sweetly to it, soothed Makar, and put a stop to his ill-temper. Wherefore Megaclo, as a token of gratitude to them, on her mother's account erected brazen pillars, and ordered them to be held in honour in all the temples. Such, then, are the Muses. This account is in Myrsilus of Lesbos.

And now, then, hear the loves of your gods, and the incredible tales of their licentiousness, and their wounds, and their bonds, and their laughings, and their fights, their servitudes too, and their banquets; and furthermore, their embraces, and tears, and sufferings, and lewd delights. Call me Poseidon, and the troop of damsels deflowered by him, Amphitrite Amymone, Alope, Melanippe, Alcyone, Hippothoe, Chione, and myriads of others; with whom, though so many, the passions of your Poseidon were not satiated.

Call me Apollo; this is Phœbus, both a holy prophet and a good adviser. But Sterope will not say that, nor Æthousa, nor Arsinoe, nor Zeuxippe, nor Prothoe, nor Marpissa, nor Hypsipyle. For Daphne alone escaped the prophet and seduction.

And, above all, let the Father of gods and men, according to you, himself come, who was so given to sexual pleasure, as to lust after all, and indulge his lust on all. For he took his fill of women, as the he-goat of the Thmuitæ did of the she-goats. And thy poems, O Homer, fill me with admiration!

> "He said, and nodded with his shadowy brows;
> Waved on the immortal head the ambrosial locks,
> And all Olympus trembled at his nod."[1]

Thou makest Zeus venerable, O Homer; and the nod which thou dost ascribe to him is most reverend. But show him only a woman's girdle, and Zeus is exposed, and his locks are dishonoured. To what a pitch of licentiousness did that Zeus of yours proceed, who spent so many nights in volup-

[1] *Iliad*, i. 527.

tnousness with Alcmene? For not even these nine nights were long to this insatiable monster. But, on the contrary, a whole lifetime were short enough for his lust; that he might beget for us the evil-averting god.

Hercules, the son of Zeus—a true son of Zeus—was the offspring of that long night, who with hard toil accomplished the twelve labours in a long time, but in one night deflowered the fifty daughters of Thestius, and thus was at once the debaucher and the bridegroom of so many virgins. It is not, then, without reason that the poets call him a cruel wretch and a nefarious scoundrel. It were tedious to recount his adulteries of all sorts, and debauching of boys. For your gods did not even abstain from boys, one having loved Hylas, another Hyacinthus, another Pelops, another Chrysippus, and another Ganymede. Let such gods as these be worshipped by your wives, and let them pray that their husbands be such as these —so temperate; that, emulating them in the same practices, they may be like the gods. Such gods let your boys be trained to worship, that they may grow up to be men with the accursed likeness of fornication on them received from the gods.

But it is only the male deities, perhaps, that are impetuous in sexual indulgence.

"The female deities stayed each in the house, for shame,"[1] says Homer; the goddesses blushing, for modesty's sake, to look on Aphrodite when she had been guilty of adultery. But these are more passionately licentious, bound in the chains of adultery; Eos having disgraced herself with Tithonus, Selene with Endymion, Nereis with Æacus, Thetis with Peleus, Demeter with Jason, Pherephatta with Adonis. And Aphrodite having disgraced herself with Ares, crossed over to Cinyra and married Anchises, and laid snares for Phaëthon, and loved Adonis. She contended with the ox-eyed Juno; and the goddesses unrobed for the sake of the apple, and presented themselves naked before the shepherd, that he might decide which was the fairest.

But come, let us briefly go the round of the games, and do

[1] *Iliad*, viii. 324.

away with those solemn assemblages at tombs, the Isthmian, Nemean, and Pythian, and finally the Olympian. At Pytho the Pythian dragon is worshipped, and the festival-assemblage of the serpent is called by the name Pythia. At the Isthmus the sea spit out a piece of miserable refuse; and the Isthmian games bewail Melicerta.

At Nemea another—a little boy, Archemorus—was buried; and the funeral games of the child are called Nemea. Pisa is the grave of the Phrygian charioteer, O Hellenes of all tribes; and the Olympian games, which are nothing else than the funeral sacrifices of Pelops, the Zeus of Phidias claims for himself. The mysteries were then, as is probable, games held in honour of the dead; so also were the oracles, and both became public. But the mysteries at Sagra[1] and in Alimus of Attica were confined to Athens. But those contests and *phalloi* consecrated to Dionysus were a world's shame, pervading life with their deadly influence. For Dionysus, eagerly desiring to descend to Hades, did not know the way; a man, by name Prosymnus, offers to tell him, not without reward. The reward was a disgraceful one, though not so in the opinion of Dionysus: it was an Aphrodisian favour that was asked of Dionysus as a reward. The god was not reluctant to grant the request made to him, and promises to fulfil it should he return, and confirms his promise with an oath. Having learned the way, he departed and again returned: he did not find Prosymnus, for he had died. In order to acquit himself of his promise to his lover, he rushes to his tomb, and burns with unnatural lust. Cutting a fig-branch that came to his hand, he shaped the likeness of the *membrum virile*, and sat over it; thus performing his promise to the dead man. As a mystic memorial of this incident, *phalloi* are raised aloft in honour of Dionysus through the various cities. "For did they not make a procession in honour of Dionysus, and sing most shameless songs in honour of the pudenda, all would go wrong," says Heraclitus. This is that Pluto and Dionysus in whose honour they give themselves up to frenzy, and play the bacchanal,—not so much, in my opinion, for the sake of

---

[1] Meursius proposed to read, "at Agra."

intoxication, as for the sake of the shameless ceremonial practised. With reason, therefore, such as have become slaves of their passions are your gods!

Furthermore, like the Helots among the Lacedemonians, Apollo came under the yoke of slavery to Admetus in Pheræ, Hercules to Omphale in Sardis. Poseidon was a drudge to Laomedon; and so was Apollo, who, like a good-for-nothing servant, was unable to obtain his freedom from his former master; and at that time the walls of Troy were built by them for the Phrygian. And Homer is not ashamed to speak of Athene as appearing to Ulysses with a golden lamp in her hand. And we read of Aphrodite, like a wanton serving-wench, taking and setting a seat for Helen opposite the adulterer, in order to entice him to intercourse.

Panyasis, too, tells us of gods in plenty besides those who acted as servants, writing thus:

> "Demeter underwent servitude, and so did the famous lame god;
> Poseidon underwent it, and Apollo too, of the silver bow,
> With a mortal man for a year. And fierce Mars
> Underwent it at the compulsion of his father."

And so on.

Agreeably to this, it remains for me to bring before you those amatory and sensuous deities of yours, as in every respect having human feelings.

> "For theirs was a mortal body."

This Homer most distinctly shows, by introducing Aphrodite uttering loud and shrill cries on account of her wound; and describing the most warlike Ares himself as wounded in the stomach by Diomede. Polemo, too, says that Athene was wounded by Ornytus; nay, Homer says that Pluto even was struck with an arrow by Hercules; and Panyasis relates that the beams of Sol were struck by the arrows of Hercules;[1] and the same Panyasis relates, that by the same Hercules Hera the goddess of marriage was wounded in sandy Pylos. Sosibius, too, relates that Hercules was wounded in the hand by the sons of Hippocoon. And if there are wounds, there

[1] *The beams of Sol or the Sun* is an emendation of Potter's. The MSS. read "*the Elean Augeas.*"

is blood. For the *ichor* of the poets is more repulsive than blood; for the putrefaction of blood is called *ichor*. Wherefore cures and means of sustenance of which they stand in need must be furnished. Accordingly mention is made of tables, and potations, and laughter, and intercourse; for men would not devote themselves to love, or beget children, or sleep, if they were immortal, and had no wants, and never grew old. Jupiter himself, when the guest of Lycaon the Arcadian, partook of a human table among the Ethiopians—a table rather inhuman and forbidden. For he satiated himself with human flesh unwittingly; for the god did not know that Lycaon the Arcadian, his entertainer, had slain his son (his name was Nyctimus), and served him up cooked before Zeus.

This is Jupiter the good, the prophetic, the patron of hospitality, the protector of suppliants, the benign, the author of omens, the avenger of wrongs; rather the unjust, the violator of right and of law, the impious, the inhuman, the violent, the seducer, the adulterer, the amatory. But perhaps when he was such he was a man; but now these fables seem to have grown old on our hands. Zeus is no longer a serpent, a swan, nor an eagle, nor a licentious man; the god no longer flies, nor loves boys, nor kisses, nor offers violence, although there are still many beautiful women, more comely than Leda, more blooming than Semele, and boys of better looks and manners than the Phrygian herdsman. Where is now that eagle? where now that swan? where now is Zeus himself? He has grown old with his feathers; for as yet he does not repent of his amatory exploits, nor is he taught continence. The fable is exposed before you: Leda is dead, the swan is dead. Seek your Jupiter. Ransack not heaven, but earth. The Cretan, in whose country he was buried, will show him to you,—I mean Callimachus, in his hymns:

"For thy tomb, O king,
The Cretans fashioned!"

For Zeus is dead, be not distressed, as Leda is dead, and the swan, and the eagle, and the libertine, and the serpent. And now even the superstitious seem, although reluctantly, yet truly, to have come to understand their error respecting the gods.

> "For not from an ancient oak, nor from a rock,
> But from men, is thy descent."[1]

But shortly after this, they will be found to be but oaks and stones. One Agamemnon is said by Staphylus to be worshipped as a Jupiter in Sparta; and Phanocles, in his book of the *Brave and Fair*, relates that Agamemnon king of the Hellenes erected the temple of Argennian Aphrodite, in honour of Argennus his friend. An Artemis, named the Strangled, is worshipped by the Arcadians, as Callimachus says in his *Book of Causes*; and at Methymna another Artemis had divine honours paid her, viz. Artemis Condylitis. There is also the temple of another Artemis—Artemis Podagra (or, the gout)—in Laconica, as Sosibius says. Polemo tells of an image of a yawning Apollo; and again of another image, reverenced in Elis, of the guzzling Apollo. Then the Eleans sacrifice to Zeus, the averter of flies; and the Romans sacrifice to Hercules, the averter of flies; and to Fever, and to Terror, whom also they reckon among the attendants of Hercules. (I pass over the Argives, who worshipped Aphrodite, opener of graves.) The Argives and Spartans reverence Artemis Chelytis, or the cougher, from χελύττειν, which in their speech signifies to cough.

Do you imagine from what source these details have been quoted? Only such as are furnished by yourselves are here adduced; and you do not seem to recognise your own writers, whom I call as witnesses against your unbelief. Poor wretches that ye are, who have filled with unholy jesting the whole compass of your life—a life in reality devoid of life!

Is not Zeus the Baldhead worshipped in Argos; and another Zeus, the avenger, in Cyprus? Do not the Argives sacrifice to Aphrodite Peribaso (the protectress),[2] and the

---

[1] *Odyss.* xix. 163.

[2] So Liddel and Scott. Commentators are generally agreed that the epithet is an obscene one, though what its precise meaning is they can only conjecture.

Athenians to Aphrodite Hetæra (the courtesan), and the Syracusans to Aphrodite Kallipygos, whom Nicander has somewhere called Kalliglutos (with beautiful rump). I pass over in silence just now Dionysus Choiropsales.[1] The Sicyonians reverence this deity, whom they have constituted the god of the muliebria—the patron of filthiness—and religiously honour as the author of licentiousness. Such, then, are their gods; such are they also who make mockery of the gods, or rather mock and insult themselves. How much better are the Egyptians, who in their towns and villages pay divine honours to the irrational creatures, than the Greeks, who worship such gods as these?

For if they are beasts, they are not adulterous or libidinous, and seek pleasure in nothing that is contrary to nature. And of what sort these deities are, what need is there further to say, as they have been already sufficiently exposed? Furthermore, the Egyptians whom I have now mentioned are divided in their objects of worship. The Syenites worship the braize-fish; and the maiotes—this is another fish—is worshipped by those who inhabit Elephantine: the Oxyrinchites likewise worship a fish which takes its name from their country. Again, the Heraclitopolites worship the ichneumon, the inhabitants of Sais and of Thebes a sheep, the Leucopolites a wolf, the Cynopolites a dog, the Memphites Apis, the Mendesians a goat. And you, who are altogether better than the Egyptians (I shrink from saying worse), who are never done laughing every day of your lives at the Egyptians, what are some of you, too, with regard to brute beasts? For of your number the Thessalians pay divine homage to storks, in accordance with ancient custom; and the Thebans to weasels, for their assistance at the birth of Hercules. And again, are not the Thessalians reported to worship ants, since they have learned that Zeus in the likeness of an ant had intercourse with Eurymedusa, the daughter of Cletor, and begot Myrmidon? Polemo, too, relates that the people who inhabit the Troad worship the mice of the country, which they call

---

[1] An obscene epithet, derived from χοῖρος, a sow, used metonymically for *muliebria*, and θλίβω, to press or rub.

Sminthoi, because they gnawed the strings of their enemies' bows; and from those mice Apollo has received his epithet of Sminthian. Heraclides, in his work, *Regarding the Building of Temples in Acarnania*, says that, at the place where the promontory of Actium is, and the temple of Apollo of Actium, they offer to the flies the sacrifice of an ox.

Nor shall I forget the Samians: the Samians, as Euphorion says, reverence the sheep. Nor shall I forget the Syrians, who inhabit Phœnicia, of whom some revere doves, and others fishes, with as excessive veneration as the Eleans do Zeus. Well, then, since those you worship are not gods, it seems to me requisite to ascertain if those are really demons who are ranked, as you say, in this second order [next the gods]. For if the lickerish and impure are demons, indigenous demons who have obtained sacred honours may be discovered in crowds throughout your cities: Menedemus among the Cythnians; among the Tenians, Callistagoras; among the Delians, Anius; among the Laconians, Astrabacus; at Phalerus, a hero affixed to the prow of ships is worshipped; and the Pythian priestess enjoined the Platæans to sacrifice to Androcrates and Democrates, and Cyclæus and Leuco while the Median war was at its height. Other demons in plenty may be brought to light by any one who can look about him a little.

"For thrice ten thousand are there in the all-nourishing earth
Of demons immortal, the guardians of articulate-speaking men."[1]

Who these guardians are, do not grudge, O Bœotian, to tell. Is it not clear that they are those we have mentioned, and those of more renown, the great demons, Apollo, Artemis, Leto, Demeter, Kore, Pluto, Hercules, and Zeus himself?

But it is from running away that they guard us, O Ascræan, or perhaps it is from sinning, as forsooth they have never tried their hand at sin themselves! In that case verily the proverb may fitly be uttered:

"The father who took no admonition admonishes his son."

If these are our guardians, it is not because they have any ardour of kindly feeling towards us, but intent on your ruin, after the manner of flatterers, they prey on your substance,

[1] Hesiod, *Works and Days*, L. i. 250.

enticed by the smoke. These demons themselves indeed confess their own gluttony, saying:

> "For with drink-offerings due, and fat of lambs,
> My altar still hath at their hands been fed;
> Such honour hath to us been ever paid."[1]

What other speech would they utter, if indeed the gods of the Egyptians, such as cats and weasels, should receive the faculty of speech, than that Homeric and poetic one which proclaims their liking for savoury odours and cookery? Such are your demons and gods, and demigods, if there are any so called, as there are demi-asses (mules); for you have no want of terms to make up compound names of impiety.

[1] *Iliad*, iv. 49.

CHAPTER III.

THE CRUELTY OF THE SACRIFICES TO THE GODS.

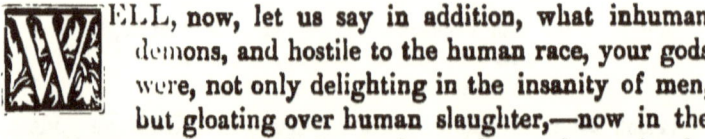ELL, now, let us say in addition, what inhuman demons, and hostile to the human race, your gods were, not only delighting in the insanity of men, but gloating over human slaughter,—now in the armed contests for superiority in the stadia, and now in the numberless contests for renown in the wars providing for themselves the means of pleasure, that they might be able abundantly to satiate themselves with the murder of human beings.

And now, like plagues invading cities and nations, they demanded cruel oblations. Thus, Aristomenes the Messenian slew three hundred human beings in honour of Ithometan Zeus, thinking that hecatombs of such a number and quality would give good omens; among whom was Theopompos, king of the Lacedemonians, a noble victim.

The Taurians, the people who inhabit the Tauric Chersonese, sacrifice to the Tauric Artemis forthwith whatever strangers they lay hands on on their coasts who have been cast adrift on the sea. These sacrifices Euripides represents in tragedies on the stage. Monimus relates, in his treatise on marvels, that at Pella, in Thessaly, a man of Achaia was slain in sacrifice to Peleus and Chiron. That the Lyctii, who are a Cretan race, slew men in sacrifice to Zeus, Anticlides shows in his *Homeward Journeys;* and that the Lesbians offered the like sacrifice to Dionysus, is said by Dosidas. The Phocæans also (for I will not pass over such as they are), Pythocles informs us in his third book, *On Concord,* offer a man as a burnt-sacrifice to the Taurian Artemis.

Erechtheus of Attica and Marius the Roman [1] sacrificed

---
[1] Plutarch, xx.

their daughters,—the former to Pherephatta, as Demaratus mentions in his first book on *Tragic Subjects;* the latter to the evil-averting deities, as Dorotheus relates in his first book of *Italian Affairs.* Philanthropic, assuredly, the demons appear, from these examples; and how shall those who revere the demons not be correspondingly pious? The former are called by the fair name of saviours; and the latter ask for safety from those who plot against their safety, imagining that they sacrifice with good omens to them, and forget that they themselves are slaying men. For a murder does not become a sacrifice by being committed in a particular spot. You are not to call it a sacred sacrifice, if one slays a man either at the altar or on the highway to Artemis or Zeus, any more than if he slew him for anger or covetousness,—other demons very like the former; but a sacrifice of this kind is murder and human butchery. Then why is it, O men, wisest of all creatures, that you avoid wild beasts, and get out of the way of the savage animals, if you fall in with a bear or lion?

".... As when some traveller spies,
Coiled in his path upon the mountain side,
A deadly snake, back he recoils in haste,—
His limbs all trembling, and his cheek all pale." [1]

But though you perceive and understand demons to be deadly and wicked, plotters, haters of the human race, and destroyers, why do you not turn out of their way, or turn them out of yours? What truth can the wicked tell, or what good can they do any one?

I can then readily demonstrate that man is better than these gods of yours, who are but demons; and can show, for instance, that Cyrus and Solon were superior to oracular Apollo. Your Phœbus was a lover of gifts, but not a lover of men. He betrayed his friend Crœsus, and forgetting the reward he had got (so careful was he of his fame), led him across the Halys to the stake. The demons love men in such a way as to bring them to the fire [unquenchable].

But O man, who lovest the human race better, and art truer than Apollo, pity him that is bound on the pyre. Do thou,

[1] *Iliad*, iii. v. 33.

O Solon, declare truth; and thou, O Cyrus, command the fire to be extinguished. Be wise, then, at last, O Crœsus, taught by suffering. He whom you worship is an ingrate; he accepts your reward, and after taking the gold plays false. "Look again to the end," O Solon. It is not the demon, but the man that tells you this. It is not ambiguous oracles that Solon utters. You shall easily take him up. Nothing but true, O Barbarian, shall you find by proof this oracle to be, when you are placed on the pyre. Whence I cannot help wondering, by what plausible reasons those who first went astray were impelled to preach superstition to men, when they exhorted them to worship wicked demons, whether it was Phoroneus or Merops, or whoever else that raised temples and altars to them; and besides, as is fabled, were the first to offer sacrifices to them. But, unquestionably, in succeeding ages men invented for themselves gods to worship. It is beyond doubt that this Eros, who is said to be among the oldest of the gods, was worshipped by no one till Charmus took a little boy and raised an altar to him in Academia,—a thing more seemly[1] than the lust he had gratified; and the lewdness of vice men called by the name of Eros, deifying thus unbridled lust. The Athenians, again, knew not who Pan was till Philippides told them.

Superstition, then, as was to be expected, having taken its rise thus, became the fountain of insensate wickedness; and not being subsequently checked, but having gone on augmenting and rushing along in full flood, it became the originator of many demons, and was displayed in sacrificing hecatombs, appointing solemn assemblies, setting up images, and building temples, which were in reality tombs: for I will not pass these over in silence, but make a thorough exposure of them, though called by the august name of temples; that is, the tombs which got the name of temples. But do ye now at length quite give up your superstition, feeling ashamed to regard sepulchres with religious veneration. In the temple of Athene in Larissa,

---

[1] If we read χαριέστερον, this is the only sense that can be put on the words. But if we read χαριστήριον, we may translate, "a memorial of gratified lust."

on the Acropolis, is the grave of Acrisius; and at Athens, on the Acropolis, is that of Cecrops, as Antiochus says in the ninth book of his *Histories*. What of Erichthonius? was he not buried in the temple of Polias? And Immarus, the son of Eumolpus and Daira, were they not buried in the precincts of the Elusinium, which is under the Acropolis; and the daughters of Celeus, were they not interred in Eleusis? Why should I enumerate to you the wives of the Hyperboreans? They were called Hyperoche and Laodice; they were buried in the Artemisium in Delos, which is in the temple of the Delian Apollo. Leandrias says that Clearchus was buried in Miletus, in the Didymæum. Following the Myndian Zeno, it were unsuitable in this connection to pass over the sepulchre of Leucophryne, who was buried in the temple of Artemis in Magnesia; or the altar of Apollo in Telmessus, which is reported to be the tomb of Telmisseus the seer. Further, Ptolemy the son of Agesarchus, in his first book about Philopator, says that Cinyras and the descendants of Cinyras were interred in the temple of Aphrodite in Paphos. But all time would not be sufficient for me, were I to go over the tombs which are held sacred by you. And if no shame for these audacious impieties steals over you, it comes to this, that you are completely dead, putting, as really you do, your trust in the dead.

"Poor wretches, what misery is this you suffer?
Your heads are enveloped in the darkness of night."[1]

---

[1] *Odyss.* xx. v. 351

CHAPTER IV.

THE ABSURDITY AND SHAMEFULNESS OF THE IMAGES BY WHICH THE GODS ARE WORSHIPPED.

IF, in addition, I take and set before you for inspection these very images, you will, as you go over them, find how truly silly is the custom in which you have been reared, of worshipping the senseless works of men's hands.

Anciently, then, the Scythians worshipped their sabres, the Arabs stones, the Persians rivers. And some, belonging to other races still more ancient, set up blocks of wood in conspicuous situations, and erected pillars of stone, which were called Xoana, from the carving of the material of which they were made. The image of Artemis in Icarus was doubtless unwrought wood, and that of the Cithæronian Here was a felled tree-trunk; and that of the Samian Here, as Aethlius says, was at first a plank, and was afterwards during the government of Proclus carved into human shape. And when the Xoana began to be made in the likeness of men, they got the name of Brete,—a term derived from Brotos (man). In Rome, the historian Varro says that in ancient times the Xoanon of Mars—the idol by which he was worshipped—was a spear, artists not having yet applied themselves to this specious pernicious art; but when art flourished, error increased. That of stones and stocks—and, to speak briefly, of dead matter—you have made images of human form, by which you have produced a counterfeit of piety, and slandered the truth, is now as clear as can be; but such proof as the point may demand must not be declined.

That the statue of Zeus at Olympia, and that of Polias at

Athens, were executed of gold and ivory by Phidias, is known by everybody; and that the image of Here in Samos was formed by the chisel of Euclides, Olympichus relates in his *Samiaca*. Do not, then, entertain any doubt, that of the gods called at Athens venerable, Scopas made two of the stone called Lychnis, and Calos the one which they are reported to have had placed between them, as Polemon shows in the fourth of his books addressed to Timæus. Nor need you doubt respecting the images of Zeus and Apollo at Patara, in Lycia, which Phidias executed, as well as the lions that recline with them; and if, as some say, they were the work of Bryxis, I do not dispute,—you have in him another maker of images. Whichever of these you like, write down. Furthermore, the statues nine cubits in height of Poseidon and Amphitrite, worshipped in Tenos, are the work of Telesius the Athenian, as we are told by Philochorus. Demetrius, in the second book of his *Argolics*, writes of the image of Here in Tiryns, both that the material was pear-tree and the artist was Argus.

Many, perhaps, may be surprised to learn that the Palladium which is called the Diopetes — that is, fallen from heaven—which Diomede and Ulysses are related to have carried off from Troy and deposited at Demophoon, was made of the bones of Pelops, as the Olympian Jove of other bones —those of the Indian wild beast. I adduce as my authority Dionysius, who relates this in the fifth part of his *Cycle*. And Apellas, in the *Delphics*, says that there were two Palladia, and that both were fashioned by men. But that no one may suppose that I have passed over them through ignorance, I shall add that the image of Dionysus Morychus at Athens was made of the stones called Phellata, and was the work of Simon the son of Eupalamus, as Polemo says in a letter. There were also two other sculptors of Crete, as I think: they were called Scyles and Dipoenus; and these executed the statues of the Dioscuri in Argos, and the image of Hercules in Tiryns, and the effigy of the Munychian Artemis in Sicyon.

Why should I linger over these, when I can point out to you the great deity himself, and show you who he was,— whom indeed, conspicuously above all, we hear to have been considered worthy of veneration? Him they have dared to speak of as made without hands—I mean the Egyptian Serapis. For some relate that he was sent as a present by the people of Sinope to Ptolemy Philadelphus, king of the Egyptians, who won their favour by sending them corn from Egypt when they were perishing with famine; and that this idol was an image of Pluto; and Ptolemy, having received the statue, placed it on the promontory which is now called Racotis; where the temple of Serapis was held in honour, and the sacred enclosure borders on the spot; and that Blistichis the courtesan having died in Canopus, Ptolemy had her conveyed there, and buried beneath the fore-mentioned shrine.

Others say that the Serapis was a Pontic idol, and was transported with solemn pomp to Alexandria. Isidore alone says that it was brought from the Seleucians, near Antioch, who also had been visited with a dearth of corn, and had been fed by Ptolemy. But Athenodorus the son of Sandon, while wishing to make out the Serapis to be ancient, has somehow slipped into the mistake of proving it to be an image fashioned by human hands. He says that Sesostris the Egyptian king, having subjugated the most of the Hellenic races, on his return to Egypt brought a number of craftsmen with him. Accordingly he ordered a statue of Osiris, his ancestor, to be executed in sumptuous style; and the work was done by the artist Bryaxis, not the Athenian, but another of the same name, who employed in its execution a mixture of various materials. For he had filings of gold, and silver, and lead, and in addition, tin; and of Egyptian stones not one was wanting, and there were fragments of sapphire, and hematite, and emerald, and topaz. Having ground down and mixed together all these ingredients, he gave to the composition a blue colour, whence the darkish hue of the image; and having mixed the whole with the colouring matter that was left over from the funeral of Osiris and Apis, moulded the Serapis, the name of which points to its connection with sepulture and its construction from funeral materials, compounded as it is of Osiris and Apis, which together make Osirapis.

Another new deity was added to the number with great

religious pomp in Egypt, and was near being so in Greece by the king of the Romans, who deified Antinous, whom he loved as Zeus loved Ganymede, and whose beauty was of a very rare order: for lust is not easily restrained, destitute as it is of fear; and men now observe the sacred nights of Antinous, the shameful character of which the lover who spent them with him knew well. Why reckon him among the gods, who is honoured on account of uncleanness? And why do you command him to be lamented as a son? And why should you enlarge on his beauty? Beauty blighted by vice is loathsome. Do not play the tyrant, O man, over beauty, nor offer foul insult to youth in its bloom. Keep beauty pure, that it may be truly fair. Be king over beauty, not its tyrant. Remain free, and then I shall acknowledge thy beauty, because thou hast kept its image pure: then will I worship that true beauty which is the archetype of all who are beautiful. Now the grave of the debauched boy is the temple and town of Antinous. For just as temples are held in reverence, so also are sepulchres, and pyramids, and mausoleums, and labyrinths, which are temples of the dead, as the others are sepulchres of the gods. As teacher on this point, I shall produce to you the Sybil prophetess:

"Not the oracular lie of Phœbus,
Whom silly men called God, and falsely termed Prophet;
But the oracles of the great God, who was not made by men's hands,
Like dumb idols of sculptured stone."[1]

She also predicts the ruin of the temple, foretelling that that of the Ephesian Artemis would be engulphed by earthquakes and rents in the ground, as follows:

"Prostrate on the ground Ephesus shall wail, weeping by the shore,
And seeking a temple that has no longer an inhabitant."

She says also that the temple of Isis and Serapis would be demolished and burned:

"Isis, thrice-wretched goddess, thou shalt linger by the streams of the Nile;
Solitary, frenzied, silent, on the sands of Acheron."

---

[1] Vulg. *Sybillini*, p. 253.

Then she proceeds :

> " And thou, Serapis, covered with a heap of white stones,
> Shalt lie a huge ruin in thrice-wretched Egypt."

But if you attend not to the prophetess, hear at least your own philosopher, the Ephesian Heraclitus, upbraiding images with their senselessness : " And to these images they pray, with the same result as if one were to talk to the walls of his house." For are they not to be wondered at who worship stones, and place them before the doors, as if capable of activity ? They worship Hermes as a god, and place Aguieus as a doorkeeper. For if people upbraid them with being devoid of sensation, why worship them as gods ? And if they are thought to be endowed with sensation, why place them before the door ? The Romans, who ascribed their greatest successes to Fortune, and regarded her as a very great deity, took her statue to the privy, and erected it there, assigning to the goddess as a fitting temple—the necessary. But senseless wood and stone, and rich gold, care not a whit for either savoury odour, or blood, or smoke, by which, being at once honoured and fumigated, they are blackened ; no more do they for honour or insult. And these images are more worthless than any animal. I am at a loss to conceive how objects devoid of sense were deified, and feel compelled to pity as miserable wretches those that wander in the mazes of this folly : for if some living creatures have not all the senses, as worms and caterpillars, and such as even from the first appear imperfect, as moles and the shrew-mouse, which Nicander says is blind and uncouth ; yet are they superior to those utterly senseless idols and images. For they have some one sense,— say, for example, hearing, or touching, or something analogous to smell or taste ; while images do not possess even one sense. There are many creatures that have neither sight, nor hearing, nor speech, such as the genus of oysters, which yet live and grow, and are affected by the changes of the moon. But images, being motionless, inert, and senseless, are bound, nailed, glued,—are melted, filed, sawed, polished, carved. The senseless earth is dishonoured by the makers of images, who change it by their art from its proper nature, and induce men to worship it; and the makers of gods worship not gods and demons, but in my view earth and art, which go to make up images. For, in sooth, the image is only dead matter shaped by the craftsman's hand. But *we* have no sensible image of sensible matter, but an image that is perceived by the mind alone,—God, who alone is truly God.

And again, when involved in calamities, the superstitious worshippers of stones, though they have learned by the event that senseless matter is not to be worshipped, yet, yielding to the pressure of misfortune, become the victims of their superstition; and though despising the images, yet not wishing to appear wholly to neglect them, are found fault with by those gods by whose names the images are called.

For Dionysius the tyrant, the younger, having stripped off the golden mantle from the statue of Jupiter in Sicily, ordered him to be clothed in a woollen one, remarking facetiously that the latter was better than the golden one, being lighter in summer and warmer in winter. And Antiochus of Cyzicus, being in difficulties for money, ordered the golden statue of Zeus, fifteen cubits in height, to be melted; and one like it, of less valuable material, plated with gold, to be erected in place of it. And the swallows and most birds fly to these statues, and void their excrement on them, paying no respect either to Olympian Zeus, or Epidaurian Asclepius, or even to Athene Polias, or the Egyptian Serapis; but not even from them have you learned the senselessness of images. But it has happened that miscreants or enemies have assailed and set fire to temples, and plundered them of their votive gifts, and melted even the images themselves, from base greed of gain. And if a Cambyses or a Darius, or any other madman, has made such attempts, and if one has killed the Egyptian Apis, I laugh at him killing their god, while pained at the outrage being perpetrated for the sake of gain. I will therefore willingly forget such villany, looking on acts like these more as deeds of covetousness, than as a proof of the impotence of idols. But fire and earthquakes are shrewd enough not to feel shy or frightened at either demons or idols, any more than at pebbles heaped by the waves on the shore.

I know fire to be capable of exposing and curing superstition. If thou art willing to abandon this folly, the element of fire shall light thy way. This same fire burned the temple in Argos, with Chrysis the priestess; and that of Artemis in Ephesus the second time after the Amazons. And the Capitol in Rome was often wrapped in flames; nor did the fire spare the temple of Serapis, in the city of the Alexandrians. At Athens it demolished the temple of the Eleutherian Dionysus; and as to the temple of Apollo at Delphi, first a storm assailed it, and then the discerning fire utterly destroyed it. This is told as the preface of what the fire promises. And the makers of images, do they not shame those of you who are wise into despising matter? The Athenian Phidias inscribed on the finger of the Olympian Jove, Pantarkes [1] is beautiful. It was not Zeus that was beautiful in his eyes, but the man he loved. And Praxiteles, as Posidippus relates in his book about Cnidus, when he fashioned the statue of Aphrodite of Cnidus, made it like the form of Cratine, of whom he was enamoured, that the miserable people might have the paramour of Praxiteles to worship. And when Phryne the courtesan, the Thespian, was in her bloom, all the painters made their pictures of Aphrodite copies of the beauty of Phryne; as, again, the sculptors at Athens made their Mercuries like Alcibiades. It remains for you to judge whether you ought to worship courtesans. Moved, as I believe, by such facts, and despising such fables, the ancient kings unblushingly proclaimed themselves gods, as this involved no danger from men, and thus taught that on account of their glory they were made immortal. Ceux, the son of Eolus, was styled Zeus by his wife Alcyone; Alcyone, again, being by her husband styled Hera. Ptolemy the Fourth was called Dionysus; and Mithridates of Pontus was also called Dionysus; and Alexander wished to be considered the son of Ammon, and to have his statue made horned by the sculptors—eager to disgrace the beauty of the human form by the addition of a horn. And not kings only, but pri-

[1] Pantarkes is said to have been the name of a boy loved by Phidias; but as the word signifies "all-assisting," "all-powerful," it might also be made to apply to Zeus.

vate persons dignified themselves with the names of deities, as Menecrates the physician, who took the name of Zeus. What need is there for me to instance Alexarchus? He, having been by profession a grammarian, assumed the character of the sungod, as Aristus of Salamis relates. And why mention Nicagorus? He was a native of Zela [in Pontus], and lived in the days of Alexander. Nicagorus was styled Hermes, and used the dress of Hermes, as he himself testifies. And whilst whole nations, and cities with all their inhabitants, sinking into self-flattery, treat the myths about the gods with contempt, at the same time men themselves, assuming the air of equality with the gods, and being puffed up with vainglory, vote themselves extravagant honours. There is the case of the Macedonian Philip of Pella, the son of Amyntor, to whom they decreed divine worship in Cynosargus, although his collar-bone was broken, and he had a lame leg, and had one of his eyes knocked out. And again that of Demetrius, who was raised to the rank of the gods; and where he alighted from his horse on his entrance into Athens is the temple of Demetrius *the Alighter;* and altars were raised to him everywhere, and nuptials with Athene assigned to him by the Athenians. But he disdained the goddess, as he could not marry the statue; and taking the courtesan Lamia, he ascended the Acropolis, and lay with her on the couch of Athene, showing to the old virgin the postures of the young courtesan.

There is no cause for indignation, then, at Hippo, who immortalized his own death. For this Hippo ordered the following elegy to be inscribed on his tomb:

"This is the sepulchre of Hippo, whom Destiny
Made, through death, equal to the immortal gods."

Well done, Hippo! thou showest to us the delusion of men. If they did not believe thee speaking, now that thou art dead, let them become thy disciples. This is the oracle of Hippo; let us consider it. The objects of your worship were once men, and in process of time died; and fable and time have raised them to honour. For somehow, what is present is wont to be despised through familiarity; but what is past, being separated through the obscurity of time from the temporary censure that attached to it, is invested with honour by fiction, so that the present is viewed with distrust, the past with admiration. Exactly in this way is it, then, that the dead men of antiquity, being reverenced through the long prevalence of delusion respecting them, are regarded as gods by posterity. As grounds of your belief in these, there are your mysteries, your solemn assemblies, bonds and wounds, and weeping deities.

"Woe, woe! that fate decrees my best-belov'd,
Sarpedon, by Patroclus' hand to fall."[1]

The will of Zeus was overruled; and Zeus being worsted, laments for Sarpedon. With reason, therefore, have you yourselves called them shades and demons, since Homer, paying Athene and the other divinities sinister honour, has styled them demons:

"She her heavenward course pursued
To join the immortals in the abode of Jove."[2]

How, then, can shades and demons be still reckoned gods, being in reality unclean and impure spirits, acknowledged by all to be of an earthy and watery nature, sinking downwards by their own weight, and flitting about graves and tombs, about which they appear dimly, being but shadowy phantasms? Such things are your gods—shades and shadows; and to these add those maimed, wrinkled, squinting divinities the Litæ, daughters of Thersites rather than of Zeus. So that Bion—wittily, as I think—says, How in reason could men pray Zeus for a beautiful progeny,—a thing he could not obtain for himself?

The incorruptible being, as far as in you lies, you sink in the earth; and that pure and holy essence you have buried in the grave, robbing the divine of its true nature.

Why, I pray you, have you assigned the prerogatives of God to what are no gods? Why, let me ask, have you forsaken heaven to pay divine honour to earth? What else is gold, or silver, or steel, or iron, or brass, or ivory, or precious stones? Are they not earth, and of the earth?

Are not all these things which you look on the progeny of one mother—the earth?

[1] *Iliad*, xvi. 433.   [2] *Iliad*, i. v. 22; μετὰ δαίμονας ἄλλους.

which your authors introduce, urge me to cry out, though I would fain be silent. Oh the godlessness! You have turned heaven into a stage; the Divine has become a drama; and what is sacred you have acted in comedies under the masks of demons, travestying true religion by your demon-worship [superstition].

"But he, striking the lyre, began to sing beautifully."[1]

Sing to us, Homer, that beautiful song

"About the amours of Ares and Venus with the beautiful crown:
How first they slept together in the palace of Hephæstus
Secretly; and he gave many gifts, and dishonoured the bed and chamber of king Hephæstus."

Stop, O Homer, the song! It is not beautiful; it teaches adultery, and we are prohibited from polluting our ears with hearing about adultery: for we are they who bear about with us, in this living and moving image of our human nature, the likeness of God,—a likeness which dwells with us, takes counsel with us, associates with us, is a guest with us, feels with us, feels for us. We have become a consecrated offering to God for Christ's sake: we are the chosen generation, the royal priesthood, the holy nation, the peculiar people, who once were not a people, but are now the people of God; who, according to John, are not of those who are beneath, but have learned all from Him who came from above; who have come to understand the dispensation of God; who have learned to walk in newness of life. But these are not the sentiments of the many; but, casting off shame and fear, they depict in their houses the unnatural passions of the demons. Accordingly, wedded to impurity, they adorn their bed-chambers with painted tablets hung up in them, regarding licentiousness as religion; and lying in bed, in the midst of their embraces, they look on that Aphrodite locked in the embrace of her paramour. And in the hoops of their rings they cut a representation of the amorous bird that fluttered round Leda,—having a strong predilection for representations of effeminacy,—and use a seal stamped with an impression of the licentiousness of Zeus. Such are

[1] *Odyss.* viii. v. 266.

examples of your voluptuousness, such are the theologies of vice, such are the instructions of your gods, who commit fornication along with you; for what one wishes, that he thinks, according to the Athenian orator. And of what kind, on the other hand, are your other images? Diminutive Pans, and naked girls, and drunken Satyrs, and *erecta pudenda*, painted naked in pictures disgraceful for filthiness. And more than this: you are not ashamed in the eyes of all to look at representations of all forms of licentiousness which are portrayed in public places, but set them up and guard them with scrupulous care, consecrating these pillars of shamelessness at home, as if, forsooth, they were the images of your gods, depicting on them equally the postures of Philænis and the labours of Heracles. Not only the use of these, but the sight of them, and the very hearing of them, we denounce as deserving the doom of oblivion. Your ears are debauched, your eyes commit fornication, your looks commit adultery before you embrace. O ye that have done violence to man, and have devoted to shame what is divine in this handiwork of God, you disbelieve everything that you may indulge your passions, and that ye may believe in idols, because you have a craving after their licentiousness, but disbelieve God, because you cannot bear a life of self-restraint. You have hated what was better, and valued what was worse, having been spectators indeed of virtue, but actors of vice. Happy, therefore, so to say, alone are all those with one accord,

"Who shall refuse to look on any temples
And altars, worthless seats of dumb stones,
And idols of stone, and images made by hands,
Stained with the life's-blood, and with sacrifices
Of quadrupeds, and bipeds, and fowls, and butcheries of wild beasts."[1]

For we are expressly prohibited from exercising a deceptive art: "For thou shalt not make," says the prophet, "the likeness of anything which is in the heaven above or in the earth beneath."[2]

For can we possibly any longer suppose the Demeter, and

[1] Sibyl. Justin Martyr. *Cohort. ad Græcos*, p. 81; English Transl. (A.N. Lib.), p. 304. [2] Ex. xx. 4.

the Kore, and the mystic Iacchus of Praxiteles, to be gods, and not rather regard the art of Leucippus, or the hands of Apelles, which clothed the material with the form of the divine glory, as having a better title to the honour? But while you bestow the greatest pains that the image may be fashioned with the most exquisite beauty possible, you exercise no care to guard against your becoming like images for stupidity. Accordingly, with the utmost clearness and brevity, the prophetic word condemns this practice: "For all the gods of the nations are the images of demons; but God made the heavens, and what is in heaven."[1] Some, however, who have fallen into error, I know not how, worship God's work instead of God Himself,—the sun and the moon, and the rest of the starry choir,—absurdly imagining these, which are but instruments for measuring time, to be gods; "for by His word they were established, and all their host by the breath of His mouth."[2]

Human art, moreover, produces houses, and ships, and cities, and pictures. But how shall I tell what God makes? Behold the whole universe; it is His work: and the heaven, and the sun, and angels, and men, are the works of His fingers.[3] How great is the power of God! His bare volition was the creation of the universe. For God alone made it, because He alone is truly God. By the bare exercise of volition He creates; His mere willing was followed by the springing into being of what He willed. Consequently the choir of philosophers are in error, who indeed most nobly confess that man was made for the contemplation of the heavens, but who worship the objects that appear in the heavens and are apprehended by sight. For if the heavenly bodies are not the works of men, they were certainly created for man. Let none of you worship the sun, but set his desires on the Maker of the sun; nor deify the universe, but seek after the Creator of the universe. The only refuge, then, which remains for him who would reach the portals of salvation is divine wisdom. From this, as from a sacred asylum, the man who presses after salvation, can be dragged by no demon.

[1] Ps. xcvi. 5.   [2] Ps. xxxiii. 6.   [3] Ps. viii. 4.

CHAPTER V.

THE OPINIONS OF THE PHILOSOPHERS RESPECTING GOD.

LET us then run over, if you choose, the opinions of the philosophers, to which they give boastful utterance, respecting the gods; that we may discover philosophy itself, through its conceit making an idol of matter; although we are able to show, as we proceed, that even while deifying certain demons, it has a dream of the truth. The elements were designated as the first principles of all things by some of them: by Thales of Miletus, who celebrated water, and Anaximenes, also of Miletus, who celebrated air as the first principle of all things, and was followed afterwards by Diogenes of Apollonia. Parmenides of Elia introduced fire and earth as gods; one of which, namely fire, Hippasus of Metapontum and Heraclitus of Ephesus supposed a divinity. Empedocles of Agrigentum fell in with a multitude, and, in addition to those four elements, enumerates disagreement and agreement. Atheists surely these are to be reckoned, who through an unwise wisdom worshipped matter, who did not indeed pay religious honour to stocks and stones, but deified earth, the mother of these,— who did not make an image of Poseidon, but revered water itself. For what else, according to the original signification, is Poseidon, but a moist substance? the name being derived from *posis* (drink); as, beyond doubt, the warlike Ares is so called, from *arsis* (rising up) and *anæresis* (destroying). For this reason mainly, I think, many fix a sword into the ground, and sacrifice to it as to Ares. The Scythians have a practice of this nature, as Eudoxus tells us in the second book of his *Travels*. The Sauromatæ, too, a tribe of the

Scythians, worship a sabre, as Ikesius says in his work on *Mysteries*.

This was also the case with Heraclitus and his followers, who worshipped fire as the first cause; for this fire others named Hephæstus. The Persian Magi, too, and many of the inhabitants of Asia, worshipped fire; and besides them, the Macedonians, as Diogenes relates in the first book of his *Persica*. Why specify the Sauromatæ, who are said by Nymphodorus, in his *Barbaric Customs*, to pay sacred honours to fire? or the Persians, or the Medes, or the Magi? These, Dino tells us, sacrifice beneath the open sky, regarding fire and water as the only images of the gods.

Nor have I failed to reveal their ignorance; for, however much they think to keep clear of error in one form, they slide into it in another.

They have not supposed stocks and stones to be images of the gods, like the Greeks; nor Ibises and Ichneumons, like the Egyptians; but fire and water, as philosophers. Berosus, in the third book of his *Chaldaics*, shows that it was after many successive periods of years that men worshipped images of human shape, this practice being introduced by Artaxerxes, the son of Darius, and father of Ochus, who first set up the image of Aphrodite Anaitis at Babylon and Susa; and Ecbatana set the example of worshipping it to the Persians; the Bactrians, to Damascus and Sardis.

Let the philosophers, then, own as their teachers the Persians, or the Sauromatæ, or the Magi, from whom they have learned the impious doctrine of regarding as divine certain first principles, being ignorant of the great First Cause, the Maker of all things, and Creator of those very first principles, the unbeginning God, but reverencing "these weak and beggarly elements,"[1] as the apostle says, which were made for the service of man. And of the rest of the philosophers who, passing over the elements, have eagerly sought after something higher and nobler, some have descanted on the Infinite, of whom were Anaximander of Miletus, Anaxagoras of Clazomenæ, and the Athenian Archelaus, both of

[1] Gal. iv. 9.

whom set Mind (νοῦς) above Infinity; while the Milesian Leucippus and the Chian Metrodorus apparently inculcated two first principles—fulness and vacuity. Democritus of Abdera, while accepting these two, added to them images (εἴδωλα); while Alcmæon of Crotona supposed the stars to be gods, and endowed with life (I will not keep silence as to their effrontery). Xenocrates of Chalcedon indicates that the planets are seven gods, and that the universe, composed of all these, is an eighth. Nor will I pass over those of the Porch, who say that the Divinity pervades all matter, even the vilest, and thus clumsily disgrace philosophy. Nor do I think will it be taken ill, having reached this point, to advert to the Peripatetics. The father of this sect, not knowing the Father of all things, thinks that He who is called the Highest is the soul of the universe; that is, he supposes the soul of the world to be God, and so is pierced by his own sword. For by first limiting the sphere of Providence to the orbit of the moon, and then by supposing the universe to be God, he confutes himself, inasmuch as he teaches that that which is without God is God. And that Eresian Theophrastus, the pupil of Aristotle, conjectures at one time heaven, and at another spirit, to be God. Epicurus alone I shall gladly forget, who carries impiety to its full length, and thinks that God takes no charge of the world. What, moreover, of Heraclides of Pontus? He is dragged everywhere to the images—the εἴδωλα—of Democritus.

CHAPTER VI.

BY DIVINE INSPIRATION PHILOSOPHERS SOMETIMES HIT ON THE TRUTH.

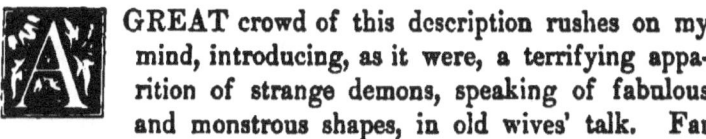GREAT crowd of this description rushes on my mind, introducing, as it were, a terrifying apparition of strange demons, speaking of fabulous and monstrous shapes, in old wives' talk. Far from enjoining men to listen to such tales are we, who avoid the practice of soothing our crying children, as the saying is, by telling them fabulous stories, being afraid of fostering in their minds the impiety professed by those who, though wise in their own conceit, have no more knowledge of the truth than infants. For why (in the name of truth!) do you make those who believe you subject to ruin and corruption, dire and irretrievable? Why, I beseech you, fill up life with idolatrous images, by feigning the winds, or the air, or fire, or earth, or stones, or stocks, or steel, or this universe, to be gods; and, prating loftily of the heavenly bodies in this much vaunted science of astrology, not astronomy, to those men who have truly wandered, talk of the wandering stars as gods? It is the Lord of the spirits, the Lord of the fire, the Maker of the universe, Him who lighted up the sun, that I long for. I seek after God, not the works of God. Whom shall I take as a helper in my inquiry? We do not, if you have no objection, wholly disown Plato. How, then, is God to be searched out, O Plato? "For both to find the Father and Maker of this universe is a work of difficulty; and having found Him, to declare Him fully, is impossible."[1]

Why so? by Himself, I beseech you! For He can by no

[1] *Timæus.*

means be expressed. Well done, Plato! Thou hast touched on the truth. But do not flag. Undertake with me the inquiry respecting the Good. For into all men whatever, especially those who are occupied with intellectual pursuits, a certain divine effluence has been instilled; wherefore, though reluctantly, they confess that God is one, indestructible, unbegotten, and that somewhere above in the tracts of heaven, in His own peculiar appropriate eminence, whence He surveys all things, He has an existence true and eternal.

> "Tell me what I am to conceive God to be,
> Who sees all things, and is Himself unseen,"

Euripides says. Accordingly, Menander seems to me to have fallen into error when he said:

> "O sun! for thou, first of gods, ought to be worshipped,
> By whom it is that we are able to see the other gods,"

For the sun never could show me the true God; but that healthful Word, that is the Sun of the soul, by whom alone, when He arises in the depths of the soul, the eye of the soul itself is irradiated. Whence accordingly, Democritus, not without reason, says, "that a few of the men of intellect, raising their hands upwards to what we Greeks now call the air (ἠέρ), called the whole expanse Zeus, or God: He, too, knows all things, gives and takes away, and He is King of all."

Of the same sentiments is Plato, who somewhere alludes to God thus: "Around the King of all are all things, and He is the cause of all good things." Who, then, is the King of all? God, who is the measure of the truth of all existence. As, then, the things that are to be measured are contained in the measure, so also the knowledge of God measures and comprehends truth. And the truly holy Moses says: "There shall not be in thy bag a balance and a balance, great or small, but a true and just balance shall be to thee,"[1] deeming the balance and measure and number of the whole to be God. For the unjust and unrighteous idols are hid at home in the bag, and, so to speak, in the polluted soul. But the only just measure is the only true God, always just, continuing the self-same; who measures all things, and weighs

[1] Deut. xxv. 13, 15.

them by righteousness as in a balance, grasping and sustaining universal nature in equilibrium. "God, therefore, as the old saying has it, occupying the beginning, the middle, and the end of all that is in being, keeps the straight course, while He makes the circuit of nature; and justice always follows Him, avenging those who violate the divine law."

Whence, O Plato, is that hint of the truth which thou givest? Whence this rich copiousness of diction, which proclaims piety with oracular utterance? The tribes of the barbarians, he says, are wiser than these; I know thy teachers, even if thou wouldst conceal them. You have learned geometry from the Egyptians, astronomy from the Babylonians; the charms of healing you have got from the Thracians; the Assyrians also have taught you many things; but for the laws that are consistent with truth, and your sentiments respecting God, you are indebted to the Hebrews,

> "Who do not worship through vain deceits
> The works of men, of gold, and brass, and silver, and ivory,
> And images of dead men, of wood and stone,
> Which other men, led by their foolish inclinations, worship;
> But raise to heaven pure arms:
> When they rise from bed, purifying themselves with water,
> And worship alone the Eternal, who reigns for evermore."

And let it not be this one man alone—Plato; but, O philosophy, hasten to produce many others also, who declare the only true God to be God, through His inspiration, if in any measure they have grasped the truth. For Antisthenes did not think out this doctrine of the Cynics; but it is in virtue of his being a disciple of Socrates that he says, "that God is not like to any; wherefore no one can know Him from an image." And Xenophon the Athenian would have in his own person committed freely to writing somewhat of the truth, and given the same testimony as Socrates, had he not been afraid of the cup of poison, which Socrates had to drink. But he hints nothing less; he says: "How great and powerful He is who moves all things, and is Himself at rest, is manifest; but what He is in form is not revealed. The sun himself, intended to be the source of light to all around, does not deem it fitting to allow himself to be looked at; but if any one audaciously gazes on him, he is deprived of sight." Whence, then, does the son of Gryllus learn his wisdom? Is it not manifestly from the prophetess of the Hebrews,[1] who prophesies in the following style?—

> "What flesh can see with the eye the celestial,
> The true, the immortal God, who inhabits the vault of heaven?
> Nay, men born mortal cannot even stand
> Before the rays of the sun."

Cleanthes Pisadeus,[2] the Stoic philosopher, who exhibits not a poetic theogony, but a true theology, has not concealed what sentiments he entertained respecting God:

> "If you ask me what is the nature of the good, listen:
> That which is regular, just, holy, pious,
> Self-governing, useful, fair, fitting,
> Grave, independent, always beneficial;
> That feels no fear or grief; profitable, painless,
> Helpful, pleasant, safe, friendly;
> Held in esteem, agreeing with itself, honourable;
> Humble, careful, meek, zealous,
> Perennial, blameless, ever-during:
> Mean is every one who looks to opinion
> With the view of obtaining some advantage from it."

Here, as I think, he clearly teaches of what nature God is; and that the common opinion and religious customs enslave those that follow them, but seek not after God.

We must not either keep the Pythagoreans in the background, who say: "God is one; and He is not, as some suppose, outside of this frame of things, but within it; but, in all the entireness of His being, is in the whole circle of existence, surveying all nature, and blending in harmonious union the whole,—the author of all His own forces and works, the giver of light in heaven, and Father of all,—the mind and vital power of the whole world,—the mover of all things." For the knowledge of God, these utterances, written by those we have mentioned through the inspiration of God, and selected by us, may suffice even for the man that has but small power to examine into truth.

---

[1] The *Sibyl.*   [2] Or Asseus, native of Asso.

CHAPTER VII.

THE POETS ALSO BEAR TESTIMONY TO THE TRUTH.

LET poetry also approach to us (for philosophy alone will not suffice): poetry which is wholly occupied with falsehood—which scarcely will make confession of the truth, but will rather own to God its deviations into fable. Let whoever of those poets chooses advance first. Aratus considers that the power of God pervades all things:

" That all may be secure,
Him ever they propitiate first and last,
Hail, Father! great marvel, great gain to man."

Thus also the Ascræan Hesiod dimly speaks of God:

" For He is the King of all, and monarch
Of the immortals; and there is none that may vie with Him in power."

Also on the stage they reveal the truth:

" Look on the ether and heaven, and regard that as God,"

says Euripides. And Sophocles, the son of Sophilus, says:

" One, in truth, one is God,
Who made both heaven and the far-stretching earth,
And ocean's blue wave, and the mighty winds;
But many of us mortals, deceived in heart,
Have set up for ourselves, as a consolation in our afflictions,
Images of the gods of stone, or wood, or brass,
Or gold, or ivory;
And, appointing to those sacrifices and vain festal assemblages,
Are accustomed thus to practise religion."

In this venturous manner has he on the stage brought truth before the spectators. But the Thracian Orpheus, the son of Œagrus, hierophant and poet at once, after his exposition of the orgies, and his theology of idols, introduces a palinode of truth with true solemnity, though tardily singing the strain:

> "I shall utter to whom it is lawful; but let the doors be closed,
> Nevertheless, against all the profane. But do thou hear,
> O Musæus, offspring of the light-bringing moon,
> For I will declare what is true. And let not these things
> Which once appeared in your breast rob you of dear life;
> But looking to the divine word, apply yourself to it,
> Keeping right *the seat of intellect and feeling;* and walk well
> In the straight path, and to the immortal King of the universe alone
> Direct your gaze."

Then proceeding, he clearly adds:

> "He is one, self-proceeding; and from Him alone all things proceed,
> And in them He Himself exerts his activity: no mortal
> Beholds Him, but He beholds all."

Thus far Orpheus at last understood that he had been in error:

> "But linger no longer, O man, endued with varied wisdom;
> But turn and retrace your steps, and propitiate God."

For if, at the most, the Greeks, having received certain scintillations of the divine word, have given forth some utterances of truth, they bear indeed witness that the force of truth is not hidden, and at the same time expose their own weakness in not having arrived at the end. For I think it has now become evident to all, that those who do or speak aught without the word of truth are like people compelled to walk without feet. Let the strictures on your gods, which the poets, impelled by the force of truth, introduce in their comedies, shame you into salvation. Menander, for instance, the comic poet, in his drama of the *Charioteer*, says:

> "No god pleases me that goes about
> With an old woman, and enters houses
> Carrying a trencher."

For such are the begging priests of Cybele. Hence Antisthenes replies appropriately to their request for alms:

> "I do not maintain the mother of the gods,
> For the gods maintain her."

Again, the same writer of comedy, expressing his dissatisfaction with the common usages, tries to expose the impious arrogance of the prevailing error in the drama of the *Priestess*, sagely declaring:

> "If a man drags the Deity
> Whither he will by the sound of cymbals,

He that does this is greater than the Deity;
But these are the instruments of audacity and means of living
Invented by men."

And not only Menander, but Homer also, and Euripides, and other poets in great numbers, expose your gods, and are wont to rate them, and that soundly too. For instance, they call Aphrodite dog-fly, and Hephæstus a cripple. Helen says to Aphrodite:

"Thy godship abdicate!
Renounce Olympus!"[1]

And of Dionysus, Homer writes without reserve:

"He, mid their frantic orgies, in the groves
Of lovely Nyssa, put to shameful rout
The youthful Bacchus' nurses; they in fear,
Dropped each her thyrsus, scattered by the hand
Of fierce Lycurgus, with an ox-goad armed."[2]

Worthy truly of the Socratic school is Euripides, who fixes his eye on truth, and despises the spectators of his plays. On one occasion, Apollo,

"Who inhabits the sanctuary that is in the middle of the earth,
Dispensing most certain oracles to mortals,"

is thus exposed:

"It was in obedience to him that I killed her who brought me forth;
Him do you regard as stained with guilt—put him to death;
It was he that sinned, not I, uninstructed as I was
In right and justice."[3]

He introduces Heracles, at one time mad, at another drunk and gluttonous. How should he not so represent the god who, when entertained as a guest, ate green figs to flesh, uttering discordant howls, that even his barbarian host remarked it? In his drama of *Ion*, too, he barefacedly brings the gods on the stage:

"How, then, is it right for you, who have given laws to mortals,
To be yourselves guilty of wrong?
And if—what will never take place, yet I will state the supposition—
You will give satisfaction to men for your adulteries,
You, Poseidon, and you, Zeus, the ruler of heaven,—
You will, in order to make recompense for your misdeeds,
Have to empty your temples."

---

[1] *Il.* iii. 405.   [2] *Il.* vi. 132.   [3] *Orestes*, 590.   [4] *Ion*, 422.

CHAPTER VIII.

THE TRUE DOCTRINE IS TO BE SOUGHT IN THE PROPHETS.

IT is now time, as we have despatched in order the other points, to go to the prophetic Scriptures; for the oracles present us with the appliances necessary for the attainment of piety, and so establish the truth. The divine Scriptures and institutions of wisdom form the short road to salvation. Devoid of embellishment, of outward beauty of diction, of wordiness and seductiveness, they raise up humanity strangled by wickedness, teaching men to despise the casualties of life; and with one and the same voice remedying many evils, they at once dissuade us from pernicious deceit, and clearly exhort us to the attainment of the salvation set before us. Let the Sibyl prophetess, then, be the first to sing to us the song of salvation:

> "So He is all sure and unerring:
> Come, follow no longer darkness and gloom;
> See, the sun's sweet-glancing light shines gloriously.
> Know, and lay up wisdom in your hearts:
> There is one God, who sends rains, and winds, and earthquakes,
> Thunderbolts, famines, plagues, and dismal sorrows,
> And snows and ice. But why detail particulars?
> He reigns over heaven, He rules earth, He truly is;"—

where, in remarkable accordance with inspiration, she compares delusion to darkness, and the knowledge of God to the sun and light, and subjecting both to comparison, shows the choice we ought to make. For falsehood is not dissipated by the bare presentation of the truth, but by the practical improvement of the truth it is ejected and put to flight.

Jeremiah the prophet, gifted with consummate wisdom, or

rather the Holy Spirit in Jeremiah, exhibits God. "Am I a God at hand," he says, "and not a God afar off? Shall a man do ought in secret, and I not see him? Do I not fill heaven and earth? saith the Lord."[1]

And again by Isaiah, "Who shall measure heaven with a span, and the whole earth with his hand?"[2] Behold God's greatness, and be filled with amazement. Let us worship Him of whom the prophet says, "Before Thy face the hills shall melt, as wax melteth before the fire!"[3] This, says he, is the God "whose throne is heaven, and His footstool the earth; and if He open heaven, quaking will seize thee."[4] Will you hear, too, what this prophet says of idols? "And they shall be made a spectacle of in the face of the sun, and their carcases shall be meat for the fowls of heaven and the wild beasts of the earth; and they shall putrefy before the sun and the moon, which they have loved and served; and their city shall be burned down."[5] He says, too, that the elements and the world shall be destroyed. "The earth," he says, "shall grow old, and the heaven shall pass away; but the word of the Lord endureth for ever." What, then, when again God wishes to show Himself by Moses: "Behold ye, behold ye, that I AM, and there is no other God beside me. I will kill, and I will make to live; I will strike, and I will heal; and there is none who shall deliver out of my hands."[6] But do you wish to hear another seer? You have the whole prophetic choir, the associates of Moses. What the Holy Spirit says by Hosea, I will not shrink from quoting: "Lo, I am He that appointeth the thunder, and createth spirit; and His hands have established the host of heaven."[7] And once more by Isaiah. And this utterance I will repeat: "I am," he says, "I am the Lord; I who speak righteousness, announce truth. Gather yourselves together, and come. Take counsel together, ye that are saved from the nations. They have not known, they who set up the block of wood, their carved work, and pray to gods who

---

[1] Jer. xxiii. 24.   [2] Isa. xl. 12.   [3] Isa. lxiv. 1, 2.
[4] Isa. lxvi. 1.   [5] Jer. viii. 2, xxx. 20, iv. 6.   [6] Deut. xxxii. 39.
[7] Amos iv. 13.

will not save them."[1] Then proceeding: "I am God, and there is not beside me a just God, and a Saviour: there is none except me. Turn to me, and ye will be saved, ye that are from the end of the earth. I am God, and there is no other; by myself I swear."[2] But against the worshippers of idols he is exasperated, saying, "To whom will ye liken the Lord, or to what likeness will ye compare Him? Has not the artificer made the image, or the goldsmith melted the gold and plated it with gold?"[3]—and so on. Be not therefore idolaters, but even now beware of the threatenings; "for the graven images and the works of men's hands shall wail, or rather they that trust in them,"[4] for matter is devoid of sensation. Once more he says, "The Lord will shake the cities that are inhabited, and grasp the world in His hand like a nest."[5] Why repeat to you the mysteries of wisdom, and sayings from the writings of the son of the Hebrews, the master of wisdom? "The Lord created me the beginning of His ways, in order to His works."[6] And, "The Lord giveth wisdom, and from His face proceed knowledge and understanding."[7] "How long wilt thou lie in bed, O sluggard; and when wilt thou be aroused from sleep?"[8] "but if thou show thyself no sluggard, as a fountain thy harvest shall come,"[9] the "Word of the Father, the benign light, the Lord that bringeth light, faith to all, and salvation."[10] For "the Lord who created the earth by His power," as Jeremiah says, "has raised up the world by His wisdom;"[11] for wisdom, which is His word, raises us up to the truth, who have fallen prostrate before idols, and is itself the first resurrection from our fall. Whence Moses, the man of God, dissuading from all idolatry, beautifully exclaims, "Hear, O Israel, the Lord thy God is one Lord; and thou shalt worship the Lord thy God, and Him only shalt thou serve."[12] "Now therefore be wise, O men," according to that blessed psalmist David; "lay hold on instruction, lest the Lord be angry, and ye perish from the

---

[1] Isa. xlv. 19, 20. [2] Isa. xlv. 21-23. [3] Isa. xl. 18, 19.
[4] Isa. x. 10, 11. [5] Isa. x. 14. [6] Prov. viii. 22.
[7] Prov. xi. 6. [8] Prov. vi. 9. [9] Prov. vi. 11.
[10] Prov. vi. 23. [11] Jer. x. 12. [12] Deut. xi. 4, 13, x. 20.

way of righteousness, when His wrath has quickly kindled. Blessed are all they who put their trust in Him."[1] But already the Lord, in His surpassing pity, has inspired the song of salvation, sounding like a battle march, "Sons of men, how long will ye be slow of heart? Why do you love vanity, and seek after a lie?"[2] What, then, is the vanity, and what the lie? The holy apostle of the Lord, reprehending the Greeks, will show thee : " Because that, when they knew God, they glorified Him not as God, neither were thankful; but became vain in their imaginations, and changed the glory of God into the likeness of corruptible man, and worshipped and served the creature more than the Creator."[3] And verily this is the God who "in the beginning made the heaven and the earth."[4] But you do not know God, and worship the heaven, and how shall you escape the guilt of impiety? Hear again the prophet speaking: "The sun shall suffer eclipse, and the heaven be darkened; but the Almighty shall shine for ever: while the powers of the heavens shall be shaken, and the heavens stretched out and drawn together shall be rolled as a parchment-skin (for these are the prophetic expressions), and the earth shall flee away from before the face of the Lord."[5]

[1] Ps. ii. 12, 13.   [2] Ps. iv. 3.   [3] Rom. i. 21, 23, 25.   [4] Gen. i. 1.
[5] This is made up of several passages, as Isa. xiii. 10, Ezek. xxxii. 7, Joel ii. 10, 31, iii. 15.

CHAPTER IX.

"THAT THOSE GRIEVOUSLY SIN WHO DESPISE OR NEGLECT GOD'S GRACIOUS CALLING."

I COULD adduce ten thousand scriptures of which not "one tittle shall pass away"[1] without being fulfilled; for the mouth of the Lord the Holy Spirit hath spoken these things. "Do not any longer," he says, "my son, despise the chastening of the Lord, nor faint when thou art rebuked of Him."[2] O surpassing love for man! Not as a teacher speaking to his pupils, not as a master to his domestics, nor as God to men, but as a father, does the Lord gently admonish His children. Thus Moses confesses that "he was filled with quaking and terror"[3] while he listened to God speaking concerning the Word. And art not thou afraid as thou hearest the voice of the Divine Word? Art not thou distressed? Do you not fear, and hasten to learn of Him,—that is, to salvation,—dreading wrath, loving grace, eagerly striving after the hope set before us, that you may shun the judgment threatened? Come, come, O my young people! For if you become not again as little children, and be born again, as saith the Scripture, you shall not receive the truly existent Father, nor shall you ever enter into the kingdom of heaven. For in what way is a stranger permitted to enter? Well, as I take it, then, when he is enrolled and made a citizen, and receives one to stand to him in the relation of father, then will he be occupied with the Father's concerns, then shall he be deemed worthy to be made His heir, then will he share the kingdom of the Father with His own dear Son. For

[1] Matt. v. 18.   [2] Prov. iii. 11.   [3] Heb. xii. 21.

this is the first-born church, composed of many good children; these are "the first-born enrolled in heaven, who hold high festival with so many myriads of angels." We, too, are first-born sons, who are reared by God, who are the genuine friends of the First-born, who first of all other men attained to the knowledge of God, who first were wrenched away from our sins, first severed from the devil. And now the more benevolent God is, the more impious men are; for He desires us from slaves to become sons, while they scorn to become sons. O the prodigious folly of being ashamed of the Lord! He offers freedom, you flee into bondage; He bestows salvation, you sink down into destruction; He confers everlasting life, you wait for punishment, and prefer the fire which the Lord "has prepared for the devil and his angels."[1] Wherefore the blessed apostle says: "I testify in the Lord, that ye walk no longer as the Gentiles walk, in the vanity of their mind; having their understanding darkened, being alienated from the life of God through the ignorance that is in them, because of the hardness of their heart: who, being past feeling, have given themselves over to lasciviousness, to work all uncleanness and concupiscence."[2] After the accusation of such a witness, and his invocation of God, what else remains for the unbelieving than judgment and condemnation? And the Lord, with ceaseless assiduity, exhorts, terrifies, urges, rouses, admonishes; He awakes from the sleep of darkness, and raises up those who have wandered in error. "Awake," He says, "thou that sleepest, and arise from the dead, and Christ shall give thee light,"[3]—Christ, the Sun of the Resurrection, He "who was born before the morning star,"[4] and with His beams bestows life. Let no one then despise the Word, lest he unwittingly despise himself. For the Scripture somewhere says, "To-day, if ye will hear His voice, harden not your hearts, as in the provocation, in the day of temptation in the wilderness, when your fathers proved me by trial."[5] And what was the trial? If you wish to learn, the Holy Spirit will show you: "And saw my works," He

---

[1] Matt. xxv. 41, 46. [2] Eph. iv. 17–19. [3] Eph. v. 14.
[4] Ps. cx. 3. [5] Ps. xcv. 8, 9.

says, "forty years. Wherefore I was grieved with that generation, and said, They do always err in heart, and have not known my ways. So I sware in my wrath, they shall not enter into my rest."[1] Look to the threatening! Look to the exhortation! Look to the punishment! Why, then, should we any longer change grace into wrath, and not receive the word with open ears, and entertain God as a guest in pure spirits? For great is the grace of His promise, "if to-day we hear His voice."[2] And that to-day is lengthened out day by day, while it is called to-day. And to the end the to-day and the instruction continue; and then the true to-day, the never-ending day of God, extends over eternity. Let us then ever obey the voice of the divine word. For the to-day signifies eternity. And day is the symbol of light; and the light of men is the Word, by whom we behold God. Rightly, then, to those that have believed and obey, grace will superabound; while with those that have been unbelieving, and err in heart, and have not known the Lord's ways, which John commanded to make straight and to prepare, God is incensed, and those He threatens.

And, indeed, the old Hebrew wanderers in the desert received typically the end of the threatening; for they are said not to have entered into the rest, because of unbelief, till, having followed the successor of Moses, they learned by experience, though late, that they could not be saved otherwise than by believing on Jesus. But the Lord, in His love to man, invites all men to the knowledge of the truth, and for this end sends the Paraclete. What, then, is this knowledge? Godliness; and "godliness," according to Paul, "is profitable for all things, having the promise of the life that now is, and of that which is to come."[3] If eternal salvation were to be sold, for how much, O men, would you propose to purchase it? Were one to estimate the value of the whole of Pactolus, the fabulous river of gold, he would not have reckoned up a price equivalent to salvation.

Do not, however, faint. You may, if you choose, purchase salvation, though of inestimable value, with your own re-

[1] Ps. xcv. 9-11.   [2] Ps. xcv. 7.   [3] 1 Tim. i. 14.

sources, love and living faith, which will be reckoned a suitable price. This recompense God cheerfully accepts; "for we trust in the living God, who is the Saviour of all men, especially of those who believe."[1]
But the rest, round whom the world's growths have fastened, as the rocks on the sea-shore are covered over with seaweed, make light of immortality, like the old man of Ithaca, eagerly longing to see, not the truth, not the fatherland in heaven, not the true light, but smoke. But godliness, that makes man as far as can be like God, designates God as our suitable teacher, who alone can worthily assimilate man to God. This teaching the apostle knows as truly divine. "Thou, O Timothy," he says, "from a child hast known the holy letters, which are able to make thee wise unto salvation, through faith that is in Christ Jesus."[2] For truly holy are those letters that sanctify and deify; and the writings or volumes that consist of those holy letters and syllables, the same apostle consequently calls "inspired of God, being profitable for doctrine, for reproof, for correction, for instruction in righteousness, that the man of God may be perfect, thoroughly furnished to every good work."[3] No one will be so impressed by the exhortations of any of the saints, as he is by the words of the Lord Himself, the lover of man. For this, and nothing but this, is His only work—the salvation of man. Therefore He Himself, urging them on to salvation, cries, "The kingdom of heaven is at hand."[4] Those men that draw near through fear, He converts. Thus also the apostle of the Lord, beseeching the Macedonians, becomes the interpreter of the divine voice, when he says, "The Lord is at hand; take care that ye be not apprehended empty."[5] But are ye so devoid of fear, or rather of faith, as not to believe the Lord Himself, or Paul, who in Christ's stead thus entreats: "Taste and see that Christ is God?"[6] Faith will lead you in; experience will teach you; Scripture will train you, for it says, "Come hither, O children; listen to

[1] 1 Tim. iv. 10.   [2] 2 Tim. iii. 15.   [3] 1 Tim. iii. 16, 17.
[4] Matt. iv. 17.   [5] Phil. iv. 5.
[6] Ps. xxxiv. 8, where Clem. has read Χριστός for χρηστός.

me, and I will teach you the fear of the Lord." Then, as to those who already believe, it briefly adds, " What man is he that desireth life, that loveth to see good days?"[1] It is we, we shall say—we who are the devotees of good, we who eagerly desire good things. Hear, then, ye who are far off, hear ye who are near: the word has not been hidden from any; light is common, it shines "on all men." No one is a Cimmerian in respect to the word. Let us haste to salvation, to regeneration; let us who are many haste that we may be brought together into one love, according to the union of the essential unity; and let us, by being made good, conformably follow after union, seeking after the good Monad.

The union of many in one, issuing in the production of divine harmony out of a medley of sounds and division, becomes one symphony following one choir-leader and teacher, the Word, reaching and resting in the same truth, and crying Abba, Father. This, the true utterance of His children, God accepts with gracious welcome—the first-fruits He receives from them.

[1] Ps. xxxiv. 12.

CHAPTER X.

ANSWER TO THE OBJECTION OF THE HEATHEN, THAT IT WAS NOT RIGHT TO ABANDON THE CUSTOMS OF THEIR FATHERS.

BUT you say it is not creditable to subvert the customs handed down to us from our fathers. And why, then, do we not still use our first nourishment, milk, to which our nurses accustomed us from the time of our birth? Why do we increase or diminish our patrimony, and not keep it exactly the same as we got it? Why do we not still vomit on our parents' breasts, or still do the things for which, when infants, and nursed by our mothers, we were laughed at, but have corrected ourselves, even if we did not fall in with good instructors? Then, if excesses in the indulgence of the passions, though pernicious and dangerous, yet are accompanied with pleasure, why do we not in the conduct of life abandon that usage which is evil, and provocative of passion, and godless, even should our fathers feel hurt, and betake ourselves to the truth, and seek Him who is truly our Father, rejecting custom as a deleterious drug? For of all that I have undertaken to do, the task I now attempt is the noblest, viz. to demonstrate to you how inimical this insane and most wretched custom is to godliness. For a boon so great, the greatest ever given by God to the human race, would never have been hated and rejected, had not you been carried away by custom, and then shut your ears against us; and just as unmanageable horses throw off the reins, and take the bit between their teeth, you rush away from the arguments addressed to you, in your eager desire to shake yourselves clear of us, who seek to guide the chariot of your life, and, impelled by your folly, dash towards the precipices of destruction, and regard the holy word of God as an accursed thing. The reward of your choice, therefore, as described by Sophocles, follows:

"The mind a blank, useless ears, vain thoughts."

And you know not that, of all truths, this is the truest, that the good and godly shall obtain the good reward, inasmuch as they held goodness in high esteem; while, on the other hand, the wicked shall receive meet punishment. For the author of evil, torment has been prepared; and so the prophet Zecharias threatens him: "He that hath chosen Jerusalem rebuke thee; lo, is not this a brand plucked from the fire?"[1] What an infatuated desire, then, for voluntary death is this, rooted in men's minds! Why do they flee to this fatal brand, with which they shall be burned, when it is within their power to live nobly according to God, and not according to custom? For God bestows life freely; but evil custom, after our departure from this world, brings on the sinner unavailing remorse with punishment. *By sad experience, even a child knows* how superstition destroys and piety saves. Let any of you look at those who minister before the idols, their hair matted, their persons disgraced with filthy and tattered clothes; who never come near a bath, and let their nails grow to an extraordinary length, like wild beasts; many of them castrated, who show the idol's temples to be in reality graves or prisons. These appear to me to bewail the gods, not to worship them, and their sufferings to be worthy of pity rather than piety. And seeing these things, do you still continue blind, and will you not look up to the Ruler of all, the Lord of the universe? And will you not escape from those dungeons, and flee to the mercy that comes down from heaven? For God, of His great love to man, comes to the help of man, as the mother-bird flies to one of her young that has fallen out of the nest; and if a serpent open its mouth to swallow the little bird, "the mother flutters round, uttering cries of grief over her dear progeny;"[2] and God the Father seeks His creature, and heals his transgression, and pursues the serpent, and recovers the young one, and incites it to fly up to the nest.

[1] Zech. iii. 2.   [2] *Iliad*, ii. 315.

Thus dogs that have strayed, track out their master by the scent; and horses that have thrown their riders, come to their master's call if he but whistle. " The ox," it is said, "knoweth his owner, and the ass his master's crib; but Israel hath not known me."[1] What, then, of the Lord? He remembers not our ill desert; He still pities, He still urges us to repentance.

And I would ask you, if it does not appear to you monstrous, that you men who are God's handiwork, who have received your souls from Him, and belong wholly to God, should be subject to another master, and, what is more, serve the tyrant instead of the rightful King—the evil one instead of the good? For, in the name of truth, what man in his senses turns his back on good, and attaches himself to evil? What, then, is he who flees from God to consort with demons? Who, that may become a son of God, prefers to be in bondage? Or who is he that pursues his way to Erebus, when it is in his power to be a citizen of heaven, and to cultivate Paradise, and walk about in heaven and partake of the tree of life and immortality, and, cleaving his way through the sky in the track of the luminous cloud, behold, like Elias, the rain of salvation? Some there are, who, like worms wallowing in marshes and mud in the streams of pleasure, feed on foolish and useless delights—swinish men. For swine, it is said, like mud better than pure water; and, according to Democritus, "doat upon dirt."

Let us not then be enslaved or become swinish; but, as true children of the light, let us raise our eyes and look on the light, lest the Lord discover us to be spurious, as the sun does the eagles. Let us therefore repent, and pass from ignorance to knowledge, from foolishness to wisdom, from licentiousness to self-restraint, from unrighteousness to righteousness, from godlessness to God. It is an enterprise of noble daring to take our way to God; and the enjoyment of many other good things is within the reach of the lovers of righteousness, who pursue eternal life, specially those things to which God Himself alludes, speaking by Isaiah: "There is an inheritance for those who serve the Lord."[2] Noble

---

[1] Isa. i. 3. [2] Isa. liv. 17.

and desirable is this inheritance: not gold, not silver, not raiment, which the moth assails, and things of earth which are assailed by the robber, whose eye is dazzled by worldly wealth; but it is that treasure of salvation to which we must hasten, by becoming lovers of the Word. Thence praiseworthy works descend to us, and fly with us on the wing of truth. This is the inheritance with which the eternal covenant of God invests us, conveying the everlasting gift of grace; and thus our loving Father—the true Father—ceases not to exhort, admonish, train, love us. For He ceases not to save, and advises the best course: "Become righteous," says the Lord.[1] Ye that thirst, come to the water; and ye that have no money, come, and buy and drink without money.[2] He invites to the laver, to salvation, to illumination, all but crying out and saying, The land I give thee, and the sea, my child, and heaven too; and all the living creatures in them I freely bestow upon thee. Only, O child, thirst for thy Father; God shall be revealed to thee without price; the truth is not made merchandise of. He gives thee all creatures that fly and swim, and those on the land. These the Father has created for thy thankful enjoyment. What the bastard, who is a son of perdition, foredoomed to be the slave of mammon, has to buy for money, He assigns to thee as thine own, even to His own son who loves the Father; for whose sake He still works, and to whom alone He promises, saying, "The land shall not be sold in perpetuity," for it is not destined to corruption. "For the whole land is mine;" and it is thine too, if thou receive God. Wherefore the Scripture, as might have been expected, proclaims good news to those who have believed. "The saints of the Lord shall inherit the glory of God and His power." What glory, tell me, O blessed One, which "eye hath not seen, nor ear heard, nor hath it entered into the heart of man;"[3] and "they shall be glad in the kingdom of their Lord for ever and ever! Amen." You have, O men, the divine promise of grace; you have heard, on the other hand, the threatening of punishment:

---

[1] Isa. liv. 17, where Sept. reads, "ye shall be righteous."
[2] Isa. lv. 1.   [3] 1 Cor. ii. 9.

by these the Lord saves, teaching men by fear and grace. Why do we delay? Why do we not shun the punishment? Why do we not receive the free gift? Why, in fine, do we not choose the better part, God instead of the evil one, and prefer wisdom to idolatry, and take life in exchange for death? "Behold," He says, "I have set before your face death and life."[1] The Lord tries you, that "you may choose life." He counsels you as a father to obey God. "For if ye hear me," He says, "and be willing, ye shall eat the good things of the land:"[2] this is the grace attached to obedience. "But if ye obey me not, and are unwilling, the sword and fire shall devour you:"[3] this is the penalty of disobedience. For the mouth of the Lord—the law of truth, the word of the Lord—hath spoken these things. Are you willing that I should be your good counsellor? Well, do you hear. I, if possible, will explain. You ought, O men, when reflecting on the Good, to have brought forward a witness inborn and competent, viz. faith, which of itself, and from its own resources, chooses at once what is best, instead of occupying yourselves in painfully inquiring whether what is best ought to be followed. For, allow me to tell you, you ought to doubt whether you should get drunk, but you get drunk before reflecting on the matter; and whether you ought to do an injury, but you do injury with the utmost readiness. The only thing you make the subject of question is, whether God should be worshipped, and whether this wise God and Christ should be followed: and this you think requires deliberation and doubt, and know not what is worthy of God. Have faith in us, as you have in drunkenness, that you may be wise; have faith in us, as you have in injury, that you may live. But if, acknowledging the conspicuous trustworthiness of the virtues, you wish to trust them, come and I will set before you in abundance, materials of persuasion respecting the Word. But do you—for your ancestral customs, by which your minds are preoccupied, divert you from the truth,—do you now hear what is the real state of the case as follows.

And let not any shame of this name preoccupy you, which

[1] Deut. xxx. 15.   [2] Isa. i. 20.   [3] Isa. i. 20, xxxiii. 11.

does great harm to men, and seduces them from salvation. Let us then openly strip for the contest, and nobly strive in the arena of truth, the holy Word being the judge, and the Lord of the universe prescribing the contest. For 'tis no insignificant prize, the guerdon of immortality which is set before us. Pay no more regard, then, if you are rated by some of the low rabble who lead the dance of impiety, and are driven on to the same pit by their folly and insanity, makers of idols and worshippers of stones. For these have dared to deify men,—Alexander of Macedon, for example, whom they canonized as the thirteenth god, whose pretensions Babylon confuted, which showed him dead. I admire, therefore, the divine sophist. Theocritus was his name. After Alexander's death, Theocritus, holding up the vain opinions entertained by men respecting the gods, to ridicule before his fellow-citizens, said: "Men, keep up your hearts as long as you see the gods dying sooner than men." And, truly, he who worships gods that are visible, and the promiscuous rabble of creatures begotten and born, and attaches himself to them, is a far more wretched object than the very demons. For God is by no manner of means unrighteous, as the demons are, but in the very highest degree righteous; and nothing more resembles God than one of us when he becomes righteous in the highest possible degree:

"Go into the way, the whole tribe of you handicraftsmen,
 Who worship Jove's fierce-eyed daughter,[1] the working goddess,
 With fans duly placed, fools that ye are"—

fashioners of stones, and worshippers of them. Let your Phidias, and Polycletus, and your Praxiteles and Apelles too, come, and all that are engaged in mechanical arts, who, being themselves of the earth, are workers of the earth. "For then," says a certain prophecy, "the affairs here turn out unfortunately, when men put their trust in images." Let the meaner artists, too—for I will not stop calling—come. None of these ever made a breathing image, or out of earth moulded soft flesh. Who liquefied the marrow? or who solidified the bones? Who stretched the nerves? who distended the veins?

[1] Minerva.

Who poured the blood into them? Or who spread the skin? Who ever could have made eyes capable of seeing? Who breathed spirit into the lifeless form? Who bestowed righteousness? Who promised immortality? The Maker of the universe alone: the Great Artist and Father has formed us, such a living image as man is. But your Olympian Jove, the image of an image, greatly out of harmony with truth, is the senseless work of Attic hands. For the image of God is His Word, the genuine Son of Mind, the Divine Word, the archetypal light of light; and the image of the Word is the true man, the mind which is in man, who is therefore said to have been made "in the image and likeness of God,"[1] assimilated to the Divine Word in the affections of the soul, and therefore rational; but effigies sculptured in human form, the earthly image of that part of man which is visible and earth-born, are but a perishable impress of humanity, manifestly wide of the truth. That life, then, which is occupied with so much earnestness about matter, seems to me to be nothing else than full of insanity. And custom, which has made you taste bondage and unreasonable care, is fostered by vain opinion; and ignorance, which has proved to the human race the cause of unlawful rites and delusive shows, and also of deadly plagues and hateful images, has, by devising many shapes of demons, stamped on all that follow it the mark of long-continued death. Receive, then, the water of the word; wash, ye polluted ones; purify yourselves from custom, by sprinkling yourselves with the drops of truth. The pure must ascend to heaven. Thou art a man, if we look to that which is most common to thee and others—seek Him who created thee; thou art a son, if we look to that which is thy peculiar prerogative—acknowledge thy Father. But do you still continue in your sins, engrossed with pleasures? To whom shall the Lord say, "Yours is the kingdom of heaven?" Yours, whose choice is set on God, if you will; yours, if you will only believe, and comply with the brief terms of the announcement; which the Ninevites having obeyed, instead of the destruction they looked for, obtained a signal deliver-

---
[1] Gen. i. 26.

ance. How, then, may I ascend to heaven, is it said? The Lord is the way; a strait way, but leading from heaven, strait in truth, but leading back to heaven, strait, despised on earth; broad, adored in heaven.

Then, he that is uninstructed in the word, has ignorance as the excuse of his error; but as for him into whose ears instruction has been poured, and who deliberately maintains his incredulity in his soul, the wiser he appears to be, the more harm will his understanding do him; for he has his own sense as his accuser for not having chosen the best part. For man has been otherwise constituted by nature, so as to have fellowship with God. As, then, we do not compel the horse to plough, or the bull to hunt, but set each animal to that for which it is by nature fitted; so, placing our finger on what is man's peculiar and distinguishing characteristic above other creatures, we invite him—born, as he is, for the contemplation of heaven, and being, as he is, a truly heavenly plant—to the knowledge of God, counselling him to furnish himself with what is his sufficient provision for eternity, namely piety. Practise husbandry, we say, if you are a husbandman; but while you till your fields, know God. Sail the sea, you who are devoted to navigation, yet call the whilst on the heavenly Pilot. Has knowledge taken hold of you while engaged in military service? Listen to the commander, who orders what is right. As those, then, who have been overpowered with sleep and drunkenness, do ye awake; and using your eyes a little, consider what mean those stones which you worship, and the expenditure you frivolously lavish on matter. Your means and substance you squander on ignorance, even as you throw away your lives to death, having found no other end of your vain hope than this. Not only unable to pity yourselves, you are incapable even of yielding to the persuasions of those who commiserate you; enslaved as you are to evil custom, and, clinging to it voluntarily till your last breath, you are hurried to destruction: "because light is come into the world, and men have loved the darkness rather than the light,"[1] while they could sweep away those

[1] John iii. 19.

hindrances to salvation, pride, and wealth, and fear, repeating this poetic utterance:

> "Whither do I bear these abundant riches? and whither
> Do I myself wander?"[1]

If you wish, then, to cast aside these vain phantasies, and bid adieu to evil custom, say to vain opinion:

> "Lying dreams, farewell; you were then nothing."

For what, think you, O men, is the Hermes of Typho, and that of Andocides, and that of Amyetus? Is it not evident to all that they are stones, as is the veritable Hermes himself? As the Halo is not a god, and as the Iris is not a god, but are states of the atmosphere and of the clouds; and as, likewise, a day is not a god, nor a year, nor time, which is made up of these, so neither is sun nor moon, by which each of those mentioned above is determined. Who, then, in his right senses, can imagine Correction, and Punishment, and Justice, and Retribution to be gods? For neither the Furies, nor the Fates, nor Destiny are gods, since neither Government, nor Glory, nor Wealth are gods, which last [as Plutus] painters represent as blind. But if you deify Modesty, and Love, and Venus, let these be followed by Infamy, and Passion, and Beauty, and Intercourse. Therefore Sleep and Death cannot reasonably any more be regarded as twin deities, being merely changes which take place naturally in living creatures; no more will you with propriety call Fortune, or Destiny, or the Fates goddesses. And if Strife and Battle be not gods, no more are Ares and Enyo. Still further, if the lightnings, and thunderbolts, and rains are not gods, how can fire and water be gods? how can shooting stars and comets, which are produced by atmospheric changes? He who calls Fortune a god, let him also so call Action. If, then, none of these, nor of the images formed by human hands, and destitute of feeling, is held to be a God, while a providence exercised about us is evidently the result of a divine power,[2] it remains only

---

[1] *Odyss.* xiii. 203.

[2] A translation in accordance with the Latin version would run thus: "While a certain previous conception of divine power is nevertheless discovered within us." But adopting that in the text the argument is:

to acknowledge this, that He alone who is truly God, only truly is and subsists. But those who are insensible to this are like men who have drunk mandrake or some other drug. May God grant that you may at length awake from this slumber, and know God; and that neither Gold, nor Stone, nor Tree, nor Action, nor Suffering, nor Disease, nor Fear, may appear in your eyes as a god. For there are, in sooth, "on the fruitful earth thrice ten thousand" demons, not immortal, nor indeed mortal; for they are not endowed with sensation, so as to render them capable of death, but only things of wood and stone, that hold despotic sway over men insulting and violating life through the force of custom. "The earth is the Lord's," it is said, "and the fulness thereof."[1] Then why darest thou, while luxuriating in the bounties of the Lord, to ignore the Sovereign Ruler? "Leave my earth," the Lord will say to thee. "Touch not the water which I bestow. Partake not of the fruits of the earth produced by my husbandry." Give to God recompense for your sustenance; acknowledge thy Master. Thou art God's creature. What belongs to Him, how can it with justice be alienated? For that which is alienated, being deprived of the properties that belonged to it, is also deprived of truth. For, after the fashion of Niobe, or, to express myself more mystically, like the Hebrew woman called by the ancients Lot's wife, are ye not turned into a state of insensibility? This woman, we have heard, was turned into stone for her love of Sodom. And those who are godless, addicted to impiety, hard-hearted and foolish, are Sodomites. Believe that these utterances are addressed to you from God. For think not that stones, and stocks, and birds, and serpents are sacred things, and men are not; but, on the contrary, regard men as truly sacred, and take beasts and stones for what they are. For there are miserable wretches of human kind, who consider that God

there is unquestionably a providence implying the exertion of divine power. That power is not exercised by idols or heathen gods. The only other alternative is, that it is exercised by the one self-existent God.

[1] Ps. xxiv. 1; 1 Cor. x. 26, 28.

utters His voice by the raven and the jackdaw, but says nothing by man; and honour the raven as a messenger of God. But the man of God, who croaks not, nor chatters, but speaks rationally and instructs lovingly, alas, they persecute; and while he is inviting them to cultivate righteousness, they try inhumanly to slay him, neither welcoming the grace which comes from above, nor fearing the penalty. For they believe not God, nor understand His power, whose love to man is ineffable; and His hatred of evil is inconceivable. His anger augments punishment against sin; His love bestows blessings on repentance. It is the height of wretchedness to be deprived of the help which comes from God. Hence this blindness of eyes and dulness of hearing are more grievous than other inflictions of the evil one; for the one deprives them of heavenly vision, the other robs them of divine instruction. But ye, thus maimed as respects the truth, blind in mind, deaf in understanding, are not grieved, are not pained, have had no desire to see heaven and the Maker of heaven, nor, by fixing your choice on salvation, have sought to hear the Creator of the universe, and to learn of Him; for no hindrance stands in the way of him who is bent on the knowledge of God. Neither childlessness, nor poverty, nor obscurity, nor want, can hinder him who eagerly strives after the knowledge of God; nor does any one who has conquered[1] by brass or iron the true wisdom for himself choose to exchange it, for it is vastly preferred to everything else. Christ is able to save in every place. For he that is fired with ardour and admiration for righteousness, being the lover of One who needs nothing, needs himself but little, having treasured up his bliss in nothing but himself and God, where is neither moth,[2] robber, nor pirate, but the eternal Giver of good. With justice, then, have you been compared to those serpents who shut their ears against the charmers. For "their mind," says the Scripture, "is like the serpent, like the deaf adder,

---

[1] The expression "conquered by brass or iron" is borrowed from Homer (*Il.* viii. 534). Brass, or copper, and iron were the metals of which arms were made.

[2] Matt. vi. 20, 21.

which stoppeth her ear, and will not hear the voice of the charmers."[1] But allow yourselves to feel the influence of the charming strains of sanctity, and receive that mild word of ours, and reject the deadly poison, that it may be granted to you to divest yourselves as much as possible of destruction, as they[2] have been divested of old age. Hear me, and do not stop your ears; do not block up the avenues of hearing, but lay to heart what is said. Excellent is the medicine of immortality! Stop at length your grovelling reptile motions. "For the enemies of the Lord," says Scripture, "shall lick the dust."[3] Raise your eyes from earth to the skies, look up to heaven, admire the sight, cease watching with outstretched head the heel of the righteous, and hindering the way of truth. Be wise and harmless. Perchance the Lord will endow you with the wing of simplicity (for He has resolved to give wings to those that are earth-born), that you may leave your holes and dwell in heaven. Only let us with our whole heart repent, that we may be able with our whole heart to contain God. "Trust in Him, all ye assembled people; pour out all your hearts before Him."[4] He says to those that have newly abandoned wickedness, "He pities them, and fills them with righteousness." Believe Him who is man and God; believe, O man. Believe, O man, the living God, who suffered and is adored. Believe, ye slaves, Him who died; believe, all ye of human kind, Him who alone is God of all men. Believe, and receive salvation as your reward. Seek God, and your soul shall live. He who seeks God is busying himself about his own salvation. Hast thou found God?—then thou hast life. Let us then seek, in order that we may live. The reward of seeking is life with God. "Let all who seek Thee be glad and rejoice in Thee; and let them say continually, God be magnified."[5] A noble hymn of God is an immortal man, established in righteousness, in whom the oracles of truth are engraved. For where but in a soul that is wise can you write truth? where love? where

---

[1] Ps. lviii. 4, 5.
[2] "They" seems to refer to sanctity and the word.
[3] Ps. lxxii. 9.   [4] Ps. lxii. 8.   [5] Ps. lxx. 4.

reverence? where meekness? Those who have had these
divine characters impressed on them, ought, I think, to regard
wisdom as a fair port whence to embark, to whatever lot in life
they turn; and likewise to deem it the calm haven of salvation: wisdom, by which those who have betaken themselves to
the Father, have proved good fathers to their children; and
good parents to their sons, those who have known the Son;
and good husbands to their wives, those who remember the
Bridegroom; and good masters to their servants, those who
have been redeemed from utter slavery. Oh, happier far the
beasts than men involved in error! who live in ignorance as
you, but do not counterfeit the truth. There are no tribes
of flatterers among them. Fishes have no superstition: the
birds worship not a single image; only they look with admiration on heaven, since, deprived as they are of reason,
they are unable to know God. So are you not ashamed for
living through so many periods of life in impiety, making
yourselves more irrational than the irrational creatures? You
were boys, then striplings, then youths, then men, but never
as yet were you good. If you have respect for old age, be wise,
now that you have reached life's sunset; and albeit at the close
of life, acquire the knowledge of God, that the end of life may
to you prove the beginning of salvation. You have become
old in superstition; as young, enter on the practice of piety.
God regards you as innocent children. Let, then, the Athenian follow the laws of Solon, and the Argive those of Phoroneus, and the Spartan those of Lycurgus: but if thou enrol
thyself as one of God's people, heaven is thy country, God
thy lawgiver. And what are the laws? "Thou shalt not
kill; thou shalt not commit adultery; thou shalt not seduce
boys; thou shalt not steal; thou shalt not bear false witness;
thou shalt love the Lord thy God."[1] And the complements
of these are those laws of reason and words of sanctity
which are inscribed on men's hearts: "Thou shalt love thy
neighbour as thyself; to him who strikes thee on the cheek,
present also the other;"[2] "thou shalt not lust, for by lust
alone thou hast committed adultery."[3] How much better,

[1] Ex. xx. 13-16; Deut. vi. 3.   [2] Luke vi. 29.   [3] Matt. v. 28.

therefore, is it for men from the beginning not to wish to desire things forbidden, than to obtain their desires! But ye are not able to endure the austerity of salvation; but as we delight in sweet things, and prize them higher for the agreeableness of the pleasure they yield, while, on the other hand, those bitter things which are distasteful to the palate are curative and healing, and the harshness of medicines strengthens people of weak stomach, thus custom pleases and tickles; but custom pushes into the abyss, while truth conducts to heaven. Harsh it is at first, but a good nurse of youth; and it is at once the decorous place where the household maids and matrons dwell together, and the sage council-chamber. Nor is it difficult to approach, or impossible to attain, but is very near us in our very homes; as Moses, endowed with all wisdom, says, while referring to it, it has its abode in three departments of our constitution—in the hands, the mouth, and the heart: a meet emblem this of truth, which is embraced by these three things in all—will, action, speech. And be not afraid lest the multitude of pleasing objects which rise before you withdraw you from wisdom. You yourself will spontaneously surmount the frivolousness of custom, as boys when they have become men throw aside their toys. For with a celerity unsurpassable, and a benevolence to which we have ready access, the divine power, casting its radiance on the earth, hath filled the universe with the seed of salvation. For it was not without divine care that so great a work was accomplished in so brief a space by the Lord, who, though despised as to appearance, was in reality adored, the expiator of sin, the Saviour, the clement, the Divine Word, He that is truly most manifest Deity, He that is made equal to the Lord of the universe; because He was His Son, and the Word was in God, not disbelieved in by all when He was first preached, nor altogether unknown when, assuming the character of man, and fashioning Himself in flesh, He enacted the drama of human salvation: for He was a true champion and a fellow-champion with the creature. And being communicated most speedily to men, having dawned from His Father's counsel quicker than the sun, with the most perfect ease He made God shine on us. Whence He was and what He was, He showed by what He taught and exhibited, manifesting Himself as the Herald of the Covenant, the Reconciler, our Saviour, the Word, the fount of life, the giver of peace, diffused over the whole face of the earth; by whom, so to speak, the universe has already become an ocean of blessings.

CHAPTER XI.

HOW GREAT ARE THE BENEFITS CONFERRED ON MAN THROUGH THE ADVENT OF CHRIST.

CONTEMPLATE a little, if agreeable to you, the divine beneficence. The first man, when in Paradise, sported free, because he was the child of God; but when he succumbed to pleasure (for the serpent allegorically signifies pleasure crawling on its belly, earthly wickedness nourished for fuel to the flames), was as a child seduced by lusts, and grew old in disobedience; and by disobeying his Father, dishonoured God. Such was the influence of pleasure. Man, that had been free by reason of simplicity, was found fettered to sins. The Lord then wished to release him from his bonds, and clothing Himself with flesh—O divine mystery!—vanquished the serpent, and enslaved the tyrant death; and, most marvellous of all, man that had been deceived by pleasure, and bound fast to corruption, had his hands unloosed, and was set free. O mystic wonder! The Lord was laid low, and man rose up; and he that fell from Paradise receives as the reward of obedience something greater [than Paradise]—namely, heaven itself. Wherefore, since the Word Himself has come to us from heaven, we need not, I reckon, go any more in search of human learning to Athens and the rest of Greece, and to Ionia. For if we have as our teacher Him that filled the universe with His holy energies in creation, salvation, beneficence, legislation, prophecy, teaching, we have the Teacher from whom all instruction comes; and the whole world, with Athens and Greece, has already become the domain of the Word. For you, who believed the poetical fable which designated Minos the Cretan as the bosom friend of Zeus, will not refuse to believe that we who have become the disciples of God have received the only true wisdom; and that which the chiefs of philosophy only guessed at, the disciples of Christ have both apprehended and proclaimed. And the one whole Christ is not divided: "There is neither barbarian, nor Jew, nor Greek, neither male nor female, but a new man,"[1] transformed by God's Holy Spirit. Further, the other counsels and precepts are unimportant, and respect particular things,—as, for example, if one may marry, take part in public affairs, beget children; but the only command that is universal, and over the whole course of existence, at all times and in all circumstances, tends to the highest end, viz. life, is piety,—all that is necessary, in order that we may live for ever, being that we live in accordance with it. Philosophy, however, as the ancients say, is "a long-lived exhortation, wooing the eternal love of wisdom;" while the commandment of the Lord is far-shining, "enlightening the eyes." Receive Christ, receive sight, receive thy light,

"In order that you may know well both God and man."[2]

"Sweet is the Word that gives us light, precious above gold and gems; it is to be desired above honey and the honey-comb."[3] For how can it be other than desirable, since it has filled with light the mind which had been buried in darkness, and given keenness to the "light-bringing eyes" of the soul? For just as, had the sun not been in existence, night would have brooded over the universe notwithstanding the other luminaries of heaven; so, had we not known the Word, and been illuminated by Him, we should have been nowise different from fowls that are being fed, fattened in darkness, and nourished for death. Let us then admit the light, that we may admit God; let us admit the light, and become disciples to the Lord. This, too, He has been promised to the Father: "I will declare Thy name to my brethren; in the midst of the church will I praise Thee."[4] Praise and declare to me Thy Father God; Thy utterances save; Thy hymn teaches that

[1] Gal. iii. 28, vi. 15. [2] *Iliad*, v. 128.
[3] Ps. xix. 11. [4] Ps. xxii. 23.

hitherto I have wandered in error, seeking God. But since Thou leadest me to the light, O Lord, and I find God through Thee, and receive the Father from Thee, I become "Thy fellow-heir,"[1] since Thou "wert not ashamed of me as Thy brother."[2] Let us put away, then, let us put away oblivion of the truth, viz. ignorance; and removing the darkness which obstructs, as dimness of sight, let us contemplate the only true God, first raising our voice in this hymn of praise: Hail, O light! For in us, buried in darkness, shut up in the shadow of death, light has shone forth from heaven, purer than the sun, sweeter than life here below. That light is eternal life; and whatever partakes of it lives. But night fears the light, and hiding itself in terror, gives place to the day of the Lord. Sleepless light is now over all, and the west has given credence to the east. For this was the end of the new creation. For "the Sun of Righteousness," who drives His chariot over all, pervades equally all humanity, like "His Father, who makes His sun to rise on all men," and distils on them the dew of the truth. He hath changed sunset into sunrise, and through the cross brought death to life; and having wrenched man from destruction, He hath raised him to the skies, transplanting mortality into immortality, and translating earth to heaven—He, the husbandman of God,

"Pointing out the favourable signs and rousing the nations
To good works, putting them in mind of the true sustenance;"[3]

having bestowed on us the truly great, divine, and inalienable inheritance of the Father, deifying man by heavenly teaching, putting His laws into our minds, and writing them on our hearts. What laws does He inscribe? "That all shall know God, from small to great;" and, "I will be merciful to them," says God, "and will not remember their sins."[4] Let us receive the laws of life, let us comply with God's expostulations; let us become acquainted with Him, that He may be gracious. And though God needs nothing, let us render to Him the grateful recompense of a thankful heart and of piety, as a kind of house-rent for our dwelling here below.

[1] Rom. viii. 17.
[2] Heb. ii. 11.
[3] Aratus.
[4] Heb. viii. 10-12; Jer. xxxi. 33, 34.

"Gold for brass,
A hundred oxen's worth for that of nine;"[1]

that is, for your little faith He gives you the earth of so great extent to till, water to drink and also to sail on, air to breathe, fire to do your work, a world to dwell in; and He has permitted you to conduct a colony from here to heaven: with these important works of His hand, and benefits in such numbers, He has rewarded your little faith. Then, those who have put faith in necromancers, receive from them amulets and charms, to ward off evil forsooth; and will you not allow the heavenly Word, the Saviour, to be bound on to you as an amulet, and, by trusting in God's own charm, be delivered from passions which are the diseases of the mind, and rescued from sin?—for sin is eternal death. Surely utterly dull and blind, and, like moles, doing nothing but eat, you spend your lives in darkness, surrounded with corruption. But it is truth which cries, "The light shall shine forth from the darkness." Let the light then shine in the hidden part of man, that is, the heart; and let the beams of knowledge arise to reveal and irradiate the hidden inner man, the disciple of the Light, the familiar friend and fellow-heir of Christ; especially now that we have come to know the most precious and venerable name of the good Father, who to a pious and good child gives gentle counsels, and commands what is salutary for His child. He who obeys Him has the advantage in all things, follows God, obeys the Father, knows Him though wandering, loves God, loves his neighbour, fulfils the commandment, seeks the prize, claims the promise. But it has been God's fixed and constant purpose to save the flock of men: for this end the good God sent the good Shepherd. And the Word, having unfolded the truth, showed to men the height of salvation, that either repenting they might be saved, or refusing to obey, they might be judged. This is the proclamation of righteousness: to those that obey, glad tidings; to those that disobey, judgment. The loud trumpet, when sounded, collects the soldiers, and proclaims war. And shall not Christ, breathing a strain of peace to the ends of the earth, gather

[1] Il. vi. 236.

together His own soldiers, the soldiers of peace? Well, by His blood, and by the word, He has gathered the bloodless host of peace, and assigned to them the kingdom of heaven. The trumpet of Christ is His gospel. He hath blown it, and we have heard. "Let us array ourselves in the armour of peace, putting on the breastplate of righteousness, and taking the shield of faith, and binding our brows with the helmet of salvation; and the sword of the Spirit, which is the word of God,"[1] let us sharpen. So the apostle in the spirit of peace commands. These are our invulnerable weapons: armed with these, let us face the evil one; "the fiery darts of the evil one" let us quench with the sword-points dipped in water, that have been baptized by the Word, returning grateful thanks for the benefits we have received, and honouring God through the Divine Word. "For while thou art yet speaking," it is said, "He will say, Behold, I am beside thee."[2] O this holy and blessed power, by which God has fellowship with men! Better far, then, is it to become at once the imitator and the servant of the best of all beings; for only by holy service will any one be able to imitate God, and to serve and worship Him only by imitating Him. The heavenly and truly divine love comes to men thus, when in the soul itself the spark of true goodness, kindled in the soul by the Divine Word, is able to burst forth into flame; and, what is of the highest importance, salvation runs parallel with sincere willingness— choice and life being, so to speak, yoked together. Wherefore this exhortation of the truth alone, like the most faithful of our friends, abides with us till our last breath, and is to the whole and perfect spirit of the soul the kind attendant on our ascent to heaven. What, then, is the exhortation I give you? I urge you to be saved. This Christ desires. In one word, He freely bestows life on you. And who is He? Briefly learn. The Word of truth, the Word of incorruption, that regenerates man by bringing him back to the truth—the goad that urges to salvation—He who expels destruction and pursues death—He who builds up the temple of God in men, that He may cause God to take up

[1] Eph. vi. 14-17.   [2] Isa. lviii. 9.

His abode in men. Cleanse the temple; and pleasures and amusements abandon to the winds and the fire, as a fading flower; but wisely cultivate the fruits of self-command, and present thyself to God as an offering of first-fruits, that there may be not the work alone, but also the grace of God; and both are requisite, that the friend of Christ may be rendered worthy of the kingdom, and be counted worthy of the kingdom.

CHAPTER XII.

EXHORTATION TO ABANDON THEIR OLD ERRORS AND LISTEN TO THE INSTRUCTIONS OF CHRIST.

ET us then avoid custom as we would a dangerous headland, or the threatening Charybdis, or the mythic sirens. It chokes man, turns him away from truth, leads him away from life: custom is a snare, a gulf, a pit, a mischievous winnowing fan.

"Urge the ship beyond that smoke and billow."[1]

Let us shun, fellow-mariners, let us shun this billow; it vomits forth fire: it is a wicked island, heaped with bones and corpses, and in it sings a fair courtesan, Pleasure, delighting with music for the common ear.

"Hie thee hither, far-famed Ulysses, great glory of the Achæans;
Moor the ship, that thou mayest hear a diviner voice."[2]

She praises thee, O mariner, and calls thee illustrious; and the courtesan tries to win to herself the glory of the Greeks. Leave her to prey on the dead; a heavenly spirit comes to thy help: pass by Pleasure, she beguiles.

"Let not a woman with flowing train cheat you of your senses,
With her flattering prattle seeking your hurt."

Sail past the song; it works death. Exert your will only, and you have overcome ruin; bound to the wood of the cross, thou shalt be freed from destruction: the word of God will be thy pilot, and the Holy Spirit will bring thee to anchor in the haven of heaven. Then shalt thou see my God, and be initiated into the sacred mysteries, and come to the fruition of those things which are laid up in heaven

[1] *Odys.* xii. 226.   [2] *Odys.* xii. 184.

reserved for me, which "ear hath not heard, nor have they entered into the heart of any."[1]

> " And in sooth methinks I see two suns,
> And a double Thebes,"[2]

said one frenzy-stricken in the worship of idols, intoxicated with mere ignorance. I would pity him in his frantic intoxication, and thus frantic I would invite him to the sobriety of salvation; for the Lord welcomes a sinner's repentance, and not his death.

Come, O madman, not leaning on the thyrsus, not crowned with ivy; throw away the mitre, throw away the fawn-skin; come to thy senses. I will show thee the Word, and the mysteries of the Word, expounding them after thine own fashion. This is the mountain beloved of God, not the subject of tragedies like Cithæron, but consecrated to dramas of the truth,—a mount of sobriety, shaded with forests of purity; and there revel on it not the Mænades, the sisters of Semele, who was struck by the thunderbolt, practising in their initiatory rites unholy division of flesh, but the daughters of God, the fair lambs, who celebrate the holy rites of the Word, raising a sober choral dance. The righteous are the chorus; the music is a hymn of the King of the universe. The maidens strike the lyre, the angels praise, the prophets speak; the sound of music issues forth, they run and pursue the jubilant band; those that are called make haste, eagerly desiring to receive the Father.

Come thou also, O aged man, leaving Thebes, and casting away from thee both divination and Bacchic frenzy, allow thyself to be led to the truth. I give thee the staff [of the cross] on which to lean. Haste, Tiresias; believe, and thou wilt see. Christ, by whom the eyes of the blind recover sight, will shed on thee a light brighter than the sun; night will flee from thee, fire will fear, death will be gone; thou, old man, who saw not Thebes, shalt see the heavens. O truly sacred mysteries! O stainless light! My way is lighted with torches, and I survey the heavens and God; I become holy whilst I am initiated.

[1] 1 Cor. ii. 9.   [2] Eurip. *Bacch.* 916.

The Lord is the hierophant, and seals while illuminating him who is initiated, and presents to the Father him who believes, to be kept safe for ever. Such are the revelries of my mysteries. If it is thy wish, be thou also initiated; and thou shalt join the choir along with angels around the unbegotten and indestructible and the only true God, the Word of God, raising the hymn with us. This Jesus, who is eternal, the one great High Priest of the one God and of His Father, prays for and exhorts men.

"Hear, ye myriad tribes, rather whoever among men are endowed with reason, both barbarians and Greeks. I call on the whole race of men, whose creator I am, by the will of the Father. Come to me, that you may be put in your due rank under the one God and the one Word of God; and do not only have the advantage of the irrational creatures in the possession of reason; for to you of all mortals I grant the enjoyment of immortality. For I want, I want to impart to you this grace, bestowing on you the perfect boon of immortality; and I confer on you both the Word and the knowledge of God, my complete self. This am I, this God wills, this is symphony, this the harmony of the Father, this is the Son, this is Christ, this the Word of God, the arm of the Lord, the power of the universe, the will of the Father; of which things there were images of old, but not all adequate. I desire to restore you according to the original model, that ye may become also like me. I anoint you with the unguent of faith, by which you throw off corruption, and show you the naked form of righteousness by which you ascend to God. Come to me, all ye that labour and are heavy laden, and I will give you rest. Take my yoke upon you, and learn of me; for I am meek and lowly in heart: and ye shall find rest to your souls. For my yoke is easy, and my burden light."[1]

Let us haste, let us run, my fellow-men—us, who are God-loving and God-like images of the Word. Let us haste, let us run, let us take His yoke, let us receive, to conduct us to immortality, the good charioteer of men. Let us love

[1] Matt. xi. 28, 29, 30.

Christ. He led the colt with its parent; and having yoked the team of humanity to God, directs His chariot to immortality, hastening clearly to fulfil, by driving now into heaven, what He shadowed forth before by riding into Jerusalem. A spectacle most beautiful to the Father is the eternal Son crowned with victory. Let us aspire, then, after what is good; let us become God-loving men, and obtain the greatest of all things which are incapable of being harmed —God and life. Our helper is the Word; let us put confidence in Him; and never let us be visited with such a craving for silver and gold, and glory, as for the Word of truth Himself. For it will not, it will not be pleasing to God Himself if we value least those things which are worth most, and hold in the highest estimation the manifest enormities and the utter impiety of folly, and ignorance, and thoughtlessness, and idolatry. For not improperly the sons of the philosophers consider that the foolish are guilty of profanity and impiety in whatever they do; and describing ignorance itself as a species of madness, allege that the multitude are nothing but madmen. There is therefore no room to doubt, the Word will say, whether it is better to be sane or insane; but holding on to truth with our teeth, we must with all our might follow God, and in the exercise of wisdom regard all things to be, as they are, His; and besides, having learned that we are the most excellent of His possessions, let us commit ourselves to God, loving the Lord God, and regarding this as our business all our life long. And if what belongs to friends be reckoned common property, and man be the friend of God— for through the mediation of the Word has he been made the friend of God—then accordingly all things become man's, because all things are God's, and the common property of both the friends, God and man.

It is time, then, for us to say that the pious Christian alone is rich and wise, and of noble birth, and thus call and believe him to be God's image, and also His likeness,[1] having become

---

[1] Clement here draws a distinction, frequently made by early Christian writers, between the image and likeness of God. Man never loses the image of God; but as the likeness consists in moral resemblance, he

righteous and holy and wise by Jesus Christ, and so far already like God. Accordingly this grace is indicated by the prophet, when he says, "I said that ye are gods, and all sons of the Highest."[1] For us, yea us, He has adopted, and wishes to be called the Father of us alone, not of the unbelieving. Such is then our position who are the attendants of Christ.

> "As are men's wishes, so are their words;
> As are their words, so are their deeds;
> And as their works, such is their life."

Good is the whole life of those who have known Christ.

Enough, methinks, of words, though, impelled by love to man, I might have gone on to pour out what I had from God, that I might exhort to what is the greatest of blessings—salvation. For discourses concerning the life which has no end, are not readily brought to the end of their disclosures. To you still remains this conclusion, to choose which will profit you most—judgment or grace. For I do not think there is even room for doubt which of these is the better; nor is it allowable to compare life with destruction.

may lose it, and he recovers it only when he becomes righteous, holy, and wise.

[1] Ps. lxxxii. 6.

THE INSTRUCTOR
(PÆDAGOGUS).

1:1

THE INSTRUCTOR.
BOOK I.

CHAPTER I.

THE OFFICE OF THE INSTRUCTOR.

AS there are these three things in the case of man, habits, actions, and passions; habits are the department appropriated by *hortatory* discourse the guide to piety, which, like the ship's keel, is laid beneath for the building up of faith; in which, rejoicing exceedingly, and abjuring our old opinions, through salvation we renew our youth, singing with the hymning prophecy, "How good is God to Israel, to such as are upright in heart!"[1] All actions, again, are the province of *preceptive* discourse; while *persuasive* discourse applies itself to heal the passions. It is, however, one and the self-same word which rescues man from the custom of this world in which he has been reared, and trains him up in the one salvation of faith in God.

When, then, the heavenly guide, the Word, was inviting men to salvation, the appellation of *hortatory* was properly applied to Him: this same word was called rousing (the whole from a part). For the whole of piety is hortatory, engendering in the kindred faculty of reason a yearning after true life now and to come. But now, being at once curative and preceptive, following in His own steps, He makes what had been prescribed the subject of persuasion, promising the cure of the passions within us. Let us then designate this Word appropriately by the one name *Tutor* (or *Pædagogue*, or *Instructor*).

[1] Ps. lxxiii. 1.

The Instructor being practical, not theoretical, His aim is thus to improve the soul, not to teach, and to train it up to a virtuous, not to an intellectual life. Although this same word is didactic, but not in the present instance. For the word which, in matters of doctrine, explains and reveals, is that whose province it is to teach. But our Educator[1] being practical, first exhorts to the attainment of right dispositions and character, and then persuades us to the energetic practice of our duties, enjoining on us pure commandments, and exhibiting to such as come after representations of those who formerly wandered in error. Both are of the highest utility,—that which assumes the form of counselling to obedience, and that which is presented in the form of example; which latter is of two kinds, corresponding to the former duality,—the one having for its purpose that we should choose and imitate the good, and the other that we should reject and turn away from the opposite.

Hence accordingly ensues the healing of our passions, in consequence of the assuagements of those examples; the Pædagogue strengthening our souls, and by His benign commands, as by gentle medicines, guiding the sick to the perfect knowledge of the truth.

There is a wide difference between health and knowledge; for the latter is produced by learning, the former by healing. One, who is ill, will not therefore learn any branch of instruction till he is quite well. For neither to learners nor to the sick is each injunction invariably expressed similarly; but to the former in such a way as to lead to knowledge, and to the latter to health. As, then, for those of us who are diseased in body a physician is required, so also those who are diseased in soul require a pædagogue to cure our maladies; and then a teacher, to train and guide the soul to all requisite knowledge when it is made able to admit the revelation of the Word. Eagerly desiring, then, to perfect us by a gradation conducive to salvation, suited for efficacious discipline, a beautiful arrangement is observed by the all-benignant Word, who first exhorts, then trains, and finally teaches.

[1] The pædagogus.

CHAPTER II.

OUR INSTRUCTOR'S TREATMENT OF OUR SINS.

NOW, O you, my children, our Instructor is like His Father God, whose son He is, sinless, blameless, and with a soul devoid of passion; God in the form of man, stainless, the minister of His Father's will, the Word who is God, who is in the Father, who is at the Father's right hand, and with the form of God is God. He is to us a spotless image; to Him we are to try with all our might to assimilate our souls. He is wholly free from human passions; wherefore also He alone is judge, because He alone is sinless. As far, however, as we can, let us try to sin as little as possible. For nothing is so urgent in the first place as deliverance from passions and disorders, and then the checking of our liability to fall into sins that have become habitual. It is best, therefore, not to sin at all in any way, which we assert to be the prerogative of God alone; next to keep clear of voluntary transgressions, which is characteristic of the wise man; thirdly, not to fall into many involuntary offences, which is peculiar to those who have been excellently trained. Not to continue long in sins, let that be ranked last. But this also is salutary to those who are called back to repentance, to renew the contest.

And the Instructor, as I think, very beautifully says, through Moses: "If any one die suddenly by him, straightway the head of his consecration shall be polluted, and shall be shaved,"[1] designating involuntary sin as sudden death. And He says that it pollutes by defiling the soul: wherefore He prescribes the cure with all speed, advising the head to be

[1] Num. vi. 9.

instantly shaven; that is, counselling the locks of ignorance which shade the reason to be shorn clean off, that reason (whose seat is in the brain), being left bare of the dense stuff of vice, may speed its way to repentance. Then after a few remarks He adds, "The days before are not reckoned irrational,"[1] by which manifestly sins are meant which are contrary to reason. The involuntary act He calls "*sudden*," the sin he calls "irrational." Wherefore the Word, the Instructor, has taken the charge of us, in order to the prevention of sin, which is contrary to reason.

Hence consider the expression of Scripture, "Therefore these things saith the Lord;" the sin that had been committed before is held up to reprobation by the succeeding expression "therefore," according to which the righteous judgment follows. This is shown conspicuously by the prophets, when they said, "Hadst thou not sinned, He would not have uttered these threatenings." "Therefore thus saith the Lord;" "Because thou hast not heard these words, therefore these things the Lord;" and, "Therefore, behold, the Lord saith." For prophecy is given by reason both of obedience and disobedience: for obedience, that we may be saved; for disobedience, that we may be corrected.

Our Instructor, the Word, therefore cures the unnatural passions of the soul by means of exhortations. For with the highest propriety the help of bodily diseases is called the healing art—an art acquired by human skill. But the paternal Word is the only Pæonian physician of human infirmities, and the holy charmer of the sick soul. "Save," it is said, "Thy servant, O my God, who trusteth in Thee. Pity me, O Lord; for I will cry to Thee all the day."[2] For a while the "physician's art," according to Democritus, "heals the diseases of the body; wisdom frees the soul from passion." But the good Instructor, the Wisdom, the Word of the Father, who made man, cares for the whole nature of His creature; the all-sufficient Physician of humanity, the Saviour, heals both body and soul. "Rise up," He said to the paralytic; "take the bed on which thou liest, and go away home;"[3]

[1] Num. vi. 2.   [2] Ps. lxxxvi. 2, 3.   [3] Mark ii. 11.

and straightway the infirm man received strength. And to the dead He said, "Lazarus, go forth;" and the dead man issued from his coffin such as he was ere he died, having undergone resurrection. Further, He heals the soul itself by precepts and gifts—by precepts indeed, in course of time, but being liberal in His gifts, He says to us sinners, "Thy sins be forgiven thee."[1]

We, however, as soon as He conceived the thought, became His children, having had assigned us the best and most secure rank by His orderly arrangement, which first circles about the world, the heavens, and the sun's circuits, and occupies itself with the motions of the rest of the stars for man's behoof, and then busies itself with man himself, on whom all its care is concentrated; and regarding him as its greatest work, regulated his soul by wisdom and temperance, and tempered the body with beauty and proportion. And whatever in human actions is right and regular, is the result of the inspiration of its rectitude and order.

[1] John xi. 23.

CHAPTER III.

THE PHILANTHROPY OF THE INSTRUCTOR.

THE Lord ministers all good and all help, both as man and as God: as God, forgiving our sins; and as man, training us not to sin. Man is therefore justly dear to God, since he is His workmanship. The other works of creation He made by the word of command alone, but man He framed by Himself, by His own hand, and breathed into him what was peculiar to Himself. What, then, was fashioned by Him, and after His likeness, either was created by God Himself as being desirable on its own account, or was formed as being desirable on account of something else. If, then, man is an object desirable for itself, then He who is good loved what is good, and the love-charm is within even in man, and is that very thing which is called the inspiration [or breath] of God; but if man was a desirable object on account of something else, God had no other reason for creating him, than that unless he came into being, it was not possible for God to be a good Creator, or for man to arrive at the knowledge of God. For God would not have accomplished that on account of which man was created otherwise than by the creation of man; and what hidden power in willing God possessed, He carried fully out by the forth-putting of His might externally in the act of creating, receiving from man what He made man;[1] and

---

[1] Bishop Kaye (*Some Account of the Writings and Opinions of Clement of Alexandria*, p. 48) translates, "receiving from man that which made man (that on account of which man was made)." But it seems more likely that Clement refers to the ideal man in the divine mind, whom he identifies elsewhere with the Logos, the ἄνθρωπος ἀπαθής, of whom man

whom He had He saw, and what He wished that came to pass; and there is nothing which God cannot do. Man, then, whom God made, is desirable for himself, and that which is desirable on his account is allied to him to whom it is desirable on his account; and this, too, is acceptable and liked.

But what is loveable, and is not also loved by Him? And man has been proved to be loveable; consequently man is loved by God. For how shall he not be loved for whose sake the only-begotten Son is sent from the Father's bosom, the Word of faith, the faith which is superabundant; the Lord Himself distinctly confessing and saying, "For the Father Himself loveth you, because ye have loved me;"[1] and again, "And hast loved them as Thou hast loved me?"[2] What, then, the Master desires and declares, and how He is disposed in deed and word, how He commands what is to be done, and forbids the opposite, has already been shown.

Plainly, then, the other kind of discourse, the didactic, is powerful and spiritual, observing precision, occupied in the contemplation of mysteries. But let it stand over for the present. Now, it is incumbent on us to return His love, who lovingly guides us to that life which is best; and to live in accordance with the injunctions of His will, not only fulfilling what is commanded, or guarding against what is forbidden, but turning away from some examples, and imitating others as much as we can, and thus to perform the works of the Master according to His similitude, and so fulfil what Scripture says as to our being made in His image and likeness. For, wandering in life as in deep darkness, we need a guide that cannot stumble or stray; and our guide is the best, not blind, as the Scripture says, "leading the blind into pits."[3] But the Word is keen-sighted, and scans the recesses of the heart. As, then, that is not light which enlightens not, nor motion that moves not, nor loving which loves not, so neither

was the image. The reader will notice that Clement speaks of man as existing in the divine mind before his creation, and creation is represented by God's *seeing* what He had previously within Him merely as a hidden power.

[1] John xvi. 27.   [2] John xvii. 23.   [3] Matt. xv. 14.

is that good which profits not, nor guides to salvation. Let us then aim at the fulfilment of the commandments by the works of the Lord; for the Word Himself also, having openly become flesh,[1] exhibited the same virtue, both practical and contemplative. Wherefore let us regard the Word as law, and His commands and counsels as the short and straight paths to immortality; for His precepts are full of persuasion, not of fear.

[1] John i. 14.

CHAPTER IV.

MEN AND WOMEN ALIKE UNDER THE INSTRUCTOR'S CHARGE.

LET us, then, embracing more and more this good obedience, give ourselves to the Lord, clinging to what is surest, the cable of faith in Him, and understanding that the virtue of man and woman is the same. For if the God of both is one, the Master of both is also one; one church, one temperance, one modesty; their food is common, marriage an equal yoke; respiration, sight, hearing, knowledge, hope, obedience, love, all alike. And those whose life is common, have common grace and a common salvation; common to them are love and training. "For in this world," he says, "they marry, and are given in marriage,"[1] in which alone the female is distinguished from the male; "but in that world it is so no more." There the rewards of this social and holy life, which is based on conjugal union, are laid up, not for male and female, but for man, the sexual desire which divided humanity being removed. Common therefore, too, to men and women, is the name of man. For this reason I think the Attics called, not boys only, but girls, παιδάριον, using it as a word of common gender; if Menander the comic poet, in *Rhapizomena*, appears to any one a sufficient authority, who thus speaks:

> "My little daughter; for by nature
> The child (παιδάριον) is most loving."

Ἄρνες, too, the word for lambs, is a common name of simplicity for the male and female animal.

Now the Lord Himself will feed us as His flock for ever. Amen. But without a shepherd, neither can sheep nor any other animal live, nor children without a tutor, nor domestics without a master.

[1] Luke xx. 34.

CHAPTER V.

ALL WHO WALK ACCORDING TO TRUTH ARE CHILDREN OF GOD.

THAT, then, Pædagogy is the training of children (παίδων αγωγή), is clear from the word itself. It remains for us to consider the children whom Scripture points to; then to give the pædagogue charge of them. We are the children. In many ways Scripture celebrates us, and describes us in manifold figures of speech, giving variety to the simplicity of the faith by diverse names. Accordingly, in the gospel, "the Lord, standing on the shore, says to the disciples"—they happened to be fishing—"and called aloud, Children, have ye any meat?"[1] —addressing those that were already in the position of disciples as children. "And they brought to Him," it is said, "children, that He might put His hands on them and bless them; and when His disciples hindered them, Jesus said, Suffer the children, and forbid them not to come to me, for of such is the kingdom of heaven."[2] What the expression means, the Lord Himself shall declare, saying, "Except ye be converted, and become as little children, ye shall not enter into the kingdom of heaven;"[3] not in that place speaking figuratively of regeneration, but setting before us, for our imitation, the simplicity that is in children.

The prophetic spirit also distinguishes us as children. "Plucking," it is said, "branches of olives or palms, the children went forth to meet the Lord, and cried, saying, Hosanna to the Son of David! Blessed is He that cometh in the name of the Lord;"[4] light, and glory, and praise, with

[1] John xxi. 4, 5. [2] Matt. xix. 14. [3] Matt. xviii. 3. [4] Matt. xxi. 9.

supplication to the Lord: for this is the meaning of the expression Hosanna when rendered into Greek. And the Scripture appears to me, in allusion to the prophecy just mentioned, reproachfully to upbraid the thoughtless: "Have ye never read, Out of the mouths of babes and sucklings Thou hast perfected praise?"[1] In this way the Lord in the Gospels spurs on His disciples, urging them to attend to Him, hastening as He was to the Father; rendering His hearers more eager by the intimation that after a little He was to depart, and showing them that it was requisite that they should take more unsparing advantage of the truth than ever before, as the Word was to ascend to heaven. Again, therefore, He calls them children; for He says, "Children, a little while I am with you."[2] And, again, He likens the kingdom of heaven to children sitting in the market-places and saying, "We have piped unto you, and ye have not danced; we have mourned, and ye have not lamented;"[3] and whatever else He added agreeably thereto. And it is not alone the gospel that holds these sentiments. Prophecy also agrees with it. David accordingly says, "*Praise, O children, the Lord; praise the name of the Lord.*"[4] It says also by Esaias, "*Here am I, and the children that God hath given me.*"[5] Are you amazed, then, to hear that men who belong to the nations are sons in the Lord's sight? You do not in that case appear to give ear to the Attic dialect, from which you may learn that beautiful, comely, and freeborn young maidens are still called παιδίσκαι, and servant-girls παιδισκάρια; and that those last also are, on account of the bloom of youth, called by the flattering name of young maidens.

And when He says, "Let my lambs stand on my right,"[6] He alludes to the simple children, as if they were sheep and lambs in nature, not men; and the lambs He counts worthy of preference, from the superior regard He has to that tenderness and simplicity of disposition in men which constitutes innocence. Again, when He says, "as sucking calves," He again alludes figuratively to us; and "as an innocent and

[1] Matt. xxi. 16; Ps. viii. 3.   [2] John xiii. 33.   [3] Matt. xi. 16, 17.
[4] Ps. cxiii. 18.   [5] Isa. viii.   [6] Matt. xxv. 33.

gentle dove," [1] the reference is again to us. Again, by Moses, He commands "two young pigeons or a pair of turtles to be offered for sin;" [2] thus saying, that the harmlessness and innocence and placable nature of these tender young birds are acceptable to God, and explaining that like is an expiation for like. Further, the timorousness of the turtle-doves typifies fear in reference to sin.

And that He calls us chickens the Scripture testifies: " As a hen gathereth her chickens under her wings." [3] Thus are we the Lord's chickens; the Word thus marvellously and mystically describing the simplicity of childhood. For sometimes He calls us children, sometimes chickens, sometimes infants, and at other times sons, and "a new people," and "a recent people." "And my servants shall be called by a new name" [4] (a new name, He says, fresh and eternal, pure and simple, and childlike and true), which shall be blessed on the earth. And again, He figuratively calls us colts unyoked to vice, not broken in by wickedness; but simple, and bounding joyously to the Father alone; not such horses "as neigh after their neighbours' wives, that are under the yoke, and are female-mad;" [5] but free and new-born, jubilant by means of faith, ready to run to the truth, swift to speed to salvation, that tread and stamp under foot the things of the world.

"Rejoice greatly, O daughter of Sion; tell aloud, O daughter of Jerusalem: behold, thy King cometh, just, meek, and bringing salvation; meek truly is He, and riding on a beast of burden, and a young colt." [6] It was not enough to have said colt alone, but He added to it also *young*, to show the youth of humanity in Christ, and the eternity of simplicity, which shall know no old age. And we who are little ones being such colts, are reared up by our divine colt-tamer. But if the new man in Scripture is represented by the ass, this ass is also a colt. "And he bound," it is said, "the colt to the vine," having bound this simple and childlike people to the word, whom He figuratively represents as a vine. For the

---

[1] Matt. x. 16.   [2] Lev. xv. 29, xii. 8; Luke ii. 24.
[3] Matt. xxiii. 37.   [4] Isa. lxv. 15, 16.
[5] Jer. v. 8.   [6] Zech. ix. 9; Gen. xlix. 11.

vine produces wine, as the Word produces blood, and both drink for health to men—wine for the body, blood for the spirit.

And that He also calls us lambs, the Spirit by the mouth of Isaiah is an unimpeachable witness: "He will feed His flock like a shepherd, He will gather the lambs with His arm,"[1]—using the figurative appellation of lambs, which are still more tender than sheep, to express simplicity. And we also in truth, honouring the fairest and most perfect objects in life with an appellation derived from the word child, have named training παιδεία, and discipline παιδαγωγία. Discipline (παιδαγωγία) we declare to be right guiding from childhood to virtue. Accordingly, our Lord revealed more distinctly to us what is signified by the appellation of children. On the question arising among the apostles, "which of them should be the greater," Jesus placed a little child in the midst, saying, "Whosoever shall humble himself as this little child, the same shall be the greater in the kingdom of heaven."[2] He does not then use the appellation of children on account of their very limited amount of understanding from their age, as some have thought. Nor, if He says, "Except ye become as these children, ye shall not enter into the kingdom of God," are His words to be understood as meaning "without learning." We, then, who are infants, no longer roll on the ground, nor creep on the earth like serpents as before, crawling with the whole body about senseless lusts; but, stretching upwards in soul, loosed from the world and our sins, touching the earth on tiptoe so as to appear to be in the world, we pursue holy wisdom, although this seems folly to those whose wits are whetted for wickedness. Rightly, then, are those called children who know Him who is God alone as their Father, who are simple, and infants, and guileless, who are lovers of the horns of the unicorns.[3]

To those, therefore, that have made progress in the word, He has proclaimed this utterance, bidding them dismiss anxious

---

[1] Isa. xl. 11. [2] Matt. xviii. 1.

[3] Theodoret explains this to mean that, as the animal referred to has only one horn, so those brought up in the practice of piety worship only one God.

care of the things of this world, and exhorting them to adhere to the Father alone, in imitation of children. Wherefore also in what follows He says: "Take no anxious thought for the morrow; sufficient unto the day is the evil thereof."[1] Thus He enjoins them to lay aside the cares of this life, and depend on the Father alone. And he who fulfils this commandment is in reality a child and a son to God and to the world,—to the one as deceived, to the other as beloved. And if we have one Master in heaven, as the Scripture says, then by common consent those on the earth will be rightly called disciples. For so is the truth, that perfection is with the Lord, who is always teaching, and infancy and childishness with us, who are always learning. Thus prophecy hath honoured *perfection*, by applying to it the appellation *man*. For instance, by David, He says of the devil: "The Lord abhors the man of blood;"[2] he calls him man, as perfect in wickedness. And the Lord is called man, because He is perfect in righteousness. Directly in point is the instance of the apostle, who says, writing the Corinthians: "For I have espoused you to one man, that I may present you as a chaste virgin to Christ,"[3] whether as children or saints, but to the Lord alone. And writing to the Ephesians, he has unfolded in the clearest manner the point in question, speaking to the following effect: "Till we all attain to the unity of the faith, and of the knowledge of God, to a perfect man, to the measure of the stature of the fulness of Christ: that we be no longer children, tossed to and fro by every wind of doctrine, by the craft of men, by their cunning in the stratagems of deceit; but, speaking the truth in love, may grow up to Him in all things,"[4]—saying these things in order to the edification of the body of Christ, who is the head and man, the only one perfect in righteousness; and we who are children guarding against the blasts of heresies, which blow to our inflation; and not putting our trust in fathers who teach us otherwise, are then made perfect when we are the church, having received Christ the head. Then it is right to notice, with respect to the appellation of infant (νήπιος), that τὸ νήπιον is not pre-

[1] Matt. vi. 34. [2] Ps. v. 6. [3] 2 Cor. xi. 2. [4] Eph. iv. 13-15.

dicated of the silly: for the silly man is called νηπύτιος; and νήπιος is νεήπιος (since he that is tender-hearted is called ἤπιος), as being one that has newly become gentle and meek in conduct. This the blessed Paul most clearly pointed out when he said, "When we might have been burdensome as the apostles of Christ, we were gentle (ἤπιοι) among you, as a nurse cherisheth her children."[1] The child (νήπιος) is therefore gentle (ἤπιος), and therefore more tender, delicate, and simple, guileless, and destitute of hypocrisy, straightforward and upright in mind, which is the basis of simplicity and truth. For He says, "Upon whom shall I look, but upon him who is gentle and quiet?"[2] For such is the virgin speech, tender, and free of fraud; whence also a virgin is wont to be called "a tender bride," and a child "tender-hearted." And we are tender who are pliant to the power of persuasion, and are easily drawn to goodness, and are mild, and free of the stain of malice and perverseness, for the ancient race was perverse and hard-hearted; but the band of infants, the new people which we are, is delicate as a child. On account of the hearts of the innocent, the apostle, in the Epistle to the Romans, owns that he rejoices, and furnishes a kind of definition of children, so to speak, when he says, "I would have you wise toward good, but simple towards evil."[3] For the name of child, νήπιος, is not understood by us privatively, though the sons of the grammarians make the νη a privative particle. For if they call us who follow after childhood foolish, see how they utter blasphemy against the Lord, in regarding those as foolish who have betaken themselves to God. But if, which is rather the true sense, they themselves understand the designation children of simple ones, we glory in the name. For the new minds, which have newly become wise, which have sprung into being according to the new covenant, are infantile in the old folly. Of late, then, God was known by the coming of Christ: "For no man knoweth God but the Son, and he to whom the Son shall reveal Him."[4]

[1] 1 Thess. ii. 6, 7. [2] Isa. lxvi. 2.
[3] Rom. xvi. 19. [4] Matt. xi. 27; Luke x. 28.

In contradistinction, therefore, to the older people, the new people are called young, having learned the new blessings; and we have the exuberance of life's morning prime in this youth which knows no old age, in which we are always growing to maturity in intelligence, are always young, always mild, always new: for those must necessarily be new, who have become partakers of the new Word. And that which participates in eternity is wont to be assimilated to the incorruptible: so that to us appertains the designation of the age of childhood, a lifelong spring-time, because the truth that is in us, and our habits saturated with the truth, cannot be touched by old age; but Wisdom is ever blooming, ever remains consistent and the same, and never changes. "Their children," it is said, "shall be borne upon their shoulders, and fondled on their knees; as one whom his mother comforteth, so also shall I comfort you."[1] The mother draws the children to herself; and we seek our mother the church. Whatever is feeble and tender, as needing help on account of its feebleness, is kindly looked on, and is sweet and pleasant, anger changing into help in the case of such: for thus horses' colts, and the little calves of cows, and the lion's whelp, and the stag's fawn, and the child of man, are looked upon with pleasure by their fathers and mothers. Thus also the Father of the universe cherishes affection towards those who have fled to Him; and having begotten them again by His Spirit to the adoption of children, knows them as gentle, and loves those alone, and aids and fights for them; and therefore He bestows on them the name of child. The word Isaac I also connect with child. Isaac means laughter. He was seen sporting with his wife and helpmeet Rebecca by the prying king.[2] The king, whose name was Abimelech, appears to me to represent a supramundane wisdom contemplating the mystery of sport. They interpret Rebecca to mean endurance. O wise sport, laughter also assisted by endurance, and the king as spectator! The spirit of those that are children in Christ, whose lives are ordered in endurance, rejoice. And this is the divine sport. "Such a sport, of his own,

[1] Isa. lxvi. 12, 13.   [2] Gen. xxvi. 8.

Jove sports," says Heraclitus. For what other employment is seemly for a wise and perfect man, than to sport and be glad in the endurance of what is good, and, in the administration of what is good, holding festival with God? That which is signified by the prophet may be interpreted differently,—namely, of our rejoicing for salvation, as Isaac. He also, delivered from death, laughed, sporting and rejoicing with his spouse, who was the type of the Helper of our salvation, the church, to whom the stable name of endurance is given; for this cause surely, because she alone remains to all generations, rejoicing ever, subsisting as she does by the endurance of us believers, who are the members of Christ. And the witness of those that have endured to the end, and the rejoicing on their account, is the mystic sport, and the salvation accompanied with decorous solace which brings us aid.

The King, then, who is Christ, beholds from above our laughter, and looking through the window, as the Scripture says, views the thanksgiving, and the blessing, and the rejoicing, and the gladness, and furthermore the endurance which works together with them and their embrace: views His church, showing only His face, which was wanting to the church, which is made perfect by her royal Head. And where, then, was the door by which the Lord showed Himself? The flesh by which He was manifested. He is Isaac (for the narrative may be interpreted otherwise), who is a type of the Lord, a child as a son; for he was the son of Abraham, as Christ the Son of God, and a sacrifice as the Lord, but he was not immolated as the Lord. Isaac only bore the wood of the sacrifice, as the Lord the wood of the cross. And he laughed mystically, prophesying that the Lord should fill us with joy, who have been redeemed from corruption by the blood of the Lord. Isaac did everything but suffer, as was right, yielding the precedence in suffering to the Word. Furthermore, there is an intimation of the divinity of the Lord in His not being slain. For Jesus rose again after His burial, having suffered no harm, like Isaac released from sacrifice. And in defence of the point to be established, I shall adduce another consideration of the greatest weight. The Spirit calls the Lord Himself a child, thus prophesying by Esaias: "Lo, to us a child has been born, to us a son has been given, on whose own shoulder the government shall be; and His name has been called the Angel of great Counsel." Who, then, is this infant child? He according to whose image we are made little children. By the same prophet is declared His greatness: "Wonderful, Counsellor, Mighty God, Everlasting Father, Prince of Peace; that He might fulfil His discipline: and of His peace there shall be no end."[1] O the great God! O the perfect child! The Son in the Father, and the Father in the Son. And how shall not the discipline of this child be perfect, which extends to all, leading as a schoolmaster us as children, who are His little ones? He has stretched forth to us those hands of His that are conspicuously worthy of trust. To this child additional testimony is borne by John, "the greatest prophet among those born of women:"[2] "Behold the Lamb of God!"[3] For since Scripture calls the infant children lambs, it has also called Him—God the Word—who became man for our sakes, and who wished in all points to be made like to us—"the Lamb of God"—Him, namely, that is the Son of God, the child of the Father.

[1] Isa. ix. 6. [2] Luke vii. 28. [3] John i. 29, 36.

CHAPTER VI.

THE NAME CHILDREN DOES NOT IMPLY INSTRUCTION IN ELEMENTARY PRINCIPLES.

WE have ample means of encountering those who are given to carping. For we are not termed children and infants with reference to the childish and contemptible character of our education, as those who are inflated on account of knowledge have calumniously alleged. Straightway, on our regeneration, we attained that perfection after which we aspired. For we were illuminated, which is to know God. He is not then imperfect who knows what is perfect. And do not reprehend me when I profess to know God; for so it was deemed right to speak to the Word, and He is free.[1] For at the moment of the Lord's baptism there sounded a voice from heaven, as a testimony to the Beloved, "Thou art my beloved Son, to-day have I begotten Thee." Let us then ask at the wise, Is Christ, begotten to-day, already perfect, or—what were most monstrous—imperfect? If the latter, there is some addition He requires yet to make. But for Him to make any addition to His knowledge is absurd, since He is God. For none can be superior to the Word, or the teacher of the only Teacher. Will they not then own, though reluctant, that the perfect Word born of the perfect Father was begotten in perfection, according to œconomic fore-ordination? And if He was perfect, why was He, the perfect one, baptized? It was necessary, they say, to fulfil the profession that pertained to humanity. Most excellent. Well, I assert, simultaneously with His baptism by John, He becomes perfect? Manifestly. He did not then learn anything more from him? Certainly

[1] In allusion apparently to John viii. 35, 36.

not. But He is perfected by the washing—of baptism—alone, and is sanctified by the descent of the Spirit? Such is the case. The same also takes place in our case, whose exemplar Christ became. Being baptized, we are illuminated; illuminated, we become sons; being made sons, we are made perfect; being made perfect, we are made immortal. "I," says He, "have said that ye are gods, and all sons of the Highest."[1] This work is variously called grace,[2] and illumination, and perfection, and washing: washing, by which we cleanse away our sins; grace, by which the penalties accruing to transgressions are remitted; and illumination, by which that holy light of salvation is beheld, that is, by which we see God clearly. Now we call that perfect which wants nothing. For what is yet wanting to him who knows God? For it were truly monstrous that that which is not complete should be called a gift (or act) of God's grace. Being perfect, He consequently bestows perfect gifts. As at His command all things were made, so on His bare wishing to bestow grace, ensues the perfecting of His grace. For the future of time is anticipated by the power of His volition.

Further release from evils is the beginning of salvation. We then alone, who first have touched the confines of life, are already perfect; and we already live who are separated from death. Salvation, accordingly, is the following of Christ: "For that which is in Him is life."[3] "Verily, verily, I say unto you, He that heareth my words, and believeth on Him that sent me, hath eternal life, and cometh not into condemnation, but hath passed from death to life."[4] Thus believing alone, and regeneration, is perfection in life; for God is never weak. For as His will is work, and this[5] is named the world; so also His counsel is the salvation of men, and this has been called the church. He knows, therefore, whom He has called, and whom He has saved; and at one and the same time He called and saved them. "For ye are," says the apostle, "taught of God."[6] It is not then allowable to think of what is taught by Him as imperfect; and what

---

[1] Ps. lxxxii. 6. [2] χάρισμα. [3] John i. 4.
[4] John v. 24. [5] viz. the result of His will. [6] 1 Thess. iv. 9.

is learned from Him is the eternal salvation of the eternal Saviour, to whom be thanks for ever and ever. Amen. And he who is only regenerated—as the name necessarily indicates—and is enlightened, is delivered forthwith from darkness, and on the instant receives the light.

As, then, those who have shaken off sleep forthwith become all awake within; or rather, as those who try to remove a film that is over the eyes, do not supply to them from without the light which they do not possess, but removing the obstacle from the eyes, leave the pupil free; thus also we who are baptized, having wiped off the sins which obscure the light of the Divine Spirit, have the eye of the spirit free, unimpeded, and full of light, by which alone we contemplate the Divine, the Holy Spirit flowing down to us from above. This is the eternal adjustment of the vision, which is able to see the eternal light, since like loves like; and that which is holy, loves that from which holiness proceeds, which has appropriately been termed light. "Once ye were darkness, now are ye light in the Lord."[1] Hence I am of opinion man was called by the ancients φώς.[2] But he has not yet received, say they, the perfect gift. I also assent to this; but he is in the light, and the darkness comprehendeth him not. There is nothing intermediate between light and darkness. But the end is reserved till the resurrection of those who believe; and it is not the reception of some other thing, but the obtaining of the promise previously made. For we do not say that both take place together at the same time—both the arrival at the end, and the anticipation of that arrival. For eternity and time are not the same, neither is the attempt and the final result; but both have reference to the same thing, and one and the same person is concerned in both. Faith, so to speak, is the attempt generated in time; the final result is the attainment of the promise, secured for eternity. Now the Lord Himself has most clearly revealed the equality of salvation, when He said: "For this is the will of my Father, that every one that seeth the Son, and believeth on Him, should have everlasting life; and I will raise him up in the

[1] Eph. v. 8.   φῶς, light; φώς, a man.

last day."[1] As far as possible in this world, which is what he means by the last day, and which is preserved till the time that it shall end, we believe that we are made perfect. Wherefore He says, "He that believeth on the Son hath everlasting life."[2] If, then, those who have believed have life, what remains beyond the possession of eternal life? Nothing is wanting to faith, as it is perfect and complete in itself. If aught is wanting to it, it is not wholly perfect. But faith is not lame in any respect; nor after our departure from this world does it make us who have believed, and received without distinction the earnest of future good, wait; but having in anticipation grasped by faith that which is future, after the resurrection we receive it as present, in order that that may be fulfilled which was spoken, "Be it according to thy faith."[3] And where faith is, there is the promise; and the consummation of the promise is rest. So that in illumination what we receive is knowledge, and the end of knowledge is rest—the last thing conceived as the object of aspiration. As, then, inexperience comes to an end by experience, and perplexity by finding a clear outlet, so by illumination must darkness disappear. The darkness is ignorance, through which we fall into sins, purblind as to the truth. Knowledge, then, is the illumination we receive, which makes ignorance disappear, and endows us with clear vision. Further, the abandonment of what is bad is the adopting[4] of what is better. For what ignorance has bound ill, is by knowledge loosed well; those bonds are with all speed slackened by human faith and divine grace, our transgressions being taken away by one Pæonian medicine, the baptism of the Word. We are washed from all our sins, and are no longer entangled in evil. This is the one grace of illumination, that our characters are not the same as before our washing. And since knowledge springs up with illumination, shedding its beams around the mind, the moment we hear, we who were untaught become disciples. Does this, I ask, take place on the advent of this

---

[1] John vi. 40.   [2] John iii. 36.   [3] Matt. ix. 29.
[4] Migne's text has ἀποκάλυψις. The emendation ἀπόληψις is preferable.

instruction? You cannot tell the time. For instruction leads to faith, and faith with baptism is trained by the Holy Spirit. For that faith is the one universal salvation of humanity, and that there is the same equality before the righteous and loving God, and the same fellowship between Him and all, the apostle most clearly showed, speaking to the following effect: "Before faith came, we were kept under the law, shut up unto the faith which should afterwards be revealed, so that the law became our schoolmaster to bring us to Christ, that we might be justified by faith; but after that faith is come, we are no longer under a schoolmaster."[1] Do you not hear that we are no longer under that law which was accompanied with fear, but under the Word, the master of free choice? Then he subjoined the utterance, clear of all partiality: "For ye are all the children of God through faith in Christ Jesus. For as many as were baptized into Christ have put on Christ. There is neither Jew nor Greek, there is neither bond nor free, there is neither male nor female: for ye are all one in Christ Jesus."[2] There are not, then, in the same Word some "illuminated (gnostics); and some animal (or natural) men;" but all who have abandoned the desires of the flesh are equal and spiritual before the Lord. And again he writes in another place: "For by one spirit are we all baptized into one body, whether Jews or Greeks, whether bond or free, and we have all drunk of one cup."[3] Nor were it absurd to employ the expressions of those who call the reminiscence of better things the filtration of the spirit, understanding by filtration the separation of what is baser, that results from the reminiscence of what is better. There follows of necessity, in him who has come to the recollection of what is better, repentance for what is worse. Accordingly, they confess that the spirit in repentance retraces its steps. In the same way, therefore, we also, repenting of our sins, renouncing our iniquities, purified by baptism, speed back to the eternal light, children to the Father. Jesus therefore, rejoicing in spirit, said: "I thank Thee, O Father, God of heaven and earth, that Thou hast hid these things from the

[1] Gal. iii. 23-25.   [2] Gal. iii. 26-28.   [3] 1 Cor. xii. 13.

wise and prudent, and hast revealed them to babes;"[1] the Master and Teacher applying the name babes to us, who are readier to embrace salvation than the wise in the world, who, thinking themselves wise, are inflated with pride. And He exclaims in exultation and exceeding joy, as if lisping with the children, "Even so, Father; for so it seemed good in Thy sight."[2] Wherefore those things which have been concealed from the wise and prudent of this present world have been revealed to babes. Truly, then, are we the children of God, who have put aside the old man, and stripped off the garment of wickedness, and put on the immortality of Christ; that we may become a new, holy people by regeneration, and may keep the man undefiled. And a babe, as God's little one, is cleansed from fornication and wickedness. With the greatest clearness the blessed Paul has solved for us this question in his First Epistle to the Corinthians, writing thus: "Brethren, be not children in understanding; howbeit in malice be children, but in understanding be men."[3] And the expression, "When I was a child, I thought as a child, I spake as a child,"[4] points out his mode of life according to the law, according to which, thinking childish things, he persecuted, and speaking childish things he blasphemed the Word, not as having yet attained to the simplicity of childhood, but as being in its folly; for the word νήπιον has two meanings.[5] "When I became a man," again Paul says, "I put away childish things."[6] It is not incomplete size of stature, nor a definite measure of time, nor additional secret teachings in things that are manly and more perfect, that the apostle, who himself professes to be a preacher of childishness, alludes to when he sends it, as it were, into banishment; but he applies the name "children" to those who are under the law, who are terrified by fear as children are by bugbears; and "men" to us who are obedient to the Word and masters of ourselves, who have believed, and are saved by voluntary choice, and are rationally, not irrationally, frightened by terror.

[1] Luke x. 21. [2] Luke x. 21. [3] 1 Cor. xiv. 20. [4] 1 Cor. xiii. 11.
[5] viz. simple or innocent as a child, and *foolish* as a child.
[6] 1 Cor. xiii. 11.

Of this the apostle himself shall testify, calling as he does the Jews heirs according to the first covenant, and us heirs according to promise: "*Now I say, as long as the heir is a child, he differeth nothing from a servant, though he be lord of all; but is under tutors and governors, till the time appointed by the father. So also we, when we were children, were in bondage under the rudiments of the world; but when the fulness of the time was come, God sent forth His Son, made of a woman, made under the law, to redeem them that were under the law, that we might receive the adoption of sons*"[1] by Him. See how He has admitted those to be children who are under fear and sins; but has conferred manhood on those who are under faith, by calling them sons, in contradistinction from the children that are under the law: "For thou art no more a servant," he says, "but a son; and if a son, then an heir through God."[2] What, then, is lacking to the son after inheritance? Wherefore the expression, "When I was a child," may be elegantly expounded thus: that is, when I was a Jew (for he was a Hebrew by extraction) I thought as a child, when I followed the law; but after becoming a man, I no longer entertain the sentiments of a child, that is, of the law, but of a man, that is, of Christ, whom alone the Scripture calls man, as we have said before. "I put away childish things." But the childhood which is in Christ is maturity, as compared with the law. Having reached this point, we must defend our childhood. And we have still to explain what is said by the apostle: "I have fed you with milk (as children in Christ), not with meat; for ye were not able, neither yet are ye now able."[3] For it does not appear to me that the expression is to be taken in a Jewish sense; for I shall oppose to it also that scripture, "I will bring you into that good land which flows with milk and honey."[4] A very great difficulty arises in reference to the comparison of these scriptures, when we consider. For if the infancy which is characterized by the milk is the beginning of faith in Christ, then it is disparaged as childish and imperfect. How is the rest that comes after the meat, the rest of the man who is perfect and endowed with knowledge,

[1] Gal. iv. 1-5. [2] Gal. iv. 7. [3] 1 Cor. iii. 2. [4] Ex. iii. 8.

again distinguished by infant milk? Does not this, as explaining a parable, mean something like this, and is not the expression to be read somewhat to the following effect: "*I have fed you with milk in Christ;*" and after a slight stop, let us add, "*as children,*" that by separating the words in reading we may make out some such sense as this: I have instructed you in Christ with simple, true, and natural nourishment,—namely, that which is spiritual: for such is the nourishing substance of milk swelling out from breasts of love. So that the whole matter may be conceived thus: As nurses nourish new-born children on milk, so do I also by the Word, the milk of Christ, instilling into you spiritual nutriment.

Thus, then, the milk which is perfect is perfect nourishment, and brings to that consummation which cannot cease. Wherefore also the same milk and honey were promised in the rest. Rightly, therefore, the Lord again promises milk to the righteous, that the Word may be clearly shown to be both, "the Alpha and Omega, beginning and end;"[1] the Word being figuratively represented as milk. Something like this Homer oracularly declares against his will, when he calls righteous men milk-fed (γαλακτοφάγοι). So also may we take the scripture: "And I, brethren, could not speak unto you as unto spiritual, but as unto carnal, even as unto babes in Christ;"[2] so that the carnal may be understood as those recently instructed, and still babes in Christ. For he called those who had already believed on the Holy Spirit spiritual, and those newly instructed and not yet purified carnal; whom with justice he calls still carnal, as minding equally with the heathen the things of the flesh: "For whereas there is among you envy and strife, are ye not carnal, and walk as men?"[3] "Wherefore also I have given you milk to drink," he says; meaning, I have instilled into you the knowledge which, from instruction, nourishes up to life eternal. But the expression, "I have given you to drink" (ἐπότισα), is the symbol of perfect appropriation. For those who are full-grown are said to drink, babes to suck. "For my blood," says the Lord, "is true drink."[4] In saying, therefore, "I have given

[1] Rev. i. 8.   [2] 1 Cor. iii. 1.   [3] 1 Cor. iii. 3.   [4] John vi. 56.

you milk to drink," has he not indicated the knowledge of the truth, the perfect gladness in the Word, who is the milk? And what follows next, "not meat, for ye were not able," may indicate the clear revelation in the future world, like food, face to face. "For now we see as through a glass," the same apostle says, "but then face to face."[1] Wherefore also he has added, "neither yet are ye now able, for ye are still carnal," minding the things of the flesh,—desiring, loving, feeling jealousy, wrath, envy. "For we are no more in the flesh,"[2] as some suppose. For with it [they say], having the face which is like an angel's, we shall see the promise face to face. How then, if that is truly the promise after our departure hence, say they that they know "what eye hath not known, nor hath entered into the mind of man," who have not perceived by the Spirit, but received from instruction "what ear hath not heard,"[3] or that ear alone which "was rapt up into the third heaven?"[4] But it even then was commanded to preserve it unspoken.

But if human wisdom, as it remains to understand, is the glorying in knowledge, hear the law of Scripture: "Let not the wise man glory in his wisdom, and let not the mighty man glory in his might; but let him that glorieth glory in the Lord."[5] But we are God-taught, and glory in the name of Christ. How then are we not to regard the apostle as attaching this sense to the milk of the babes? And if we who preside over the churches are shepherds after the image of the good Shepherd, and you the sheep, are we not to regard the Lord as preserving consistency in the use of figurative speech, when He speaks also of the milk of the flock? And to this meaning we may secondly accommodate the expression, "I have given you milk to drink, and not given you food, for ye are not yet able," regarding the meat not as something different from the milk, but the same in substance. For the very same Word is fluid and mild as milk, or solid and compact as meat. And entertaining this view, we may regard the proclamation of the gospel, which is universally diffused, as milk;

[1] 1 Cor. xiii. 12.   [2] Rom. viii. 9.   [3] 1 Cor. ii. 9.
[4] 2 Cor. xii. 2-4.   [5] Jer. ix. 23; 1 Cor. i. 31; 2 Cor. x. 17.

and as meat, faith, which from instruction is compacted into a foundation, which, being more substantial than hearing, is likened to meat, and assimilates to the soul itself nourishment of this kind. Elsewhere the Lord, in the Gospel according to John, brought this out by symbols, when He said: "Eat ye my flesh, and drink my blood;"[1] describing distinctly by metaphor the drinkable properties of faith and the promise, by means of which the Church, like a human being consisting of many members, is refreshed and grows, is welded together and compacted of both,—of faith, which is the body, and of hope, which is the soul; as also the Lord of flesh and blood. For in reality the blood of faith is hope, in which faith is held as by a vital principle. And when hope expires, it is as if blood flowed forth; and the vitality of faith is destroyed. If, then, some would oppose, saying that by milk is meant the first lessons—as it were, the first food—and that by meat is meant those spiritual cognitions to which they attain by raising themselves to knowledge, let them understand that, in saying that meat is solid food, and the flesh and blood of Jesus, they are brought by their own vainglorious wisdom to the true simplicity. For the blood is found to be an original product in man, and some have consequently ventured to call it the substance of the soul. And this blood, transmuted by a natural process of assimilation in the pregnancy of the mother, through the sympathy of parental affection, effloresces and grows old, in order that there may be no fear for the child. Blood, too, is the moister part of flesh, being a kind of liquid flesh; and milk is the sweeter and finer part of blood. For whether it be the blood supplied to the fœtus, and sent through the navel of the mother, or whether it be the menses themselves shut out from their proper passage, and by a natural diffusion, bidden by the all-nourishing and creating God, proceed to the already swelling breasts, and by the heat of the spirits transmuted, [whether it be the one or the other] that is formed into food desirable for the babe, that which is changed is the blood. For of all the members, the breasts have the most sympathy with the womb. When

[1] John vi. 54.

there is parturition, the vessel by which blood was conveyed to the fœtus is cut off: there is an obstruction of the flow, and the blood receives an impulse towards the breasts; and on a considerable rush taking place, they are distended, and change the blood to milk in a manner analogous to the change of blood into pus in ulceration. Or if, on the other hand, the blood from the veins in the vicinity of the breasts, which have been opened in pregnancy, is poured into the natural hollows of the breasts; and the spirit discharged from the neighbouring arteries being mixed with it, the substance of the blood, still remaining pure, it becomes white by being agitated like a wave; and by an interruption such as this is changed by frothing it, like what takes place with the sea, which at the assaults of the winds, the poets say, "spits forth briny foam." Yet still the essence is supplied by the blood.

In this way also the rivers, borne on with rushing motion, and fretted by contact with the surrounding air, murmur forth foam. The moisture in our mouth, too, is whitened by the breath. What an absurdity[1] is it, then, not to acknowledge that the blood is converted into that very bright and white substance by the breath! The change it suffers is in quality, not in essence. You will certainly find nothing else more nourishing, or sweeter, or whiter than milk. In every respect, accordingly, it is like spiritual nourishment, which is sweet through grace, nourishing as life, bright as the day of Christ.

The blood of the Word has been also exhibited as milk. Milk being thus provided in parturition, is supplied to the infant; and the breasts, which till then looked straight towards the husband, now bend down towards the child, being taught to furnish the substance elaborated by nature in a way easily received for salutary nourishment. For the breasts are not like fountains full of milk, flowing in ready prepared; but, by effecting a change in the nutriment, form the milk in themselves, and discharge it. And the nutriment suitable and wholesome for the new-formed and new-born babe is

[1] The emendation ἀπολήρησις is adopted instead of the reading in the text.

elaborated by God, the nourisher and the Father of all that are generated and regenerated,—as manna, the celestial food of angels, flowed down from heaven on the ancient Hebrews. Even now, in fact, nurses call the first-poured drink of milk by the same name as that food—manna. Further, pregnant women, on becoming mothers, discharge milk. But the Lord Christ, the fruit of the Virgin, did not pronounce the breasts of women blessed, nor selected them to give nourishment; but when the kind and loving Father had rained down the Word, Himself became spiritual nourishment to the good. O mystic marvel! The universal Father is one, and one the universal Word; and the Holy Spirit is one and the same everywhere, and one is the only virgin mother. I love to call her the Church. This mother, when alone, had not milk, because alone she was not a woman. But she is at once virgin and mother—pure as a virgin, loving as a mother. And calling her children to her, she nurses them with holy milk, viz. with the Word for childhood. Therefore she had not milk; for the milk was this child fair and comely, the body of Christ, which nourishes by the Word the young brood, which the Lord Himself brought forth in throes of the flesh, which the Lord Himself swathed in His precious blood. O amazing birth! O holy swaddling bands! The Word is all to the child, both father and mother, and tutor and nurse. "Eat ye my flesh," He says, "and drink my blood."[1] Such is the suitable food which the Lord ministers, and He offers His flesh and pours forth His blood, and nothing is wanting for the children's growth. O amazing mystery! We are enjoined to cast off the old and carnal corruption, as also the old nutriment, receiving in exchange another new regimen, that of Christ, receiving Him if we can, to hide Him within; and that, enshrining the Saviour in our souls, we may correct the affections of our flesh.

But you are not inclined to understand it thus, but perchance more generally. Hear it also in the following way. The flesh figuratively represents to us the Holy Spirit; for the flesh was created by Him. The blood points out

[1] John vi. 53, 54.

to us the Word, for as rich blood the Word has been infused into life; and the union of both is the Lord, the food of the babes—the Lord who is Spirit and Word. The food—that is, the Lord Jesus—that is, the Word of God, the Spirit made flesh, the heavenly flesh sanctified. The nutriment is the milk of the Father, by which alone we infants are nourished. The Word Himself, then, the beloved One, and our nourisher, hath shed His own blood for us, to save humanity; and by Him, we, believing on God, flee to the Word, "the care-soothing breast" of the Father. And He alone, as is befitting, supplies us children with the milk of love, and those only are truly blessed who suck this breast. Wherefore also Peter says: "Laying therefore aside all malice, and all guile, and hypocrisy, and envy, and evil speaking, as new-born babes, desire the milk of the word, that ye may grow by it to salvation; if ye have tasted that the Lord is Christ."[1] And were one to concede to them that the meat was something different from the milk, then how shall they avoid being transfixed on their own spit, through want of consideration of nature? For in winter, when the air is condensed, and prevents the escape of the heat enclosed within, the food, transmuted and digested and changed into blood, passes into the veins, and these, in the absence of exhalation, are greatly distended, and exhibit strong pulsations; consequently also nurses are then fullest of milk. And we have shown a little above, that on pregnancy blood passes into milk by a change which does not affect its substance, just as in old people yellow hair changes to grey. But again in summer, the body, having its pores more open, affords greater facility for diaphoretic action in the case of the food, and the milk is least abundant, since neither is the blood full, nor is the whole nutriment retained. If, then, the digestion of the food results in the production of blood, and the blood becomes milk, then blood is a preparation for milk, as blood is for a human being, and the grape for the vine. With milk, then, the Lord's nutriment, we are nursed directly we are born; and as soon

[1] 1 Pet. ii. 1-3. Clement here reads Χριστός, *Christ*, for χρηστός, *gracious*, in Text. Rec.

as we are regenerated, we are honoured by receiving the good news of the hope of rest, even the Jerusalem above, in which it is written that milk and honey fall in showers, receiving through what is material the pledge of the sacred food. "For meats are done away with,"[1] as the apostle himself says; but this nourishment on milk leads to the heavens, rearing up citizens of heaven, and members of the angelic choirs. And since the Word is the gushing fountain of life, and has been called a river of olive oil, Paul, using appropriate figurative language, and calling Him milk, adds: "I have given you to drink;"[2] for we drink in the word, the nutriment of the truth. In truth, also liquid food is called drink; and the same thing may somehow be both meat and drink, according to the different aspects in which it is considered, just as cheese is the solidification of milk, or milk solidified; for I am not concerned here to make a nice selection of an expression, only to say that one substance supplies both articles of food. Besides, for children at the breast, milk alone suffices; it serves both for meat and drink. "I," says the Lord, "have meat to eat that ye know not of. My meat is to do the will of Him that sent me."[3] You see another kind of food which, similarly with milk, represents figuratively the will of God. Besides, also, the completion of His own passion He called catachrestically "a cup,"[4] when He alone had to drink and drain it. Thus to Christ the fulfilling of His Father's will was food; and to us infants, who drink the milk of the word of the heavens, Christ Himself is food. Hence seeking is called sucking; for to those babes that seek the Word, the Father's breasts of love supply milk.

Further, the Word declares Himself to be the bread of heaven. "For Moses," He says, "gave you not that bread from heaven, but my Father giveth you the true bread from heaven. For the bread of God is He that cometh down from heaven, and giveth life to the world. And the bread which I will give is my flesh, which I will give for the life of the world."[5] Here is to be noted the mystery of the bread, inas-

---

[1] 1 Cor. vi. 13.   [2] 1 Cor. iii. 2.   [3] John iv. 32-34.
[4] Matt. xx. 22, etc.   [5] John vi. 32, 33, 51.

much as He speaks of it as flesh, and as flesh, consequently, that has risen through fire, as the wheat springs up from decay and germination; and, in truth, it has risen through fire for the joy of the church, as bread baked. But this will be shown by and by more clearly in the chapter on the resurrection. But since He said, "And the bread which I will give is my flesh," and since flesh is moistened with blood, and blood is figuratively termed wine, we are bidden know that, as bread, crumbled into a mixture of wine and water, seizes on the wine and leaves the watery portion, so also the flesh of Christ, the bread of heaven, absorbs the blood; that is, those among men who are heavenly, nourishing them up to immortality, and leaving only to destruction the lusts of the flesh.

Thus in many ways the Word is figuratively described, as meat, and flesh, and food, and bread, and blood, and milk. The Lord is all these, to give enjoyment to us who have believed on Him. Let no one then think it strange, when we say that the Lord's blood is figuratively represented as milk. For is it not figuratively represented as wine? "Who washes," it is said, "His garment in wine, His robe in the blood of the grape."[1] In His own Spirit He says He will deck the body of the Word; as certainly by His own Spirit He will nourish those who hunger for the Word.

And that the blood is the Word, is testified by the blood of Abel, the righteous interceding with God. For the blood would never have uttered a voice, had it not been regarded as the Word: for the righteous man of old is the type of the new righteous one; and the blood of old that interceded, intercedes in the place of the new blood. And the blood that is the Word cries to God, since it intimated that the Word was to suffer.

Further, this flesh, and the blood in it, are by a mutual sympathy moistened and increased by the milk. And the process of formation of the seed in conception ensues when it has mingled with the pure residue of the menses, which remains. For the force that is in the seed coagulating the substances of the blood, as the rennet curdles milk, effects the essential

[1] Gen. xlix. 11.

part of the formative process. For a suitable blending conduces to fruitfulness; but extremes are adverse, and tend to sterility. For when the earth itself is flooded by excessive rain, the seed is swept away, while in consequence of scarcity it is dried up; but when the sap is viscous, it retains the seed, and makes it germinate. Some also hold the hypothesis, that the seed of an animal is in substance the foam of the blood, which being by the natural heat of the male agitated and shaken out, in copulation is turned into foam, and deposited in the seminal veins. For Diogenes Apolliouates will have it, that hence is derived the word *aphrodisia*.

From all this it is therefore evident, that the essential principle of the human body is blood. The contents of the stomach, too, at first are milky, a coagulation of fluid; then the same coagulated substance is changed into blood; but when it is formed into a compact consistency in the womb, by the natural and warm spirit by which the embryo is fashioned, it becomes a living creature. Further also, the child after birth is nourished by the same blood. For the flow of milk is the product of the blood; and the source of nourishment is the milk; by which a woman is shown to have brought forth a child, and to be truly a mother, by which also she receives a potent charm of affection. Wherefore the Holy Spirit in the apostle, using the voice of the Lord, says mystically, "I have given you milk to drink."[1] For if we have been regenerated unto Christ, He who has regenerated us nourishes us with His own milk, the Word; for it is proper that what has procreated should forthwith supply nourishment to that which has been procreated. And as the regeneration was conformably spiritual, so also was the nutriment of man spiritual. In all respects, therefore, and in all things, we are brought into union with Christ, into relationship through His blood, by which we are redeemed; and into sympathy, in consequence of the nourishment which flows from the Word; and into immortality, through His guidance:

"Among men the bringing up of children
Often produces stronger impulses to love than the procreating of them."

---

[1] 1 Cor. iii. 2.

The same blood and milk of the Lord is therefore the symbol of the Lord's passion and teaching. Wherefore each of us babes is permitted to make our boast in the Lord, while we proclaim:

"Yet of a noble sire and noble blood I boast me sprung."[1]

And that milk is produced from blood by a change, is already clear; yet we may learn it from the flocks and herds. For these animals, in the time of the year which we call spring, when the air has more humidity, and the grass and meadows are juicy and moist, are first filled with blood, as is shown by the distension of the veins of the swollen vessels; and from the blood the milk flows more copiously. But in summer, again, the blood being burnt and dried up by the heat, prevents the change, and so they have less milk.

Further, milk has a most natural affinity for water, as assuredly the spiritual washing has for the spiritual nutriment. Those, therefore, that swallow a little cold water, in addition to the above-mentioned milk, straightway feel benefit; for the milk is prevented from souring by its combination with water, not in consequence of any antipathy between them, but in consequence of the water taking kindly to the milk while it is undergoing digestion.

And such as is the union of the Word with baptism, is the agreement of milk with water; for it receives it alone of all liquids, and admits of mixture with water, for the purpose of cleansing, as baptism for the remission of sins. And it is mixed naturally with honey also, and this for cleansing along with sweet nutriment. For the Word blended with love at once cures our passions and cleanses our sins; and the saying,

"Sweeter than honey flowed the stream of speech,"[2]

seems to me to have been spoken of the Word, who is honey. And prophecy oft extols Him "above honey and the honeycomb."[3]

Furthermore, milk is mixed with sweet wine; and the mixture is beneficial, as when suffering is mixed in the cup in order to immortality. For the milk is curdled by the wine, and separated, and whatever adulteration is in it is drained

[1] *Il.* xiv. 113.   [2] *Il.* i. 248.   [3] Ps. xix. 10.

off. And in the same way, the spiritual communion of faith with suffering man, drawing off as serous matter the lusts of the flesh, commits man to eternity, along with those who are divine, immortalizing him.

Further, many also use the fat of milk, called butter, for the lamp, plainly indicating by this enigma the abundant unction of the Word, since He alone it is who nourishes the infants, makes them grow, and enlightens them. Wherefore also the Scripture says respecting the Lord, "He fed them with the produce of the fields; they sucked honey from the rock, and oil from the solid rock, butter of kine, and milk of sheep, with fat of lambs;"[1] and what follows He gave them. But he that prophesies the birth of the child says: "Butter and honey shall He eat."[2] And it occurs to me to wonder how some dare call themselves perfect and gnostics, with ideas of themselves above the apostle, inflated and boastful, when Paul even owned respecting himself, "Not that I have already attained, or am already perfect; but I follow after, if that I may apprehend that for which I am apprehended of Christ. Brethren, I count not myself to have apprehended: but this one thing I do, forgetting the things which are behind, and stretching forth to those that are before, I press toward the mark, for the prize of the high calling in Christ Jesus."[3] And yet he reckons himself perfect, because he has been emancipated from his former life, and strives after the better life, not as perfect in knowledge, but as aspiring after perfection. Wherefore also he adds, "As many of us as are perfect, are thus minded,"[4] manifestly describing perfection as the renunciation of sin, and regeneration into the faith of the only perfect One, and forgetting our former sins.

[1] Deut. xxxii. 13, 14.
[2] Isa. vii. 15.
[3] Phil. iii. 12-14.
[4] Phil. iii. 15.

CHAPTER VII.

WHO THE INSTRUCTOR IS, AND RESPECTING HIS INSTRUCTION.

SINCE, then, we have shown that all of us are by Scripture called children; and not only so, but that we who have followed Christ are figuratively called babes; and that the Father of all alone is perfect, for the Son is in Him, and the Father is in the Son; it is time for us in due course to say who our Instructor is.

He is called Jesus. Sometimes He calls Himself a shepherd, and says, "I am the good Shepherd."[1] According to a metaphor drawn from shepherds, who lead the sheep, is hereby understood the Instructor, who leads the children—the Shepherd who tends the babes. For the babes are simple, being figuratively described as sheep. "And they shall all," it is said, "be one flock, and one shepherd."[2] The Word, then, who leads the children to salvation, is appropriately called *the Instructor*[3] (Pædagogue).

With the greatest clearness, accordingly, the Word has spoken respecting Himself by Hosea: "I am your Instructor."[4] Now piety is instruction, being the learning of the service of God, and training in the knowledge of the truth, and right guidance which leads to heaven. And the word "instruction"[5] is employed variously. For there is the instruction of him who is led and learns, and that of him who leads and teaches; and there is, thirdly, the guidance itself; and fourthly, what is taught, as the commandments enjoined.

---

[1] John x. 11.   [2] John x. 16.   [3] παιδαγωγός.
[4] παιδευτής; Hos. v. 2.   [5] παιδαγωγία.

Now the instruction which is of God is the right direction of truth to the contemplation of God, and the exhibition of holy deeds in everlasting perseverance.

As therefore the general directs the phalanx, consulting the safety of his soldiers, and the pilot steers the vessel, desiring to save the passengers; so also the Instructor guides the children to a saving course of conduct, through solicitude for us; and, in general, whatever we ask in accordance with reason from God to be done for us, will happen to those who believe in the Instructor. And just as the helmsman does not always yield to the winds, but sometimes, turning the prow towards them, opposes the whole force of the hurricanes; so the Instructor never yields to the blasts that blow in this world, nor commits the child to them like a vessel to make shipwreck on a wild and licentious course of life; but, wafted on by the favouring breeze of the Spirit of truth, stoutly holds on to the child's helm,—his ears, I mean,—until He bring him safe to anchor in the haven of heaven.

What is called by men an ancestral custom passes away in a moment, but the divine guidance is a possession which abides for ever.

They say that Phœnix was the instructor of Achilles, and Adrastus of the children of Crœsus; and Leonides of Alexander, and Nausithous of Philip. But Phœnix was women-mad, Adrastus was a fugitive. Leonides did not curtail the pride of Alexander, nor Nausithous reform the drunken Pellæan. No more was the Thracian Zopyrus able to check the fornication of Alcibiades; but Zopyrus was a bought slave, and Ticinnus, the tutor of the children of Themistocles, was a lazy domestic. They say also that he invented the Sicinnian dance. Those have not escaped our attention who are called royal instructors among the Persians; whom, in number four, the kings of the Persians select with the greatest care from all the Persians, and set over their sons. But the children only learn the use of the bow, and on reaching maturity have sexual intercourse with sisters, and mothers, and women, wives and courtesans innumerable, practised in intercourse like the wild boars.

But our Instructor is the holy God Jesus, the Word, who is the guide of all humanity. The loving God Himself is our Instructor. Somewhere in song the Holy Spirit says with regard to Him, "He provided sufficiently for the people in the wilderness. He led him about in the thirst of summer heat in a dry land, and instructed him, and kept him as the apple of His eye, as an eagle protects her nest, and shows her fond solicitude for her young, spreads abroad her wings, takes them, and bears them on her back. The Lord alone led them, and there was no strange god with them."[1] Clearly, I trow, has the Scripture exhibited the Instructor in the account it gives of His guidance.

Again, when He speaks in His own person, He confesses Himself to be the Instructor: "I am the Lord thy God, who brought thee out of the land of Egypt."[2] Who, then, has the power of leading in and out? Is it not the Instructor? This was He who appeared to Abraham, and said to him, "I am thy God, be accepted before me;"[3] and in a way most befitting an instructor, forms him into a faithful child, saying, "And be blameless; and I will make my covenant between me and thee, and thy seed." There is the communication of the Instructor's friendship. And He most manifestly appears as Jacob's instructor. He says accordingly to him, "Lo, I am with thee, to keep thee in all the way in which thou shalt go; and I will bring thee back into this land: for I will not leave thee till I do what I have told thee."[4] He is said, too, to have wrestled with Him. "And Jacob was left alone, and there wrestled with him a man (the Instructor) till the morning."[5] This was the man who led, and brought, and wrestled with, and anointed the athlete Jacob against evil.[6] Now that the Word was at once Jacob's trainer and the Instructor of humanity [appears from this]—"He asked," it is said, "His name, and said to him, Tell me what is thy name." And he said, "Why is it that thou askest my name?" For He reserved the new name for the new people—the babe; and was as yet unnamed, the Lord God not having yet become

---

[1] Deut. xxxii. 10-12.   [2] Ex. xx. 1.   [3] Gen. xvii. 1, 2.
[4] Gen. xxviii. 15.   [5] Gen. xxxii. 24.   [6] Or, "against the evil one."

man. Yet Jacob called the name of the place, "Face of God." "For I have seen," he says, "God face to face; and my life is preserved."[1] The face of God is the Word by whom God is manifested and made known. Then also was he named Israel, because he saw God the Lord. It was God, the Word, the Instructor, who said to him again afterwards, "Fear not to go down into Egypt."[2] See how the Instructor follows the righteous man, and how He anoints the athlete, teaching him to trip up his antagonist.

It is He also who teaches Moses to act as instructor. For the Lord says, "If any one sin before me, him will I blot out of my book; but now, go and lead this people into the place which I told thee."[3] Here He is the teacher of the art of instruction. For it was really the Lord that was the instructor of the ancient people by Moses; but He is the instructor of the new people by Himself, face to face. "For behold," He says to Moses, "my angel shall go before thee," representing the evangelical and commanding power of the Word, but guarding the Lord's prerogative. "In the day on which I will visit them,"[4] He says, "I will bring their sins on them; that is, on the day on which I will sit as judge I will render the recompense of their sins." For the same who is Instructor is judge, and judges those who disobey Him; and the loving Word will not pass over their transgression in silence. He reproves, that they may repent. For "the Lord willeth the repentance of the sinner rather than his death."[5] And let us as babes, hearing of the sins of others, keep from similar transgressions, through dread of the threatening, that we may not have to undergo like sufferings. What, then, was the sin which they committed? "For in their wrath they slew men, and in their impetuosity they hamstrung bulls. Cursed be their anger."[6] Who, then, would train us more lovingly than He? Formerly the older people had an old covenant, and the law disciplined the people with fear, and the Word was an angel; but to the fresh and new people has also been given a new covenant, and the

[1] Gen. xxxii. 30.   [2] Gen. xlvi. 3.   [3] Ex. xxxii. 33, 34.
[4] Ex. xxxii. 33, 34.   [5] Ezek. xviii. 23, 32.   [6] Gen. xlix. 6.

Word has appeared, and fear is turned to love, and that mystic angel is born—Jesus. For this same Instructor said then, "Thou shalt fear the Lord God;"[1] but to us He has addressed the exhortation, "Thou shalt love the Lord thy God."[2] Wherefore also this is enjoined on us: "Cease from your own works, from your old sins;" "Learn to do well;" "Depart from evil, and do good;" "Thou hast loved righteousness, and hated iniquity." This is my new covenant written in the old letter. The newness of the word must not, then, be made ground of reproach. But the Lord hath also said in Jeremiah: "Say not that I am a youth: before I formed thee in the belly I knew thee, and before I brought thee out of the womb I sanctified thee."[3] Such allusions prophecy can make to us, destined in the eye of God to faith before the foundation of the world; but now babes, through the recent fulfilment of the will of God, according to which we are born now to calling and salvation. Wherefore also He adds, "I have set thee for a prophet to the nations,"[4] saying that he must prophesy, so that the appellation of "youth" should not become a reproach to those who are called babes.

Now the law is ancient grace given through Moses by the Word. Wherefore also the Scripture says, "The law was given through Moses,"[5] not by Moses, but by the Word, and through Moses His servant. Wherefore it was only temporary; but eternal grace and truth were by Jesus Christ. Mark the expressions of Scripture: of the law only is it said "was given;" but truth being the grace of the Father, is the eternal work of the Word; and it is not said to *be given*, but *to be* by Jesus, *without whom nothing was*.[6] Presently, therefore, Moses prophetically, giving place to the perfect Instructor the Word, predicts both the name and the office of Instructor, and committing to the people the commands of obedience, sets before them the Instructor. "A prophet," says he, "like me shall God raise up to you of your brethren," pointing out Jesus the Son of God, by an allusion to Jesus

[1] Deut. vi. 2.   [2] Matt. xxii. 37.   [3] Jer. i. 7.
[4] Jer. i. 5.   [5] John i. 17.   [6] John i. 3.

the son of Nun; for the name of Jesus predicted in the law was a shadow of Christ. He adds, therefore, consulting the advantage of the people, "Him shall ye hear;"[1] and, "The man who will not hear that Prophet,"[2] him He threatens. Such a name, then, he predicts as that of the Instructor, who is the author of salvation. Wherefore prophecy invests Him with a rod, a rod of discipline, of rule, of authority; that those whom the persuasive word heals not, the threatening may heal; and whom the threatening heals not, the rod may heal; and whom the rod heals not, the fire may devour. "There shall come forth," it is said, " a rod out of the root of Jesse."[3]

See the care, and wisdom, and power of the Instructor: "He shall not judge according to opinion, nor according to report; but He shall dispense judgment to the humble, and reprove the sinners of the earth." And by David: "The Lord instructing, hath instructed me, and not given me over to death."[4] For to be chastised of the Lord, and instructed, is deliverance from death. And by the same prophet He says: "Thou shalt rule them with a rod of iron."[5] Thus also the apostle, in the Epistle to the Corinthians, being moved, says, "What will ye? Shall I come unto you with a rod, or in love, in the spirit of meekness?"[6] Also, "The Lord shall send the rod of strength out of Sion,"[7] He says by another prophet. And this same rod of instruction, "Thy rod and staff have comforted me,"[8] said some one else. Such is the power of the Instructor—sacred, soothing, saving.

[1] Deut. xviii. 15. [2] Deut. xviii. 19. [3] Isa. xi. 1, 3, 4.
[4] Ps. cxviii. 18. [5] Ps. ii. 9. [6] 1 Cor. iv. 21.
[7] Ps. cx. 2. [8] Ps. xxiii. 4.

CHAPTER VIII.

AGAINST THOSE WHO THINK THAT WHAT IS JUST IS NOT GOOD.

AT this stage some rise up, saying that the Lord, by reason of the rod, and threatening, and fear, is not good; misapprehending, as appears, the scripture which says, "And he that feareth the Lord will turn to his heart;"[1] and most of all, oblivious of His love, in that for us He became man. For more suitably to Him, the prophet prays in these words: "Remember us, for we are dust;"[2] that is, Sympathize with us; for Thou knowest from personal experience of suffering the weakness of the flesh. In this respect, therefore, the Lord the Instructor is most good and unimpeachable, sympathizing as He does from the exceeding greatness of His love with the nature of each man. "For there is nothing which the Lord hates."[3] For assuredly He does not hate anything, and yet wish that which He hates to exist. Nor does He wish anything not to exist, and yet become the cause of existence to that which He wishes not to exist. Nor does He wish anything not to exist which yet exists. If, then, the Word hates anything, He does not wish it to exist. But nothing exists, the cause of whose existence is not supplied by God. Nothing, then, is hated by God, nor yet by the Word. For both are one—that is, God. For He has said, "In the beginning the Word was in God, and the Word was God."[4] If then He hates none of the things which He has made, it follows that He loves them. Much more than the rest, and

[1] Ecclus. xxi. 7.
[2] Ps. ciii. 14.
[3] Wisd. xi. 25.
[4] John i. 1.

with reason, will He love man, the noblest of all objects created by Him, and a God-loving being. Therefore God is loving; consequently the Word is loving.

But he who loves anything wishes to do it good. And that which does good must be every way better than that which does not good. But nothing is better than the Good. The Good, then, does good. And God is admitted to be good. God therefore does good. And the Good, in virtue of its being good, does nothing else than do good. Consequently God does all good. And He does no good to man without caring for him, and He does not care *for* him without taking care *of* him. For that which does good purposely, is better than what does not good purposely. But nothing is better than God. And to do good purposely, is nothing else than to take care of man. God therefore cares for man, and takes care of him. And He shows this practically, in instructing him by the Word, who is the true coadjutor of God's love to man. But the good is not said to be good, on account of its being possessed of virtue; as also righteousness is not said to be good on account of its possessing virtue —for it is itself virtue—but on account of its being in itself and by itself good.

In another way the useful is called good, not on account of its pleasing, but of its doing good. All which, therefore, is righteousness, being a good thing, both as virtue and as desirable for its own sake, and not as giving pleasure; for it does not judge in order to win favour, but dispenses to each according to his merits. And the beneficial follows the useful. Righteousness, therefore, has characteristics corresponding to all the aspects in which goodness is examined, both possessing equal properties equally. And things which are characterized by equal properties are equal and similar to each other. Righteousness is therefore a good thing.

"How then," say they, "if the Lord loves man, and is good, is He angry and punishes?" We must therefore treat of this point with all possible brevity; for this mode of treatment is advantageous to the right training of the children, occupying the place of a necessary help. For many of the passions are cured by punishment, and by the inculcation of the sterner precepts, as also by instruction in certain principles. For reproof is, as it were, the surgery of the passions of the soul; and the passions are, as it were, an abscess of the truth,[1] which must be cut open by an incision of the lancet of reproof.

Reproach is like the application of medicines, dissolving the callosities of the passions, and purging the impurities of the lewdness of the life; and in addition, reducing the excrescences of pride, restoring the patient to the healthy and true state of humanity.

Admonition is, as it were, the regimen of the diseased soul, prescribing what it must take, and forbidding what it must not. And all these tend to salvation and eternal health.

Furthermore, the general of an army, by inflicting fines and corporeal punishments with chains and the extremest disgrace on offenders, and sometimes even by punishing individuals with death, aims at good, doing so for the admonition of the officers under him.

Thus also He who is our great General, the Word, the Commander-in-chief of the universe, by admonishing those who throw off the restraints of His law, that He may effect their release from the slavery, error, and captivity of the adversary, brings them peacefully to the sacred concord of citizenship.

As, therefore, in addition to persuasive discourse, there is the hortatory and the consolatory form; so also, in addition to the laudatory, there is the inculpatory and reproachful. And this latter constitutes the art of censure. Now censure is a mark of good-will, not of ill-will. For both he who is a friend and he who is not, reproach; but the enemy does so in scorn, the friend in kindness. It is not, then, from hatred that the Lord chides men; for He Himself suffered for us, whom He might have destroyed for our faults. For the Instructor also, in virtue of His being good, with consummate art glides into censure by rebuke; rousing the sluggishness of the mind by His sharp words as by a scourge. Again

[1] For ἀληθείας, there are the readings ἀπαθείας and ἀτιμίας.

in turn He endeavours to exhort the same persons. For those who are not induced by praise are spurred on by censure; and those whom censure calls not forth to salvation, being as dead, are by denunciation roused to the truth. "For the stripes and correction of wisdom are in all time." "For teaching a fool is gluing a potsherd; and sharpening to sense a hopeless blockhead is bringing earth to sensation."[1] Wherefore He adds plainly, "rousing the sleeper from deep sleep," which of all things else is likest death.

Further, the Lord shows very clearly of Himself, when, describing figuratively His manifold and in many ways serviceable culture,—He says, "I am the true vine, and my Father is the husbandman." Then He adds, "Every branch in me that beareth not fruit He taketh away; and every branch that beareth fruit He pruneth, that it may bring forth more fruit."[2] For the vine that is not pruned grows to wood. So also man. The Word—the knife—clears away the wanton shoots; compelling the impulses of the soul to fructify, not to indulge in lust. Now, reproof addressed to sinners has their salvation for its aim, the word being harmoniously adjusted to each one's conduct; now with tightened, now with relaxed cords. Accordingly it was very plainly said by Moses, "Be of good courage: God has drawn near to try you, that His fear may be among you, that ye sin not."[3] And Plato, who had learned from this source, says beautifully: "For all who suffer punishment are in reality treated well, for they are benefited; since the spirit of those who are justly punished is improved." And if those who are corrected receive good at the hands of justice, and, according to Plato, what is just is acknowledged to be good, fear itself does good, and has been found to be for men's good. "For the soul that feareth the Lord shall live, for their hope is in Him who saveth them."[4] And this same Word who inflicts punishment is judge; regarding whom Esaias also says, "The Lord has assigned Him to our sins,"[5] plainly as a corrector and reformer of sins. Wherefore He alone is

[1] Ecclus. xxii. 6–8.   [2] John xv. 1, 2.   [3] Ex. xx. 20.
[4] Ecclus. xxxiv. 14, 15.   [5] Isa. liii. 6.

able to forgive our iniquities, who has been appointed by the Father, Instructor of us all; He alone it is who is able to distinguish between disobedience and obedience. And while He threatens, He manifestly is unwilling to inflict evil to execute His threatenings; but by inspiring men with fear, He cuts off the approach to sin, and shows His love to man, still delaying, and declaring what they shall suffer if they continue sinners, and is not as a serpent, which the moment it fastens on its prey devours it.

God, then, is good. And the Lord speaks many a time and oft before He proceeds to act. "For my arrows," He says, "will make an end of them; they shall be consumed with hunger, and be eaten by birds; and there shall be incurable tetanic incurvature. I will send the teeth of wild beasts upon them, with the rage of serpents creeping on the earth. Without, the sword shall make them childless; and out of their chambers shall be fear."[1] For the Divine Being is not angry in the way that some think; but often restrains, and always exhorts humanity, and shows what ought to be done. And this is a good device, to terrify lest we sin. "For the fear of the Lord drives away sins, and he that is without fear cannot be justified,"[2] says the Scripture. And God does not inflict punishment from wrath, but for the ends of justice; since it is not expedient that justice should be neglected on our account. Each one of us, who sins, with his own free-will chooses punishment, and the blame lies with him who chooses.[3] God is without blame. "But if our unrighteousness commend the righteousness of God, what shall we say? Is God unrighteous, who taketh vengeance? God forbid."[4] He says, therefore, threatening, "I will sharpen my sword, and my hand shall lay hold on judgment; and I will render justice to mine enemies, and requite those who hate me. I will make mine arrows drunk with blood, and my sword shall devour flesh from the blood of the wounded."[5] It is clear, then, that those who are not at enmity with the truth, and do not hate the Word, will not hate their own salvation, but will

[1] Deut. xxxii. 23–25. [2] Ecclus. i. 27, 28. [3] Plato, *Rep.* x. 617 E.
[4] Rom. iii. 5, 6. [5] Deut. xxxii. 41, 42.

escape the punishment of enmity. "The crown of wisdom," then, as the book of Wisdom says, " is the fear of the Lord."[1] Very clearly, therefore, by the prophet Amos has the Lord unfolded His method of dealing, saying, " I have overthrown you, as God overthrew Sodom and Gomorrah; and ye shall be as a brand plucked from the fire: and yet ye have not returned unto me, saith the Lord."[2]

See how God, through His love of goodness, seeks repentance; and by means of the plan He pursues of threatening silently, shows His own love for man. "I will avert," He says, "my face from them, and show what shall happen to them."[3] For where the face of the Lord looks, there is peace and rejoicing; but where it is averted, there is the introduction of evil. The Lord, accordingly, does not wish to look on evil things; for He is good. But on His looking away, evil arises spontaneously through human unbelief. "Behold, therefore," says Paul, "the goodness and severity of God: on them that fell, severity; but upon thee, goodness, if thou continue in His goodness,"[4] that is, in faith in Christ.

Now hatred of evil attends the good man, in virtue of His being in nature good. Wherefore I will grant that He punishes the disobedient (for punishment is for the good and advantage of him who is punished, for it is the correction of a refractory subject); but I will not grant that He wishes to take vengeance. Revenge is retribution for evil, imposed for the advantage of him who takes the revenge. He will not desire us to take revenge, who teaches us "to pray for those that despitefully use us."[5] But that God is good, all willingly admit; and that the same God is just, I require not many more words to prove, after adducing the evangelical utterance of the Lord; He speaks of Him as one, "That they all may be one; as Thou, Father, art in me, and I in Thee, that they also may be one in us: that the world also may believe that Thou hast sent me. And the glory which thou hast given me I have given them; that they may be one, as we are

[1] Ecclus. i. 22. [2] Amos iv. 11. [3] Deut. xxxii. 20.
[4] Rom. xi. 22. [5] Matt. v. 44.

one: I in them, and Thou in me, that they may be made perfect in one."[1] God is one, and beyond the one, and above the Monad itself. Wherefore also the particle "Thou," having a demonstrative emphasis, points out God, who alone truly is, "who was, and is, and is to come," in which three divisions of time the one name (ὁ ὤν), "who is,"[2] has its place. And that He who alone is God is also alone and truly righteous, our Lord in the Gospel itself shall testify, saying, "Father, I will that they also whom Thou hast given me be with me where I am; that they may behold my glory, which Thou hast given me: for Thou lovedst me before the foundation of the world. O righteous Father, the world hath not known Thee: but I have known Thee, and these have known that Thou hast sent me. And I have declared to them Thy name, and will declare it."[3] This is He "that visits the iniquities of the fathers upon the children, to them that hate Him, and shows mercy to those that love Him."[4] For He who placed some "on the right hand, and others on the left,"[5] conceived as Father, being good, is called that which alone He is—"good;"[6] but as He is the Son in the Father, being his Word, from their mutual relation, the name of power being measured by equality of love, He is called righteous. "He will judge," He says, "a man according to his works,"[7]—a good balance, even God having made known to us the face of righteousness in the person of Jesus, by whom also, as by even scales, we know God. Of this also the book of Wisdom plainly says, "For mercy and wrath are with Him, for He alone is Lord of both," Lord of propitiations, and pouring forth wrath according to the abundance of His mercy. "So also is His reproof."[8] For the aim of mercy and of reproof is the salvation of those who are reproved.

Now, that the God and Father of our Lord Jesus is good, the Word Himself will again avouch: "For He is kind to the unthankful and the evil;" and further, when He says, "Be merciful, as your Father is merciful."[9] Still further also He plainly says, "None is good, but my Father, who is

[1] John xvii. 21-23.   [2] Ex. iii. 14.   [3] John xvii. 24-26.
[4] Ex. xx. 5, 6.   [5] Matt. xx. 21, xxv. 33.   [6] Matt. xix. 17.
[7] Ecclus. xvi. 13.   [8] Ecclus. xvi. 12, 3.   [9] Luke vi. 35, 36.

in heaven."[1] In addition to these, again He says, "My Father makes His sun to shine on all."[2] Here it is to be noted that He proclaims His Father to be good, and to be the Creator. And that the Creator is just, is not disputed. And again he says, "My Father sends rain on the just, and on the unjust." In respect of His sending rain, He is the Creator of the waters, and of the clouds. And in respect of His doing so on all, He holds an even balance justly and rightly. And as being good, He does so on just and unjust alike.

Very clearly, then, we conclude Him to be one and the same God, thus. For the Holy Spirit has sung, "I will look to the heavens, the works of Thy hands;"[3] and, "He who created the heavens dwells in the heavens;" and, "Heaven is Thy throne."[4] And the Lord says in His prayer, "Our Father, who art in heaven."[5] And the heavens belong to Him, who created the world. It is indisputable, then, that the Lord is the Son of the Creator. And if the Creator above all is confessed to be just, and the Lord to be the Son of the Creator; then the Lord is the Son of Him who is just. Wherefore also Paul says, "But now the righteousness of God without the law is manifested;"[6] and again, that you may better conceive of God, "even the righteousness of God by the faith of Jesus Christ upon all that believe; for there is no difference."[7] And, witnessing further to the truth, he adds after a little, "through the forbearance of God, in order to show that He is just, and that Jesus is the justifier of him who is of faith." And that he knows that what is just is good, appears by his saying, "So that the law is holy, and the commandment holy, and just, and good,"[8] using both names to denote the same power. But "no one is good," except His Father. It is this same Father of His, then, who being one is manifested by many powers. And this was the import of the utterance, "No man knew the Father,"[9] who was Himself everything before the coming of the Son. So

[1] Matt. xix. 17. [2] Matt. v. 45. [3] Ps. viii. 4.
[4] Ps. ii. 4, xi. 5, ciii. 19. [5] Matt. vi. 9. [6] Rom. iii. 21, 22.
[7] Rom. iii. 26. [8] Rom. vii. 12. [9] Luke x. 22; John xvii. 25.

that it is veritably clear that the God of all is only one good, just Creator, and the Son in the Father, to whom be glory for ever and ever, Amen. But it is not inconsistent with the saving Word, to administer rebuke dictated by solicitude. For this is the medicine of the divine love to man, by which the blush of modesty breaks forth, and shame at sin supervenes. For if one must censure, it is necessary also to rebuke; when it is the time to wound the apathetic soul not mortally, but salutarily, securing exemption from everlasting death by a little pain.

Great is the wisdom displayed in His instruction, and manifold the modes of His dealing in order to salvation. For the Instructor testifies to the good, and summons forth to better things those that are called; dissuades those that are hastening to do wrong from the attempt, and exhorts them to turn to a better life. For the one is not without testimony, when the other has been testified to; and the grace which proceeds from the testimony is very great. Besides, the feeling of anger (if it is proper to call His admonition anger) is full of love to man, God condescending to emotion on man's account; for whose sake also the Word of God became man.

CHAPTER IX.

THAT IT IS THE PREROGATIVE OF THE SAME POWER TO BE BENEFICENT AND TO PUNISH JUSTLY. ALSO THE MANNER OF THE INSTRUCTION OF THE LOGOS.

ITH all His power, therefore, the Instructor of humanity, the Divine Word, using all the resources of wisdom, devotes Himself to the saving of the children, admonishing, upbraiding, blaming, chiding, reproving, threatening, healing, promising, favouring; and as it were, by many reins, curbing the irrational impulses of humanity. To speak briefly, therefore, the Lord acts towards us as we do towards our children. "Hast thou children? correct them," is the exhortation of the book of Wisdom, "and bend them from their youth. Hast thou daughters? attend to their body, and let not thy face brighten towards them,"[1]—although we love our children exceedingly, both sons and daughters, above aught else whatever. For those who speak with a man merely to please him, have little love for him, seeing they do not pain him; while those that speak for his good, though they inflict pain for the time, do him good for ever after. It is not immediate pleasure, but future enjoyment, that the Lord has in view.

Let us now proceed to consider the mode of His loving discipline, with the aid of the prophetic testimony.

Admonition, then, is the censure of loving care, and produces understanding. Such is the Instructor in His admonitions, as when He says in the gospel, "How often would I have gathered thy children, as a bird gathers her young ones under her wings, and ye would not!"[2] And again, the

---
[1] Ecclus. vii. 25, 26.   [2] Matt. xxiii. 37.

Scripture admonishes, saying, "And they committed adultery with stock and stone, and burnt incense to Baal."[1] For it is a very great proof of His love, that, though knowing well the shamelessness of the people that had kicked and bounded away, He notwithstanding exhorts them to repentance, and says by Ezekiel, "Son of man, thou dwellest in the midst of scorpions; nevertheless, speak to them, if peradventure they will hear."[2] Further, to Moses He says, "Go and tell Pharaoh to send my people forth; but I know that he will not send them forth."[3] For He shows both things: both His divinity in His foreknowledge of what would take place, and His love in affording an opportunity for repentance to the self-determination of the soul. He admonishes also by Esaias, in His care for the people, when He says, "This people honour me with their lips, but their heart is far from me." What follows is reproving censure: "In vain do they worship me, teaching for doctrines the commandments of men."[4] Here His loving care, having shown their sin, shows salvation side by side.

Upbraiding is censure on account of what is base, conciliating to what is noble. This is shown by Jeremiah: "They were female-mad horses; each one neighed after his neighbour's wife. Shall I not visit for these things? saith the Lord: shall not my soul be avenged on such a nation as this?"[5] He everywhere interweaves fear, because "the fear of the Lord is the beginning of sense."[6] And again, by Hosea, He says, "Shall I not visit them? for they themselves were mingled with harlots, and sacrificed with the initiated; and the people that understood embraced a harlot."[7] He shows their offence to be clearer, by declaring that they understood, and thus sinned wilfully. Understanding is the eye of the soul; wherefore also Israel means, "he that sees God"—that is, he that understands God.

Complaint is censure of those who are regarded as despising or neglecting. He employs this form when He says by Esaias: "Hear, O heaven; and give ear, O earth: for the

[1] Jer. iii. 9, vii. 9, xi. 13, xxxii. 29.   [2] Ezek. ii. 6, 7.
[3] Ex. iii. 18, 19.   [4] Isa. xxix. 13.   [5] Jer. v. 8, 9.   [6] Prov. i. 7.
[7] Hos. iv. 11; "understood not" in the Septuagint.

Lord hath spoken, I have begotten and brought up children, but they have disregarded me. The ox knoweth his owner, and the ass his master's crib: but Israel hath not known me."[1] For how shall we not regard it fearful, if he that knows God, shall not recognise the Lord; but while the ox and the ass, stupid and foolish animals, will know him who feeds them, Israel is found to be more irrational than these? And having, by Jeremiah, complained against the people on many grounds, He adds: "And they have forsaken me, saith the Lord."[2]

Invective[3] is a reproachful upbraiding, or chiding censure. This mode of treatment the Instructor employs in Isaiah, when He says, "Woe to you, children revolters. Thus saith the Lord, Ye have taken counsel, but not by me; and made compacts, but not by my Spirit."[4] He uses the very bitter mordant of fear in each case repressing[5] the people, and at the same time turning them to salvation; as also wool that is undergoing the process of dyeing is wont to be previously treated with mordants, in order to prepare it for taking on a fast colour.

Reproof is the bringing forward of sin, laying it before one. This form of instruction He employs as in the highest degree necessary, by reason of the feebleness of the faith of many. For He says by Esaias, "Ye have forsaken the Lord, and have provoked the Holy One of Israel to anger."[6] And He says also by Jeremiah: "Heaven was astonished at this, and the earth shuddered exceedingly. For my people have committed two evils; they have forsaken me, the fountain of living waters, and have hewn out to themselves broken cisterns, which will not be able to hold water."[7] And again, by the same: "Jerusalem hath sinned a sin; therefore it became commotion. All that glorified her dishonoured her, when they saw her baseness."[8] And He uses the bitter and biting[9] language of reproof in His consolations

---

[1] Isa. i. 2, 3.   [2] Jer. i. 16, ii. 13, 19.   [3] Or, rebuke.   [4] Isa. xxx. 1.
[5] Lowth conjectures ἐπιστομῶν or ἐπιστομίζων, instead of ἀναστομῶν.
[6] Isa. i. 4.   [7] Jer. ii. 12, 13.   [8] Lam. i. 8.
[9] H. reads δηκτικόν, for which the text has ἐπιδεικτικόν.

by Solomon, tacitly alluding to the love for children that characterizes His instruction: "My son, despise not thou the chastening of the Lord; nor faint when thou art rebuked of Him: for whom the Lord loveth He chasteneth, and scourgeth every son whom He receiveth;"[1] "For a man who is a sinner escapes reproof."[2] Consequently, therefore, the Scripture says, "Let the righteous reprove and correct me; but let not the oil of the sinner anoint my head."[3]

Bringing one to his senses ($\phi\rho\acute{\epsilon}\nu\omega\sigma\iota\varsigma$) is censure, which makes a man think. Neither from this form of instruction does he abstain, but says by Jeremiah, "How long shall I cry, and you not hear? So your ears are uncircumcised."[4] O blessed forbearance! And again, by the same: "All the heathen are uncircumcised, but this people is uncircumcised in heart:"[5] "for the people are disobedient; children," says He, "in whom is not faith."[6]

Visitation is severe rebuke. He uses this species in the Gospel: "O Jerusalem, Jerusalem, that killest the prophets, and stonest them that are sent unto thee!" The reduplication of the name gives strength to the rebuke. For he that knows God, how does he persecute God's servants? Wherefore He says, "Your house is left desolate; for I say unto you, Henceforth ye shall not see me, till ye shall say, Blessed is He that cometh in the name of the Lord."[7] For if you do not receive His love, ye shall know His power.

Denunciation is vehement speech. And He employs denunciation as medicine, by Isaiah, saying, "Ah, sinful nation, lawless sons, people full of sins, wicked seed!"[8] And in the Gospel by John He says, "Serpents, brood of vipers."[9]

Accusation is censure of wrong-doers. This mode of instruction He employs by David, when He says: "The people whom I knew not served me, and at the hearing of the ear obeyed me. Sons of strangers lied to me, and halted from

---

[1] Prov. iii. 12. [2] Ecclus. xxxii. 21. [3] Ps. cxli. 5.
[4] Jer. vi. 10. [5] Jer. ix. 26. [6] Isa. xxx. 9.
[7] Matt. xxiii. 37-39. [8] Isa. i. 4.

[9] Nothing similar to this is found in the fourth Gospel; the reference may be to the words of the Baptist, Matt. iii. 7, Luke iii. 7.

their ways."[1] And by Jeremiah: "And I gave her a writing of divorcement, and covenant-breaking Judah feared not."[2] And again: "And the house of Israel disregarded me; and the house of Judah lied to the Lord."[3]

Bewailing one's fate is latent censure, and by artful aid ministers salvation as under a veil. He made use of this by Jeremiah: "How did the city sit solitary that was full of people! She that ruled over territories became as a widow; she came under tribute; weeping, she wept in the night."[4]

Objurgation is objurgatory censure. Of this help the Divine Instructor made use by Jeremiah, saying, "Thou hadst a whore's forehead; thou wast shameless towards all; and didst not call me to the house, who am thy father, and lord of thy virginity."[5] "And a fair and graceful harlot skilled in enchanted potions."[6] With consummate art, after applying to the virgin the opprobrious name of whoredom, He thereupon calls her back to an honourable life by filling her with shame.

Indignation is a rightful upbraiding; or upbraiding on account of ways exalted above what is right. In this way He instructed by Moses, when He said, "Faulty children, a generation crooked and perverse, do ye thus requite the Lord? This people is foolish, and not wise. Is not this thy father who acquired thee?"[7] He says also by Isaiah, "Thy princes are disobedient, companions of thieves, loving gifts, following after rewards, not judging the orphans."[8]

In fine, the system He pursues to inspire fear is the source of salvation. And it is the prerogative of goodness to save: "The mercy of the Lord is on all flesh, while He reproves, corrects, and teaches as a shepherd His flock. He pities those who receive His instruction, and those who eagerly seek union with Him."[9] And with such guidance He guarded the six hundred thousand footmen that were brought together in the hardness of heart in which they were found; scourging, pitying, striking, healing, in compassion and discipline: "For

---

[1] Ps. xviii. 43–45.   [2] Jer. iii. 8.   [3] Jer. v. 11, 12.
[4] Lam. i. 1, 2.   [5] Jer. iii. 3, 4.   [6] Nahum iii. 4.
[7] Deut. xxxii. 5, 6.   [8] Isa. i. 23.   [9] Ecclus. xviii. 13, 14.

according to the greatness of His mercy, so is His rebuke." [1] For it is indeed noble not to sin ; but it is good also for the sinner to repent; just as it is best to be always in good health, but well to recover from disease. So He commands by Solomon : "Strike thou thy son with the rod, that thou mayest deliver his soul from death." [2] And again : "Abstain not from chastising thy son, but correct him with the rod ; for he will not die." [3]

For reproof and rebuke, as also the original term implies, are the stripes of the soul, chastising sins, preventing death, and leading to self-control those carried away to licentiousness. Thus also Plato, knowing reproof to be the greatest power for reformation, and the most sovereign purification, in accordance with what has been said, observes, "that he who is in the highest degree impure is uninstructed and base, by reason of his being unreproved in those respects in which he who is destined to be truly happy ought to be purest and best."

For if rulers are not a terror to a good work, how shall God, who is by nature good, be a terror to him who sins not ? "If thou doest evil, be afraid," [4] says the apostle. Wherefore the apostle himself also in every case uses stringent language to the churches, after the Lord's example ; and conscious of his own boldness, and of the weakness of his hearers, he says to the Galatians: "Am I your enemy, because I tell you the truth ?" [5] Thus also people in health do not require a physician, do not require him as long as they are strong ; but those who are ill need his skill. Thus also we who in our lives are ill of shameful lusts and reprehensible excesses, and other inflammatory effects of the passions, need the Saviour. And He administers not only mild, but also stringent medicines. The bitter roots of fear then arrest the eating sores of our sins. Wherefore also fear is salutary, if bitter. Sick, we truly stand in need of the Saviour ; having wandered, of one to guide us ; blind, of one to lead us to the light ; thirsty, "of the fountain of life, of which whosoever partakes, shall no

[1] Ecclus. xvi. 12. [2] Prov. xxiii. 14. [3] Prov. xxiii. 13.
[4] Rom. xiii. 3, 4. [5] Gal. iv. 16.

longer thirst;"[1] dead, we need life; sheep, we need a shepherd; we who are children need a tutor, while universal humanity stands in need of Jesus; so that we may not continue intractable and sinners to the end, and thus fall into condemnation, but may be separated from the chaff, and stored up in the paternal garner. "For the fan is in the Lord's hand, by which the chaff due to the fire is separated from the wheat."[2] You may learn, if you will, the crowning wisdom of the all-holy Shepherd and Instructor, of the omnipotent and paternal Word, when He figuratively represents Himself as the Shepherd of the sheep. And He is the Tutor of the children. He says therefore by Ezekiel, directing His discourse to the elders, and setting before them a salutary description of His wise solicitude: "And that which is lame I will bind up, and that which is sick I will heal, and that which has wandered I will turn back; and I will feed them on my holy mountain."[3] Such are the promises of the good Shepherd.

Feed us, the children, as sheep. Yea, Master, fill us with righteousness, Thine own pasture; yea, O Instructor, feed us on Thy holy mountain the church, which towers aloft, which is above the clouds, which touches heaven. "And I will be," He says, "their Shepherd,"[4] and will be near them, as the garment to their skin. He wishes to save my flesh by enveloping it in the robe of immortality, and He hath anointed my body. "They shall call me," He says, "and I will say, Here am I."[5] Thou didst hear sooner than I expected, Master. "And if they pass over, they shall not slip,"[6] saith the Lord. For we who are passing over to immortality shall not fall into corruption, for He shall sustain us. For so He has said, and so He has willed. Such is our Instructor, righteously good. "I came not," He says, "to be ministered unto, but to minister."[7] Wherefore He is introduced in the Gospel "wearied,"[8] because toiling for us,

[1] John iv. 13, 14.
[2] Matt. iii. 12; Luke iii. 17.
[3] Ezek. xxxiv. 14, 15, 16.
[4] Ezek. xxxiv. 14-16.
[5] Isa. lviii. 9.
[6] Isa. xliii. 2.
[7] Matt. xx. 28; Mark x. 45.
[8] John iv. 6.

and promising "to give His life a ransom for many."[1] For him alone who does so He owns to be the good shepherd. Generous, therefore, is He who gives for us the greatest of all gifts, His own life; and beneficent exceedingly, and loving to men, in that, when He might have been Lord, He wished to be a brother man; and so good was He that He died for us.

Further, His righteousness cried, "If ye come straight to me, I also will come straight to you; but if ye walk crooked, I also will walk crooked, saith the Lord of hosts;"[2] meaning by the crooked ways the chastisements of sinners. For the straight and natural way which is indicated by the *Iota* of the name of Jesus is His goodness, which is firm and sure towards those who have believed at hearing: "When I called, ye obeyed not, saith the Lord; but set at nought my counsels, and heeded not my reproofs."[3] Thus the Lord's reproof is most beneficial. David also says of them, "A perverse and provoking race; a race which set not their heart aright, and whose spirit was not faithful with God: they kept not the covenant of God, and would not walk in His law."[4]

Such are the causes of provocation for which the Judge comes to inflict punishment on those that would not choose a life of goodness. Wherefore also afterwards He assailed them more roughly; in order, if possible, to drag them back from their impetuous rush towards death. He therefore tells by David the most manifest cause of the threatening: "They believed not in His wonderful works. When He slew them, they sought after Him, and turned and inquired early after God; and remembered that God was their Helper, and God the Most High their Redeemer."[5] Thus He knew that they turned for fear, while they despised His love: for, for the most part, that goodness which is always mild is despised; but He who admonishes by the loving fear of righteousness is reverenced.

There is a twofold species of fear, the one of which is

---

[1] Matt. xx. 28.
[2] Here Clement gives the sense of various passages, *e.g.* Jer. vi., Lev. xxvi.
[3] Prov. i. 24, 25. [4] Ps. lxxviii. 8, 10. [5] Ps. lxxviii. 32-35.

accompanied with reverence, such as citizens show towards good rulers, and we towards God, as also right-minded children towards their fathers. "For an unbroken horse turns out unmanageable, and a son who is let take his own way turns out reckless."[1] The other species of fear is accompanied with hatred, which slaves feel towards hard masters, and the Hebrews felt, who made God a master, not a father. And as far as piety is concerned, that which is voluntary and spontaneous differs much, nay entirely, from what is forced. "For He," it is said, "is merciful; He will heal their sins, and not destroy them, and fully turn away His anger, and not kindle all His wrath."[2] See how the justice of the Instructor, which deals in rebukes, is shown; and the goodness of God, which deals in compassions. Wherefore David—that is, the Spirit by him—embracing them both, sings of God Himself, "Justice and judgment are the preparation of His throne: mercy and truth shall go before Thy face."[3] He declares that it belongs to the same power both to judge and to do good. For there is power over both together, and judgment separates that which is just from its opposite. And He who is truly God is just and good; who is Himself all, and all is He; for He is God, the only God.

For as the mirror is not evil to an ugly man because it shows him what like he is; and as the physician is not evil to the sick man because he tells him of his fever,—for the physician is not the cause of the fever, but only points out the fever;—so neither is He, that reproves, ill-disposed towards him who is diseased in soul. For He does not put the transgressions on him, but only shows the sins which are there; in order to turn him away from similar practices. So God is good on His own account, and just also on ours, and He is just because He is good. And His justice is shown to us by His own Word from there from above, whence the Father was. For before He became Creator He was God; He was good. And therefore He wished to be Creator and Father. And the nature of that love was the source of righteousness —the cause, too, of His lighting up His sun, and sending

[1] Ecclus. xxx. 8. [2] Ps. lxxviii. 38. [3] Ps. lxxxix. 14.

down His own Son. And He first announced the good righteousness that is from heaven, when He said, "No man knoweth the Son, but the Father; nor the Father, but the Son."[1] This mutual and reciprocal knowledge is the symbol of primeval justice. Then justice came down to men both in the letter and in the body, in the Word and in the law, constraining humanity to saving repentance; for it was good. But do you not obey God? Then blame yourself, who drag to yourself the judge.

[1] Luke x. 22.

CHAPTER X.

THAT THE SAME GOD, BY THE SAME WORD, RESTRAINS FROM SIN BY THREATENING, AND SAVES HUMANITY BY EXHORTING.

IF, then, we have shown that the plan of dealing stringently with humanity is good and salutary, and necessarily adopted by the Word, and conducive to repentance and the prevention of sins; we shall have now to look in order at the mildness of the Word. For He has been demonstrated to be just. He sets before us His own inclinations which invite to salvation; by which, in accordance with the Father's will, He wishes to make known to us the good and the useful. Consider these. The good (τὸ καλόν) belongs to the panegyrical form of speech, the useful to the persuasive. For the hortatory and the dehortatory are a form of the persuasive, and the laudatory and inculpatory of the panegyrical.

For the persuasive style of sentence in one form becomes hortatory, and in another dehortatory. So also the panegyrical in one form becomes inculpatory, and in another laudatory. And in these exercises the Instructor, the Just One, who has proposed our advantage as His aim, is chiefly occupied. But the inculpatory and dehortatory forms of speech have been already shown us; and we must now handle the persuasive and the laudatory, and, as on a beam, balance the equal scales of justice. The exhortation to what is useful, the Instructor employs by Solomon, to the following effect: "I exhort you, O men; and I utter my voice to the sons of men. Hear me; for I will speak of excellent things;"[1]

[1] Prov. viii. 4, 6.

and so on. And He counsels what is salutary: for counsel has for its end, choosing or refusing a certain course; as He does by David, when He says, "Blessed is the man who walketh not in the counsels of the ungodly, and standeth not in the way of sinners, and sitteth not in the chair of pestilences; but his will is in the law of the Lord."[1] And there are three departments of counsel: That which takes examples from past times; as what the Hebrews suffered when they worshipped the golden calf, and what they suffered when they committed fornication, and the like. The second, whose meaning is understood from the present times, as being apprehended by perception; as it was said to those who asked the Lord, "If He was the Christ, or shall we wait for another? Go and tell John, the blind receive their sight, the deaf hear, the lepers are cleansed, the dead are raised up; and blessed is he who shall not be offended in me."[2] Such was that which David said when he prophesied, "As we have heard, so have we seen."[3] And the third department of counsel consists of what is future, by which we are bidden guard against what is to happen; as also that was said, "They that fall into sins shall be cast into outer darkness, where there shall be wailing and gnashing of teeth,"[4] and the like. So that from these things it is clear that the Lord, going the round of all the methods of curative treatment, calls humanity to salvation.

By encouragement He assuages sins, reducing lust, and at the same time inspiring hope for salvation. For He says by Ezekiel, "If ye return with your whole heart, and say, Father, I will hear you, as a holy people."[5] And again He says, "Come all to me, who labour, and are heavy laden, and I will give you rest;"[6] and that which is added the Lord speaks in His own person. And very clearly He calls to goodness by Solomon, when He says, "Blessed is the man who hath found wisdom, and the mortal who hath found understanding."[7] "For the good is found by him who seeks it, and is

[1] Ps. i. 1, 2. [2] Matt. xi. 5, 6; Luke vii. 19, 22, 23.
[3] Ps. xlviii. 8. [4] Matt. xxii. 13, xxv. 30.
[5] Ezek. xviii. xxxiii. [6] Matt. xi. 28.   [7] Prov. iii. 13.

wont to be seen by him who has found it."[1] By Jeremiah, too, He sets forth prudence, when He says, "Blessed are we, Israel; for what is pleasing to God is known by us;"[2]— and it is known by the Word, by whom we are blessed and wise. For wisdom and knowledge are mentioned by the same prophet, when he says, "Hear, O Israel, the commandments of life, and give ear to know understanding."[3] By Moses, too, by reason of the love He has to man, He promises a gift to those who hasten to salvation. For He says, "And I will bring you into the good land, which the Lord sware to your fathers."[4] And further, "And I will bring you into the holy mountain, and make you glad,"[5] He says by Isaiah. And still another form of instruction is benediction. "And blessed is he," He saith by David, "who has not sinned; and he shall be as the tree planted near the channels of the waters, which will yield its fruit in its season, and his leaf shall not wither"[6] (by this He made an allusion to the resurrection); "and whatsoever he shall do shall prosper with him." Such He wishes us to be, that we may be blessed. Again, showing the opposite scale of the balance of justice, He says, "But not so the ungodly—not so; but as the dust which the wind sweeps away from the face of the earth."[7] By showing the punishment of sinners, and their easy dispersion, and carrying off by the wind, the Instructor dissuades from crime by means of punishment; and by holding up the merited penalty, shows the benignity of His beneficence in the most skilful way, in order that we may possess and enjoy its blessings. He invites us to knowledge also, when He says by Jeremiah, "Hadst thou walked in the way of God, thou wouldst have dwelt for ever in peace;"[8] for, exhibiting there the reward of knowledge, He calls the wise to the love of it. And, granting pardon to him who has erred, He says, "Turn, turn, as a grape-gatherer to his basket."[9] Do you see the goodness of justice, in that it counsels to repentance?

---

[1] In Prov. ii. 4. 5, iii. 15, Jer. ii. 24, we have the sense of these verses.
[2] Baruch iv. 4.   [3] Baruch iii. 9.   [4] Deut. xxxi. 20.
[5] Isa. lvi. 7.   [6] Ps. i. 1–3.   [7] Ps. i. 4.
[8] Baruch iii. 13.   [9] Jer. vi. 9.

And still further, by Jeremiah, He enlightens in the truth those who have erred. "Thus saith the Lord, Stand in the ways, and look, and ask for the eternal paths of the Lord, what is the good path, and walk in it, and ye shall find purification for your souls."[1] And in order to promote our salvation, He leads us to repentance. Wherefore He says, "If thou repent, the Lord will purify thy heart, and the heart of thy seed."[2] We might have adduced, as supporters on this question, the philosophers who say that only the perfect man is worthy of praise, and the bad man of blame. But since some slander beatitude, as neither itself taking any trouble, nor giving any to any one else, thus not understanding its love to man; on their account, and on account of those who do not associate justice with goodness, the following remarks are added. For it were a legitimate inference to say, that rebuke and censure are suitable to men, since they say that all men are bad; but God alone is wise, from whom cometh wisdom, and alone perfect, and therefore alone worthy of praise. But I do not employ such language. I say, then, that praise or blame, or whatever resembles praise or blame, are medicines most essential of all to men. Some are ill to cure, and, like iron, are wrought into shape with fire, and hammer, and anvil, that is, with threatening, and reproof, and chastisement; while others, cleaving to faith itself, as self-taught, and as acting of their own free-will, grow by praise:

"For virtue that is praised
Grows like a tree."

And comprehending this, as it seems to me, the Samian Pythagoras gives the injunction:

"When you have done base things, rebuke *yourself*;
But when you have done good things, be glad."

Chiding is also called admonishing; and the etymology of admonishing (νουθέτησις) is (νοῦ ἐνθεματισμός) putting of understanding into one; so that rebuking is bringing one to one's senses.

But there are myriads of injunctions to be found, whose aim is the attainment of what is good, and the avoidance of

[1] Jer. vi. 16.   [2] Deut. xxx. 6.

what is evil. "For there is no peace to the wicked, saith the Lord."¹ Wherefore by Solomon He commands the children to beware: "My son, let not sinners deceive thee, and go not after their ways; and go not, if they entice thee, saying, Come with us, share with us in innocent blood, and let us hide unjustly the righteous man in the earth; let us put him out of sight all alive as he is into Hades."² This is accordingly likewise a prediction concerning the Lord's passion. And by Ezekiel, the life supplies commandments: "The soul that sinneth shall die; but he that doeth righteousness shall be righteous. He eateth not upon the mountains, and hath not set his eyes on the devices of the house of Israel, and will not defile his neighbour's wife, and will not approach to a woman in her separation, and will not oppress a man, and will restore the debtor's pledge, and will not take plunder: he will give his bread to the hungry, and clothe the naked. His money he will not give on usury, and will not take interest; and he will turn away his hand from wrong, and will execute righteous judgment between a man and his neighbour. He has walked in my statutes, and kept my judgments to do them. This is a righteous man. He shall surely live, saith the Lord."³ These words contain a description of the conduct of Christians, a notable exhortation to the blessed life, which is the reward of a life of goodness—everlasting life.

¹ Isa. lvii. 21, xlviii. 22. ² Prov. i. 10-12. ³ Ezek. xviii. 4-9.

CHAPTER XI.

THAT THE WORD INSTRUCTED BY THE LAW AND THE PROPHETS.

THE mode of His love and His instruction we have shown as we could. Wherefore He Himself, declaring Himself very beautifully, likened Himself to a grain of mustard-seed;[1] and pointed out the spirituality of the word that is sown, and the productiveness of its nature, and the magnificence and conspicuousness of the power of the word; and besides, intimated that the pungency and the purifying virtue of punishment are profitable on account of its sharpness. By the little grain, as it is figuratively called, He bestows salvation on all humanity abundantly. Honey, being very sweet, generates bile, as goodness begets contempt, which is the cause of sinning. But mustard lessens bile, that is, anger, and stops inflammation, that is, pride. From which Word springs the true health of the soul, and its eternal happy temperament (εὐκρασία).

Accordingly, of old He instructed by Moses, and then by the prophets. Moses, too, was a prophet. For the law is the training of refractory children. "Having feasted to the full," accordingly, it is said, "they rose up to play;"[2] senseless repletion with victuals being called χόρτασμα (fodder), not βρῶμα (food). And when, having senselessly filled themselves, they senselessly played; on that account the law was given them, and terror ensued for the prevention of transgressions and for the promotion of right actions, securing attention, and so winning to obedience to the true Instructor, being one and the same Word, and reducing to conformity

[1] Matt. xiii. 31; Luke xiii. 19.   [2] Ex. xxxii. 6; 1 Cor. x. 7.

with the urgent demands of the law. For Paul says that it was given to be a "schoolmaster to bring us to Christ."[1] So that from this it is clear, that one alone, true, good, just, in the image and likeness of the Father, His Son Jesus, the Word of God, is our Instructor; to whom God hath entrusted us, as an affectionate father commits his children to a worthy tutor, expressly charging us, "This is my beloved Son: hear Him."[2] The divine Instructor is trustworthy, adorned as He is with three of the fairest ornaments—knowledge, benevolence, and authority of utterance;—with knowledge, for He is the paternal wisdom: "All wisdom is from the Lord, and with Him for evermore;"—with authority of utterance, for He is God and Creator: "For all things were made by Him, and without Him was not anything made;"[3]—and with benevolence, for He alone gave Himself a sacrifice for us: "For the good Shepherd giveth His life for the sheep;"[4] and He has so given it. Now, benevolence is nothing but wishing to do good to one's neighbour for his sake.

[1] Gal. iii. 24. [2] Matt. xvii. 5. [3] John i. 3. [4] John x. 11.

CHAPTER XII.

THE INSTRUCTOR CHARACTERIZED BY THE SEVERITY AND BENIGNITY OF PATERNAL AFFECTION.

HAVING now accomplished those things, it were a fitting sequel that our instructor Jesus should draw for us the model of the true life, and train humanity in Christ.

Nor is the cast and character of the life He enjoins very formidable; nor is it made altogether easy by reason of His benignity. He enjoins His commands, and at the same time gives them such a character that they may be accomplished.

The view I take is, that He Himself formed man of the dust, and regenerated him by water; and made him grow by his Spirit; and trained him by His word to adoption and salvation, directing him by sacred precepts; in order that, transforming earth-born man into a holy and heavenly being by His advent, He might fulfil to the utmost that divine utterance, "Let us make man in our own image and likeness."[1] And, in truth, Christ became the perfect realization of what God spake; and the rest of humanity is conceived as being created merely in His image.

But let us, O children of the good Father—nurslings of the good Instructor—fulfil the Father's will, listen to the Word, and take on the impress of the truly saving life of our Saviour; and meditating on the heavenly mode of life according to which we have been deified, let us anoint ourselves with the perennial immortal bloom of gladness—that ointment of sweet fragrance—having a clear example of immortality in the walk and conversation of the Lord; and

[1] Gen. i. 26.

following the footsteps of God, to whom alone it belongs to consider, and whose care it is to see to, the way and manner in which the life of men may be made more healthy. Besides, He makes preparation for a self-sufficing mode of life, for simplicity, and for girding up our loins, and for free and unimpeded readiness of our journey; in order to the attainment of an eternity of beatitude, teaching each one of us to be his own storehouse. For He says, "Take no anxious thought for to-morrow,"[1] meaning that the man who has devoted himself to Christ ought to be sufficient to himself, and servant to himself, and moreover lead a life which provides for each day by itself. For it is not in war, but in peace, that we are trained. War needs great preparation, and luxury craves profusion; but peace and love, simple and quiet sisters, require no arms nor excessive preparation. The Word is their sustenance.

Our superintendence in instruction and discipline is the office of the Word, from whom we learn frugality and humility, and all that pertains to love of truth, love of man, and love of excellence. And so, in a word, being assimilated to God by a participation in moral excellence, we must not retrograde into carelessness and sloth. But labour, and faint not. Thou shalt be what thou dost not hope, and canst not conjecture. And as there is one mode of training for philosophers, another for orators, and another for athletes; so is there a generous disposition, suitable to the choice that is set upon moral loveliness, resulting from the training of Christ. And in the case of those who have been trained according to this influence, their gait in walking, their sitting at table, their food, their sleep, their going to bed, their regimen, and the rest of their mode of life, acquire a superior dignity. For such a training as is pursued by the Word is not overstrained, but is of the right tension. Thus, therefore, the Word has been called also the Saviour, seeing He has found out for men those rational medicines which produce vigour of the senses and salvation; and devotes Himself to watching for the favourable moment, reproving evil, exposing the causes of evil affections,

[1] Matt. vi. 34.

and striking at the roots of irrational lusts, pointing out what we ought to abstain from, and supplying all the antidotes of salvation to those who are diseased. For the greatest and most regal work of God is the salvation of humanity. The sick are vexed at a physician, who gives no advice bearing on their restoration to health. But how shall we not acknowledge the highest gratitude to the divine Instructor, who is not silent, who omits not those threatenings that point towards destruction, but discloses them, and cuts off the impulses that tend to them; and who indoctrinates in those counsels which result in the true way of living? We must confess, therefore, the deepest obligations to Him. For what else do we say is incumbent on the rational creature—I mean man—than the contemplation of the Divine? I say, too, that it is requisite to contemplate human nature, and to live as the truth directs, and to admire the Instructor and His injunctions, as suitable and harmonious to each other. According to which image also we ought, conforming ourselves to the Instructor, and making the word and our deeds agree, to live a real life.

CHAPTER XIII.

VIRTUE RATIONAL, SIN IRRATIONAL.

EVERYTHING that is contrary to right reason is sin. Accordingly, therefore, the philosophers think fit to define the most generic passions thus: lust, as desire disobedient to reason; fear, as weakness disobedient to reason; pleasure, as an elation of the spirit disobedient to reason. If, then, disobedience in reference to reason is the generating cause of sin, how shall we escape the conclusion, that obedience to reason—the Word—which we call faith, will of necessity be the efficacious cause of duty? For virtue itself is a state of the soul rendered harmonious by reason in respect to the whole life. Nay, to crown all, philosophy itself is pronounced to be the cultivation of right reason; so that, necessarily, whatever is done through error of reason is transgression, and is rightly called (ἁμάρτημα) sin. Since, then, the first man sinned and disobeyed God, it is said, "And man became like to the beasts:"[1] being rightly regarded as irrational, he is likened to the beasts. Whence Wisdom says: "The horse for covering; the libidinous and the adulturer is become like to an irrational beast."[2] Wherefore also it is added: "He neighs, whoever may be sitting on him." The man, it is meant, no longer speaks; for he who transgresses against reason is no longer rational, but an irrational animal, given up to lusts by which he is ridden (as a horse by his rider).

But that which is done right, in obedience to reason, the followers of the Stoics call προσῆκον and καθῆκον, that is, incumbent and fitting. What is fitting is incumbent. And

[1] Ps. xlix. 12, 20.   [2] Ecclus. xxxiii. 6.

obedience is founded on commands. And these being, as they are, the same as counsels—having truth for their aim, train up to the ultimate goal of aspiration, which is conceived of as the *end* (τέλος). And the end of piety is eternal rest in God. And the beginning of eternity is our end. The right operation of piety perfects duty by works; whence, according to just reasoning, duties consist in actions, not in sayings. And Christian conduct is the operation of the rational soul in accordance with a correct judgment and aspiration after the truth, which attains its destined end through the body, the soul's consort and ally. Virtue is a will in conformity to God and Christ in life, rightly adjusted to life everlasting. For the life of Christians, in which we are now trained, is a system of reasonable actions—that is, of those things taught by the Word—an unfailing energy which we have called faith. The system is the commandments of the Lord, which, being divine statutes and spiritual counsels, have been written for ourselves, being adapted for ourselves and our neighbours. Moreover, they turn back on us, as the ball rebounds on him that throws it by the repercussion. Whence also duties are essential for divine discipline, as being enjoined by God, and furnished for our salvation. And since, of those things which are necessary, some relate only to life here, and others, which relate to the blessed life yonder, wing us for flight hence; so, in an analogous manner, of duties, some are ordained with reference to life, others for the blessed life. The commandments issued with respect to natural life are published to the multitude; but those that are suited for living well, and from which eternal life springs, we have to consider, as in a sketch, as we read them out of the Scriptures.

BOOK II.

CHAPTER I.

ON EATING.

KEEPING, then, to our aim, and selecting the scriptures which bear on the usefulness of training for life, we must now compendiously describe what the man who is called a Christian ought to be during the whole of his life. We must accordingly begin with ourselves, and how we ought to regulate ourselves. We have therefore, preserving a due regard to the symmetry of this work, to say how each of us ought to conduct himself in respect to his body, or rather how to regulate the body itself. For whenever any one, who has been brought away by the Word from external things, and from attention to the body itself to the mind, acquires a clear view of what happens according to nature in man, he will know that he is not to be earnestly occupied about external things, but about what is proper and peculiar to man—to purge the eye of the soul, and to sanctify also his flesh. For he that is clean rid of those things which constitute him still dust, what else has he more serviceable than himself for walking in the way which leads to the comprehension of God?

Some men, in truth, live that they may eat, as the irrational creatures, "whose life is their belly, and nothing else." But the Instructor enjoins us to eat that we may live. For neither is food our business, nor is pleasure our aim; but both are on account of our life here, which the Word is training up to immortality. Wherefore also there is discrimination to be employed in reference to food. And it is to be simple, truly plain, suiting precisely simple and artless children—as ministering to life, not to luxury. And the life to which it conduces consists of two things—health and strength; to which plainness of fare is most suitable, being conducive both to digestion and lightness of body, from which come growth, and health, and right strength, not strength that is wrong or dangerous and wretched, as is that of athletes produced by compulsory feeding.

We must therefore reject different varieties, which engender various mischiefs, such as a depraved habit of body and disorders of the stomach, the taste being vitiated by an unhappy art—that of cookery, and the useless art of making pastry. For people dare to call by the name of food their dabbling in luxuries, which glides into mischievous pleasures. Antiphanes, the Delian physician, said that this variety of viands was the one cause of disease; there being people who dislike the truth, and through various absurd notions abjure moderation of diet, and put themselves to a world of trouble to procure dainties from beyond seas.

For my part, I am sorry for this disease, while they are not ashamed to sing the praises of their delicacies, giving themselves great trouble to get lampreys in the Straits of Sicily, the eels of the Mæander, and the kids found in Melos, and the mullets in Sciathus, and the mussels of Pelorus, the oysters of Abydos, not omitting the sprats found in Lipara, and the Mantinican turnip; and furthermore, the beetroot that grows among the Ascræans: they seek out the cockles of Methymna, the turbots of Attica, and the thrushes of Daphnis, and the reddish-brown dried figs, on account of which the ill-starred Persian marched into Greece with five hundred thousand men. Besides these, they purchase birds from Phasis, the Egyptian snipes, and the Median peafowl. Altering these by means of condiments, the gluttons gape for the sauces. "Whatever earth and the depths of the sea, and the unmeasured space of the air produce," they cater for their gluttony. In their greed and solicitude, the gluttons seem absolutely to sweep the world with a drag-net to gratify their luxurious tastes. These gluttons, surrounded with the sound of hissing frying-pans, and wearing their whole life away at the pestle and mortar, cling to matter like fire. More than that, they emasculate plain food, namely bread, by straining off the nourishing part of the grain, so that the necessary part of food becomes matter of reproach to luxury. There is no limit to epicurism among men. For it has driven them to sweetmeats, and honey-cakes, and sugar-plums; inventing a multitude of desserts, hunting after all manner of dishes. A man like this seems to me to be all jaw, and nothing else. "Desire not," says the Scripture, "rich men's dainties;"[1] for they belong to a false and base life. They partake of luxurious dishes, which a little after go to the dunghill. But we who seek the heavenly bread must rule the belly, which is beneath heaven, and much more the things which are agreeable to it, which "God shall destroy,"[2] says the apostle, justly execrating gluttonous desires. For "meats are for the belly,"[3] for on them depends this truly carnal and destructive life; whence[4] some, speaking with unbridled tongue, dare to apply the name *agapè*[5] to pitiful suppers, redolent of savour and sauces. Dishonouring the good and saving work of the Word, the consecrated *agape*, with pots and pouring of sauce; and by drink and delicacies and smoke desecrating that name, they are deceived in their idea, having expected that the promise of God might be bought with suppers. Gatherings for the sake of mirth, and such entertainments as are called by ourselves, we name rightly suppers, dinners, and banquets, after the example of the Lord. But such entertainments the Lord has not called *agapæ*. He says accordingly somewhere, "When thou art called to a wedding, recline not on the highest couch; but when thou art called, fall into the lowest place;"[6] and elsewhere, "When thou makest a dinner or a supper;" and again, "But when thou makest an entertainment, call the poor,"[7] for whose sake chiefly a supper ought to be made. And further, "A certain man made a

---

[1] Prov. xxiii. 3.
[2] 1 Cor. vi. 13.
[3] 1 Cor. vi. 13.
[4] ὅθεν, an emendation for ὅν.
[5] Love, or love-feast, a name applied by the ancients to public entertainments.
[6] Luke xiv. 8, 10.
[7] Luke xiv. 12, 13.

great supper, and called many."[1] But I perceive whence the specious appellation of suppers flowed: "from the gullets and furious love for suppers"—according to the comic poet. For, in truth, "to many, many things are on account of the supper." For they have not yet learned that God has provided for His creature (man I mean) food and drink, for sustenance, not for pleasure; since the body derives no advantage from extravagance in viands. For, quite the contrary, those who use the most frugal fare are the strongest and the healthiest, and the noblest; as domestics are healthier and stronger than their masters, and husbandmen than the proprietors; and not only more robust, but wiser, as philosophers are wiser than rich men. For they have not buried the mind beneath food, nor deceived it with pleasures. But love (*agape*) is in truth celestial food, the banquet of reason. "It beareth all things, endureth all things, hopeth all things. Love never faileth."[2] "Blessed is he who shall eat bread in the kingdom of God."[3] But the hardest of all cases is for charity, which faileth not, to be cast from heaven above to the ground into the midst of sauces. And do you imagine that I am thinking of a supper that is to be done away with? "For if," it is said, "I bestow all my goods, and have not love, I am nothing."[4] On this love alone depend the law and the Word; and if "thou shalt love the Lord thy God and thy neighbour," this is the celestial festival in the heavens. But the earthly is called a supper, as has been shown from Scripture. For the supper is made for love, but the supper is not love (*agape*); only a proof of mutual and reciprocal kindly feeling. "Let not, then, your good be evil spoken of; for the kingdom of God is not meat and drink," says the apostle, in order that the meal spoken of may not be conceived as ephemeral, "but righteousness, and peace, and joy in the Holy Ghost."[5] He who eats of this meal, the best of all, shall possess the kingdom of God, fixing his regards here on the holy assembly of love, the heavenly church. Love, then, is something pure and worthy of God,

[1] Luke xiv. 16.   [2] 1 Cor. xiii. 7, 8.   [3] Luke xiv. 15.
[4] 1 Cor. xiii. 3.   [5] Rom. xiv. 16, 17.

and its work is communication. "And the care of discipline is love," as Wisdom says; "and love is the keeping of the law."[1] And these joys have an inspiration of love from the public nutriment, which accustoms to everlasting dainties. Love (*agape*), then, is not a supper. But let the entertainment depend on love. For it is said, "Let the children whom Thou hast loved, O Lord, learn that it is not the products of fruits that nourish man; but it is Thy word which preserves those who believe on Thee."[2] "For the righteous shall not live by bread."[3] But let our diet be light and digestible, and suitable for keeping awake, unmixed with diverse varieties. Nor is this a point which is beyond the sphere of discipline. For love is a good nurse for communication; having as its rich provision sufficiency, which, presiding over diet measured in due quantity, and treating the body in a healthful way, distributes something from its resources to those near us. But the diet which exceeds sufficiency injures a man, deteriorates his spirit, and renders his body prone to disease. Besides, those dainty tastes, which trouble themselves about rich dishes, drive to practices of ill-repute, daintiness, gluttony, greed, voracity, insatiability. Appropriate designations of such people as so indulge are flies, weasels, flatterers, gladiators, and the monstrous tribes of parasites—the one class surrendering reason, the other friendship, and the other life, for the gratification of the belly; crawling on their bellies, beasts in human shape after the image of their father, the voracious beast. People first called the abandoned ἀσώτους, and so appear to me to indicate their end, understanding them as those who are (ἀσώστους) unsaved, excluding the σ. For those that are absorbed in pots, and exquisitely prepared niceties of condiments, are they not plainly abject, earth-born, leading an ephemeral kind of life, as if they were not to live [hereafter]? Those the Holy Spirit, by Isaiah, denounces as wretched, depriving them tacitly of the name of love (*agape*), since their feasting was not in accordance with the word. "But they made mirth, killing calves, and sacrificing sheep, saying, Let us eat

[1] Wisd. vi. 19.   [2] Wisd. xvi. 17.   [3] Deut. viii. 3; Matt. iv. 4.

and drink, for to-morrow we die." And that He reckons such luxury to be sin, is shown by what He adds, "And your sin shall not be forgiven you till you die,"[1]—not conveying the idea that death, which deprives of sensation, is the forgiveness of sin, but meaning that death of salvation which is the recompense of sin. "Take no pleasure in abominable delicacies," says Wisdom.[2] At this point, too, we have to advert to what are called things sacrificed to idols, in order to show how we are enjoined to abstain from them. Polluted and abominable those things seem to me, to the blood of which, fly

"Souls from Erebus of inanimate corpses."—*Odyss.* xi. 37.

"For I would not that ye should have fellowship with demons,"[3] says the apostle; since the food of those who are saved and those who perish is separate. We must therefore abstain from these viands not for fear (because there is no power in them); but on account of our conscience, which is holy, and out of detestation of the demons to which they are dedicated, are we to loathe them; and further, on account of the instability of those who regard many things in a way that makes them prone to fall, "whose conscience, being weak, is defiled: for meat commendeth us not to God."[4] "For it is not that which entereth in that defileth a man, but that which goeth out of his mouth."[5] The natural use of food is then indifferent. "For neither if we eat are we the better," it is said, "nor if we eat not are we the worse."[6] But it is inconsistent with reason, for those that have been made worthy to share divine and spiritual food, to partake of the tables of demons. "Have we not power to eat and to drink," says the apostle, "and to lead about wives?" But by keeping pleasures under command we prevent lusts. See, then, that this power of yours never "become a stumbling-block to the weak."

For it were not seemly that we, after the fashion of the rich man's son in the Gospel,[7] should, as prodigals, abuse the Father's gifts; but we should use them, without undue

[1] Isa. xxii. 13. [2] Ecclus. xviii. 32. [3] 1 Cor. x. 20.
[4] 1 Cor. viii. 7, 8. [5] Matt. xv. 11. [6] 1 Cor. viii. 8.
[7] Luke xv. 11.

attachment to them, as having command over ourselves. For we are enjoined to reign and rule over meats, not to be slaves to them. It is an admirable thing, therefore, to raise our eyes aloft to what is true, to depend on that divine food above, and to satiate ourselves with the exhaustless contemplation of that which truly exists, and so taste of the only sure and pure delight. For such is the *agape*, which, the food that comes from Christ shows that we ought to partake of. But totally irrational, futile, and not human is it for those that are of the earth, fattening themselves like cattle, to feed themselves up for death; looking downwards on the earth, and bending ever over tables; leading a life of gluttony; burying all the good of existence here in a life that by and by will end; courting voracity alone, in respect to which cooks are held in higher esteem than husbandmen. For we do not abolish social intercourse, but look with suspicion on the snares of custom, and regard them as a calamity. Wherefore daintiness is to be shunned, and we are to partake of few and necessary things. "And if one of the unbelievers call us to a feast, and we determine to go" (for it is a good thing not to mix with the dissolute), the apostle bids us "eat what is set before us, asking no questions for conscience sake."[1] Similarly he has enjoined to purchase "what is sold in the shambles," without curious questioning.[2]

We are not, then, to abstain wholly from various kinds of food, but only are not to be taken up about them. We are to partake of what is set before us, as becomes a Christian, out of respect to him who has invited us; by a harmless and moderate participation in the social meeting; regarding the sumptuousness of what is put on the table as a matter of indifference, despising the dainties, as after a little destined to perish. "Let him who eateth, not despise him who eateth not; and let him who eateth not, not judge him who eateth."[3] And a little way on he explains the reason of the command, when he says, "He that eateth, eateth to the Lord, and giveth God thanks; and he that eateth not, to the Lord he eateth not, and giveth God thanks."[4] So that

[1] 1 Cor. x. 27. [2] 1 Cor. x. 25. [3] Rom. xiv. 3. [4] Rom. xiv. 6.

the right food is thanksgiving. And he who gives thanks does not occupy his time in pleasures. And if we would persuade any of our fellow-guests to virtue, we are all the more on this account to abstain from those dainty dishes; and so exhibit ourselves as a bright pattern of virtue, such as we ourselves have in Christ. "For if any of such meats make a brother to stumble, I shall not eat it as long as the world lasts," says he, "that I may not make my brother stumble."[1] I gain the man by a little self-restraint. "Have we not power to eat and to drink?"[2] And "we know"—he says the truth—"that an idol is nothing in the world; but we have only one true God, of whom are all things, and one Lord Jesus. But," he says, "through thy knowledge thy weak brother perishes, for whom Christ died; and they that wound the conscience of the weak brethren sin against Christ."[3] Thus the apostle, in his solicitude for us, discriminates in the case of entertainments, saying, that "if any one called a brother be found a fornicator, or an adulterer, or an idolater, with such an one not to eat;"[4] neither in discourse or food are we to join, looking with suspicion on the pollution thence proceeding, as on the tables of the demons. "It is good, then, neither to eat flesh nor to drink wine,"[5] as both he and the Pythagoreans acknowledge. For this is rather characteristic of a beast; and the fumes arising from them being dense, darken the soul. If one partakes of them, he does not sin. Only let him partake temperately, not dependent on them, nor gaping after fine fare. For a voice will whisper to him, saying, "Destroy not the work of God for the sake of food."[6] For it is the mark of a silly mind to be amazed and stupified at what is presented at vulgar banquets, after the rich fare which is in the word; and much sillier to make one's eyes the slaves of the delicacies, so that one's greed is, so to speak, carried round by the servants. And how foolish for people to raise themselves on the couches, all but pitching their faces into the dishes, stretching out from the couch as from a nest, according to the common saying, "that they may

[1] 1 Cor. viii. 13.   [2] 1 Cor. ix. 14.   [3] 1 Cor. viii. 6, 11, 12.
[4] 1 Cor. v. 11.   [5] Rom. xiv. 21.   [6] Rom. xiv. 20.

catch the wandering steam by breathing it in!" And how senseless, to besmear their hands with the condiments, and to be constantly reaching to the sauce, cramming themselves immoderately and shamelessly, not like people tasting, but ravenously seizing! For you may see such people, liker swine or dogs for gluttony than men, in such a hurry to feed themselves full, that both jaws are stuffed out at once, the veins about the face raised, and besides, the perspiration running all over, as they are tightened with their insatiable greed, and panting with their excess; the food pushed with unsocial eagerness into their stomach, as if they were stowing away their victuals for provision for a journey, not for digestion. Excess, which in all things is an evil, is very highly reprehensible in the matter of food. Gluttony, called ὀψοφαγία, is nothing but excess in the use of relishes (ὄψον); and λαιμαργία is insanity with respect to the gullet; and γαστριμαργία is excess with respect to food—insanity in reference to the belly, as the name implies; for μάργος is a madman. The apostle, checking those that transgress in their conduct at entertainments, says: "For every one taketh beforehand in eating his own supper; and one is hungry, and another drunken. Have ye not houses to eat and to drink in? Or despise ye the church of God, and shame those who have not?"[1] And among those who have, they, who eat shamelessly and are insatiable, shame themselves. And both act badly; the one by paining those who have not, the other by exposing their own greed in the presence of those who have. Necessarily, therefore, against those who have cast off shame and unsparingly abuse meals, the insatiable to whom nothing is sufficient, the apostle, in continuation, again breaks forth in a voice of displeasure: "So that, my brethren, when ye come together to eat, wait for one another. And if any one is hungry, let him eat at home, that ye come not together to condemnation."[2]

From all slavish habits[3] and excess we must abstain, and touch what is set before us in a decorous way; keeping the

[1] 1 Cor. xi. 21, 22.   [2] 1 Cor. xi. 33, 34.
[3] Literally, "slave-manners," the conduct to be expected from slaves.

hand and couch and chin free of stains; preserving the grace of the countenance undisturbed, and committing no indecorum in the act of swallowing; but stretching out the hand at intervals in an orderly manner. We must guard against speaking anything while eating: for the voice becomes disagreeable and inarticulate when it is confined by full jaws; and the tongue, pressed by the food and impeded in its natural energy, gives forth a compressed utterance. Nor is it suitable to eat and to drink simultaneously. For it is the very extreme of intemperance to confound the times whose uses are discordant. And "whether ye eat or drink, do all to the glory of God,"[1] aiming after true frugality, which the Lord also seems to me to have hinted at when He blessed the loaves and the cooked fishes with which He feasted the disciples, introducing a beautiful example of simple food. That fish then which, at the command of the Lord, Peter caught, points to digestible and God-given and moderate food. And by those who rise from the water to the bait of righteousness, He admonishes us to take away luxury and avarice, as the coin from the fish; in order that He might displace vainglory; and by giving the stater to the tax-gatherers, and "rendering to Cæsar the things which are Cæsar's," might preserve "to God the things which are God's."[2] The stater is capable of other explanations not unknown to us, but the present is not a suitable occasion for their treatment. Let the mention we make for our present purpose suffice, as it is not unsuitable to the flowers of the Word; and we have often done this, drawing to the urgent point of the question the most beneficial fountain, in order to water those who have been planted by the Word. "For if it is lawful for me to partake of all things, yet all things are not expedient."[3] For those that do all that is lawful, quickly fall into doing what is unlawful. And just as righteousness is not attained by avarice, nor temperance by excess; so neither is the regimen of a Christian formed by indulgence; for the table of truth is far from lascivious dainties. For though it was chiefly for men's sake that all things were made, yet it is not good to use all things, nor

[1] 1 Cor. x. 31.   [2] Matt. xxii. 21.   [3] 1 Cor. x. 23.

at all times. For the occasion, and the time, and the mode, and the intention, materially turn the balance with reference to what is useful, in the view of one who is rightly instructed; and this is suitable, and has influence in putting a stop to a life of gluttony, which wealth is prone to choose, not that wealth which sees clearly, but that abundance which makes a man blind with reference to gluttony. No one is poor as regards necessaries, and a man is never overlooked. For there is one God who feeds the fowls and the fishes, and, in a word, the irrational creatures; and not one thing whatever is wanting to them, though "they take no thought for their food."[1] And we are better than they, being their lords, and more closely allied to God, as being wiser; and we were made, not that we might eat and drink, but that we might devote ourselves to the knowledge of God. "For the just man who eats is satisfied in his soul, but the belly of the wicked shall want,"[2] filled with the appetites of insatiable gluttony. Now lavish expense is adapted not for enjoyment alone, but also for social communication. Wherefore we must guard against those articles of food which persuade us to eat when we are not hungry, bewitching the appetite. For is there not within a temperate simplicity a wholesome variety of eatables? Bulbs,[3] olives, certain herbs, milk, cheese, fruits, all kinds of cooked food without sauces; and if flesh is wanted, let roast rather than boiled be set down. Have you anything to eat here? said the Lord[4] to the disciples after the resurrection; and they, as taught by Him to practise frugality, "gave Him a piece of broiled fish;" and having eaten before them, says Luke, He spoke to them what He spoke. And in addition to these, it is not to be overlooked that those who feed according to the Word are not debarred from dainties in the shape of honey-combs. For of articles of food, those are the most suitable which are fit for immediate use without fire, since they are readiest; and second to these are those which are simplest, as we said before. But those who bend around inflammatory tables, nourishing

---

[1] Matt. vi. 25, etc.   [2] Prov. xiii. 5.
[3] A bulbous root, much prized in Greece, which grew wild.
[4] Luke xxiv. 41-44.

their own diseases, are ruled by a most lickerish demon, whom I shall not blush to call the Belly-demon, and the worst and most abandoned of demons. He is therefore exactly like the one who is called the Ventriloquist-demon. It is far better to be happy[1] than to have a demon dwelling with us. And happiness is found in the practice of virtue. Accordingly, the apostle Matthew partook of seeds, and nuts,[2] and vegetables, without flesh. And John, who carried temperance to the extreme, "ate locusts and wild honey." Peter abstained from swine; "but a trance fell on him," as is written in the Acts of the Apostles, "and he saw heaven opened, and a vessel let down on the earth by the four corners, and all the four-footed beasts and creeping things of the earth and the fowls of heaven in it; and there came a voice to him, Rise, and slay, and eat. And Peter said, Not so, Lord, for I have never eaten what is common or unclean. And the voice came again to him the second time, What God hath cleansed, call not thou common."[3] The use of them is accordingly indifferent to us. "For not what entereth into the mouth defileth the man,"[4] but the vain opinion respecting uncleanness. For God, when He created man, said, "All things shall be to you for meat."[5] "And herbs, with love, are better than a calf with fraud."[6] This well reminds us of what was said above, that herbs are not love, but that our meals are to be taken with love;[7] and in these the medium state is good. In all things, indeed, this is the case, and not least in the preparation made for feasting, since the extremes are dangerous, and middle courses good. And to be in no want of necessaries is the medium. For the desires which are in accordance with nature are bounded by sufficiency. The Jews had frugality enjoined on them by the law in the most systematic manner. For the Instructor, by Moses, deprived them of the use of innumerable things, adding reasons—the spiritual ones hidden; the carnal ones

---

[1] A play here on the words εὐδαίμων and δαίμων.
[2] ἀκρόδρυα, hard-shelled fruits.
[3] Acts x. 10-15.
[4] Matt. xv. 11.
[5] Gen. ix. 2, 3.
[6] Prov. xv. 17.
[7] In allusion to the agapæ, or love-feasts.

apparent, to which indeed they have trusted; in the case of some animals, because they did not part the hoof, and others because they did not ruminate their food, and others because alone of aquatic animals they were devoid of scales; so that altogether but a few were left appropriate for their food. And of those that he permitted them to touch, he prohibited such as had died, or were offered to idols, or had been strangled; for to touch these was unlawful. For since it is impossible for those who use dainties to abstain from partaking of them, he appointed the opposite mode of life, till he should break down the propensity to indulgence arising from habit. Pleasure has often produced in men harm and pain; and full feeding begets in the soul uneasiness, and forgetfulness, and foolishness. And they say that the bodies of children, when shooting up to their height, are made to grow right by deficiency in nourishment. For then the spirit, which pervades the body in order to its growth, is not checked by abundance of food obstructing the freedom of its course. Whence that truth-seeking philosopher Plato, fanning the spark of the Hebrew philosophy when condemning a life of luxury, says: "On my coming hither, the life which is here called happy, full of Italian and Syracusan tables, pleased me not by any means, [consisting as it did] in being filled twice a day, and never sleeping by night alone, and whatever other accessories attend the mode of life. For not one man under heaven, if brought up from his youth in such practices, will ever turn out a wise man, with however admirable a natural genius he may be endowed." For Plato was not unacquainted with David, who "placed the sacred ark in his city in the midst of the tabernacle;" and bidding all his subjects rejoice "before the Lord, divided to the whole host of Israel, man and woman, to each a loaf of bread, and baked bread, and a cake from the frying-pan."[1]

This was the sufficient sustenance of the Israelites. But that of the Gentiles was over-abundant. No one who uses it will ever study to become temperate, burying as he does his mind in his belly, very like the fish called ass,[2] which, Aristotle

---

[1] 1 Kings vi. 17–19, Septuagint.
[2] ὄνος, perhaps the hake or cod.

says, alone of all creatures has its heart in its stomach. This fish Epicharmus the comic poet calls "monster-paunch."

Such are the men who believe in their belly, "whose God is their belly, whose glory is in their shame, who mind earthly things." To them the apostle predicted no good when he said, "whose end is destruction."[1]

[1] Phil. iii. 19.

CHAPTER II.

ON DRINKING.

"USE a little wine," says the apostle to Timothy, who drank water, "for thy stomach's sake;"[1] most properly applying its aid as a strengthening tonic suitable to a sickly body enfeebled with watery humours; and specifying "a little," lest the remedy should, on account of its quantity, unobserved, create the necessity of other treatment.

The natural, temperate, and necessary beverage, therefore, for the thirsty is water. This was the simple drink of sobriety, which, flowing from the smitten rock, was supplied by the Lord to the ancient Hebrews.[2] It was most requisite that in their wanderings they should be temperate.

Afterwards the sacred vine produced the prophetic cluster. This was a sign to them, when trained from wandering to their rest; representing the great cluster the Word, bruised for us. For the blood of the grape—that is, the Word—desired to be mixed with water, as His blood is mingled with salvation.

And the blood of the Lord is twofold. For there is the blood of His flesh, by which we are redeemed from corruption; and the spiritual, that by which we are anointed. And to drink the blood of Jesus, is to become partaker of the Lord's immortality; the Spirit being the energetic principle of the Word, as blood is of flesh.

Accordingly, as wine is blended with water, so is the Spirit with man. And the one, the mixture of wine and water, nourishes to faith; while the other, the Spirit, conducts to immortality.

And the mixture of both—of the water and of the Word—

[1] 1 Tim. i. 25.   [2] Ex. xvii.; Num. xx.

is called *Eucharist*, renowned and glorious grace; and they who by faith partake of it are sanctified both in body and soul. For the divine mixture, man, the Father's will has mystically compounded by the Spirit and the Word. For, in truth, the spirit is joined to the soul, which is inspired by it; and the flesh, by reason of which the Word became flesh, to the Word.

I therefore admire those who have adopted an austere life, and who are fond of water, the medicine of temperance, and flee as far as possible from wine, shunning it as they would the danger of fire. It is proper, therefore, that boys and girls should keep as much as possible away from this medicine. For it is not right to pour into the burning season of life the hottest of all liquids—wine—adding, as it were, fire to fire. For hence wild impulses and burning lusts and fiery habits are kindled; and young men inflamed from within become prone to the indulgence of vicious propensities; so that signs of injury appear in their body, the members of lust coming to maturity sooner than they ought. The breasts and organs of generation, inflamed with wine, expand and swell in a shameful way, already exhibiting beforehand the image of fornication; and the body compels the wound of the soul to inflame, and shameless pulsations follow abundance, inciting the man of correct behaviour to transgression; and hence the voluptuousness of youth overpasses the bounds of modesty. And we must, as far as possible, try to quench the impulses of youth by removing the Bacchic fuel of the threatened danger; and by pouring the antidote to the inflammation, so keep down the burning soul, and keep in the swelling members, and allay the agitation of lust when it is already in commotion. And in the case of grown-up people, let those with whom it agrees sometimes partake of dinner, tasting bread only, and let them abstain wholly from drink; in order that their superfluous moisture may be absorbed and drunk up by the eating of dry food. For constant spitting and wiping off perspiration, and hastening to evacuations, is the sign of excess, from the immoderate use of liquids supplied in excessive quantity to the body. And if thirst come on, let the appetite be satisfied with a little water. For it is not proper that water should be supplied in too great profusion; in order that the food may not be drowned, but ground down in order to digestion; and this takes place when the victuals are collected into a mass, and only a small portion is evacuated.

And, besides, it suits divine studies not to be heavy with wine. "For unmixed wine is far from compelling a man to be wise, much less temperate," according to the comic poet. But towards evening, about supper-time, wine may be used, when we are no longer engaged in more serious readings. Then also the air becomes colder than it is during the day; so that the failing natural warmth requires to be nourished by the introduction of heat. But even then it must only be a little wine that is to be used; for we must not go on to intemperate potations. Those who are already advanced in life may partake more hilariously of the bowl, to warm by the harmless medicine of the vine the chill of age, which the decay of time has produced. For old men's passions are not, for the most part, stirred to such agitation as to drive them to the shipwreck of drunkenness. For being moored by reason and time, as by anchors, they stand with greater ease the storm of passions which rushes down from intemperance. They also may be permitted to indulge in pleasantry at feasts. But to them also let the limit of their potations be the point up to which they keep their reason unwavering, their memory active, and their body unmoved and unshaken by wine. People in such a state are called by those who are skilful in these matters, acrothorakes.[1] It is well, therefore, to leave off betimes, for fear of tripping.

One Artorius, in his book *On Long Life* (for so I remember), thinks that drink should be taken only till the food be moistened, that we may attain to a longer life. It is fitting, then, that some apply wine by way of physic, for the sake of health alone, and others for purposes of relaxation and enjoyment. For first wine makes the man who has drunk it more

---

[1] The exact derivation of *acrothorakes* is matter of doubt. But we have the authority of Aristotle and Erotian for believing that it was applied to those who were slightly drunk. Some regard the clause here as an interpolation.

benignant than before, more agreeable to his boon companions, kinder to his domestics, and more pleasant to his friends. But when intoxicated, he becomes violent instead. For wine being warm, and having sweet juices when duly mixed, dissolves the foul excrementitious matters by its warmth, and mixes the acrid and base humours with agreeable scents.

It has therefore been well said, "A joy of the soul and heart was wine created from the beginning, when drunk in moderate sufficiency."[1] And it is best to mix the wine with as much water as possible, and not to have recourse to it as to water, and so get enervated to drunkenness, and not pour it in as water from love of wine. For both are works of God; and so the mixture of both, of water and of wine, conduces together to health, because life consists of what is necessary and of what is useful. With water, then, which is the necessary of life, and to be used in abundance, there is also to be mixed the useful.

By an immoderate quantity of wine the tongue is impeded; the lips are relaxed; the eyes roll wildly, the sight, as it were, swimming through the quantity of moisture; and compelled to deceive, they think that everything is revolving round them, and cannot count distant objects as single. "And, in truth, methinks I see two suns,"[2] said the Theban old man in his cups. For the sight, being disturbed by the heat of the wine, frequently fancies the substance of one object to be manifold. And there is no difference between moving the eye or the object seen. For both have the same effect on the sight, which, on account of the fluctuation, cannot accurately obtain a perception of the object. And the feet are carried from beneath the man as by a flood, and hiccuping and vomiting and maudlin nonsense follow; "for every intoxicated man," according to the tragedy,[3]

> "Is conquered by anger, and empty of sense,
> And likes to pour forth much silly speech;
> And is wont to hear unwillingly,
> What evil words he with his will hath said."

---

[1] Ecclus. xxxi. 36. [2] Pentheus in Euripides, *Bacch.*
[3] Attributed to Sophocles.

And before tragedy, Wisdom cried, "Much wine drunk abounds in irritation and all manner of mistakes."[1] Wherefore most people say that you ought to relax over your cups, and postpone serious business till morning. I however think that then especially ought reason to be introduced to mix in the feast, to act the part of director (pædagogue) to wine-drinking, lest conviviality imperceptibly degenerate to drunkenness. For as no sensible man ever thinks it requisite to shut his eyes before going to sleep, so neither can any one rightly wish reason to be absent from the festive board, or can well study to lull it asleep till business is begun. But the Word can never quit those who belong to Him, not even if we are asleep; for He ought to be invited even to our sleep. For perfect wisdom, which is knowledge of things divine and human, which comprehends all that relates to the oversight of the flock of men, becomes, in reference to life, art; and so, while we live, is constantly with us, always accomplishing its own proper work, the product of which is a good life.

But the miserable wretches who expel temperance from conviviality, think excess in drinking to be the happiest life; and their life is nothing but revel, debauchery, baths, excess, urinals, idleness, drink. You may see some of them, half-drunk, staggering, with crowns round their necks like wine jars, vomiting drink on one another in the name of good fellowship; and others, full of the effects of their debauch, dirty, pale in the face, livid, and still above yesterday's bout pouring another bout to last till next morning. It is well, my friends, it is well to make our acquaintance with this picture at the greatest possible distance from it, and to frame ourselves to what is better, dreading lest we also become a like spectacle and laughing-stock to others.

It has been appropriately said, "As the furnace tests the steel blade in the process of dipping, so wine tests the heart of the haughty."[2] A debauch is the immoderate use of wine, intoxication the disorder that results from such use; crapulousness (κραιπάλη) is the discomfort and nausea that follow a debauch, so called from the head shaking (κάρα πάλλειν).

[1] Ecclus. xxx. 38.   [2] Ecclus. xxxi. 31.

Such a life as this (if life it must be called, which is spent in idleness, in agitation about voluptuous indulgences, and in the hallucinations of debauchery) the divine Wisdom looks on with contempt, and commands her children, "Be not a wine-bibber, nor spend your money in the purchase of flesh; for every drunkard and fornicator shall come to beggary, and every sluggard shall be clothed in tatters and rags."[1] For every one that is not awake to wisdom, but is steeped in wine, is a sluggard. "And the drunkard," he says, "shall be clothed in rags, and be ashamed of his drunkenness in the presence of onlookers."[2] For the wounds of the sinner are the rents of the garment of the flesh, the holes made by lusts, through which the shame of the soul within is seen—namely sin, by reason of which it will not be easy to save the garment, that has been torn away all round, that has rotted away in many lusts, and has been rent asunder from salvation.

So he adds these most monitory words: "Who has woes, who has clamour, who has contentions, who has disgusting babblings, who has unavailing remorse?"[3] You see, in all his raggedness, the lover of wine, who despises the Word Himself, and has abandoned and given himself to drunkenness. You see what threatening Scripture has pronounced against him. And to its threatening it adds again: "Whose are red eyes? Those, is it not, who tarry long at their wine, and hunt out the places where drinking goes on?" Here he shows the lover of drink to be already dead to the Word, by the mention of the blood-shot eyes,—a mark which appears on corpses, announcing to him death in the Lord. For forgetfulness of the things which tend to true life turns the scale towards destruction. With reason therefore, the Instructor, in His solicitude for our salvation, forbids us, "Drink not wine to drunkenness." Wherefore? you will ask. Because, says He, "thy mouth will then speak perverse things, and thou liest down as in the heart of the sea, and as the steersman of a ship in the midst of huge billows." Hence, too, poetry comes to our help, and says:

[1] Prov. xxiii. 20.   [2] Prov. xxiii. 21.   [3] Prov. xxiii. 29, 30.

"Let wine which has strength equal to fire come to men.
Then will it agitate them, as the north or south wind agitates the Libyan waves."

And further:

"Wine wandering in speech shows all secrets.
Soul-deceiving wine is the ruin of those who drink it."

And so on.

You see the danger of shipwreck. The heart is drowned in much drink. The excess of drunkenness is compared to the danger of the sea, in which when the body has once been sunken like a ship, it descends to the depths of turpitude, overwhelmed in the mighty billows of wine; and the helmsman, the human mind, is tossed about on the surge of drunkenness, which swells aloft; and buried in the trough of the sea, is blinded by the darkness of the tempest, having drifted away from the haven of truth, till, dashing on the rocks beneath the sea, it perishes, driven by itself into voluptuous indulgences.

With reason, therefore, the apostle enjoins, "Be not drunk with wine, in which there is much excess;" by the term excess (ἀσωτία) intimating the inconsistence of drunkenness with salvation (ἄσωστον). For if He made water wine at the marriage, He did not give permission to get drunk. He gave life to the watery element of the meaning of the law, filling with His blood the doer of it who is of Adam, that is, the whole world; supplying piety with drink from the vine of truth, the mixture of the old law and of the new word, in order to the fulfilment of the predestined time. The Scripture, accordingly, has named wine the symbol of the sacred blood; but reproving the base tippling with the dregs of wine, it says: "Intemperate is wine, and insolent is drunkenness."[1] It is agreeable, therefore, to right reason, to drink on account of the cold of winter, till the numbness is dispelled from those who are subject to feel it; and on other occasions as a medicine for the intestines. For, as we are to use food to satisfy hunger, so also are we to use drink to satisfy thirst, taking the most careful precautions against a slip: "for the introduction of wine is perilous." And thus shall our soul be

[1] Prov. xx. 1.

pure, and dry, and luminous; and the soul itself is wisest and best when dry. And thus, too, is it fit for contemplation, and is not humid with the exhalations, that rise from wine, forming a mass like a cloud. We must not therefore trouble ourselves to procure Chian wine if it is absent, or Ariousian when it is not at hand. For thirst is a sensation of want, and craves means suitable for supplying the want, and not sumptuous liquor. Importations of wines from beyond seas are for an appetite enfeebled by excess, where the soul even before drunkenness is insane in its desires. For there are the fragrant Thasian wine, and the pleasant-breathing Lesbian, and a sweet Cretan wine, and sweet Syracusan wine, and Mendusian, an Egyptian wine, and the insular Naxian, the "highly perfumed and flavoured,"[1] another wine of the land of Italy. These are many names. For the temperate drinker, one wine suffices, the product of the cultivation of the one God. For why should not the wine of their own country satisfy men's desires, unless they were to import water also, like the foolish Persian kings? The Choaspes, a river of India so called, was that from which the best water for drinking—the Choaspian—was got. As wine, when taken, makes people lovers of it, so does water too. The Holy Spirit, uttering His voice by Amos, pronounces the rich to be wretched on account of their luxury:[2] "Those that drink strained wine, and recline on an ivory couch," he says; and what else similar he adds by way of reproach.

Especial regard is to be paid to decency (as the myth represents Athene, whoever she was, out of regard to it, giving up the pleasure of the flute because of the unseemliness of the sight): so that we are to drink without contortions of the face, not greedily grasping the cup, nor before drinking making the eyes roll with unseemly motion; nor from intemperance are we to drain the cup at a draught; nor besprinkle the chin, nor splash the garments while gulping down all the liquor at once,—our face all but filling the bowl, and

---

[1] ἀνθοσμίας. Some suppose the word to be derived from the name of a town: "The Anthosmian."

[2] Amos vi. 4, 6.

drowned in it. For the gurgling occasioned by the drink rushing with violence, and by its being drawn in with a great deal of breath, as if it were being poured into an earthenware vessel, while the throat makes a noise through the rapidity of ingurgitation, is a shameful and unseemly spectacle of intemperance. In addition to this, eagerness in drinking is a practice injurious to the partaker. Do not haste to mischief, my friend. Your drink is not being taken from you. It is given you, and waits you. Be not eager to burst, by draining it down with gaping throat. Your thirst is satiated, even if you drink slower, observing decorum, by taking the beverage in small portions, in an orderly way. For that which intemperance greedily seizes, is not taken away by taking time.

"Be not mighty," he says, "at wine; for wine has overcome many."[1] The Scythians, the Celts, the Iberians, and the Thracians, all of them warlike races, are greatly addicted to intoxication, and think that it is an honourable, happy pursuit to engage in. But we, the people of peace, feasting for lawful enjoyment, not to wantonness, drink sober cups of friendship, that our friendships may be shown in a way truly appropriate to the name.

In what manner do you think the Lord drank when He became man for our sakes? As shamelessly as we? Was it not with decorum and propriety? Was it not deliberately? For rest assured, He Himself also partook of wine; for He, too, was man. And He blessed the wine, saying, "Take, drink: this is my blood"—the blood of the vine. He figuratively calls the Word "shed for many, for the remission of sins"—the holy stream of gladness. And that he who drinks ought to observe moderation, He clearly showed by what He taught at feasts. For He did not teach affected by wine. And that it was wine which was the thing blessed, He showed again, when He said to His disciples, "I will not drink of the fruit of this vine, till I drink it with you in the kingdom of my Father."[2] But that it was wine which was drunk by the Lord, He tells us again, when He spake concerning Himself, reproaching the Jews for their hardness of

[1] Ecclus. xxxi. 30. [2] Mark xiv. 25; Matt. xxvi. 29.

heart: "For the Son of man," He says, "came, and they say, Behold a glutton and a wine-bibber, a friend of publicans."[1] Let this be held fast by us against those that are called Encratites.

But women, making a profession, forsooth, of aiming at the graceful, that their lips may not be rent apart by stretching them on broad drinking cups, and so widening the mouth, drinking in an unseemly way out of alabastra quite too narrow in the mouth, throw back their heads and bare their necks indecently, as I think; and distending the throat in swallowing, gulp down the liquor as if to make bare all they can to their boon companions; and drawing hiccups like men, or rather like slaves, revel in luxurious riot. For nothing disgraceful is proper for man, who is endowed with reason; much less for woman, to whom it brings shame even to reflect of what nature she is.

"An intoxicated woman is great wrath," it is said, as if a drunken woman were the wrath of God. Why? "Because she will not conceal her shame."[2] For a woman is quickly drawn down to licentiousness, if she only set her choice on pleasures. And we have not prohibited drinking from alabastra; but we forbid studying to drink from them alone, as arrogant; counselling women to use with indifference what comes in the way, and cutting up by the roots the dangerous appetites that are in them. Let the rush of air, then, which regurgitates so as to produce hiccup, be emitted silently.

But by no manner of means are women to be allowed to uncover and exhibit any part of their person, lest both fall,—the men by being excited to look, they by drawing on themselves the eyes of the men.

But always must we conduct ourselves as in the Lord's presence, lest He say to us, as the apostle in indignation said to the Corinthians, "When ye come together, this is not to eat the Lord's supper."[3]

To me, the star called by the mathematicians Acephalus (headless), which is numbered before the wandering star, his head resting on his breast, seems to be a type of the

[1] Matt. xi. 19.   [2] Ecclus. xxvi. 11.   [3] 1 Cor. xi. 20.

gluttonous, the voluptuous, and those that are prone to drunkenness. For in such[1] the faculty of reasoning is not situated in the head, but among the intestinal appetites, enslaved to lust and anger. For just as Elpenor broke his neck through intoxication,[2] so the brain, dizzied by drunkenness, falls down from above, with a great fall to the liver and the heart, that is, to voluptuousness and anger: as the sons of the poets say Hephæstus was hurled by Zeus from heaven to earth.[3] "The trouble of sleeplessness, and bile, and cholic, are with an insatiable man," it is said.[4]

Wherefore also Noah's intoxication was recorded in writing, that, with the clear and written description of his transgression before us, we might guard with all our might against drunkenness. For which cause they who covered the shame[5] of his drunkenness are blessed by the Lord. The Scripture accordingly, giving a most comprehensive compend, has expressed all in one word: "To an instructed man sufficiency is wine, and he will rest in his bed."[6]

[1] τούτοις, an emendation for τούτῳ. [2] *Odyss.* xi. 65.
[3] *Iliad*, i. 589.   [4] Ecclus. xxxi. 23.   [5] Shem and Japheth.
[6] See Ecclus. xxxi. 22, where, however, we have a different reading.

CHAPTER III.

ON COSTLY VESSELS.

AND so the use of cups made of silver and gold, and of others inlaid with precious stones, is out of place, being only a deception of the vision. For if you pour any warm liquid into them, the vessels becoming hot, to touch them is painful. On the other hand, if you pour in what is cold, the material changes its quality, injuring the mixture, and the rich potion is hurtful. Away, then, with Thericleian cups and Antigonides, and Canthari, and goblets, and Lepastæ,[1] and the endless shapes of drinking vessels, and wine-coolers, and wine-pourers also. For, on the whole, gold and silver, both publicly and privately, are an invidious possession when they exceed what is necessary, seldom to be acquired, difficult to keep, and not adapted for use. The elaborate vanity, too, of vessels in glass chased, more apt to break on account of the art, teaching us to fear while we drink, is to be banished from our well-ordered constitution. And silver couches, and pans and vinegar-saucers, and trenchers and bowls; and besides these, vessels of silver and gold, some for serving food, and others for other uses which I am ashamed to name, of easily cleft cedar and thyine wood, and ebony, and tripods fashioned of ivory, and couches with silver feet and inlaid with ivory, and folding-doors of beds studded with gold and variegated with tortoise-shell, and bed-clothes of purple and other colours difficult to produce, proofs of tasteless luxury, cunning devices of envy and effeminacy,—are all to be relinquished, as having nothing whatever worth our pains. "For the time is short," as says the

[1] Limpet-shaped cups.

apostle. This then remains that we do, not make a ridiculous figure, as some are seen in the public spectacles outwardly anointed strikingly for imposing effect, but wretched within. Explaining this more clearly, he adds, "It remains that they that have wives be as though they had none, and they that buy as though they possessed not."[1] And if he speaks thus of marriage, in reference to which God says, "Multiply," how do you not think that senseless display is by the Lord's authority to be banished? Wherefore also the Lord says, "Sell what thou hast, and give to the poor; and come, follow me."[2]

Follow God, stripped of arrogance, stripped of fading display, possessed of that which is thine, which is good, what alone cannot be taken away—faith towards God, confession towards Him who suffered, beneficence towards men, which is the most precious of possessions. For my part, I approve of Plato, who plainly lays it down as a law, that a man is not to labour for wealth of gold or silver, nor to possess a useless vessel which is not for some necessary purpose, and moderate; so that the same thing may serve for many purposes, and the possession of a variety of things may be done away with. Excellently, therefore, the Divine Scripture, addressing boasters and lovers of their own selves, says, "Where are the rulers of the nations, and the lords of the wild beasts on the earth, who sport among the birds of heaven, who treasured up silver and gold, in whom men trusted, and there was no end of their substance, who fashioned silver and gold, and were full of care? There is no finding of their works. They have vanished, and gone down to Hades."[3] Such is the reward of display. For though such of us as cultivate the soil need a mattock and plough, none of us will make a pickaxe of silver or a sickle of gold, but we employ the material which is serviceable for agriculture, not what is costly. What prevents those who are capable of considering what is similar from entertaining the same sentiments with respect to household utensils, of which let use, not expense, be the measure? For tell me, does the table-knife not cut unless it be studded with

[1] 1 Cor. vii. 29, 30.   [2] Matt. xix. 21.   [3] Baruch iii. 16–19.

silver, and have its handle made of ivory? Or must we forge Indian steel in order to divide meat, as when we call for a weapon for the fight? What if the basin be of earthenware? will it not receive the dirt of the hands? or the footpan the dirt of the foot? Will the table that is fashioned with ivory feet be indignant at bearing a three-halfpenny loaf? Will the lamp not dispense light because it is the work of the potter, not of the goldsmith? I affirm that truckle-beds afford no worse repose than the ivory couch; and the goatskin coverlet being amply sufficient to spread on the bed, there is no need of purple or scarlet coverings. Yet to condemn, notwithstanding, frugality, through the stupidity of luxury, the author of mischief, what a prodigious error, what senseless conceit! See. The Lord ate from a common bowl, and made the disciples recline on the grass on the ground, and washed their feet, girded with a linen towel—He, the lowly-minded God, and Lord of the universe. He did not bring down a silver foot-bath from heaven. He asked to drink of the Samaritan woman, who drew the water from the well in an earthenware vessel, not seeking regal gold, but teaching us how to quench thirst easily. For He made use, not extravagance His aim. And He ate and drank at feasts, not digging metals from the earth, nor using vessels of gold and silver, that is, vessels exhaling the odour of rust—such fumes as the rust of smoking[1] metal gives off.

For in fine, in food, and clothes, and vessels, and everything else belonging to the house, I say comprehensively, that one must follow the institutions of the Christian man, as is serviceable and suitable to one's person, age, pursuits, time of life. For it becomes those that are servants of one God, that their possessions and furniture should exhibit the tokens of one beautiful[2] life; and that each individually should be seen in faith, which shows no difference, practising all other things which are conformable to this uniform mode of life, and harmonious with this one scheme.

What we acquire without difficulty, and use with ease, we praise, keep easily, and communicate freely. The things

[1] Or, proud.   [2] καλοῦ.

which are useful are preferable, and consequently cheap things are better than dear. In fine, wealth, when not properly governed, is a stronghold of evil, about which many casting their eyes, they will never reach the kingdom of heaven, sick for the things of the world, and living proudly through luxury. But those who are in earnest about salvation must settle this beforehand in their mind, "that all that we possess is given to us for use, and use for sufficiency, which one may attain to by a few things." For silly are they who, from greed, take delight in what they have hoarded up. "He that gathereth wages," it is said, "gathereth into a bag with holes."[1] Such is he who gathers corn and shuts it up; and he who giveth to no one, becomes poorer.

It is a farce, and a thing to make one laugh outright, for men to bring in silver urine-vases and chamber-pots of crystal as they usher in their counsellors, and for silly rich women to get gold receptacles for excrements made; so that being rich, they cannot even ease themselves except in superb way. I would that in their whole life they deemed gold fit for dung.

But now love of money is found to be the stronghold of evil, which the apostle says "is the root of all evils, which, while some coveted, they have erred from the faith, and pierced themselves through with many sorrows."[2]

But the best riches is poverty of desires; and the true magnanimity is not to be proud of wealth, but to despise it. Boasting about one's plate is utterly base. For it is plainly wrong to care much about what any one who likes may buy from the market. But wisdom is not bought with coin of earth, nor is it sold in the market-place, but in heaven. And it is sold for true coin, the immortal Word, the regal gold.

[1] Hag. i. 6.   [2] 1 Tim. vi. 10.

CHAPTER IV.

HOW TO CONDUCT OURSELVES AT FEASTS.

ET revelry keep away from our rational entertainments, and foolish vigils, too, that revel in intemperance. For revelry is an inebriating pipe, the chain[1] of an amatory bridge, that is, of sorrow. And let love, and intoxication, and senseless passions, be removed from our choir. Burlesque singing is the boon companion of drunkenness. A night spent over drink invites drunkenness, rouses lust, and is audacious in deeds of shame. For if people occupy their time with pipes, and psalteries, and choirs, and dances, and Egyptian clapping of hands, and such disorderly frivolities, they become quite immodest and intractable, beat on cymbals and drums, and make a noise on the instruments of delusion; for plainly such a banquet, as seems to me, is a theatre of drunkenness. For the apostle decrees that, "putting off the works of darkness, we should put on the armour of light, walking honestly as in the day, not spending our time in rioting and drunkenness, in chambering and wantonness."[2] Let the pipe be resigned to the shepherds, and the flute to the superstitious who are engrossed in idolatry. For, in truth, such instruments are to be banished from a temperate banquet, being more suitable to beasts than men, and the more irrational portion of mankind. For we have heard of stags being charmed by the pipe, and seduced by music into the toils, when hunted by the huntsman. And when mares are being covered, a tune is played on the flute—a nuptial song, as it were. And every improper sight and

[1] The reading ἅλυσις is here adopted. The passage is obscure.
[2] Rom. xiii. 12, 13.

sound, to speak in a word, and every shameful sensation of licentiousness—which, in truth, is privation of sensation—must by all means be excluded; and we must be on our guard against whatever pleasure titillates eye and ear, and effeminates. For the various spells of the broken strains and plaintive numbers of the Carian muse corrupt men's morals, drawing to perturbation of mind, by the licentious and mischievous art of music.

The Spirit, distinguishing from such revelry the divine service, sings, "Praise Him with sound of trumpet;" for with sound of trumpet He shall raise the dead. "Praise Him on the psaltery;" for the tongue is the psaltery of the Lord. "And praise Him on the lyre."[1] By the lyre is meant the mouth struck by the Spirit, as it were by a plectrum. "Praise with the timbrel and the dance," refers to the church meditating on the resurrection of the dead in the resounding skin. "Praise Him on the chords and organ." Our body He calls an organ, and its nerves are the strings, by which it has received harmonious tension, and when struck by the Spirit, it gives forth human voices. "Praise Him on the clashing cymbals." He calls the tongue the cymbal of the mouth, which resounds with the pulsation of the lips. Therefore He cried to humanity, "Let every breath praise the Lord," because He cares for every breathing thing which He hath made. For man is truly a pacific instrument; while other instruments, if you investigate, you will find to be warlike, inflaming to lusts, or kindling up amours, or rousing wrath.

In their wars, therefore, the Etruscans use the trumpet, the Arcadians the pipe, the Sicilians the pectides, the Cretans the lyre, the Lacedæmonians the flute, the Thracians the horn, the Egyptians the drum, and the Arabians the cymbal. The one instrument of peace, the Word alone by which we honour God, is what we employ. We no longer employ the ancient psaltery, and trumpet, and timbrel, and flute, which those expert in war and contemners of the fear of God were wont to make use of also in the choruses at their festive assemblies; that by such strains they might raise their de-

[1] Ps. cl. 3–5.

jected minds. But let our genial feeling in drinking be twofold, in accordance with the law. For "if thou shalt love the Lord thy God," and then "thy neighbour," let its first manifestation be towards God in thanksgiving and psalmody, and the second towards our neighbour in decorous fellowship. For says the apostle, "Let the Word of the Lord dwell in you richly."[1] And this Word suits and conforms Himself to seasons, to persons, to places.

In the present instance He is a guest with us. For the apostle adds again, "Teaching and admonishing one another in all wisdom, in psalms, and hymns, and spiritual songs, singing with grace in your heart to God." And again, "Whatsoever ye do in word or deed, do all in the name of the Lord Jesus, giving thanks to God and His Father." This is our thankful revelry. And even if you wish to sing and play to the harp or lyre, there is no blame. Thou shalt imitate the righteous Hebrew king in his thanksgiving to God. "Rejoice in the Lord, ye righteous; praise is comely to the upright,"[2] says the prophecy. "Confess to the Lord on the harp; play to Him on a psaltery of ten strings. Sing to Him a new song." And does not the ten-stringed psaltery indicate the Word Jesus, who is manifested by the element of the decad? And as it is befitting, before partaking of food, that we should bless the Creator of all; so also in drinking it is suitable to praise Him on partaking of His creatures. For the psalm is a melodious and sober blessing. The apostle calls the psalm "a spiritual song."[3]

Finally, before partaking of sleep, it is a sacred duty to give thanks to God, having enjoyed His grace and love, and so go straight to sleep. "And confess to Him in songs of the lips," he says, "because in His command all His good pleasure is done, and there is no deficiency in His salvation."[4]

Further, among the ancient Greeks, in their banquets over the brimming cups, a song was sung called a skolion, after the manner of the Hebrew psalms, all together raising the pæan with the voice, and sometimes also taking turns in the

[1] Col. iii. 16.   [2] Ps. xxxiii. 1-3.
[3] Eph. v. 19; Col. iii. 16.   [4] Wisd. Sirach xxxix. 20, 23.

song while they drank healths round; while those that were more musical than the rest sang to the lyre. But let amatory songs be banished far away, and let our songs be hymns to God. "Let them praise," it is said, "His name in the dance, and let them play to Him on the timbrel and psaltery."[1] And what is the choir which plays? The Spirit will show thee: "Let His praise be in the congregation (church) of the saints; let them be joyful in their King."[2] And again he adds, "The Lord will take pleasure in His people."[3] For temperate harmonies are to be admitted; but we are to banish as far as possible from our robust mind those liquid harmonies, which, through pernicious arts in the modulations of tones, train to effeminacy and scurrility. But grave and modest strains say farewell to the turbulence of drunkenness. Chromatic harmonies are therefore to be abandoned to immodest revels, and to florid and meretricious music.

[1] Ps. cxlix. 3.   [2] Ps. cxlix. 1, 2.   [3] Ps. cxlix. 4.

CHAPTER V

ON LAUGHTER.

PEOPLE who are imitators of ludicrous sensations, or rather of such as deserve derision, are to be driven from our polity [or society].

For since all forms of speech flow from mind and manners, ludicrous expressions could not be uttered, did they not proceed from ludicrous practices. For the saying, "It is not a good tree which produces corrupt fruit, nor a corrupt tree which produces good fruit,"[1] is to be applied in this case. For speech is the fruit of the mind. If, then, wags are to be ejected from our society, we ourselves must by no manner of means be allowed to stir up laughter. For it were absurd to be found imitators of things of which we are prohibited to be listeners; and still more absurd for a man to set about making himself a laughing-stock, that is, the butt of insult and derision. For if we could not endure to make a ridiculous figure, such as we see some do in processions, how could we with any propriety bear to have the inner man made a ridiculous figure of, and that to one's face? Wherefore we ought never of our own accord to assume a ludicrous character. And how, then, can we devote ourselves to being and appearing ridiculous in our conversation, thereby travestying speech, which is the most precious of all human endowments? It is therefore disgraceful to set one's self to do this; since the conversation of wags of this description is not fit for our ears, inasmuch as by the very expressions used it familiarizes us with shameful actions.

Pleasantry is allowable, not waggery. Besides, even laughter

[1] Matt. vii. 18; Luke vi. 43.

must be kept in check; for when given vent to in the right manner it indicates orderliness, but when it issues differently it shows a want of restraint.

For, in a word, whatever things are natural to men we must not eradicate from them, but rather impose on them limits and suitable times. For man is not to laugh on all occasions because he is a laughing animal, any more than the horse neighs on all occasions because he is a neighing animal. But as rational beings, we are to regulate ourselves suitably, harmoniously relaxing the austerity and over-tension of our serious pursuits, not inharmoniously breaking them up altogether.

For the seemly relaxation of the countenance in a harmonious manner—as of a musical instrument—is called a smile. So also is laughter on the face of well-regulated men termed. But the discordant relaxation of countenance in the case of women is called a giggle, and is meretricious laughter; in the case of men, a guffaw, and is savage and insulting laughter. "A fool raises his voice in laughter,"[1] says the Scripture; but a clever man smiles almost imperceptibly. The clever man in this case he calls wise, inasmuch as he is differently affected from the fool. But, on the other hand, one needs not be gloomy, only grave. For I certainly prefer a man to smile who has a stern countenance than the reverse; for so his laughter will be less apt to become the object of ridicule.

Smiling even requires to be made the subject of discipline. If it is at what is disgraceful, we ought to blush rather than smile, lest we seem to take pleasure in it by sympathy; if at what is painful, it is fitting to look sad rather than to seem pleased. For to do the former is a sign of rational human thought; the other infers suspicion of cruelty.

We are not to laugh perpetually, for that is going beyond bounds; nor in the presence of elderly persons, or others worthy of respect, unless they indulge in pleasantry for our amusement. Nor are we to laugh before all and sundry, nor in every place, nor to every one, nor about everything. For to children and women especially laughter is the cause

[1] Ecclus. xxi. 23.

of slipping into scandal. And even to appear stern serves to keep those about us at their distance. For gravity can ward off the approaches of licentiousness by a mere look. All senseless people, to speak in a word, wine

"Commands both to laugh luxuriously and to dance,"

changing effeminate manners to softness. We must consider, too, how consequently freedom of speech leads impropriety on to filthy speaking.

"And he uttered a word which had been better unsaid."[1]

Especially, therefore, in liquor crafty men's characters are wont to be seen through, stripped as they are of their mask through the caitiff licence of intoxication, through which reason, weighed down in the soul itself by drunkenness, is lulled to sleep, and unruly passions are roused, which overmaster the feebleness of the mind.

[1] *Odyss.* xiv. 461.

CHAPTER VI.

ON FILTHY SPEAKING.

FROM filthy speaking we ourselves must entirely abstain, and stop the mouths of those who practise it by stern looks and averting the face, and by what we call making a mock of one: often also by a harsher mode of speech. "For what proceedeth out of the mouth," He says, " defileth a man,"[1]—shows him to be unclean, and heathenish, and untrained, and licentious, and not select, and proper, and honourable, and temperate.

And as a similar rule holds with regard to hearing and seeing in the case of what is obscene, the divine Instructor, following the same course with both, arrays those children who are engaged in the struggle in words of modesty, as ear-guards, so that the pulsation of fornication may not penetrate to the bruising of the soul; and He directs the eyes to the sight of what is honourable, saying that it is better to make a slip with the feet than with the eyes. This filthy speaking the apostle beats off, saying, " Let no corrupt communication proceed out of your mouth, but what is good."[2] And again, " As becometh saints, let not filthiness be named among you, nor foolish talking, nor jesting, which things are not seemly, but rather giving of thanks."[3] And if " he that calls his brother a fool be in danger of the judgment," what shall we pronounce regarding him who speaks what is foolish? Is it not written respecting such : " Whosoever shall speak an idle word, shall give an account to the Lord in the day of judgment?"[4] And again, "By thy speech thou shalt be

[1] Matt. xv. 18.
[2] Eph. iv. 29.
[3] Eph. v. 3, 4.
[4] Matt. v. 22.

justified," He says, "and by thy speech thou shalt be condemned."[1] What, then, are the salutary ear-guards, and what the regulations for slippery eyes? Conversations with the righteous, preoccupying and forearming the ears against those that would lead away from the truth.

"Evil communications corrupt good manners,"
says Poetry. More nobly the apostle says, "Be haters of the evil; cleave to the good."[2] For he who associates with the saints shall be sanctified. From shameful things addressed to the ears, and words and sights, we must entirely abstain. And much more must we keep pure from shameful deeds: on the one hand, from exhibiting and exposing certain parts of the body which we ought not; and on the other, from inspection of the forbidden parts. For the modest son could not bear to look on the shameful exposure of the righteous man; and modesty covered what intoxication exposed—the spectacle of the transgression of ignorance.[3] No less ought we to keep pure from calumnious reports, to which the ears of those who have believed in Christ ought to be inaccessible.

It is on this account, as appears to me, that the Instructor does not permit us to give utterance to aught unseemly, fortifying us at an early stage against licentiousness. For He is admirable always at cutting out the roots of sins, such as, "Thou shalt not commit adultery," by "Thou shalt not lust."[4] For adultery is the fruit of lust, which is the evil root. And so likewise also in this instance the Instructor censures licence in names, and thus cuts off the licentious intercourse of excess. For licence in names produces the desire of being indecorous in conduct; and the observance of modesty in names is a training in resistance to lasciviousness. We have shown in a more exhaustive treatise, that neither in the names nor in the members of intercourse and nuptial embraces, to which appellations not in common use are applied, is there the designation of what is really obscene.

For neither are knee and leg, and such other members,

[1] Matt. xiii. 36.   [2] Rom. xii. 9.
[3] Gen. ix. 23.   [4] Ex. xx. 14, 17.

nor are the names applied to them, and the activity put forth by them, obscene. And even the secret parts of man are to be regarded as objects suggestive of modesty, not shame. It is their unlawful activity that is shameful, and deserving ignominy, and reproach, and punishment. For the only thing that is in reality shameful is wickedness, and what is done through it. In accordance with these remarks, conversation about deeds of wickedness is appropriately termed filthy [shameful] speaking, as talk about adultery and pæderasty and the like. Frivolous prating, too, is to be put to silence. " For," it is said, " in much speaking thou shalt not escape sin."[1] " Sins of the tongue, therefore, shall be punished." " There is he who is silent, and is found wise; and there is that is hated for much speech."[2] But still more, the prater makes himself the object of disgust. " For he that multiplieth speech abominates his own soul."[3]

[1] Prov. x. 19.   [2] Ecclus. xx. 5.   [3] Ecclus. xx. 8.

CHAPTER VII.

DIRECTIONS FOR THOSE WHO LIVE TOGETHER.

LET us keep away from us jibing, the originator of insult, from which strifes and contentions and enmities burst forth. Insult, we have said, is the servant of drunkenness. A man is judged, not from his deeds alone, but from his words. " In a banquet," it is said, " reprove not thy neighbour, nor say to him a word of reproach."[1] For if we are enjoined especially to associate with saints, it is a sin to jibe at a saint : " For from the mouth of the foolish," says the Scripture, " is a staff of insult,"[2]— meaning by staff the prop of insult, on which insult leans and rests. Whence I admire the apostle, who, in reference to this, exhorts us not to utter " scurrilous nor unsuitable words."[3] For if the assemblies at festivals take place on account of affection, and the end of a banquet is friendliness towards those who meet, and meat and drink accompany affection, how should not conversation be conducted in a rational manner, and puzzling people with questions be avoided from affection? For if we meet together for the purpose of increasing our good-will to each other, why should we stir up enmity by jibing? It is better to be silent than to contradict, and thereby add sin to ignorance. " Blessed," in truth, " is the man who has not made a slip with his mouth, and has not been pierced by the pain of sin;"[4] or has repented of what he has said amiss, or has spoken so as to wound no one. On the whole, let young men and young women altogether keep away from such festivals, that they may not make a slip in respect to what is unsuitable. For things to which their ears

---

[1] Ecclus. xxxi. 41.
[2] Prov. xiv. 3.
[3] Eph. v. 4.
[4] Ecclus. xiv. 1.

are unaccustomed, and unseemly sights, inflame the mind, while faith within them is still wavering; and the instability of their age conspires to make them easily carried away by lust. Sometimes also they are the cause of others stumbling, by displaying the dangerous charms of their time of life. For Wisdom appears to enjoin well: " Sit not at all with a married woman, and recline not on the elbow with her;"[1] that is, do not sup nor eat with her frequently. Wherefore he adds, "And do not join company with her in wine, lest thy heart incline to her, and by thy blood slide to ruin."[2] For the licence of intoxication is dangerous, and prone to deflower. And he names " a married woman," because the danger is greater to him who attempts to break the connubial bond.

But if any necessity arises, commanding the presence of married women, let them be well clothed—without by raiment, within by modesty. But as for such as are unmarried, it is the extremest scandal for them to be present at a banquet of men, especially men under the influence of wine. And let the men, fixing their eyes on the couch, and leaning without moving on their elbows, be present with their ears alone; and if they sit, let them not have their feet crossed, nor place one thigh on another, nor apply the hand to the chin. For it is vulgar not to bear one's self without support, and consequently a fault in a young man. And perpetually moving and changing one's position is a sign of frivolousness. It is the part of a temperate man also, in eating and drinking, to take a small portion, and deliberately, not eagerly, both at the beginning and during the courses, and to leave off betimes, and so show his indifference. "Eat," it is said, "like a man what is set before you. Be the first to stop for the sake of regimen; and, if seated in the midst of several people, do not stretch out your hand before them."[3] You must never rush forward under the influence of gluttony; nor must you, though desirous, reach out your hand till some time, inasmuch as by greed one shows an uncontrolled appetite. Nor are you, in the midst of the repast, to exhibit yourselves hugging your food like wild beasts; nor helping yourselves

[1] Ecclus. ix. 12.   [2] Ecclus. ix. 13.   [3] Ecclus. xxxi. 19-21.

to too much sauce, for man is not by nature a sauce-consumer, but a bread-eater. A temperate man, too, must rise before the general company, and retire quietly from the banquet. "For at the time for rising," it is said, "be not the last; haste home."[1] The twelve, having called together the multitude of the disciples, said, "It is not meet for us to leave the word of God and serve tables."[2] If they avoided this, much more did they shun gluttony. And the apostles themselves, writing to the brethren at Antioch, and in Syria and Cilicia, said: "It seemed good to the Holy Ghost, and to us, to lay upon you no other burden than these necessary things, to abstain from things offered to idols, and from blood, and from things strangled, and from fornication, from which, if you keep yourselves, ye shall do well."[3] But we must guard against drunkenness as against hemlock; for both drag down to death. We must also check excessive laughter and immoderate tears. For often people under the influence of wine, after laughing immoderately, then are, I know not how, by some impulse of intoxication moved to tears; for both effeminacy and violence are discordant with the word. And elderly people, looking on the young as children, may, though but very rarely, be playful with them, joking with them to train them in good behaviour. For example, before a bashful and silent youth, one might by way of pleasantry speak thus: "This son of mine (I mean one who is silent) is perpetually talking." For a joke such as this enhances the youth's modesty, by showing the good qualities that belong to him playfully, by censure of the bad qualities, which do not. For this device is instructive, confirming as it does what is present by what is not present. Such, certainly, is the intention of him who says that a water-drinker and a sober man gets intoxicated and drunk. But if there are those who like to jest at people, we must be silent, and dispense with superfluous words like full cups. For such sport is dangerous. "The mouth of the impetuous approaches to contrition."[4] "Thou shalt not receive a foolish report, nor shalt thou agree with an

[1] Ecclus. xxxii. 15.   [2] Acts vi. 2.
[3] Acts xv. 23, 28, 29.   [4] Prov. x. 14.

unjust person to be an unjust witness,"[1] neither in calumnies nor in injurious speeches, much less evil practices. I also should think it right to impose a limit on the speech of rightly regulated persons, who are impelled to speak to one who maintains a conversation with them. "For silence is the excellence of women, and the safe prize of the young; but good speech is characteristic of experienced, mature age. Speak, old man, at a banquet, for it is becoming to you. But speak without embarrassment, and with accuracy of knowledge. Youth, Wisdom also commands thee. Speak, if you must, with hesitation, on being twice asked; sum up your discourse in a few words."[2] But let both speakers regulate their discourse according to just proportion. For loudness of utterance is most insane; while an inaudible utterance is characteristic of a senseless man, for people will not hear: the one is the mark of pusillanimity, the other of arrogance. Let contentiousness in words, for the sake of a useless triumph, be banished; for our aim is to be free from perturbation. Such is the meaning of the phrase, "Peace to thee." Answer not a word before you hear. An enervated voice is the sign of effeminacy. But modulation in the voice is characteristic of a wise man, who keeps his utterance from loudness, from drawling, from rapidity, from prolixity. For we ought not to speak long or much, nor ought we to speak frivolously. Nor must we converse rapidly and rashly. For the voice itself, so to speak, ought to receive its just dues; and those who are vociferous and clamorous ought to be silenced. For this reason, the wise Ulysses chastised Thersites with stripes:

> "Only Thersites, with unmeasured words,
> Of which he had good store, to rate the chiefs,
> Not over-seemly, but wherewith he thought
> To move the crowd to laughter, brawled aloud."[3]

"For dreadful in his destruction is a loquacious man."[4] And it is with triflers as with old shoes: all the rest is worn away by evil; the tongue only is left for destruction. Wherefore Wisdom gives these most useful exhortations: "Do not

---

[1] Prov. xxiv. 28; Ex. xxiii. 1.
[2] Ecclus. xxxii. 10, 11, 13.
[3] Iliad, ii. 213.
[4] Ecclus. ix. 25.

talk trifles in the multitude of the elders." Further, eradicating frivolousness, beginning with God, it lays down the law for our regulation somewhat thus: "Do not repeat your words in your prayer."[1] Chirruping and whistling, and sounds made through the fingers, by which domestics are called, being irrational signs, are to be given up by rational men. Frequent spitting, too, and violent clearing of the throat, and wiping one's nose at an entertainment, are to be shunned. For respect is assuredly to be had to the guests, lest they turn in disgust from such filthiness, which argues want of restraint. For we are not to copy oxen and asses, whose manger and dunghill are together. For many wipe their noses and spit even whilst supping.

If any one is attacked with sneezing, just as in the case of hiccup, he must not startle those near him with the explosion, and so give proof of his bad breeding; but the hiccup is to be quietly transmitted with the expiration of the breath, the mouth being composed becomingly, and not gaping and yawning like the tragic masks. So the disturbance of hiccup may be avoided by making the respirations gently; for thus the threatening symptoms of the ball of wind will be dissipated in the most seemly way, by managing its egress so as also to conceal anything which the air forcibly expelled may bring up with it. To wish to add to the noises, instead of diminishing them, is the sign of arrogance and disorderliness. Those, too, who scrape their teeth, bleeding the wounds, are disagreeable to themselves and detestable to their neighbours. Scratching the ears and the irritation of sneezing are swinish itchings, and attend unbridled fornication. Both shameful sights and shameful conversation about them are to be shunned. Let the look be steady, and the turning and movement of the neck, and the motions of the hands in conversation, be decorous. In a word, the Christian is characterized by composure, tranquillity, calmness, and peace.

[1] Ecclus. ix. 25.

CHAPTER VIII.

ON THE USE OF OINTMENTS AND CROWNS.

THE use of crowns and ointments is not necessary for us; for it impels to pleasures and indulgences, especially on the approach of night. I know that the woman brought to the sacred supper "an alabaster box of ointment,"[1] and anointed the feet of the Lord, and refreshed Him; and I know that the ancient kings of the Hebrews were crowned with gold and precious stones. But the woman not having yet received the Word (for she was still a sinner), honoured the Lord with what she thought the most precious thing in her possession—the ointment; and with the ornament of her person, with her hair, she wiped off the superfluous ointment, while she expended on the Lord tears of repentance: "wherefore her sins are forgiven."[2]

This may be a symbol of the Lord's teaching, and of His suffering. For the feet anointed with fragrant ointment mean divine instruction travelling with renown to the ends of the earth. "For their sound hath gone forth to the ends of the earth."[3] And if I seem not to insist too much, the feet of the Lord which were anointed are the apostles, having, according to prophecy, received the fragrant unction of the Holy Ghost. Those, therefore, who travelled over the world and preached the gospel, are figuratively called the feet of the Lord, of whom also the Holy Spirit foretells in the psalm, "Let us adore at the place where His feet stood,"[4] that is, where the apostles, His feet, arrived; since, preached by them, He came to the ends of the earth. And tears are repentance;

---

[1] Matt. xxvi. 7, etc. [2] Luke vii. 47.
[3] Ps. xix. 5; Rom. x. 18. [4] Ps. cxxxii.

and the loosened hair proclaimed deliverance from the love of finery, and the affliction in patience which, on account of the Lord, attends preaching, the old vainglory being done away with by reason of the new faith.

Besides, it shows the Lord's passion, if you understand it mystically thus: the oil (ἔλαιον) is the Lord Himself, from whom comes the mercy (ἔλεος) which reaches us. But the ointment, which is adulterated oil, is the traitor Judas, by whom the Lord was anointed on the feet, being released from His sojourn in the world. For the dead are anointed. And the tears are we repentant sinners, who have believed in Him, and to whom He has forgiven our sins. And the dishevelled hair is mourning Jerusalem, the deserted, for whom the prophetic lamentations were uttered. The Lord Himself shall teach us that Judas the deceitful is meant: "He that dippeth with me in the dish, the same shall betray me."[1] You see the treacherous guest, and this same Judas betrayed the Master with a kiss. For he was a hypocrite, giving a treacherous kiss, in imitation of another hypocrite of old. And He reproves that people respecting whom it was said, "This people honour me with their lips; but their heart is far from me."[2] It is not improbable, therefore, that by the oil He means that disciple to whom was shown mercy, and by the tainted and poisoned oil the traitor.

This was, then, what the anointed feet prophesied—the treason of Judas, when the Lord went to His passion. And the Saviour Himself washing the feet of the disciples,[3] and despatching them to do good deeds, pointed out their pilgrimage for the benefit of the nations, making them beforehand fair and pure by His power. Then the ointment breathed on them its fragrance, and the work of sweet savour reaching to all was proclaimed; for the passion of the Lord has filled us with sweet fragrance, and the Hebrews with guilt. This the apostle most clearly showed, when he said, "Thanks be to God, who always makes us to triumph in Christ, and maketh manifest the savour of His knowledge by us in every place. For we are to God a sweet savour of the Lord, in them that

[1] Matt. xxvi. 23.   [2] Isa. xxix. 13.   [3] John xiii. 5.

are saved, and them that are lost; to one a savour of death unto death, to the other a savour of life unto life."[1] And the kings of the Jews using gold and precious stones and a variegated crown, the anointed ones wearing Christ symbolically on the head, were unconsciously adorned with the head of the Lord. The precious stone, or pearl, or emerald, point out the Word Himself. The gold, again, is the incorruptible Word, who admits not the poison of corruption. The Magi, accordingly, brought to Him on His birth, gold, the symbol of royalty. And this crown, after the image of the Lord, fades not as a flower.

I know, too, the words of Aristippus the Cyrenian. Aristippus was a luxurious man. He asked an answer to a sophistical proposition in the following terms: "A horse anointed with ointment is not injured in his excellence as a horse, nor is a dog which has been anointed, in his excellence as a dog; no more is a man," he added, and so finished. But the dog and horse take no account of the ointment, whilst in the case of those whose perceptions are more rational, applying girlish scents to their persons, its use is more censurable. Of these ointments there are endless varieties, such as the Brenthian, the Metallian, and the royal; the Plangonian and the Psagdian of Egypt. Simonides is not ashamed in Iambic lines to say,

"I was anointed with ointments and perfumes,
And with nard."

For a merchant was present. They use, too, the unguent made from lilies, and that from the cypress. Nard is in high estimation with them, and the ointment prepared from roses and the others which women use besides, both moist and dry, scents for rubbing and for fumigating; for day by day their thoughts are directed to the gratification of insatiable desire, to the exhaustless variety of fragrance. Wherefore also they are redolent of an excessive luxuriousness. And they fumigate and sprinkle their clothes, their bed-clothes, and their houses. Luxury all but compels vessels for the meanest uses to smell of perfume.

There are some who, annoyed at the attention bestowed on this, appear to me to be rightly so averse to perfumes on

[1] 2 Cor. ii. 14-16.

account of their rendering manhood effeminate, as to banish their compounders and vendors from well-regulated states, and banish, too, the dyers of flower-coloured wools. For it is not right that ensnaring garments and unguents should be admitted into the city of truth; but it is highly requisite for the men who belong to us to give forth the odour not of ointments, but of nobleness and goodness. And let woman breathe the odour of the true royal ointment, that of Christ, not of unguents and scented powders; and let her always be anointed with the ambrosial chrism of modesty, and find delight in the holy unguent, the Spirit. This ointment of pleasant fragrance Christ prepares for His disciples, compounding the ointment of celestial aromatic ingredients.

Wherefore also the Lord Himself is anointed with an ointment, as is mentioned by David: "Wherefore God, thy God, hath anointed thee with the oil of gladness above thy fellows; myrrh, and stacte, and cassia from thy garments."[1] But let us not unconsciously abominate unguents, like vultures or like beetles (for these, they say, when smeared with ointment, die); and let a few unguents be selected by women, such as will not be overpowering to a husband. For excessive anointings with unguents savour of a funeral, and not of connubial life. Yet oil itself is inimical to bees and insects; and some men it benefits, and some it summons to the fight; and those who were formerly friends, when anointed with it, it turns out to deadly combat.

Ointment being smooth oil, do you not think that it is calculated to render noble manners effeminate? Certainly. And as we have abandoned luxury in taste, so certainly do we renounce voluptuousness in sights and odours; lest through the senses, as through unwatched doors, we unconsciously give access into the soul to that excess which we have driven away. If, then, we say that the Lord the great High Priest offers to God the incense of sweet fragrance, let us not imagine that this is a sacrifice and sweet fragrance of incense; but let us understand it to mean, that the Lord lays the acceptable offering of love, the spiritual fragrance, on the altar.

[1] Ps. xlv. 9.

To resume: oil itself suffices to lubricate the skin, and relax the nerves, and remove any heavy smell from the body, if we require oil for this purpose. But attention to sweet scents is a bait which draws us into sensual lust. For the licentious man is led on every hand, both by his food, his bed, his conversation, by his eyes, his ears, his jaws, and by his nostrils too. As oxen are pulled by rings and ropes, so is the voluptuary by fumigations and unguents, and the sweet scents of crowns. But since we assign no place to pleasure which is linked to no use serviceable to life, come let us also distinguish here too, selecting what is useful. For there are sweet scents which neither make the head heavy nor provoke love, and are not redolent of embraces and licentious companionship, but, along with moderation, are salutary, nourishing the brain when labouring under indisposition, and strengthening the stomach. One must not therefore refrigerate himself with flowers when he wishes to supple his nerves. For their use is not wholly to be laid aside, but ointment is to be employed as a medicine and help in order to bring up the strength when enfeebled, and against catarrhs, and colds, and ennui, as the comic poet says:

"The nostrils are anointed; it being
A most essential thing for health to fill the brain with good odours."

The rubbing of the feet also with the fatness of warming or cooling unguents is practised on account of its beneficial effects; so consequently, in the case of those who are thus saturated, an attraction and flow take place from the head to the inferior members. But pleasure to which no utility attaches, induces the suspicion of meretricious habits, and is a drug provocative of the passions. Rubbing one's self with ointment is entirely different from anointing one's self with ointment. The former is effeminate, while anointing with ointment is in some cases beneficial. Aristippus the philosopher, accordingly, when anointed with ointment, said "that the wretched Cinœdi deserved to perish miserably for bringing the utility of ointment into bad repute." "Honour the physician for his usefulness," says the Scripture, "for the Most High made him; and the art of healing is of the

Lord." Then he adds, "And the compounder of unguents will make the mixture,"[1] since unguents have been given manifestly for use, nòt for voluptuousness. For we are by no means to care for the exciting properties of unguents, but to choose what is useful in them, since God hath permitted the production of oil for the mitigation of men's pains.

And silly women, who dye their grey hair and anoint their locks, grow speedily greyer by the perfumes they use, which are of a drying nature. Wherefore also those that anoint themselves become drier, and the dryness makes them greyer. For if greyness is an exsiccation of the hair, or defect of heat, the dryness drinking up the moisture which is the natural nutriment of the hair, and making it grey, how can we any longer retain a liking for unguents, through which ladies, in trying to escape grey hair, become grey? And as dogs with fine sense of smell track the wild beasts by the scent, so also the temperate scent the licentious by the superfluous perfume of unguents.

Such a use of crowns, also, has degenerated to scenes of revelry and intoxication. Do not encircle my head with a crown, for in the spring-time it is delightful to while away the time on the dewy meads, while soft and many-coloured flowers are in bloom, and, like the bees, enjoy a natural and pure fragrance. But to adorn one's self with "a crown woven from the fresh mead," and wear it at home, were unfit for a man of temperance. For it is not suitable to fill the wanton hair with rose-leaves, or violets, or lilies, or other such flowers, stripping the sward of its flowers. For a crown encircling the head cools the hair, both on account of its moisture and its coolness. Accordingly, physicians, determining by physiology that the brain is cold, approve of anointing the breast and the points of the nostrils, so that the warm exhalation passing gently through, may salutarily warm the chill. A man ought not therefore to cool himself with flowers. Besides, those who crown themselves destroy the pleasure there is in flowers: for they enjoy neither the sight of them, since they wear the crown above their eyes; nor their fragrance, since they put

[1] Ecclus. xxxviii. 1, 2, 7.

the flowers away above the organs of respiration. For the fragrance ascending and exhaling naturally, the organ of respiration is left destitute of enjoyment, the fragrance being carried away. As beauty, so also the flower delights when looked at; and it is meet to glorify the Creator by the enjoyment of the sight of beautiful objects. The use of them is injurious, and passes swiftly away, avenged by remorse. Very soon their evanescence is proved; for both fade, both the flower and beauty. Further, whoever touches them is cooled by the former, inflamed by the latter. In one word, the enjoyment of them except by sight is a crime, and not luxury. It becomes us who truly follow the Scripture to enjoy ourselves temperately, as in Paradise. We must regard the woman's crown to be her husband, and the husband's crown to be marriage; and the flowers of marriage the children of both, which the divine husbandman plucks from meadows of flesh. "Children's children are the crown of old men."[1] And the glory of children is their fathers, it is said; and our glory is the Father of all; and the crown of the whole church is Christ. As roots and plants, so also have flowers their individual properties, some beneficial, some injurious, some also dangerous. The ivy is cooling; nux emits a stupefying effluvium, as the etymology shows. The narcissus is a flower with a heavy odour; the name evinces this, and it induces a torpor (νάρκην) in the nerves. And the effluvia of roses and violets being mildly cool, relieve and prevent headaches. But we who are not only not permitted to drink with others to intoxication, but not even to indulge in much wine, do not need the crocus or the flower of the cypress to lead us to an easy sleep. Many of them also, by their odours, warm the brain, which is naturally cold, volatilizing the effusions of the head. The rose is hence said to have received its name (ῥόδον) because it emits a copious stream (ῥεῦμα) of odour (ὀδωδή). Wherefore also it quickly fades.

But the use of crowns did not exist at all among the ancient Greeks; for neither the suitors nor the luxurious Phæaceans used them. But at the games there was at first

[1] Prov. xvii. 6.

the gift to the athletes; second, the rising up to applaud; third, the strewing with leaves; lastly, the crown, Greece after the Median war having given herself up to luxury.

Those, then, who are trained by the Word are restrained from the use of crowns; and do not think that this Word, which has its seat in the brain, ought to be bound about, not because the crown is the symbol of the recklessness of revelry, but because it has been dedicated to idols. Sophocles accordingly called the narcissus "the ancient coronet of the great gods," speaking of the earth-born divinities; and Sappho crowns the Muses with the rose:

"For thou dost not share in roses from Pierin."

They say, too, that Here delights in the lily, and Artemis in the myrtle. For if the flowers were made especially for man, and senseless people have taken them not for their own proper and grateful use, but have abused them to the thankless service of demons, we must keep from them for conscience sake. The crown is the symbol of untroubled tranquillity. For this reason they crown the dead, and idols, too, on the same account, by this fact giving testimony to their being dead. For revellers do not without crowns celebrate their orgies; and when once they are encircled with flowers, at last they are inflamed excessively. We must have no communion with demons. Nor must we crown the living image of God after the manner of dead idols. For the fair crown of amaranth is laid up for those who have lived well. This flower the earth is not able to bear; heaven alone is competent to produce it. Further, it were irrational in us, who have heard that the Lord was crowned with thorns,[1] to crown ourselves with flowers, insulting thus the sacred passion of the Lord. For the Lord's crown prophetically pointed to us, who once were barren, but are placed around Him through the church of which He is the Head. But it is also a type of faith, of life in respect of the substance of the wood, of joy in respect of the appellation of crown, of danger in respect of the thorn, for there is no approaching to the Word without blood. But this platted crown

[1] Matt. xxvii. 29.

fades, and the plait of perversity is untied, and the flower withers. For the glory of those who have not believed on the Lord fades. And they crowned Jesus raised aloft, testifying to their own ignorance. For being hard of heart, they understood not that this very thing, which they called the disgrace of the Lord, was a prophecy wisely uttered: "The Lord was not known by the people"[1] which erred, which was not circumcised in understanding, whose darkness was not enlightened, which knew not God, denied the Lord, forfeited the place of the true Israel, persecuted God, hoped to reduce the Word to disgrace; and Him whom they crucified as a malefactor they crowned as a king. Wherefore the Man on whom they believed not, they shall know to be the loving God the Lord, the Just. Whom they provoked to show Himself to be the Lord, to Him when lifted up they bore witness, by encircling Him, who is exalted above every name, with the diadem of righteousness by the ever-blooming thorn. This diadem, being hostile to those who plot against Him, coerces them; and friendly to those who form the church, defends them. This crown is the flower of those who have believed on the glorified One, but covers with blood and chastises those who have not believed. It is a symbol, too, of the Lord's successful work, He having borne on His head, the princely part of His body, all our iniquities by which we were pierced. For He by His own passion rescued us from offences, and sins, and such like thorns; and having destroyed the devil, deservedly said in triumph, "O Death, where is thy sting?"[2] And we eat grapes from thorns, and figs from thistles; while those to whom He stretched forth His hands—the disobedient and unfruitful people—He lacerates into wounds. I can also show you another mystic meaning in it. For when the Almighty Lord of the universe began to legislate by the Word, and wished His power to be manifested to Moses, a godlike vision of light that had assumed a shape was shown him in the burning bush (the bush is a thorny plant); but when the Word ended the giving of the law and His stay with men, the Lord was again mystically crowned with

[1] Isa. i. 3.   [2] 1 Cor. xv. 55.

thorn. On His departure from this world to the place whence He came, He repeated the beginning of His old descent, in order that the Word beheld at first in the bush, and afterwards taken up crowned by the thorn, might show the whole to be the work of one power, He Himself being one, the Son of the Father, who is truly one, the beginning and the end of time.

But I have made a digression from the pædagogic style of speech, and introduced the didactic. I return accordingly to my subject.

To resume, then: we have showed that in the department of medicine, for healing, and sometimes also for moderate recreation, the delight derived from flowers, and the benefit derived from unguents and perfumes, are not to be overlooked. And if some say, What pleasure, then, is there in flowers to those that do not use them? let them know, then, that unguents are prepared from them, and are most useful. The Susinian ointment is made from various kinds of lilies; and it is warming, aperient, drawing, moistening, abstergent, subtle, antibilious, emollient. The Narcissinian is made from the narcissus, and is equally beneficial with the Susinian. The Myrsinian, made of myrtle and myrtle berries, is a styptic, stopping effusions from the body; and that from roses is refrigerating. For, in a word, these also were created for our use. "Hear me," it is said, "and grow as a rose planted by the streams of waters, and give forth a sweet fragrance like frankincense, and bless the Lord for His works."[1] We should have much to say respecting them, were we to speak of flowers and odours as made for necessary purposes, and not for the excesses of luxury. And if a concession must be made, it is enough for people to enjoy the fragrance of flowers; but let them not crown themselves with them. For the Father takes great care of man, and gives to him alone His own art. The Scripture therefore says, "Water, and fire, and iron, and milk, and fine flour of wheat, and honey, the blood of the grape, and oil, and clothing,—all these things are for the good of the godly."[2]

[1] Ecclus. xxxix. 17, 18, 19.   [2] Ecclus. xxxix. 31, 32.

CHAPTER IX.

ON SLEEP.

HOW, in due course, we are to go to sleep, in remembrance of the precepts of temperance, we must now say. For after the repast, having given thanks to God for our participation in our enjoyments, and for the [happy] passing of the day, our talk must be turned to sleep. Magnificence of bed-clothes, gold-embroidered carpets, and smooth carpets worked with gold, and long fine robes of purple, and costly fleecy cloaks, and manufactured rugs of purple, and mantles of thick pile, and couches softer than sleep, are to be banished.

For, besides the reproach of voluptuousness, sleeping on downy feathers is injurious, when our bodies fall down as into a yawning hollow, on account of the softness of the bedding.

For they are not convenient for sleepers turning in them, on account of the bed rising into a hill on either side of the body. Nor are they suitable for the digestion of the food, but rather for burning it up, and so destroying the nutriment. But stretching one's self on even couches, affording a kind of natural gymnasium for sleep, contributes to the digestion of the food. And those that can roll on other beds, having this, as it were, for a natural gymnasium for sleep, digest food more easily, and render themselves fitter for emergencies. Moreover, silver-footed couches argue great ostentation; and the ivory on beds, the body having left the soul, is not permissible for holy men, being a lazy contrivance for rest.

We must not occupy our thoughts about these things, for the use of them is not forbidden to those who possess them; but solicitude about them is prohibited, for happiness is not to be found in them. On the other hand, it savours of cynic vanity for a man to act as Diomede,—

"And he stretched himself under a wild bull's hide,"[1]—

unless circumstances compel.

Ulysses rectified the unevenness of the nuptial couch with a stone. Such frugality and self-help was practised not by private individuals alone, but by the chiefs of the ancient Greeks. But why speak of these? Jacob slept on the ground, and a stone served him for a pillow; and then was he counted worthy to behold the vision—that was above man. And in conformity with reason, the bed which we use must be simple and frugal, and so constructed that, by avoiding the extremes [of too much indulgence and too much endurance], it may be comfortable: if it is warm, to protect us; if cold, to warm us. But let not the couch be elaborate, and let it have smooth feet; for elaborate turnings form occasionally paths for creeping things which twine themselves about the incisions of the work, and do not slip off.

Especially is a moderate softness in the bed suitable for manhood; for sleep ought not to be for the total enervation of the body, but for its relaxation. Wherefore I say that it ought not to be allowed to come on us for the sake of indulgence, but in order to rest from action. We must therefore sleep so as to be easily awaked. For it is said, "Let your loins be girt about, and your lamps burning; and ye yourselves like to men that watch for their lord, that when he returns from the marriage, and comes and knocks, they may straightway open to him. Blessed are those servants whom the Lord, when He cometh, shall find watching."[2] For there is no use of a sleeping man, as there is not of a dead man. Wherefore we ought often to rise by night and bless God. For blessed are they who watch for Him, and so make themselves like the angels, whom we call "watchers." But a man asleep is worth nothing, any more than if he were not alive.

But he who has the light watches, "and darkness seizes not on him,"[3] nor sleep, since darkness does not. He that is illuminated is therefore awake towards God; and such an one

[1] *Iliad*, xvi. 155.   [2] Luke xii. 35-37.   [3] John i. 5.

lives. "For what was made in Him was life."[1] "Blessed is the man," says Wisdom, "who shall hear me, and the man who shall keep my ways, watching at my doors, daily observing the posts of my entrances."[2] "Let us not then sleep, as do others, but let us watch," says the Scripture, "and be sober. For they that sleep, sleep in the night; and they that be drunken, are drunken in the night," that is, in the darkness of ignorance. "But let us who are of the day be sober. For ye are all children of the light, and children of the day; we are not of the night, nor of the darkness."[3] But whoever of us is most solicitous for living the true life, and for entertaining noble sentiments, will keep awake for as long time as possible, reserving to himself only what in this respect is conducive to his own health; and that is not very usual.

But devotion to activity begets an everlasting vigil after toils. Let not food weigh us down, but lighten us; that we may be injured as little as possible by sleep, as those that swim with weights hanging to them are weighed down. But, on the other hand, let temperance raise us as from the abyss beneath to the enterprises of wakefulness. For the oppression of sleep is like death, which forces us into insensibility, cutting off the light by the closing of the eyelids. Let not us, then, who are sons of the true light, close the door against this light; but turning in on ourselves, illumining the eyes of the hidden man, and gazing on the truth itself, and receiving its streams, let us clearly and intelligibly reveal such dreams as are true.

But the hiccuping of those who are loaded with wine, and the snortings of those who are stuffed with food, and the snoring rolled in the bed-clothes, and the rumblings of pained stomachs, cover over the clear-seeing eye of the soul, by filling the mind with ten thousand phantasies. And the cause is too much food, which drags the rational part of man down to a condition of stupidity. For much sleep brings advantage neither to our bodies nor our souls; nor is it suitable at all to those processes which have truth for their object, although agreeable to nature.

[1] John i. 3, 4.   [2] Prov. viii. 34.   [3] 1 Thess. v. 5-8.

Now, just Lot (for I pass over at present the account of the economy of regeneration) would not have been drawn into that unhallowed intercourse, had he not been intoxicated by his daughters, and overpowered by sleep. If, therefore, we cut off the causes of great tendency to sleep, we shall sleep the more soberly. For those who have the sleepless Word dwelling in them, ought not to sleep the livelong night; but they ought to rise by night, especially when the days are coming to an end, and one devote himself to literature, another begin his art, the women handle the distaff, and all of us should, so to speak, fight against sleep, accustoming ourselves to this gently and gradually, so that through wakefulness we may partake of life for a longer period.

We, then, who assign the best part of the night to wakefulness, must by no manner of means sleep by day; and fits of uselessness, and napping and stretching one's self, and yawning, are manifestations of frivolous uneasiness of soul. And in addition to all, we must know this, that the need of sleep is not in the soul. For it is ceaselessly active. But the body is relieved by being resigned to rest, the soul the whilst not acting through the body, but exercising intelligence within itself. Thus also, such dreams as are true, in the view of him who reflects rightly, are the thoughts of a sober soul, undistracted for the time by the affections of the body, and counselling with itself in the best manner. For the soul to cease from activity within itself, were destruction to it. Wherefore always contemplating God, and by perpetual converse with Him inoculating the body with wakefulness, it raises man to equality with angelic grace, and from the practice of wakefulness it grasps the eternity of life.

CHAPTER X.[1]

QUÆNAM DE PROCREATIONE LIBERORUM TRACTANDA SINT.

TEMPUS autem opportunum conjunctionis solis iis relinquitur considerandum, qui juncti sunt matrimonio; qui autem matrimonio juncti sunt, iis scopus est et institutum, liberorum susceptio: finis autem, ut boni sint liberi: quemadmodum agricolæ seminis quidem dejectionis causa est, quod nutrimenti habendi curam gerat; agriculturæ autem finis est, fructuum perceptio. Multo autem melior est agricola, qui terram colit animatam: ille enim ed tempus alimentum expetens, hic vero ut universum permaneat, curam gerens, agricolæ officio fungitur: et ille quidem propter se, hic vero propter Deum plantat ac seminat. Dixit enim : " Multiplicemini;"[2] ubi hoc subaudiendum est : " Et ea ratione fit homo Dei imago, quatenus homo co-operatur ad generationem hominis." Non est quælibet terra apta ad suscipienda semina: quod si etiam sit quælibet, non tamen eidem agricolæ. Neque vero seminandum est supra petram, neque semen est contumelia afficiendum, quod quidem dux est et princeps generationis, estque substantia, quæ simul habet insitas naturæ rationes. Quæ sunt autem secundum naturam rationes, absque ratione præternaturalibus mandando meatibus, ignominia afficere, valde est impium. Videte itaque quomodo sapientissimus Moyses infrugiferam aliquando sationem symbolice repulerit: " Non comedes, inquiens, leporem, nec hyænam."[3] Non vult homines esse qualitatis eorum participes, neque eis æqualem gustare libidinem: hæc enim animalia ad explendum coitum venereum

---

[1] For obvious reasons, we have given the greater part of this chapter in the Latin version.
[2] Gen. i. 27.   [3] Deut. xiv. 7.

feruntur insano quodam furore. Ac leporem quidem dicunt quotannis multiplicare anum, pro numero annorum, quos vixit, habentem foramina : et ea ratione dum leporis esum prohibet, significat se dehortari puerorum amorem. Hyænam autem vicissim singulis annis masculinum sexum mutare in femininum : significare autem non esse illi ad adulteria prorumpendum, qui ab hyæna abstinet.

Well, I also agree that the consummately wise Moses confessedly indicates by the prohibition before us, that we must not resemble these animals ; but I do not assent to the explanation of what has been symbolically spoken. For nature never can be forced to change. What once has been impressed on it, may not be transformed into the opposite by passion. For passion is not nature, and passion is wont to deface the form, not to cast it into a new shape. Though many birds are said to change with the seasons, both in colour and voice, as the blackbird ($\kappa \acute{o}\sigma\sigma\upsilon\phi\sigma\varsigma$), which becomes yellow from black, and a chatterer from a singing-bird. Similarly also the nightingale changes by turns both its colour and note. But they do not alter their nature itself, so as in the transformation to become female from male. But the new crop of feathers, like new clothes, produces a kind of colouring of the feathers, and a little after it evaporates in the rigour of winter, as a flower when its colour fades. And in like manner the voice itself, injured by the cold, is enfeebled. For, in consequence of the outer skin being thickened by the surrounding air, the arteries about the neck being compressed and filled, press hard on the breath ; which being very much confined, emits a stifled sound. When, again, the breath is assimilated to the surrounding air and relaxed in spring, it is freed from its confined condition, and is carried through the dilated, though till then obstructed arteries, it warbles no longer a dying melody, but now gives forth a shrill note ; and the voice flows wide, and spring now becomes the song of the voice of birds.

Nequaquam ergo credendum est, hyænam unquam mutare naturam : idem enim animal non habet simul ambo pudenda maris et feminæ, sicut nonnulli existimarunt, qui prodigiose hermaphroditos finxerunt, et inter marem et feminam, hanc masculo-feminam naturam innovarunt. Valde autem falluntur, ut qui non animadverterint, quam sit filiorum amans omnium mater et genetrix Natura: quoniam enim hoc animal, hyæna inquam, est salacissimum, sub cauda ante excrementi meatum, adnatum est ei quoddam carneum tuberculum, feminino pudendo figura persimile. Nullum autem meatum habet hæc figura carnis, qui in utilem aliquam desinat partem, vel in matricem inquam, vel in rectum intestinum: tantum habet magnam concavitatem, quæ inanem excipiat libidinem, quando aversi fuerint meatus, qui in concipiendo fetu occupati sunt. Hoc ipsum autem et masculo et feminæ hyænæ adnatum est, quod sit insigniter pathica: masculus enim vicissim et agit, et patitur: unde etiam rarissime inveniri potest hyæna femina: non enim frequenter concipit hoc animal, cum in eis largiter redundet ea, quæ præter naturam est, satio. Hac etiam ratione mihi videtur Plato in *Phædro*, amorem puerorum repellens, eum appellare bestiam, quod frenum mordentes, qui se voluptatibus dedunt, libidinosi, quadrupedum coeunt more, et filios seminare conantur. Impios "autem tradidit Deus," ut ait Apostolus,[1] " in perturbationes ignominiæ: nam et feminæ eorum mutaverunt naturalem usum in eum, qui est præter naturam: similiter autem et masculi eorum, relicto usu naturali, exarserunt in desiderio sui inter se invicem, masculi in masculos turpitudinem operantes, et mercedem, quam oportuit, erroris sui in se recipientes." At vero ne libidinosissimis quidem animantibus concessit natura in excrementi meatum semen immittere: urina enim in vesicam excernitur, humefactum alimentum in ventrem, lacryma vero in oculum, sanguis in venas, sordes in aures, mucus in nares defertur: fini autem recti intestini, sedes cohæret, per quam excrementa exponuntur. Sola ergo varia in hyænis natura, superfluo coitui superfluam hanc partem excogitavit, et ideo est etiam aliquantisper concavum, ut prurientibus partibus inserviat, exinde autem excæcatur concavitas: non fuit enim res fabricata ad generationem. Hinc nobis manifestum atque adeo in confesso est, vitandos esse cum masculis concubitus, et infrugiferas sationes,

[1] Rom. i. 26, 27.

et Venerem præposteram, et quæ natura coalescere non possunt, androgynorum conjunctiones, ipsam naturam sequentibus, quæ id per partium prohibet constitutionem, ut quæ masculum non ad semen suscipiendum, sed ad id effundendum fecerit. Jeremias autem, hoc est, per ipsum loquens Spiritus, quando dicit: "Spelunca hyænæ facta est domus mea,"[1] id quod ex mortuis constabat corporibus detestans alimentum, sapienti allegoria reprehendit cultum simulacrorum: vere enim oportet ab idolis esse puram domum Dei viventis. Rursus Moyses lepore quoque vesci prohibet. Omni enim tempore coit lepus, et salit, assidente femina, eam a tergo aggrediens: est enim ex iis, quæ retro insiliunt. Concipit autem singulis mensibus, et superfetat; init autem, et parit; postquam autem peperit, statim a quovis initur lepore (neque enim uno contenta est matrimonio) et rursus concipit, adhuc lactans: habet enim matricem, cui sunt duo sinus, et non unus solus matricis vacuus sinus, est ei sufficiens sedes ad receptaculum coitus (quidquid enim est vacuum, desiderat repleri); verum accidit, ut cum uterum gerunt, altera pars matricis desiderio teneatur et libidine furiat; quocirca fiunt eis superfetationes. A vehementibus ergo appetitionibus, mutuisque congressionibus, et cum prægnantibus feminis conjunctionibus, alternisque initibus, puerorumque stupris, adulteriis et libidine abstinere, hujus nos ænigmatis adhortata est prohibitio. Idcirco aperte, et non per ænigmata Moyses prohibuit, "Non fornicaberis; non mœchaberis; pueris stuprum non inferes,"[2] inquiens. Logi itaque præscriptum totis viribus observandum, neque quidquam contra leges ullo modo faciendum est, neque mandata sunt infirmanda. Malæ enim cupiditati nomen est ὕβρις, "petulantia;" et equum cupiditatis, "petulantem" vocavit Plato, cum legisset, "Facti estis mihi equi furentes in feminas."[3] Libidines autem supplicium notum nobis facient illi, qui Sodomam accesserunt, angeli. Ii eos, qui probro illos afficere voluerunt, una cum ipsa civitate combusserunt, evidenti hoc indicio ignem, qui est fructus libidinis, describentes. Quæ enim veteribus acciderunt, sicut ante diximus, ad nos admonendos scripta sunt, ne eisdem

[1] Jer. xii. 9.   [2] Ex. xx. 14.   [3] Jer. v. 8.

teneamur vitiis, et caveamus, ne in pœnas similes incidamus. Oportet autem filios existimare, pueros; uxores autem alienas intueri tanquam proprias filias: voluptates quippe continere, ventrique et iis quæ sunt infra ventrem, dominari, est maximi imperii. Si enim ne digitum quidem temere movere permittit sapienti ratio, ut confitentur Stoici, quomodo non multo magis iis, qui sapientiam persequuntur, in eam, qua coitur, particulam dominatus est obtinendus? Atque hac quidem de causa videtur esse nominatum pudendum, quod hac corporis parte magis, quam qualibet alia, cum pudore utendum sit; natura enim sicut alimentis, ita etiam legitimis nuptiis, quantum convenit, utile est, et decet, nobis uti permisit: permisit autem appetere liberorum procreationem. Quicumque autem, quod modum excedit, persequuntur, labuntur in eo quod est secundum naturam, per congressus, qui sunt præter leges, seipsos lædentes. Ante omnia enim recte habet, ut nunquam cum adolescentibus perinde ac cum feminis, Veneris utamur consuetudine. Et ideo "non esse in petris et lapidibus seminandum" dicit, qui a Moyse factus est philosophus, "quoniam nunquam actis radicibus genitalem sit semen naturam suscepturum." Logos itaque per Moysen apertissime præcepit: "Et cum masculo non dormies feminino concubitu: est enim abominatio."[1] Accedit his, quod "ab omni quoque arvo feminino esse abstinendum" præterquam a proprio, ex divinis Scripturis colligens præclarus Plato consuluit lege illinc accepta: "Et uxori proximi tui non dabis concubitum seminis, ut polluaris apud ipsam.[2] Irrita autem sunt et adulterina concubinarum semina. Ne semina, ubi non vis tibi nasci quod seminatum est. Neque ullam omnino tange mulierem, præterquam tuam ipsius uxorem," ex qua sola tibi licet carnis voluptates percipere ad suscipiendam legitimam successionem. Hæc enim Logo sola sunt legitima. Eis quidem certe, qui divini muneris in producendo opificio sunt participes, semen non est abjiciendum, neque injuria afficiendum, neque tanquam si cornibus semen mandes seminandum est. Hic ipse ergo Moyses cum ipsis quoque prohibet uxoribus congredi, si forte

[1] Lev. xviii. 22.   [2] Lev. xviii. 20.

eas detineant purgationes menstruæ. Non enim purgamento corporis genitale semen, et quod mox homo futurum est, polluere est æquum, nec sordido materiæ profluvio, et, quæ expurgantur, inquinamentis inundare ac obruere; semen autem generationis degenerat, ineptumque redditur, si matricis sulcis privetur. Neque vero ullum unquam induxit veterum Hebræorum coeuntem cum sua uxore prægnante. Sola enim voluptas, si quis ea etiam utatur in conjugio, est præter leges, et injusta, et a ratione aliena. Rursus autem Moyses abducit viros a prægnantibus, quousque pepererint. Revera enim matrix sub vesica quidem collocata, super intestinum autem, quod rectum appellatur, posita, extendit collum inter humeros in vesica; et os colli, in quod venit semen, impletum occluditur, illa autem rursus inanis redditur, cum partu purgata fuerit: fructu autem deposito, deinde semen suscipit. Neque vero nobis turpe est ad auditorum utilitatem nominare partes, in quibus fit fetus conceptio, quæ quidem Deum fabricari non puduit. Matrix itaque sitiens filiorum procreationem, semen suscipit, probrosumque et vituperandum negat coitum, post sationem ore clauso omnino jam libidinem excludens. Ejus autem appetitiones, quæ prius in amicis versabantur complexibus, intro conversæ, in procreatione sobolis occupatæ, operantur una cum Opifice. Nefas est ergo operantem jam naturam adhuc molestia afficere, superflue ad petulantem prorumpendo libidinem. Petulantia autem, quæ multa quidem habet nomina, et multas species, cum ad hanc veneream intemperantiam deflexerit, λαγνεία, id est "lascivia," dicitur; quo nomine significatur libidinosa, publica, et incesta in coitum propensio: quæ cum aucta fuerit, magna simul morborum convenit multitudo, obsoniorum desiderium, vinolentia et amor in mulieres; luxus quoque, et simul universarum voluptatum studium; in quæ omnia tyrannidem obtinet cupiditas. His autem cognatæ innumerabiles augentur affectiones, ex quibus mores intemperantes ad summum provehuntur. Dicit autem Scriptura: "Parantur intemperantibus flagella, et supplicia humeris insipientium:"[1] vires

[1] Prov. xix. 29.

intemperantiæ, ejusque constantem tolerantiam, vocans "humeros insipientium." Quocirca, "Amove a servis tuis spes inanes, et indecoras," inquit, "cupiditates averte a me. Ventris appetitio et coitus ne me apprehendant."[1] Longe ergo sunt arcenda multifaria insidiatorum maleficia; non ad solam enim Cratetis Peram, sed etiam ad nostram civitatem non navigat stultus parasitus, nec scortator libidinosus, qui posteriori delectatur parte: non dolosa meretrix, nec ulla ejusmodi alia voluptatis bellua. Multa ergo nobis per totam vitam seminetur, quæ bona sit et honesta, occupatio. In summa ergo, vel jungi matrimonio, vel omnino a matrimonio purum esse oportet; in quæstione enim id versatur, et hoc a nobis declaratum est in libro *De continentia*. Quod si hoc ipsum, an ducenda sit uxor, veniat in considerationem: quomodo libere permittetur, quemadmodum nutrimento, ita etiam coitu semper uti, tanquam re necessaria? Ex eo ergo videri possunt nervi tanquam stamina distrahi, et in vehementi congressus intensione disrumpi. Jam vero offundit etiam caliginem sensibus, et vires enervat. Patet hoc et in animantibus rationis expertibus, et in iis, quæ in exercitatione versantur, corporibus; quorum hi quidem, qui abstinent, in certaminibus superant adversarios; illa vero a coitu abducta circumaguntur, et tantum non trahuntur, omnibus viribus et omni impetu tandem quasi enervata. "Parvam epilepsiam" dicebat "coitum" sophista Abderites morbum immedicabilem existimans. Annon enim consequuntur resolutiones, quæ exinanitionis ejusque, quod abscedit, magnitudini ascribuntur? "homo enim ex homine nascitur et evellitur." Vide damni magnitudinem: totus homo per exinanitionem coitus abstrahitur. Dicit enim: "Hoc nunc os ex ossibus meis, et caro ex carne mea."[2] Homo ergo tantum exinanitur semine, quantus videtur corpore; est enim generationis initium id, quod recedit: quin etiam conturbat ebullitio materiæ et compagem corporis labefactat et commovet. Lepide ergo ille, qui interroganti, "Quomodo adhuc se haberet ad res venereas," respondit: "Bona verba, quæso: ego vero lubentissime isthinc, tanquam ab agresti et insano domino, profugi."

[1] Ecclus. xxiii. 4, 5, 6.   [2] Gen. ii. 23.

Verum concedatur quidem et admittatur matrimonium: vult enim Dominus humanum genus repleri; sed non dicit, Estote libidinosi: nec vos, tanquam ad coitum natos, voluit esse deditos voluptati. Pudore autem nos afficiat Pædagogus, clamans per Ezechielem: " Circumcidamini fornicationem vestram." Aliquod tempus ad seminandum opportunum habent quoque rationis expertia animantia. Aliter autem coire, quam ad liberorum procreationem, est facere injuriam naturæ; qua quidem oportet magistra, quas prudenter introducit temporis commoditates, diligenter observare, senectutem, inquam, et puerilem ætatem. His enim nondum concessit, illos autem non vult amplius uxores ducere. Sed non vult homines semper dare operam matrimonio. Matrimonium autem est filiorum procreationis appetitio, non inordinata seminis excretio, quæ est et præter leges et a ratione aliena. Secundum naturam autem nobis vita universa processerit, si et ab initio cupiditates contineamus, et hominum genus, quod ex divina providentia nascitur, improbis et malitiosis non tollamus artibus: eæ enim, ut fornicationem celent, exitialia medicamenta adhibentes, quæ prorsus in perniciem ducunt, simul cum fetu omnem humanitatem perdunt. Cæterum, quibus uxores ducere concessum est, iis Pædagogo opus fuerit, ut non interdiu mystica naturæ celebrentur orgia, nec ut aliquis ex ecclesia, verbi gratia, aut ex foro mane rediens, galli more coeat, quando orationis, et lectionis, et eorum quæ interdiu facere convenit, operum tempus est. Vespere autem oportet post convivium quiescere, et post gratiarum actionem, quæ fit Deo pro bonis quæ percepimus. Non semper autem concedit tempus natura, ut peragatur congressus matrimonii; est enim eo desiderabilior conjunctio, quo diuturnior. Neque vero noctu, tanquam in tenebris, immodeste sese ac imtemperanter gerere oportet, sed verecundia, ut quæ sit lux rationis, in animo est includenda. Nihil enim a Penelope telam texente differemus, si interdiu quidem texamus dogmata temperantiæ; noctu autem ea resolvamus, cum in cubile venerimus. Si enim honestatem exercere oportet, multo magis tuæ uxori honestas est ostendenda, inhonestas vitando conjunctiones: et quod caste cum proximis verseris, fide dignum e domo adsit testimonium. Non enim potest aliquid honestum ab ea existimari, apud quam honestas in acribus illis non probatur certo quasi testimonio voluptatibus. Benevolentia autem quæ præceps fertur ad congressionem, exiguo tempore floret, et cum corpore consenescit; nonnunquam autem etiam præsenescit, flaccescente jam libidine, quando matrimonialem temperantiam meretriciæ vitiaverint libidines. Amantium enim corda sunt volucria, amorisque irritamenta exstinguuntur sæpe pœnitentia; amorque sæpe vertitur in odium, quando reprehensionem senserit satietas. Impudicorum vero verborum, et turpium figurarum, meretriciorumque osculorum, et hujusmodi lasciviarum nomina ne sunt quidem memoranda, beatum sequentibus Apostolum, qui aperte dicit: "Fornicatio autem et omnis immunditia, vel plura habendi cupiditas, ne nominetur quidem in vobis, sicut decet sanctos."[1] Recte ergo videtur dixisse quispiam: "Nulli quidem profuit coitus, recte autem cum eo agitur, quem non læserit." Nam et qui legitimus, est periculosus, nisi quatenus in liberorum procreatione versatur. De eo autem, qui est præter leges, dicit Scriptura: "Mulier meretrix apro similis reputabitur. Quæ autem viro subjecta est, turris est mortis iis, qui ea utuntur." Capro, val apro, meretricis comparavit affectionem. "Mortem" autem dixit "quæsitam," adulterium, quod committitur in meretrice, quæ custoditur. "Domum" autem, et "urbem," in qua suam exercent intemperantiam. Quin etiam quæ est apud vos poetica, quodammodo ea exprobrans, scribit:

> Tecum et adulterium est, tecum coitusque nefandus,
> Fœdus, femineusque, urbs pessima, plane impura.

Econtra autem pudicos admiratur:

> Quos desiderium tenuit nec turpe cubilis
> Alterius, nec tetra invisaque stupra tulerunt
> Ulla unquam maribus.

For many think such things to be pleasures only which are against nature, such as these sins of theirs. And those who are better than they, know them to be sins, but are overcome by pleasures, and darkness is the veil of their vicious prac-

[1] Eph. v. 3.

tices. For he violates his marriage adulterously who uses it in a meretricious way, and hears not the voice of the Instructor, crying, "The man who ascends his bed, who says in his soul, Who seeth me? darkness is around me, and the walls are my covering, and no one sees my sins. Why do I fear lest the Highest will remember?"[1] Most wretched is such a man, dreading men's eyes alone, and thinking that he will escape the observation of God. "For he knoweth not," says the Scripture, "that brighter ten thousand times than the sun are the eyes of the Most High, which look on all the ways of men, and cast their glance into hidden parts." Thus again the Instructor threatens them, speaking by Isaiah: "Woe be to those who take counsel in secret, and say, Who seeth us?"[2] For one may escape the light of sense, but that of the mind it is impossible to escape. For how, says Heraclitus, can one escape the notice of that which never sets? Let us by no means, then, veil ourselves with the darkness; for the light dwells in us. "For the darkness," it is said, "comprehendeth it not."[3] And the very night itself is illuminated by temperate reason. The thoughts of good men Scripture has named "sleepless lamps;"[4] although for one to attempt even to practise concealment, with reference to what he does, is confessedly to sin. And every one who sins, directly wrongs not so much his neighbour if he commits adultery, as himself, because he has committed adultery, besides making himself worse and less thought of. For he who sins, in the degree in which he sins, becomes worse and is of less estimation than before; and he who has been overcome by base pleasures, has now licentiousness wholly attached to him. Wherefore he who commits fornication is wholly dead to God, and is abandoned by the Word as a dead body by the spirit. For what is holy, as is right, abhors to be polluted. But it is always lawful for the pure to touch the pure. Do not, I pray, put off modesty at the same time that you put off your clothes; because it is never right for the just man to divest himself of continence. For, lo, this

[1] Ecclus. xxiii. 18, 19.　　[2] Isa. xxix. 15.　　[3] John i. 5.
[4] Wisd. vii. 10 is probably referred to.

mortal shall put on immortality; when the insatiableness of desire, which rushes into licentiousness, being trained to self-restraint, and made free from the love of corruption, shall consign the man to everlasting chastity. "For in this world they marry and are given in marriage."[1] But having done with the works of the flesh, and having been clothed with immortality, the flesh itself being pure, we pursue after that which is according to the measure of the angels.

Thus in the *Philebus*, Plato, who had been the disciple of the barbarian[2] philosophy, mystically called those Atheists who destroy and pollute, as far as in them lies, the Deity dwelling in them—that is, the Logos—by association with their vices. Those, therefore, who are consecrated to God must never live mortally (θνητῶς). "Nor," as Paul says, "is it meet to make the members of Christ the members of an harlot; nor must the temple of God be made the temple of base affections."[3] Remember the four and twenty thousand that were rejected for fornication. But the experiences of those who have committed fornication, as I have already said, are types which correct our lusts. Moreover, the Pædagogue warns us most distinctly: "Go not after thy lusts, and abstain from thine appetites;[4] for wine and women will remove the wise; and he that cleaves to harlots will become more daring. Corruption and the worm shall inherit him, and he shall be held up as public example to greater shame."[5] And again—for he wearies not of doing good—"He who averts his eyes from pleasure crowns his life."

Non est ergo justum vinci a rebus venereis, nec libidinibus stolide inhiare, nec a ratione alienis appetitionibus moveri, nec desiderare pollui. Ei autem soli, qui uxorem duxit, ut qui tunc sit agricola, serere permissum est; quando tempus sementem admittit. Adversus aliam autem intemperantiam, optimum quidem est medicamentum, ratio. Fert etiam auxilium penuria satietatis, per quam accensæ libidines prosiliunt ad voluptates.

---

[1] Matt. xxii. 30. [2] That is, the Jewish. [3] 1 Cor. vi. 15.
[4] Ecclus. xviii. 30. [5] Ecclus. xix. 2, 3, 5.

CHAPTER XI.[1]

ON CLOTHES.

WHEREFORE neither are we to provide for ourselves costly clothing any more than variety of food. The Lord Himself, therefore, dividing His precepts into what relates to the body, the soul, and thirdly, external things, counsels us to provide external things on account of the body; and manages the body by the soul (ψυχή), and disciplines the soul, saying, "Take no thought for your life (ψυχῇ), what ye shall eat; nor yet for your body, what ye shall put on; for the life is more than meat, and the body more than raiment."[2] And He adds a plain example of instruction: "Consider the ravens: for they neither sow nor reap, which have neither storehouse nor barn; and God feedeth them."[3] "Are ye not better than the fowls?"[4] Thus far as to food. Similarly He enjoins with respect to clothing, which belongs to the third division, that of things external, saying, "Consider the lilies, how they spin not, nor weave. But I say unto you, that not even Solomon was arrayed as one of these."[5] And Solomon the king plumed himself exceedingly on his riches.

What, I ask, more graceful, more gay-coloured, than flowers? What, I say, more delightful than lilies or roses? "And if God so clothe the grass, which is to-day in the field, and to-morrow is cast into the oven, how much more will He clothe you, O ye of little faith!"[6] Here the particle *what* (τί) banishes variety in food. For this is shown from the

---

[1] Chap. xi. is not a separate chapter in the Greek, but appears as part of chap. x.
[2] Luke xii. 22, 23.   [3] Luke xii. 24.   [4] Luke xii. 24.
[5] Luke xii. 27.   [6] Luke xii. 28.

scripture, "Take no thought what things ye shall eat, or what things ye shall drink." For to take thought of these things argues greed and luxury. Now eating, considered merely by itself, is the sign of necessity; repletion, as we have said, of want. Whatever is beyond that, is the sign of superfluity. And what is superfluous, Scripture declares to be of the devil. The subjoined expression makes the meaning plain. For having said, "Seek not what ye shall eat, or what ye shall drink," He added, "Neither be ye of doubtful (or lofty)[1] mind." Now pride and luxury make men waverers (or raise them aloft) from the truth; and the voluptuousness, which indulges in superfluities, leads away from the truth. Wherefore He says very beautifully, "And all these things do the nations of the world seek after."[2] The nations are the dissolute and the foolish. And what are these things which He specifies? Luxury, voluptuousness, rich cooking, dainty feeding, gluttony. These are the "What?" And of bare sustenance, dry and moist, as being necessaries, He says, "Your Father knoweth that ye need these." And if, in a word, we are naturally given to seeking, let us not destroy the faculty of seeking by directing it to luxury, but let us excite it to the discovery of truth. For He says, "Seek ye the kingdom of God, and the materials of sustenance shall be added to you."

If, then, He takes away anxious care for clothes and food, and superfluities in general, as unnecessary; what are we to imagine ought to be said of love of ornament, and dyeing of wool, and variety of colours, and fastidiousness about gems, and exquisite working of gold, and still more, of artificial hair and wreathed curls; and furthermore, of staining the eyes, and plucking out hairs, and painting with rouge and white lead, and dyeing of the hair, and the wicked arts that are employed in such deceptions? May we not very well suspect, that what was quoted a little above respecting the grass, has been said of those unornamental lovers of ornaments? For the field is the world, and we who are bedewed by the grace of God are the grass; and though cut down, we

[1] μετίωρος. [2] Matt. vi. 32.

spring up again, as will be shown at greater length in the book *On the Resurrection*. But hay figuratively designates the vulgar rabble, attached to ephemeral pleasure, flourishing for a little, loving ornament, loving praise, and being everything but truth-loving, good for nothing but to be burned with fire. "There was a certain man," said the Lord, narrating, "very rich, who was clothed in purple and scarlet, enjoying himself splendidly every day." This was the hay. "And a certain poor man named Lazarus was laid at the rich man's gate, full of sores, desiring to be filled with the crumbs which fell from the rich man's table." This is the grass. Well, the rich man was punished in Hades, being made partaker of the fire; while the other flourished again in the Father's bosom. I admire that ancient city of the Lacedæmonians which permitted harlots alone to wear flowered clothes, and ornaments of gold, interdicting respectable women from love of ornament, and allowing courtesans alone to deck themselves. On the other hand, the archons of the Athenians, who affected a polished mode of life, forgetting their manhood, wore tunics reaching to the feet, and had on the crobulus—a kind of knot of the hair— adorned with a fastening of gold grasshoppers, to show their origin from the soil, forsooth, in the ostentation of licentiousness. Now rivalry of these archons extended also to the other Ionians, whom Homer, to show their effeminacy, calls "Long-robed." Those, therefore, who are devoted to the image of the beautiful, that is, love of finery, not the beautiful itself, and who under a fair name again practise idolatry, are to be banished far from the truth, as those who by opinion,[1] not knowledge, dream of the nature of the beautiful; and so life here is to them only a deep sleep of ignorance; from which it becomes us to rouse ourselves and haste to that which is truly beautiful and comely, and desire to grasp this alone, leaving the ornaments of earth to the world, and bidding them fare-

[1] Clement uses here Platonic language, δόξα meaning opinion established on no scientific basis, which may be true or may be false, and ἐπιστήμη knowledge sure and certain, because based on the reasons of things.

well before we fall quite asleep. I say, then, that man requires clothes for nothing else than the covering of the body, for defence against excess of cold and intensity of heat, lest the inclemency of the air injure us. And if this is the object of clothing, see that one kind be not assigned to men and another to women. For it is common to both to be covered, as it is to eat and drink. The necessity, then, being common, we judge that the provision ought to be similar. For as it is common to both to require things to cover them, so also their coverings ought to be similar; although such a covering ought to be assumed as is requisite for covering the eyes of women. For if the female sex, on account of their weakness, desire more, we ought to blame the habit of that evil training, by which often men reared up in bad habits become more effeminate than women. But this must not be yielded to. And if some accommodation is to be made, they may be permitted to use softer clothes, provided they put out of the way fabrics foolishly thin, and of curious texture in the weaving; bidding farewell to embroidery of gold and Indian silks and elaborate Bombyces (silks), which is at first a worm, then from it is produced a hairy caterpillar; after which the creature suffers a new transformation into a third form which they call larva, from which a long filament is produced, as the spider's thread from the spider. For these superfluous and diaphanous materials are the proof of a weak mind, covering as they do the shame of the body with a slender veil. For luxurious clothing, which cannot conceal the shape of the body, is no more a covering. For such clothing, falling close to the body, takes its form more easily, and adhering as it were to the flesh, receives its shape, and marks out the woman's figure, so that the whole make of the body is visible to spectators, though not seeing the body itself.

Dyeing of clothes is also to be rejected. For it is remote both from necessity and truth, in addition to the fact that reproach in manners springs from it. For the use of colours is not beneficial, for they are of no service against cold; nor has it anything for covering more than other clothing, except the opprobrium alone. And the agreeableness of the colour afflicts greedy eyes, inflaming them to senseless blindness. But for those who are white and unstained within, it is most suitable to use white and simple garments. Clearly and plainly, therefore, Daniel the prophet says, "Thrones were set, and upon them sat one like the Ancient of days, and His vesture was white as snow."[1] The Apocalypse says also that the Lord Himself appeared wearing such a robe. It says also, "I saw the souls of those that had witnessed, beneath the altar, and there was given to each a white robe."[2] And if it were necessary to seek for any other colour, the natural colour of truth should suffice. But garments which are like flowers are to be abandoned to Bacchic fooleries, and to those of the rites of initiation, along with purple and silver plate, as the comic poet says:

"Useful for tragedians, not for life."

And our life ought to be anything rather than a pageant. Therefore the dye of Sardis, and another of olive, and another green, a rose-coloured, and scarlet, and ten thousand other dyes, have been invented with much trouble for mischievous voluptuousness. Such clothing is for looking at, not for covering. Garments, too, variegated with gold, and those that are purple, and that piece of luxury which has its name from beasts (figured on it), and that saffron-coloured ointment-dipped robe, and those costly and many-coloured garments of flaring membranes, we are to bid farewell to, with the art itself. "For what prudent thing can these women have done," says the comedy, "who sit covered with flowers, wearing a saffron-coloured dress, painted?"

The Instructor expressly admonishes, "Boast not of the clothing of your garment, and be not elated on account of any glory, as it is unlawful."[3]

Accordingly, deriding those who are clothed in luxurious garments, He says in the Gospel: "Lo, they who live in gorgeous apparel and luxury are in earthly palaces."[4] He says in perishable palaces, where are love of display, love of popularity, and flattery and deceit. But those that wait at

[1] Dan. vii. 9.
[2] Rev. vi. 9, 11.
[3] Ecclus. xi. 4.
[4] Luke vii. 25.

the court of heaven around the King of all, are sanctified in the immortal vesture of the Spirit, that is, the flesh, and so put on incorruptibility.

As therefore she who is unmarried devotes herself to God alone, and her care is not divided, but the chaste married woman divides her life between God and her husband, while she who is otherwise disposed is devoted entirely to marriage, that is, to passion: in the same way I think the chaste wife, when she devotes herself to her husband, sincerely serves God; but when she becomes fond of finery, she falls away from God and from chaste wedlock, exchanging her husband for the world, after the fashion of that Argive courtesan, I mean Eriphyle,

"Who received gold prized above her dear husband."

Wherefore I admire the Ceian sophist,[1] who delineated like and suitable images of Virtue and Vice, representing the former of these, viz. Virtue, standing simply, white-robed and pure, adorned with modesty alone (for such ought to be the true wife, dowered with modesty). But the other, viz. Vice, on the contrary, he introduces dressed in superfluous attire, brightened up with colour not her own; and her gait and mien are depicted as studiously framed to give pleasure, forming a sketch of wanton women.

But he who follows the Word will not addict himself to any base pleasure; wherefore also what is useful in the article of dress is to be preferred. And if the Word, speaking of the Lord by David, sings, "The daughters of kings made Thee glad by honour; the queen stood at Thy right hand, clad in cloth of gold, girt with golden fringes," it is not luxurious raiment that he indicates; but he shows the immortal adornment, woven of faith, of those that have found mercy, that is, the church; in which the guileless Jesus shines conspicuous as gold, and the elect are the golden tassels. And if such must be woven[2] for the women, let us weave apparel pleasant and soft to the touch, not flowered, like pictures, to delight the

---

[1] Prodicus, of the island of Ceus.

[2] Or by a conjectural emendation of the text, "If in this we must relax somewhat in the case of women."

eye. For the picture fades in course of time, and the washing and steeping in the medicated juices of the dye wear away the wool, and render the fabrics of the garments weak; and this is not favourable to economy. It is the height of foolish ostentation to be in a flutter about peploi, and xystides, and ephaptides,[1] and "cloaks," and tunics, and "what covers shame," says Homer. For, in truth, I am ashamed when I see so much wealth lavished on the covering of the secret parts. For primeval man in paradise provided a covering for his shame of branches and leaves; and now, since sheep have been created for us, let us not be as silly as sheep, but trained by the Word, let us condemn sumptuousness of clothing, saying, "Ye are sheep's wool." Though Miletus boast, and Italy be praised, and the wool, about which many rave, be protected beneath skins,[2] yet are we not to set our hearts on it.

The blessed John, despising the locks of sheep as savouring of luxury, chose "camel's hair," and was clad in it, making himself an example of frugality and simplicity of life. For he also "ate locusts and wild honey,"[3] sweet and spiritual fare; preparing, as he was, the lowly and chaste ways of the Lord. For how possibly could he have worn a purple robe, who turned away from the pomp of cities, and retired to the solitude of the desert, to live in calmness with God, far from all frivolous pursuits—from all false show of good—from all meanness? Elias used a sheepskin mantle, and fastened the sheepskin with a girdle made of hair.[4] And Esaias, another prophet, was naked and barefooted,[5] and often was clad in sackcloth, the garb of humility. And if you call Jeremiah, he had only "a linen girdle."[6]

For as well-nurtured bodies, when stripped, show their vigour more manifestly, so also beauty of character shows its magnanimity, when not involved in ostentatious fooleries. But to drag one's clothes, letting them down to the soles of

---

[1] Various kinds of robes.
[2] Alluding to the practice of covering the fleeces of sheep with skins when the wool was very fine, to prevent it being soiled by exposure.
[3] Mark i. 6.   [4] 2 Chron. i. 8.   [5] Isa. xx. 2.   [6] Jer. xiii. 1.

his feet, is a piece of consummate foppery, impeding activity in walking, the garment sweeping the surface dirt of the ground like a broom; since even those emasculated creatures the dancers, who transfer their dumb shameless profligacy to the stage, do not despise the dress which flows away to such indignity; whose curious vestments, and appendages of fringes, and elaborate motions of figures, show the trailing of sordid effeminacy.

If one should adduce the garment of the Lord reaching down to the foot, that many-flowered coat shows the flowers of wisdom, the varied and unfading Scriptures, the oracles of the Lord, resplendent with the rays of truth. In such another robe the Spirit arrayed the Lord through David, when he sang thus: "Thou wert clothed with confession and comeliness, putting on light as a garment."[1]

As, then, in the fashioning of our clothes, we must keep clear of all strangeness, so in the use of them we must beware of extravagance. For neither is it seemly for the clothes to be above the knee, as they say was the case with the Lacedæmonian virgins; nor is it becoming for any part of a woman to be exposed. Though you may with great propriety use the language addressed to him who said, "Your arm is beautiful; yes, but it is not for the public gaze. Your thighs are beautiful; but, was the reply, for my husband alone. And your face is comely. Yes; but only for him who has married me." But I do not wish chaste women to afford cause for such praises to those who, by praises, hunt after grounds of censure; and not only because it is prohibited to expose the ankle, but because it has also been enjoined that the head should be veiled and the face covered; for it is a wicked thing for beauty to be a snare to men. Nor is it seemly for a woman to wish to make herself conspicuous, by using a purple veil. Would it were possible to abolish purple in dress, so as not to turn the eyes of spectators on the face of those that wear it! But the women, in the manufacture of all the rest of their dress, have made everything of purple, thus inflaming the lusts. And, in truth, those women who are crazy about

[1] Ps. civ. 2.

these stupid and luxurious purples, "purple (dark) death has seized,"[1] according to the poetic saying. On account of this purple, then, Tyre and Sidon, and the vicinity of the Lacedæmonian Sea, are very much desired; and their dyers and purple-fishers, and the purple fishes themselves, because their blood produces purple, are held in high esteem. But crafty women and effeminate men, who blend these deceptive dyes with dainty fabrics, carry their insane desires beyond all bounds, and export their fine linens no longer from Egypt, but some other kinds from the land of the Hebrews and the Cilicians. I say nothing of the linens made of Amorgos[2] and Byssus. Luxury has outstripped nomenclature.

The covering ought, in my judgment, to show that which is covered to be better than itself, as the image is superior to the temple, the soul to the body, and the body to the clothes. But now, quite the contrary, the body of these ladies, if sold, would never fetch a thousand Attic drachms. Buying, as they do, a single dress at the price of ten thousand talents, they prove themselves to be of less use and less value than cloth. Why in the world do you seek after what is rare and costly, in preference to what is at hand and cheap? It is because you know not what is really beautiful, what is really good, and seek with eagerness shows instead of realities, from fools who, like people out of their wits, imagine black to be white.

[1] *Iliad*, v. 88.   [2] Flax grown in the island of Amorgos.

CHAPTER XII.

ON SHOES.

OMEN fond of display act in the same manner with regard to shoes, showing also in this matter great luxuriousness. Base, in truth, are those sandals on which golden ornaments are fastened; but they are thought worth having nails driven into the soles in winding rows. Many, too, carve on them amorous embraces, as if they would by their walk communicate to the earth harmonious movement, and impress on it the wantonness of their spirit. Farewell, therefore, must be bidden to gold-plated and jewelled mischievous devices of sandals, and Attic and Sicyonian half-boots, and Persian and Tyrrhenian buskins; and setting before us the right aim, as is the habit with our truth, we are bound to select what is in accordance with nature.

For the use of shoes is partly for covering, partly for defence in case of stumbling against objects, and for saving the sole of the foot from the roughnesses of hilly paths.

Women are to be allowed a white shoe, except when on a journey, and then a greased shoe must be used. When on a journey, they require nailed shoes. Further, they ought for the most part to wear shoes; for it is not suitable for the foot to be shown naked: besides, woman is a tender thing, easily hurt. But for a man bare feet are quite in keeping, except when he is on military service. "For being shod is near neighbour to being bound."[1]

To go with bare feet is most suitable for exercise, and best

---

[1] ὑποδεῖσθαι τῷ δεδέσθαι. "Wearing boots is near neighbour to wearing bonds."

adapted for health and ease, unless where necessity prevents. But if we are not on a journey, and cannot endure bare feet, we may use slippers or white shoes; dusty-foots[1] the Attics called them, on account of their bringing the feet near the dust, as I think. As a witness for simplicity in shoes let John suffice, who avowed that "he was not worthy to unloose the latchet of the Lord's shoes."[2] For he who exhibited to the Hebrews the type of the true philosophy wore no elaborate shoes. What else this may imply, will be shown elsewhere.

[1] κονίποδις.   [2] Mark i. 7; Luke iii. 16.

CHAPTER XIII.

AGAINST EXCESSIVE FONDNESS FOR JEWELS AND GOLD ORNAMENTS.

T is childish to admire excessively dark or green stones, and things cast out by the sea on foreign shores, particles of the earth. For to rush after stones that are pellucid and of peculiar colours, and stained glass, is only characteristic of silly people, who are attracted by things that have a striking show. Thus children, on seeing the fire, rush to it, attracted by its brightness; not understanding through senselessness the danger of touching it. Such is the case with the stones which silly women wear fastened to chains and set in necklaces, amethysts, ceraunites, jaspers, topaz, and the Milesian

"Emerald, most precious ware."

And the highly prized pearl has invaded the women's apartments to an extravagant extent. This is produced in a kind of oyster like mussels, and is about the bigness of a fish's eye of large size. And the wretched creatures are not ashamed at having bestowed the greatest pains about this little oyster, when they might adorn themselves with the sacred jewel, the Word of God, whom the Scripture has somewhere called a pearl, the pure and pellucid Jesus, the eye that watches in the flesh,—the transparent Word, by whom the flesh, regenerated by water, becomes precious. For that oyster that is in the water covers the flesh all round, and out of it is produced the pearl.

We have heard, too, that the Jerusalem above is walled with sacred stones; and we allow that the twelve gates of the celestial city, by being made like precious stones, indicate the transcendent grace of the apostolic voice. For the colours are laid on in precious stones, and these colours are precious; while the other parts remain of earthy material. With these symbolically, as is meet, the city of the saints, which is spiritually built, is walled. By that brilliancy of stones, therefore, is meant the inimitable brilliancy of the spirit, the immortality and sanctity of being. But these women, who comprehend not the symbolism of Scripture, gape all they can for jewels, adducing the astounding apology, "Why may I not use what God hath exhibited?" and, "I have it by me, why may I not enjoy it?" and, "For whom were these things made, then, if not for us?" Such are the utterances of those who are totally ignorant of the will of God. For first necessaries, such as water and air, He supplies free to all; and what is not necessary He has hid in the earth and water. Wherefore ants dig, and griffins guard gold, and the sea hides the pearl-stone. But ye busy yourselves about what you need not. Behold, the whole heaven is lighted up, and ye seek not God; but gold which is hidden, and jewels, are dug up by those among us who are condemned to death.

But you also oppose Scripture, seeing it expressly cries, "Seek first the kingdom of heaven, and all these things shall be added unto you."[1] But if all things have been conferred on you, and all things allowed you, and "if all things are lawful, yet all things are not expedient,"[2] says the apostle. God brought our race into communion by first imparting what was His own, when He gave His own Word, common to all, and made all things for all. All things therefore are common, and not for the rich to appropriate an undue share. That expression, therefore, "I possess, and possess in abundance: why then should I not enjoy?" is suitable neither to the man, nor to society. But more worthy of love is that: "I have: why should I not give to those who need?" For such an one—one who fulfils the command, "Thou shalt love thy neighbour as thyself"—is perfect. For this is the true luxury —the treasured wealth. But that which is squandered on foolish lusts is to be reckoned waste, not expenditure. For

[1] Matt. vi. 33.   [2] 1 Cor. x. 23.

God has given to us, I know well, the liberty of use, but only so far as necessary; and He has determined that the use should be common. And it is monstrous for one to live in luxury, while many are in want. How much more glorious is it to do good to many, than to live sumptuously! How much wiser to spend money on human beings, than on jewels and gold! How much more useful to acquire decorous friends, than lifeless ornaments! Whom have lands ever benefited so much as conferring favours has? It remains for us, therefore, to do away with this allegation: Who, then, will have the more sumptuous things, if all select the simpler? Men, I would say, if they make use of them impartially and indifferently. But if it be impossible for all to exercise self-restraint, yet, with a view to the use of what is necessary, we must seek after what can be most readily procured, bidding a long farewell to these superfluities.

In fine, they must accordingly utterly cast off ornaments as girls' gewgaws, rejecting adornment itself entirely. For they ought to be adorned within, and show the inner woman beautiful. For in the soul alone are beauty and deformity shown. Wherefore also only the virtuous man is really beautiful and good. And it is laid down as a dogma, that only the beautiful is good. And excellence alone appears through the beautiful body, and blossoms out in the flesh, exhibiting the amiable comeliness of self-control, whenever the character like a beam of light gleams in the form. For the beauty of each plant and animal consists in its individual excellence. And the excellence of man is righteousness, and temperance, and manliness, and godliness. The beautiful man is, then, he who is just, temperate, and in a word, good, not he who is rich. But now even the soldiers wish to be decked with gold, not having read that poetical saying:

" With childish folly to the war he came,
Laden with store of gold."[1]

But the love of ornament, which is far from caring for virtue, but claims the body for itself, when the love of the beautiful has changed to empty show, is to be utterly expelled.

[1] *Iliad*, ii. 872.

For applying things unsuitable to the body, as if they were suitable, begets a practice of lying and a habit of falsehood; and shows not what is decorous, simple, and truly childlike, but what is pompous, luxurious, and effeminate. But these women obscure true beauty, shading it with gold. And they know not how great is their transgression, in fastening around themselves ten thousand rich chains; as they say that among the barbarians malefactors are bound with gold. The women seem to me to emulate these rich prisoners. For is not the golden necklace a collar, and do not the necklets which they call catheters occupy the place of chains? and indeed among the Attics they are called by this very name. The ungraceful things round the feet of women, Philemon in the *Synephebus* called ankle-fetters:

"Conspicuous garments, and a kind of a golden fetter."

What else, then, is this coveted adorning of yourselves, O ladies, but the exhibiting of yourselves fettered? For if the material does away with the reproach, the endurance [of your fetters] is a thing indifferent. To me, then, those who voluntarily put themselves into bonds seem to glory in rich calamities.

Perchance also it is such chains that the poetic fable says were thrown around Aphrodite when committing adultery, referring to ornaments as nothing but the badge of adultery. For Homer called those, too, golden chains. But now women are not ashamed to wear the most manifest badges of the evil one. For as the serpent deceived Eve, so also has ornament of gold maddened other women to vicious practices, using as a bait the form of the serpent, and by fashioning lampreys and serpents for decoration. Accordingly the comic poet Nicostratus says, "Chains, collars, rings, bracelets, serpents, anklets, ear-rings."[1]

In terms of strongest censure, therefore, Aristophanes in the *Thesmophoriazousæ* exhibits the whole array of female ornament in a catalogue:

---

[1] Ἑλλόβιον by conjecture, as more suitable to the connection than Ἑλλίβορον or Ἑλίβορον, Hellebore of the MS., though Hellebore may be intended as a comic ending.

> "Snoods, fillets, natron, and steel;
> Pumice-stone, band, back-band,
> Back-veil, paint, necklaces,
> Paints for the eyes, soft garment, hair-net,
> Girdle, shawl, fine purple border,
> Long robe, tunic, Barathrum, round tunic."

But I have not yet mentioned the principal of them. Then what?

> "Ear-pendants, jewellery, ear-rings;
> Mallow-coloured cluster-shaped anklets;
> Buckles, clasps, necklets,
> Fetters, seals, chains, rings, powders,
> Bosses, bands, olisbi, Sardian stones,
> Fans, helicters."

I am weary and vexed at enumerating the multitude of ornaments; and I am compelled to wonder how those who bear such a burden are not worried to death. O foolish trouble! O silly craze for display! They squander meretriciously wealth on what is disgraceful; and in their love for ostentation disfigure God's gifts, emulating the art of the evil one. The rich man hoarding up in his barns, and saying to himself, "Thou hast much goods laid up for many years; eat, drink, be merry," the Lord in the Gospel plainly called "fool." "For this night they shall take of thee thy soul; whose then shall those things which thou hast prepared be?"[1]

Apelles, the painter, seeing one of his pupils painting a figure loaded with gold colour to represent Helen, said to him, "Boy, being incapable of painting her beautiful, you have made her rich."

Such Helens are the ladies of the present day, not truly beautiful, but richly got up. To these the Spirit prophesies by Zephaniah: "And their silver and their gold shall not be able to deliver them in the day of the Lord's anger."[2]

But for those women who have been trained under Christ, it is suitable to adorn themselves not with gold, but with the Word, through whom alone the gold comes to light.[3]

---

[1] Luke vii. 19, 20.   [2] Zeph. i. 18.

[3] Logos is identified with reason; and it is by reason, or the ingenuity of man, that gold is discovered and brought to light.

Happy, then, would have been the ancient Hebrews, had they cast away their women's ornaments, or only melted them; but having cast their gold into the form of an ox, and paid it idolatrous worship, they consequently reaped no advantage either from their art or their attempt. But they taught our women most expressively to keep clear of ornaments. The lust which commits fornication with gold becomes an idol, and is tested by fire; for which alone luxury is reserved, as being an idol, not a reality.[1] Hence the Word, upbraiding the Hebrews by the prophet, says, "They made to Baal things of silver and gold," that is, ornaments. And most distinctly threatening, He says, "I will punish her for the days of Baalim, in which they offered sacrifice for her, and she put on her ear-rings and her necklaces."[2] And He subjoined the cause of the adornment, when He said, "And she went after her lovers, but forgot me, saith the Lord."[3]

Resigning, therefore, these baubles to the wicked master of cunning himself, let us not take part in this meretricious adornment, nor commit idolatry through a specious pretext. Most admirably, therefore, the blessed Peter[4] says, "In like manner also, that women adorn themselves not with braids, or gold, or costly array, but (which becometh women professing godliness) with good works." For it is with reason that he bids decking of themselves to be kept far from them. For, granting that they are beautiful, nature suffices. Let not art contend against nature; that is, let not falsehood strive with truth. And if they are by nature ugly, they are convicted, by the things they apply to themselves, of what they do not possess [*i.e.* of the want of beauty]. It is suitable, therefore, for women who serve Christ to adopt simplicity. For in reality simplicity provides for sanctity, by reducing redundancies to equality, and by furnishing from whatever is at hand the enjoyment sought from superfluities. For simplicity, as the name shows, is not conspicuous, is not inflated

---

[1] εἴδωλον, an appearance, an image. [2] Hos. ii. 8. [3] Hos. ii. 13.
[4] By mistake for Paul. Clement quotes here, as often, from memory (1 Tim. ii. 9, 10).

or puffed up in aught, but is altogether even, and gentle, and equal, and free of excess, and so is sufficient. And sufficiency is a condition which reaches its proper end without excess or defect. The mother of these is Justice, and their nurse "Independence;" and this is a condition which is satisfied with what is necessary, and by itself furnishes what contributes to the blessed life.

Let there, then, be in the fruits of thy hands, sacred order, liberal communication, and acts of economy. "For he that giveth to the poor, lendeth to God."[1] "And the hands of the manly shall be enriched."[2] Manly He calls those who despise wealth, and are free in bestowing it. And on your feet let active readiness to well-doing appear, and a journeying to righteousness. Modesty and chastity are collars and necklaces; such are the chains which God forges. "Happy is the man who hath found wisdom, and the mortal who knows understanding," says the Spirit by Solomon: "for it is better to buy her than treasures of gold and silver; and she is more valuable than precious stones."[3] For she is the true decoration.

And let not their ears be pierced, contrary to nature, in order to attach to them ear-rings and ear-drops. For it is not right to force nature against her wishes. Nor could there be any better ornament for the ears than true instruction, which finds its way naturally into the passages of hearing. And eyes anointed by the Word, and ears pierced for perception, make a man a hearer and contemplator of divine and sacred things, the Word truly exhibiting the true beauty "which eye hath not seen nor ear heard before."[4]

[1] Prov. xix. 17.
[2] Prov. x. 4.
[3] Prov. iii. 13–15.
[4] 1 Cor. ii. 9.

BOOK III.

CHAPTER I.

ON THE TRUE BEAUTY.

IT is then, as appears, the greatest of all lessons to know one's self. For if one knows himself, he will know God; and knowing God, he will be made like God, not by wearing gold or long robes, but by well-doing, and by requiring as few things as possible.

Now, God alone is in need of nothing, and rejoices most when He sees us bright with the ornament of intelligence; and then, too, rejoices in him who is arrayed in chastity, the sacred stole of the body. Since then the soul consists of three divisions; the intellect, which is called the reasoning faculty, is the inner man, which is the ruler of this man that is seen. And that one, in another respect, God guides. But the irascible part, being brutal, dwells near to insanity. And appetite, which is the third department, is many-shaped above Proteus, the varying sea-god, who changed himself now into one shape, now into another; and it allures to adulteries, to licentiousness, to seductions.

"At first he was a lion with ample beard."[1]

While he yet retained the ornament, the hair of the chin showed him to be a man.

"But after that a serpent, a pard, or a big sow."

Love of ornament has degenerated to wantonness. A man no longer appears like a strong wild beast,

"But he became moist water, and a tree of lofty branches."

Passions break out, pleasures overflow; beauty fades, and

[1] *Odyss.* iv. 457.

falls quicker than the leaf on the ground, when the amorous storms of lust blow on it before the coming of autumn, and is withered by destruction. For lust becomes and fabricates all things, and wishes to cheat, so as to conceal the man. But that man with whom the Word dwells does not alter himself, does not get himself up: he has the form which is of the Word; he is made like to God; he is beautiful; he does not ornament himself: his is beauty, the true beauty, for it is God; and that man becomes God, since God so wills. Heraclitus, then, rightly said, "Men are gods, and gods are men." For the Word Himself is the manifest mystery: God in man, and man God. And the Mediator executes the Father's will; for the Mediator is the Word, who is common to both—the Son of God, the Saviour of men; His Servant, our Teacher. And the flesh being a slave, as Paul testifies, how can one with any reason adorn the handmaid like a pimp? For that which is of flesh has the form of a servant. Paul says, speaking of the Lord, "Because He emptied Himself, taking the form of a servant,"[1] calling the outward man servant, previous to the Lord becoming a servant and wearing flesh. But the compassionate God Himself set the flesh free, and, releasing it from destruction, and from bitter and deadly bondage, endowed it with incorruptibility, arraying the flesh in this, the holy embellishment of eternity—immortality.

There is, too, another beauty of men—love. "And love," according to the apostle, "suffers long, and is kind; envieth not; vaunteth not itself, is not puffed up."[2] For the decking of one's self out—carrying, as it does, the look of superfluity and uselessness—is vaunting one's self. Wherefore he adds, "doth not behave itself unseemly:" for a figure which is not one's own, and is against nature, is unseemly; but what is artificial is not one's own, as is clearly explained: "seeketh not," it is said, "what is not her own." For truth calls that its own which belongs to it; but the love of finery seeks what is not its own, being apart from God, and the Word, from love.

And that the Lord Himself was uncomely in aspect, the

[1] Phil. ii. 7. [2] 1 Cor. xiii. 4.

Spirit testifies by Esaias: "And we saw Him, and He had no form nor comeliness; but His form was mean, inferior to men."[1] Yet who was more admirable than the Lord? But it was not the beauty of the flesh visible to the eye, but the true beauty of both soul and body, which He exhibited, which in the former is beneficence; in the latter—that is, the flesh—immortality.

[1] Isa. liii. 2, 3.

CHAPTER II.

AGAINST EMBELLISHING THE BODY.

IT is not, then, the aspect of the outward man, but the soul that is to be decorated with the ornament of goodness; we may say also the flesh with the adornment of temperance. But those women who beautify the outside, are unawares all waste in the inner depths, as is the case with the ornaments of the Egyptians; among whom temples with their porticos and vestibules are carefully constructed, and groves and sacred fields adjoining; the halls are surrounded with many pillars; and the walls gleam with foreign stones, and there is no want of artistic painting; and the temples gleam with gold, and silver, and amber, and glitter with parti-coloured gems from India and Ethiopia; and the shrines are veiled with gold-embroidered hangings.

But if you enter the penetralia of the enclosure, and, in haste to behold something better, seek the image that is the inhabitant of the temple, and if any priest of those that offer sacrifice there, looking grave, and singing a pæan in the Egyptian tongue, remove a little of the veil to show the god, he will give you a hearty laugh at the object of worship. For the deity that is sought, to whom you have rushed, will not be found within, but a cat, or a crocodile, or a serpent of the country, or some such beast unworthy of the temple, but quite worthy of a den, a hole, or the dirt. The god of the Egyptians appears a beast rolling on a purple couch.

So those women who wear gold, occupying themselves in curling at their locks, and engaged in anointing their cheeks, painting their eyes, and dyeing their hair, and practising the other pernicious arts of luxury, decking the covering of flesh, —in truth, imitate the Egyptians, in order to attract their infatuated lovers.

But if one withdraw the veil of the temple, — I mean the head-dress, the dye, the clothes, the gold, the paint, the cosmetics,—that is, the web consisting of them, the veil, with the view of finding within the true beauty, he will be disgusted, I know well. For he will not find the image of God dwelling within, as is meet; but instead of it a fornicator and adulteress has occupied the shrine of the soul. And the true beast will thus be detected—an ape smeared with white paint. And that deceitful serpent, devouring the understanding part of man through vanity, has the soul as its hole, filling all with deadly poisons; and injecting his own venom of deception, this pander of a dragon has changed women into whores. For love of display is not for a lady, but a courtesan. Such women care little for keeping at home with their husbands; but loosing their husbands' purse-strings, they spend its supplies on their lusts, that they may have many witnesses of their seemingly fair appearance; and, devoting the whole day to their toilet, they spend their time with their bought slaves. Accordingly they season the flesh like a pernicious sauce; and the day they bestow on the toilet shut up in their rooms, so as not to be caught decking themselves. But in the evening this spurious beauty creeps out to candlelight as out of a hole; for drunkenness and the dimness of the light aid what they have put on. The woman who dyes her hair yellow, Menander the comic poet expels from the house:

"Now get out of this house, for no chaste
Woman ought to make her hair yellow,"

nor, I would add, stain her cheeks, nor paint her eyes. Unawares the poor wretches destroy their own beauty, by the introduction of what is spurious. At the dawn of day, mangling, racking, and plastering themselves over with certain compositions, they chill the skin, furrow the flesh with poisons, and with curiously prepared washes, thus blighting their own beauty. Wherefore they are seen to be yellow from the use of cosmetics, and susceptible to disease, their flesh, which has been shaded with poisons, being now in a melting state. So they dishonour the Creator of men, as if the beauty given by Him were nothing worth. As you might expect, they become lazy in housekeeping, sitting like painted things to be looked at, not as if made for domestic economy. Wherefore in the comic poet the sensible woman says, "What can we women do wise or brilliant, who sit with hair dyed yellow, outraging the character of gentlewomen; causing the overthrow of houses, the ruin of nuptials, and accusations on the part of children?"[1] In the same way, Antiphanes the comic poet, in *Malthaca*, ridicules the meretriciousness of women in words that apply to them all, and are framed against the rubbing of themselves with cosmetics, saying:

"She comes,
She goes back, she approaches, she goes back.
She has come, she is here, she washes herself, she advances,
She is soaped, she is combed, she goes out, is rubbed,
She washes herself, looks in the glass, robes herself,
Anoints herself, decks herself, besmears herself;
And if aught is wrong, chokes [with vexation]."

Thrice, I say, not once, do they deserve to perish, who use crocodiles' excrement, and anoint themselves with the froth of putrid humours, and stain their eyebrows with soot, and rub their cheeks with white lead.

These, then, who are disgusting even to the heathen poets for their fashions, how shall they not be rejected by the truth? Accordingly another comic poet, Alexis, reproves them. For I shall adduce his words, which with extravagance of statement shame the obstinacy of their impudence. For he was not very far beyond the mark. And I cannot for shame come to the assistance of women held up to such ridicule in comedy.

Then she ruins her husband.

"For first, in comparison with gain and the spoiling of neighbours,
All else is in their eyes superfluous."

"Is one of them little? She stitches cork into her shoe-sole.
Is one tall? She wears a thin sole,
And goes out keeping her head down on her shoulder:

---

[1] Aristophanes, *Lysistrata*.

This takes away from her height. Has one no flanks?
She has something sewed on to her, so that the spectators
May exclaim on her fine shape behind. Has she a prominent stomach?
By making additions, to render it straight, such as the nurses we see
    in the comic poets,
She draws back, as it were, by these poles, the protuberance of the
    stomach in front.
Has one yellow eyebrows? She stains them with soot.
Do they happen to be black? She smears them with ceruse.
Is one very white-skinned? She rouges.
Has one any part of the body beautiful? She shows it bare.
Has she beautiful teeth? She must needs laugh,
That those present may see what a pretty mouth she has;
But if not in the humour for laughing, she passes the day within,
With a slender sprig of myrtle between her lips,
Like what cooks have always at hand when they have goats' heads to
    sell,
So that she must keep them apart the whilst, whether she will or not."

I set these quotations from the comic poets before you, since the Word most strenuously wishes to save us. And by and by I will fortify them with the divine Scriptures. For he who does not escape notice is wont to abstain from sins, on account of the shame of reproof. Just as the plastered hand and the anointed eye exhibit from their very look the suspicion of a person in illness, so also cosmetics and dyes indicate that the soul is deeply diseased.

The divine Instructor enjoins us not to approach to another's river, meaning by the figurative expression "another's river," "another's wife;" the wanton that flows to all, and out of licentiousness gives herself up to meretricious enjoyment with all. "Abstain from water that is another's," He says, "and drink not of another's well," admonishing us to shun the stream of "voluptuousness," that we may live long, and that years of life may be added to us;[1] both by not hunting after the pleasure that belongs to another, and by diverting our inclinations.

Love of dainties and love of wine, though great vices, are not of such magnitude as fondness for finery. "A full table and repeated cups" are enough to satisfy greed.

[1] Prov. ix. 18.

But to those who are fond of gold, and purple, and jewels, neither the gold that is above the earth and below it is sufficient, nor the Tyrian Sea, nor the freight that comes from India and Ethiopia, nor yet Pactolus flowing with gold; not even were a man to become a Midas would he be satisfied, but would be still poor, craving other wealth. Such people are ready to die with their gold.

And if Plutus [1] is blind, are not those women that are crazy about him, and have a fellow-feeling with him, blind too? Having, then, no limit to their lust, they push on to shamelessness. For the theatre, and pageants, and many spectators, and strolling in the temples, and loitering in the streets, that they may be seen conspicuously by all, are necessary to them. For those that glory in their looks, not in heart,[2] dress to please others. For as the brand shows the slave, so do gaudy colours the adulteress. "For though thou clothe thyself in scarlet, and deck thyself with ornaments of gold, and anoint thine eyes with stibium, in vain is thy beauty,"[3] says the Word by Jeremiah. Is it not monstrous, that while horses, birds, and the rest of the animals, spring and bound from the grass and meadows, rejoicing in ornament that is their own, in mane, and natural colour, and varied plumage; woman, as if inferior to the brute creation, should think herself so unlovely as to need foreign, and bought, and painted beauty?

Head-dresses and varieties of head-dresses, and elaborate braidings, and infinite modes of dressing the hair, and costly specimens of mirrors, in which they arrange their costume,— hunting after those that, like silly children, are crazy about their figures,—are characteristic of women who have lost all sense of shame. If any one were to call these courtesans, he would make no mistake, for they turn their faces into masks. But us the Word enjoins "to look not on the things that are seen, but the things that are not seen; for the things that are seen are temporal, but the things that are not seen are eternal."[4]

But what passes beyond the bounds of absurdity, is that

---

[1] Wealth.   [2] 1 Thess. ii. 17.   [3] Jer. iv. 30.   [4] 2 Cor. iv. 18.

they have invented mirrors for this artificial shape of theirs, as if it were some excellent work or masterpiece. The deception rather requires a veil thrown over it. For as the Greek fable has it, it was not a fortunate thing for the beautiful Narcissus to have been the beholder of his own image. And if Moses commanded men to make not an image to represent God by art, how can these women be right, who by their own reflection produce an imitation of their own likeness, in order to the falsifying of their face? Likewise also, when Samuel the prophet was sent to anoint one of the sons of Jesse for king, and on seeing the eldest of his sons to be fair and tall, produced the anointing oil, being delighted with him, the Lord said to him, "Look not to his appearance, nor the height of his stature: for I have rejected him. For man looketh on the eyes, but the Lord into the heart." [1]

And he anointed not him that was comely in person, but him that was comely in soul. If, then, the Lord counts the natural beauty of the body inferior to that of the soul, what thinks He of spurious beauty, rejecting utterly as He does all falsehood? "For we walk by faith, not by sight." [2] Very clearly the Lord accordingly teaches by Abraham, that he who follows God must despise country, and relations, and possessions, and all wealth, by making him a stranger. And therefore also He called him His friend, who had despised the substance which he had possessed at home. For he was of good parentage, and very opulent; and so with three hundred and eighteen servants of his own he subdued the four kings who had taken Lot captive.

Esther alone we find justly adorned. The spouse adorned herself mystically for her royal husband; but her beauty turns out the redemption price of a people that were about to be massacred. And that decoration makes women courtesans, and men effeminate and adulterers, the tragic poet is a witness; thus discoursing:

"He that judged the goddesses,
As the myth of the Argives has it, having come from Phrygia

---

[1] 1 Sam. xvi. 7.   [2] 2 Cor. v. 7.

> To Lacedæmon, arrayed in flowery vestments,
> Glittering with gold and barbaric luxury,
> Loving, departed, carrying away her he loved,
> Helen, to the folds of Ida, having found that
> Menelaus was away from home."[1]

O adulterous beauty! Barbarian finery and effeminate luxury overthrew Greece; Lacedæmonian chastity was corrupted by clothes, and luxury, and graceful beauty; barbaric display proved Jove's daughter a courtesan.

They had no instructor to restrain their lusts, nor one to say, "Do not commit adultery;" nor, "Lust not;" or, "Travel not by lust into adultery;" or further, "Influence not thy passions by desire of adornment."

What an end was it that ensued to them, and what woes they endured, who would not restrain their self-will! Two continents were convulsed by unrestrained pleasures, and all was thrown into confusion by a barbarian boy. The whole of Hellas puts to sea; the ocean is burdened with the weight of continents; a protracted war breaks out, and fierce battles are waged, and the plains are crowded with dead: the barbarian assails the fleet with outrage; wickedness prevails, and the eye of that poetic Jove looks on the Thracians:

> "The barbarian plains drink noble blood,
> And the streams of the rivers are choked with dead bodies."

Breasts are beaten in lamentations, and grief desolates the land; and all the feet, and the summits of many-fountained Ida, and the cities of the Trojans, and the ships of the Achæans, shake.

Where, O Homer, shall we flee and stand? Show us a spot of ground that is not shaken!

> "Touch not the reins, inexperienced boy,
> Nor mount the seat, not having learned to drive."[2]

Heaven delights in two charioteers, by whom alone the chariot of fire is guided. For the mind is carried away by pleasure; and the unsullied principle of reason, when not instructed by the Word, slides down into licentiousness, and gets a fall as the due reward of its transgression. An example

---

[1] *Iphigenia in Aulis*, 71. [2] *Phaethon* of Euripides.

of this are the angels, who renounced the beauty of God for a beauty which fades, and so fell from heaven to earth.[1]

The Shechemites, too, were punished by an overthrow for dishonouring the holy virgin. The grave was their punishment, and the monument of their ignominy leads to salvation.

[1] Gen. vi. 1, 2.

CHAPTER III.

AGAINST MEN WHO EMBELLISH THEMSELVES.

TO such an extent, then, has luxury advanced, that not only are the female sex deranged about this frivolous pursuit, but men also are infected with the disease. For not being free of the love of finery, they are not in health; but inclining to voluptuousness, they become effeminate, cutting their hair in an ungentlemanly and meretricious way, clothed in fine and transparent garments, chewing mastich, smelling of perfume. What can one say on seeing them? Like one who judges people by their foreheads, he will divine them to be adulterers and effeminate, addicted to both kinds of venery, haters of hair, destitute of hair, detesting the bloom of manliness, and adorning their locks like women. "Living for unholy acts of audacity, these fickle wretches do reckless and nefarious deeds," says the Sibyl. For their service the towns are full of those who take out hair by pitch-plasters, shave, and pluck out hairs from these womanish creatures. And shops are erected and opened everywhere; and adepts at this meretricious fornication make a deal of money openly by those who plaster themselves, and give their hair to be pulled out in all ways by those who make it their trade, feeling no shame before the onlookers or those who approach, nor before themselves, being men. Such are those addicted to base passions, whose whole body is made smooth by the violent tuggings of pitch-plasters. It is utterly impossible to get beyond such effrontery. If nothing is left undone by them, neither shall anything be left unspoken by me. Diogenes, when he was being sold, chiding like a teacher one of these degenerate creatures, said very manfully, "Come, youngster, buy for yourself a man," chastising his meretriciousness by an ambiguous speech. But for those who are men to shave and smooth themselves, how ignoble! As for dyeing of hair, and anointing of grey locks, and dyeing them yellow, these are practices of abandoned effeminates; and their feminine combing of themselves is a thing to be let alone. For they think, that like serpents they divest themselves of the old age of their head by painting and renovating themselves. But though they do doctor the hair cleverly, they will not escape wrinkles, nor will they elude death by tricking time. For it is not dreadful, it is not dreadful to appear old, when you are not able to shut your eyes to the fact that you are so.

The more, then, a man hastes to the end, the more truly venerable is he, having God alone as his senior, since He is the eternal aged One, He who is older than all things. Prophecy has called him the "Ancient of days; and the hair of His head was as pure wool," says the prophet.[1] "And none other," says the Lord, "can make the hair white or black."[2] How, then, do these godless ones work in rivalry with God, or rather violently oppose Him, when they transmute the hair made white by Him? "The crown of old men is great experience,"[3] says Scripture; and the hoary hair of their countenance is the blossom of large experience. But these dishonour the reverence of age, the head covered with grey hairs. It is not, it is not possible for him to show the soul true who has a fraudulent head. "But ye have not so learned Christ; if so be that ye have heard Him, and have been taught by Him, as the truth is in Jesus: that ye put off, concerning the former conversation, the old man (not the hoary man, but him that is) corrupt according to deceitful lusts; and be renewed (not by dyeings and ornaments), but in the spirit of your mind; and put on the new man, which after God is created in righteousness and true holiness."[4]

But for one who is a man to comb himself and shave himself with a razor, for the sake of fine effect, to arrange his hair at the looking-glass, to shave his cheeks, pluck hairs out

[1] Dan. vii. 9.   [2] Matt. v. 36.
[3] Ecclus. xxv. 6.   [4] Eph. iv. 20-24.

of them, and smooth them, how womanly! And, in truth, unless you saw them naked, you would suppose them to be women. For although not allowed to wear gold, yet out of effeminate desire they enwreath their latches and fringes with leaves of gold; or, getting certain spherical figures of the same metal made, they fasten them to their ankles, and hang them from their necks. This is a device of enervated men, who are dragged to the women's apartments, amphibious and lecherous beasts. For this is a meretricious and impious form of snare. For God wished women to be smooth, and rejoice in their locks alone growing spontaneously, as a horse in his mane; but has adorned man, like the lions, with a beard, and endowed him, as an attribute of manhood, with shaggy breasts,—a sign this of strength and rule. So also cocks, which fight in defence of the hens, he has decked with combs, as it were helmets; and so high a value does God set on these locks, that He orders them to make their appearance on men simultaneously with discretion, and, delighted with a venerable look, has honoured gravity of countenance with grey hairs. But wisdom, and discriminating judgments that are hoary with wisdom, attain maturity with time, and by the vigour of long experience give strength to old age, producing grey hairs, the admirable flower of venerable wisdom, conciliating confidence. This, then, the mark of the man, the beard, by which he is seen to be a man, is older than Eve, and is the token of the superior nature. In this God deemed it right that he should excel, and dispersed hair over man's whole body. Whatever smoothness and softness was in him He abstracted from his side when He formed the woman Eve, adapted to the reception of seed, his help in generation and household management, while he (for he had parted with all smoothness) remained a man, and shows himself man. And to him has been assigned action, as to her suffering; for what is shaggy is drier and warmer than what is smooth. Wherefore males have both more hair and more heat than females, animals that are entire than the emasculated, perfect than imperfect. It is therefore impious to desecrate the symbol of manhood, hairiness. But the embellishment of smoothing (for I am warned by the Word), if it is to attract men, is the act of an effeminate person,—if to attract women, is the act of an adulterer; and both must be driven as far as possible from our society. "But the very hairs of your head are all numbered," says the Lord;[1] those on the chin, too, are numbered, and those on the whole body. There must be therefore no plucking out, contrary to God's appointment, which has counted[2] them in according to His will. "Know ye not yourselves," says the apostle, "that Christ Jesus is in you?"[3] Whom, had we known as dwelling in us, I know not how we could have dared to dishonour. But the using of pitch to pluck out hair (I shrink from even mentioning the shamelessness connected with this process), and in the act of bending back and bending down, the uncovering openly of nature's unmentionable parts, stepping out and bending backwards in shameful postures, yet not ashamed of themselves, conducting themselves without shame in the midst of the youth, and in the gymnasium, where the prowess of man is tested: the following of this unnatural practice, is it not the extreme of licentiousness? For those who engage in such practices in public will scarcely behave with modesty to any at home. Their want of shame in public attests their unbridled licentiousness in private. For he who in the light of day denies his manhood, will prove himself manifestly a woman by night. "There shall not be," said the Word by Moses, "a harlot of the daughters of Israel; there shall not be a fornicator of the sons of Israel."[4]

But the pitch does good, it is said. Nay, it defames, say I. No one who entertains right sentiments would wish to appear a fornicator, were he not the victim of that vice, and study to defame the beauty of his form. No one would, I say, voluntarily choose to do this. "For if God foreknew those who are called, according to His purpose, to be conformed to the image of His Son," for whose sake, according to the blessed

---

[1] Matt. x. 30.
[2] ἐγκαταριθμημένην seems to be here used in a middle, not a passive sense, as καταριθμημένος is sometimes.
[3] 2 Cor. xiii. 5.   [4] Deut. xxiii. 17.

apostle, He has appointed "Him to be the first-born among many brethren,"[1] are they not godless who treat with indignity the body which is of like form with the Lord?

The man, who would be beautiful, must adorn, that which is the most beautiful thing in man, his mind, which every day he ought to exhibit in greater comeliness; and should pluck out not hairs, but lusts. I pity the boys possessed by the slave-dealers, that are decked for dishonour. But they are not treated with ignominy by themselves, but by command the wretches are adorned for base gain. But how disgusting are those who willingly practise the things to which, if compelled, they would, if they were men, die rather than do?

But life has reached this pitch of licentiousness through the wantonness of wickedness, and lasciviousness is diffused over the cities, having become law. Beside them women stand in the stews, offering their own flesh for hire for lewd pleasure, and boys, taught to deny their sex, act the part of women.

Luxury has deranged all things; it has disgraced man. A luxurious niceness seeks everything, attempts everything, forces everything, coerces nature. Men play the part of women, and women that of men, contrary to nature; women are at once wives and husbands: no passage is closed against libidinousness; and their promiscuous lechery is a public institution, and luxury is domesticated. O miserable spectacle! horrible conduct! Such are the trophies of your social licentiousness which are exhibited: the evidence of these deeds are the prostitutes. Alas for such wickedness! Besides, the wretches know not how many tragedies the uncertainty of intercourse produces. For fathers, unmindful of children of theirs that have been exposed, often without their knowledge, have intercourse with a son that has debauched himself, and daughters that are prostitutes; and licence in lust shows them to be the men that have begotten them. These things your wise laws allow: people may sin legally; and the execrable indulgence in pleasure they call a thing indifferent. They who commit adultery against nature think themselves

[1] Rom. viii. 28, 29.

free from adultery. Avenging justice follows their audacious deeds, and, dragging on themselves inevitable calamity, they purchase death for a small sum of money. The miserable dealers in these wares sail, bringing a cargo of fornication, like wine or oil; and others, far more wretched, traffic in pleasures as they do in bread and sauce, not heeding the words of Moses, " Do not prostitute thy daughter, to cause her to be a whore, lest the land fall to whoredom, and the land become full of wickedness."[1]

Such was predicted of old, and the result is notorious: the whole earth has now become full of fornication and wickedness. I admire the ancient legislators of the Romans: these detested effeminacy of conduct; and the giving of the body to feminine purposes, contrary to the law of nature, they judged worthy of the extremest penalty, according to the righteousness of the law.

For it is not lawful to pluck out the beard, man's natural and noble ornament.

"A youth with his first beard: for with this, youth is most graceful."

By and by he is anointed, delighting in the beard "on which descended" the prophetic "ointment"[2] with which Aaron was honoured.

And it becomes him who is rightly trained, on whom peace has pitched its tent, to preserve peace also with his hair.

What, then, will not women with strong propensities to lust practise, when they look on men perpetrating such enormities? Rather we ought not to call such as these men, but lewd wretches (βατάλοι), and effeminate (γύνιδες), whose voices are feeble, and whose clothes are womanish both in feel and dye. And such creatures are manifestly shown to be what they are from their external appearance, their clothes, shoes, form, walk, cut of their hair, look. " For from his look shall a man be known," says the Scripture, " and from meeting a man the man is known: the dress of a man, the step of his foot, the laugh of his teeth, tell tales of him."[3]

For these, for the most part, plucking out the rest of their hair, only dress that on the head, all but binding their locks

[1] Lev. xix. 29.   [2] Ps. cxxxiii. 2.   [3] Ecclus. xix. 26, 27.

with fillets like women. Lions glory in their shaggy hair, but are armed by their hair in the fight; and boars even are made imposing by their mane; the hunters are afraid of them when they see them bristling their hair.

"The fleecy sheep are loaded with their wool."[1]

And their wool the loving Father has made abundant for thy use, O man, having taught thee to shear their fleeces. Of the nations, the Celts and Scythians wear their hair long, but do not deck themselves. The bushy hair of the barbarian has something fearful in it; and its auburn (ξανθόν) colour threatens war, the hue being somewhat akin to blood. Both these barbarian races hate luxury. As clear witnesses will be produced by the German, the Rhine;[2] and by the Scythian, the waggon. Sometimes the Scythian despises even the waggon: its size seems sumptuousness to the barbarian; and leaving its luxurious ease, the Scythian man leads a frugal life. For a house sufficient, and less encumbered than the waggon, he takes his horse, and mounting it, is borne where he wishes. And when faint with hunger, he asks his horse for sustenance; and he offers his veins, and supplies his master with all he possesses—his blood. To the nomad the horse is at once conveyance and sustenance; and the warlike youth of the Arabians (these are other nomads) are mounted on camels. They sit on breeding camels; and these feed and run at the same time, carrying their masters the whilst, and bear the house with them. And if drink fail the barbarians, they milk them; and after that their food is spent, they do not spare even their blood, as is reported of furious wolves. And these, gentler than the barbarians, when injured, bear no remembrance of the wrong, but sweep bravely over the desert, carrying and nourishing their masters at the same time.

Perish, then, the savage beasts whose food is blood! For it is unlawful for men, whose body is nothing but flesh elaborated of blood, to touch blood. For human blood has become a partaker of the Word: it is a participant of grace by the

[1] Hesiod, *Works and Days*, i. 232.
[2] Of which they drink.

Spirit; and if any one injure him, he will not escape unnoticed. Man may, though naked in body, address the Lord. But I approve the simplicity of the barbarians: loving an unencumbered life, the barbarians have abandoned luxury. Such the Lord calls us to be—naked of finery, naked of vanity, wrenched from our sins, bearing only the wood of life, aiming only at salvation.

CHAPTER IV.

WITH WHOM WE ARE TO ASSOCIATE.

BUT really I have unwittingly deviated in spirit from the order, to which I must now revert, and must find fault with having large numbers of domestics. For, avoiding working with their own hands and serving themselves, men have recourse to servants, purchasing a great crowd of fine cooks, and of people to lay out the table, and of others to divide the meat skilfully into pieces. And the staff of servants is separated into many divisions: some labour for their gluttony, carvers and seasoners, and the compounders and makers of sweetmeats, and honey-cakes, and custards; others are occupied with their too numerous clothes; others guard the gold, like griffins; others keep the silver, and wipe the cups, and make ready what is needed to furnish the festive table; others rub down the horses; and a crowd of cup-bearers exert themselves in their service, and herds of beautiful boys, like cattle, from whom they milk away their beauty. And male and female assistants at the toilet are employed about the ladies—some for the mirrors, some for the head-dresses, others for the combs. Many are eunuchs; and these panders serve without suspicion those that wish to be free to enjoy their pleasures, because of the belief that they are unable to indulge in lust. But a true eunuch is not one who is unable, but one who is unwilling, to indulge in pleasure. The Word, testifying by the prophet Samuel to the Jews, who had transgressed when the people asked for a king, promised not a loving lord, but threatened to give them a self-willed and voluptuous tyrant, "who shall," He says, "take your daughters to be perfumers, and cooks, and bakers,"[1]

[1] 1 Sam. viii. 13.

ruling by the law of war, not desiring a peaceful administration. And there are many Celts, who bear aloft on their shoulders women's litters. But workers in wool, and spinners, and weavers, and female work and housekeeping, are nowhere. But those who impose on the women, spend the day with them, telling them silly amatory stories, and wearing out body and soul with their false acts and words. "Thou shalt not be with many," it is said, "for evil, nor give thyself to a multitude;"[1] for wisdom shows itself among few, but disorder in a multitude. But it is not for grounds of propriety, on account of not wishing to be seen, that they purchase bearers, for it were commendable if out of such feelings they put themselves under a covering; but it is out of luxuriousness that they are carried on their domestics' shoulders, and desire to make a show.

So, opening the curtain, and looking keenly round on all that direct their eyes towards them, they show their manners; and often bending forth from within, disgrace this superficial propriety by their dangerous restlessness. "Look not round," it is said, "in the streets of the city, and wander not in its lonely places."[2] For that is, in truth, a lonely place, though there be a crowd of the licentious in it, where no wise man is present.

And these women are carried about over the temples, sacrificing and practising divination day by day, spending their time with fortune-tellers, and begging priests, and disreputable old women; and they keep up old wives' whisperings over their cups, learning charms and incantations from soothsayers, to the ruin of the nuptial bonds. And some men they keep; by others they are kept; and others are promised them by the diviners. They know not that they are cheating themselves, and giving up themselves as a vessel of pleasure to those that wish to indulge in wantonness; and exchanging their purity for the foulest outrage, they think what is the most shameful ruin a great stroke of business. And there are many ministers to this meretricious licentiousness, insinuating

[1] Ex. xxiii. 2.   [2] Ecclus. xi. 31.

themselves, one from one quarter, another from another. For the licentious rush readily into uncleanness, like swine rushing to that part of the hold of the ship which is depressed. Whence the Scripture most strenuously exhorts, "Introduce not every one into thy house, for the snares of the crafty are many."[1] And in another place, "Let just men be thy guests, and in the fear of the Lord let thy boast remain."[2] Away with fornication. "For know this well," says the apostle, "that no fornicator, or unclean person, or covetous man, who is an idolater, hath any inheritance in the kingdom of Christ and of God."[3]

But these women delight in intercourse with the effeminate. And crowds of abominable creatures (κιναίδες) flow in, of unbridled tongue, filthy in body, filthy in language; men enough for lewd offices, ministers of adultery, giggling and whispering, and shamelessly making through their noses sounds of lewdness and fornication to provoke lust, endeavouring to please by lewd words and attitudes, inciting to laughter, the precursor of fornication. And sometimes, when inflamed by any provocation, either these fornicators, or those that follow the rabble of abominable creatures to destruction, make a sound in their nose like a frog, as if they had got anger dwelling in their nostrils. But those who are more refined than these keep Indian birds and Median pea-fowls, and recline with peak-headed[4] creatures; playing with satyrs, delighting in monsters. They laugh when they hear Thersites; and these women, purchasing Thersiteses highly valued, pride themselves not in their husbands, but in those wretches which are a burden on the earth, and overlook the chaste widow, who is of far higher value than a Melitæan pup, and look askance at a just old man, who is lovelier in my estimation than a monster purchased for money. And though maintaining parrots and curlews, they do not receive the orphan child; but they expose children that are born at home, and take up the young of birds, and prefer irrational to rational creatures; although they ought to undertake the maintenance of old

---

[1] Ecclus. xi. 31.   [2] Ecclus. ix. 22.   [3] Eph. v. 3.
[4] Φοξός, in allusion to Thersites, to which Homer applies this epithet.

people with a character for sobriety, who are fairer in my mind than apes, and capable of uttering something better than nightingales; and to set before them that saying, "He that pitieth the poor lendeth to the Lord;"[1] and this, "Inasmuch as ye have done it unto the least of these my brethren, ye have done it to me."[2] But these, on the other hand, prefer ignorance to wisdom, turning their wealth into stone, that is, into pearls and Indian emeralds. And they squander and throw away their wealth on fading dyes, and bought slaves; like crammed fowls scraping the dung of life. "Poverty," it is said, "humbles a man."[3] By poverty is meant that niggardliness by which the rich are poor, having nothing to give away.

[1] Prov. xix. 17.   [2] Matt. xxv. 40.   [3] Prov. x. 4.

CHAPTER V.

BEHAVIOUR IN THE BATHS.

AND of what sort are their baths? Houses skilfully constructed, compact, portable, transparent, covered with fine linen. And gold-plated chairs, and silver ones, too, and ten thousand vessels of gold and silver, some for drinking, some for eating, some for bathing, are carried about with them. Besides these, there are even braziers of coals; for they have arrived at such a pitch of self-indulgence, that they sup and get drunk while bathing. And articles of silver with which they make a show, they ostentatiously set out in the baths, and thus display perchance their wealth out of excessive pride, but chiefly the capricious ignorance, through which they brand effeminate men, who have been vanquished by women; proving at least that they themselves cannot meet and cannot sweat without a multitude of vessels, although poor women who have no display equally enjoy their baths. The dirt of wealth, then, has an abundant covering of censure. With this, as with a bait, they hook the miserable creatures that gape at the glitter of gold. For dazzling thus those fond of display, they artfully try to win the admiration of their lovers, who after a little insult them naked. They will scarce strip before their own husbands, affecting a plausible pretence of modesty; but any others who wish, may see them at home shut up naked in their baths. For there they are not ashamed to strip before spectators, as if exposing their persons for sale. But Hesiod advises
"Not to wash the skin in the women's bath."[1]
The baths are opened promiscuously to men and women; and

[1] Hes. *Works and Days,* ii. 371.

there they strip for licentious indulgence (for from looking, men get to loving), as if their modesty had been washed away in the bath. Those who have not become utterly destitute of modesty shut out strangers; but bathe with their own servants, and strip naked before their slaves, and are rubbed by them; giving to the crouching menial liberty to lust, by permitting fearless handling. For those who are introduced before their naked mistresses while in the bath, study to strip themselves in order to audacity in lust, casting off fear in consequence of the wicked custom. The ancient athletes, ashamed to exhibit a man naked, preserved their modesty by going through the contest in drawers; but these women, divesting themselves of their modesty along with their chemise, wish to appear beautiful, but contrary to their wish are simply proved to be wicked. For through the body itself the wantonness of lust shines clearly; as in the case of dropsical people, the water covered by the skin. Disease in both is known from the look. Men, therefore, affording to women a noble example of truth, ought to be ashamed at their stripping before them, and guard against these dangerous sights; " for he who has looked curiously," it is said, " hath sinned already."[1] At home, therefore, they ought to regard with modesty parents and domestics; in the ways, those they meet; in the baths, women; in solitude, themselves; and everywhere the Word, who is everywhere, "and without Him was not anything."[2] For so only shall one remain without falling, if he regard God as ever present with him.

[1] Matt. v. 28.   [2] John i. 3.

CHAPTER VI.

THE CHRISTIAN ALONE RICH.

RICHES are then to be partaken of rationally, bestowed lovingly, not sordidly, or pompously; nor is the love of the beautiful to be turned into self-love and ostentation; lest perchance some one say to us, "His horse, or land, or domestic, or gold, is worth fifteen talents; but the man himself is dear at three coppers."

Take away, then, directly the ornaments from women, and domestics from masters, and you will find masters in no respect different from bought slaves in step, or look, or voice, so like are they to their slaves. But they differ in that they are feebler than their slaves, and have a more sickly upbringing.

This best of maxims, then, ought to be perpetually repeated, "That the good man, being temperate and just," treasures up his wealth in heaven. He who has sold his worldly goods, and given them to the poor, finds the imperishable treasure, "where is neither moth nor robber." Blessed truly is he, "though he be insignificant, and feeble, and obscure;" and he is truly rich with the greatest of all riches. "Though a man, then, be richer than Cinyras and Midas, and is wicked," and haughty as he who was luxuriously clothed in purple and fine linen, and despised Lazarus, "he is miserable, and lives in trouble," and shall not live. Wealth seems to me to be like a serpent, which will twist round the hand and bite; unless one knows how to lay hold of it without danger by the point of the tail. And riches, wriggling either in an experienced or inexperienced grasp, are dexterous at adhering and biting; unless one, despising them, use them skilfully, so as to crush the creature by the charm of the Word, and himself escape unscathed.

But, as is reasonable, he alone, who possesses what is worth most, turns out truly rich, though not recognised as such. And it is not jewels, or gold, or clothing, or beauty of person, that are of high value, but virtue; which is the Word given by the Instructor to be put in practice. This is the Word, who abjures luxury, but calls self-help as a servant, and praises frugality, the progeny of temperance. "Receive," he says, "instruction, and not silver, and knowledge rather than tested gold; for Wisdom is better than precious stones, nor is anything that is valuable equal in worth to her."[1] And again: "Acquire me rather than gold, and precious stones, and silver; for my produce is better than choice silver."[2]

But if we must distinguish, let it be granted that he is rich who has many possessions, loaded with gold like a dirty purse; but the righteous alone is graceful, because grace is order, observing a due and decorous measure in managing and distributing. "For there are those who sow and reap more,"[3] of whom it is written, "He hath dispersed, he hath given to the poor; his righteousness endureth for ever."[4] So that it is not he who has and keeps, but he who gives away, that is rich; and it is giving away, not possession, which renders a man happy; and the fruit of the Spirit is generosity. It is in the soul, then, that riches are. Let it, then, be granted that good things are the property only of good men; and Christians are good. Now, a fool or a libertine can neither have any perception of what is good, nor obtain possession of it. Accordingly, good things are possessed by Christians alone. And nothing is richer than these good things; therefore these alone are rich. For righteousness is true riches; and the Word is more valuable than all treasure, not accruing from cattle and fields, but given by God—riches which cannot be taken away. The soul alone is its treasure. It is the best possession to its possessor, rendering man truly blessed. For he whose it is to desire nothing that is not in our power,

[1] Prov. viii. 10, 11.   [2] Prov. viii. 19.
[3] Prov. xi. 24.   [4] Ps. cxii. 9.

and to obtain by asking from God what he piously desires, does he not possess much, nay all, having God as his everlasting treasure? "To him that asks," it is said, "shall be given, and to him that knocketh it shall be opened."[1] If God denies nothing, all things belong to the godly.

[1] Matt. vii. 7, 8.

CHAPTER VII.

FRUGALITY A GOOD PROVISION FOR THE CHRISTIAN.

DELICACIES spent on pleasures become a dangerous shipwreck to men; for this voluptuous and ignoble life of the many is alien to true love for the beautiful and to refined pleasures. For man is by nature an erect and majestic being, aspiring after the good as becomes the creature of the One. But the life which crawls on its belly is destitute of dignity, is scandalous, hateful, ridiculous. And to the divine nature voluptuousness is a thing most alien; for this is for a man to be like sparrows in feeding, and swine and goats in lechery. For to regard pleasure as a good thing, is the sign of utter ignorance of what is excellent. Love of wealth displaces a man from the right mode of life, and induces him to cease from feeling shame at what is shameful; if only, like a beast, he has power to eat all sorts of things, and to drink in like manner, and to satiate in every way his lewd desires. And so very rarely does he inherit the kingdom of God. For what end, then, are such dainty dishes prepared, but to fill one belly? The filthiness of gluttony is proved by the privies into which our bellies discharge the refuse of our food. For what end do they collect so many cupbearers, when they might satisfy themselves with one cup? For what the chests of clothes? and the gold ornaments for what? Those things are prepared for clothes-stealers, and scoundrels, and for greedy eyes. "But let alms and faith not fail thee,"[1] says the Scripture.

Look, for instance, to Elias the Thesbite, in whom we have a beautiful example of frugality, when he sat down beneath

[1] Prov. iii. 5.

the thorn, and the angel brought him food. "It was a cake of barley and a jar of water."[1] Such the Lord sent as best for him. We, then, on our journey to the truth, must be unencumbered. "Carry not," said the Lord, "purse, nor scrip, nor shoes;"[2] that is, possess not wealth, which is only treasured up in a purse; fill not your own stores, as if laying up produce in a bag, but communicate to those who have need. Do not trouble yourselves about horses and servants, who, as bearing burdens when the rich are travelling, are allegorically called shoes.

We must, then, cast away the multitude of vessels, silver and gold drinking cups, and the crowd of domestics, receiving as we have done from the Instructor the fair and grave attendants, Self-help and Simplicity. And we must walk suitably to the Word; and if there be a wife and children, the house is not a burden, having learned to change its place along with the sound-minded traveller. The wife who loves her husband must be furnished for travel similarly to her husband. A fair provision for the journey to heaven is theirs who bear frugality with chaste gravity. And as the foot is the measure of the shoe, so also is the body of what each individual possesses. But that which is superfluous, what they call ornaments and the furniture of the rich, is a burden, not an ornament to the body. He who climbs to the heavens by force, must carry with him the fair staff of beneficence, and attain to the true rest by communicating to those who are in distress. For the Scripture avouches, "that the true riches of the soul are a man's ransom,"[3] that is, if he is rich, he will be saved by distributing it. For as gushing wells, when pumped out, rise again to their former measure, so giving away, being the benignant spring of love, by communicating of its drink to the thirsty, again increases and is replenished, just as the milk is wont to flow into the breasts that are sucked or milked. For he who has the almighty God, the Word, is in want of nothing, and never is in straits for what he needs. For the Word is a possession that wants nothing, and is the cause of all abundance. If one say that he has

---

[1] 1 Kings xix. 4, 6. [2] Luke x. 4. [3] Prov. xiii. 8.

often seen the righteous man in need of food, this is rare, and happens only where there is not another righteous man. Notwithstanding let him read what follows: "For the righteous man shall not live by bread alone, but by the word of the Lord,"[1] who is the true bread, the bread of the heavens. The good man, then, can never be in difficulties so long as he keeps intact his confession towards God. For it appertains to him to ask and to receive whatever he requires from the Father of all; and to enjoy what is his own, if he keep the Son. And this also appertains to him, to feel no want.

This Word, who trains us, confers on us the true riches. Nor is the growing rich an object of envy to those who possess through Him the privilege of wanting nothing. He that has this wealth shall inherit the kingdom of God.

[1] Deut. viii. 3; Matt. iv. 4.

CHAPTER VIII.

SIMILITUDES AND EXAMPLES A MOST IMPORTANT PART OF RIGHT INSTRUCTION.

AND if any one of you shall entirely avoid luxury, he will, by a frugal upbringing, train himself to the endurance of involuntary labours, by employing constantly voluntary afflictions as training exercises for persecutions; so that when he comes to compulsory labours, and fears, and griefs, he will not be unpractised in endurance.

Wherefore we have no country on earth, that we may despise earthly possessions. And frugality[1] is in the highest degree rich, being equal to unfailing expenditure, bestowed on what is requisite, and to the degree requisite. For τέλη has the meaning of expenses.

How a husband is to live with his wife, and respecting self-help, and housekeeping, and the employment of domestics; and further, with respect to the time of marriage, and what is suitable for wives, we have treated in the discourse concerning marriage. What pertains to discipline alone is reserved now for description, as we delineate the life of Christians. The most indeed has been already said, and laid down in the form of disciplinary rules. What still remains we shall subjoin; for examples are of no small moment in determining to salvation.

---

[1] The word used by Clement here for frugality is εὐτίλεια, and he supposes the word to mean originally "spending well." A proper way of spending money is as good as unfailing riches, since it always has enough for all that is necessary.

See, says the tragedy,

"The consort of Ulysses was not killed
By Telemachus; for she did not take a husband in addition to a husband,
But in the house the marriage-bed remains unpolluted."[1]

Reproaching foul adultery, he showed the fair image of chastity in affection to her husband.

The Lacedæmonians compelling the Helots, their servants (Helots is the name of their servants), to get drunk, exhibited their drunken pranks before themselves, who were temperate, for cure and correction.

Observing, accordingly, their unseemly behaviour, in order that they themselves might not fall into like censurable conduct, they trained themselves, turning the reproach of the drunkards to the advantage of keeping themselves free from fault.

For some men being instructed are saved; and others, self-taught, either aspire after or seek virtue.

"He truly is the best of all who himself perceives all things."[2]
Such is Abraham, who sought God.

"And good, again, is he who obeys him who advises well."[3]
Such are those disciples who obeyed the Word. Wherefore the former was called "friend," the latter "apostles;" the one diligently seeking, and the other preaching one and the same God. And both are peoples, and both these have hearers, the one who is profited through seeking, the other who is saved through finding.

"But whoever neither himself perceives, nor, hearing another,
Lays to heart—he is a worthless man."[4]

The other people is the Gentile—useless; this is the people that followeth not Christ. Nevertheless the Instructor, lover of man, helping in many ways, partly exhorts, partly upbraids. Others having sinned, He shows us their baseness, and exhibits the punishment consequent upon it, alluring while admonishing, planning to dissuade us in love from evil, by the exhibition of those who have suffered from it before.

[1] Euripid. *Orestes*, 587.
[2] Hesiod, *Works and Days*, i. 291.   [3] *Ibid.*   [4] *Ibid.*

By which examples He very manifestly checked those who had been evil-disposed, and hindered those who were daring like deeds; and others He brought to a foundation of patience; others He stopped from wickedness; and others He cured by the contemplation of what is like, bringing them over to what is better.

For who, when following one in the way, and then on the former falling into a pit, would not guard against incurring equal danger, by taking care not to follow him in his slip? What athlete, again, who has learned the way to glory, and has seen the combatant who had preceded him receiving the prize, does not exert himself for the crown, imitating the elder one?

Such images of divine wisdom are many; but I shall mention one instance, and expound it in a few words. The fate of the Sodomites was judgment to those who had done wrong, instruction to those who hear. The Sodomites having, through much luxury, fallen into uncleanness, practising adultery shamelessly, and burning with insane love for boys; the All-seeing Word, whose notice those who commit impieties cannot escape, cast His eye on them. Nor did the sleepless guard of humanity observe their licentiousness in silence; but dissuading us from the imitation of them, and training us up to His own temperance, and falling on some sinners, lest lust being unavenged, should break loose from all the restraints of fear, ordered Sodom to be burned, pouring forth a little of the sagacious fire on licentiousness; lest lust, through want of punishment, should throw wide the gates to those that were rushing into voluptuousness. Accordingly, the just punishment of the Sodomites became to men an image of the salvation which is well calculated for men. For those who have not committed like sins with those who are punished, will never receive a like punishment. By guarding against sinning, we guard against suffering. "For I would have you to know," says Jude, "that God, having once saved His people from the land of Egypt, afterwards destroyed them that believed not; and the angels which kept not their first estate, but left their own habitation, He hath reserved to the judgment of the great day, in everlasting chains under darkness of the savage angels."[1] And a little after he sets forth, in a most instructive manner, representations of those that are judged: "Woe unto them, for they have gone in the way of Cain, and run greedily after the error of Balaam, and perished in the gainsaying of Core." For those, who cannot attain the privilege of adoption, fear keeps from growing insolent. For punishments and threats are for this end, that fearing the penalty we may abstain from sinning. I might relate to you punishments for ostentation, and punishments for vainglory, not only for licentiousness; and adduce the censures pronounced on those whose hearts are bad through wealth,[2] in which censures the Word through fear restrains from evil acts. But sparing prolixity in my treatise, I shall bring forward the following precepts of the Instructor, that you may guard against His threatenings.

[1] Jude 5, 6.
[2] Following Lowth's conjecture of κακοφρόνων instead of that of the text, κακότροπος.

CHAPTER IX.

WHY WE ARE TO USE THE BATH.

THERE are, then, four reasons for the bath (for from that point I digressed in my oration), for which we frequent it: for cleanliness, or heat, or health, or lastly, for pleasure. Bathing for pleasure is to be omitted. For unblushing pleasure must be cut out by the roots; and the bath is to be taken by women for cleanliness and health, by men for health alone. To bathe for the sake of heat is a superfluity, since one may restore what is frozen by the cold in other ways. Constant use of the bath, too, impairs strength and relaxes the physical energies, and often induces debility and fainting. For in a way the body drinks, like trees, not only by the mouth, but also over the whole body in bathing, by what they call the pores. In proof of this, often people, when thirsty, by going afterwards into the water, have assuaged their thirst. Unless, then, the bath is for some use, we ought not to indulge in it. The ancients called them places for fulling[1] men, since they wrinkle men's bodies sooner than they ought, and by cooking them, as it were, compel them to become prematurely old. The flesh, like iron, being softened by the heat, hence we require cold, as it were, to temper and give an edge. Nor must we bathe always; but if one is a little exhausted, or, on the other hand, filled to repletion, the bath is to be forbidden, regard being had to the age of the body and the season of the year. For the bath is not beneficial to all, or always, as those who are skilled in these things own. But due proportion, which on all occasions we call as our helper in life, suffices for us. For

[1] ἀνθρωπογναφεῖα.

we must not so use the bath as to require an assistant, nor are we to bathe constantly and often in the day as we frequent the market-place. But to have the water poured over us by several people is an outrage on our neighbours, through fondness for luxuriousness, and is done by those who will not understand that the bath is common to all the bathers equally.

But most of all is it necessary to wash the soul in the cleansing Word (sometimes the body too, on account of the dirt which gathers and grows to it, sometimes also to relieve fatigue). "Woe unto you, scribes and Pharisees, hypocrites!" saith the Lord, "for ye are like to whited sepulchres. Without, the sepulchre appears beautiful, but within it is full of dead men's bones and all uncleanness."[1] And again He says to the same people, "Woe unto you! for ye cleanse the outside of the cup and platter, but within are full of uncleanness. Cleanse first the inside of the cup, that the outside may be clean also."[2] The best bath, then, is what rubs off the pollution of the soul, and is spiritual. Of which prophecy speaks expressly: "The Lord will wash away the filth of the sons and daughters of Israel, and will purge the blood from the midst of them"[3]—the blood of crime and the murders of the prophets. And the mode of cleansing, the Word subjoined, saying, "by the spirit of judgment and the spirit of burning." The bathing of the body, which is carnal, is accomplished by water alone, as often in the country where there is not a bath.

[1] Matt. xxiii. 27.   [2] Matt. xxiii. 25, 26.   [3] Isa. iv. 4.

CHAPTER X.

THE EXERCISES SUITED TO A GOOD LIFE.

THE gymnasium is sufficient for boys, even if a bath is within reach. And even for men to prefer gymnastic exercises by far to the baths, is perchance not bad, since they are in some respect conducive to the health of young men, and produce exertion—emulation to aim at not only a healthy habit of body, but courageousness of soul. When this is done without dragging a man away from better employments, it is pleasant, and not unprofitable. Nor are women to be deprived of bodily exercise. But they are not to be encouraged to engage in wrestling or running, but are to exercise themselves in spinning, and weaving, and superintending the cooking if necessary. And they are, with their own hand, to fetch from the store, what we require. And it is no disgrace for them to apply themselves to the mill. Nor is it a reproach to a wife—housekeeper and helpmeet—to occupy herself in cooking, so that it may be palatable to her husband. And if she shake up the couch, reach drink to her husband when thirsty, set food on the table as neatly as possible, and so give herself exercise tending to sound health, the Instructor will approve of a woman like this, who "stretches forth her arms to useful tasks, rests her hands on the distaff, opens her hand to the poor, and extends her wrist to the beggar."[1]

She who emulates Sarah is not ashamed of that highest of ministries, helping wayfarers. For Abraham said to her, "Haste, and knead three measures of meal, and make cakes."[2] "And Rachel, the daughter of Laban, came," it is said,

---

[1] Prov. xxxi. 19, 20, Septuagint.   [2] Gen. xviii. 6.

"with her father's sheep."[1] Nor was this enough; but to teach humility it is added, "for she fed her father's sheep."[2] And innumerable such examples of frugality and self-help, and also of exercises, are furnished by the Scriptures. In the case of men, let some strip and engage in wrestling; let some play at the small ball, especially the game they call Pheninda,[3] in the sun. To others who walk into the country, or go down into the town, the walk is sufficient exercise. And were they to handle the hoe, this stroke of economy in agricultural labour would not be ungentlemanly.

I had almost forgot to say that the well-known Pittacus, king of Miletus, practised the laborious exercise of turning the mill.[4] It is respectable for a man to draw water for himself, and to cut billets of wood which he is to use himself. Jacob fed the sheep of Laban that were left in his charge, having as a royal badge "a rod of storax,"[5] which aimed by its wood to change and improve nature. And reading aloud is often an exercise to many. But let not such athletic contests, as we have allowed, be undertaken for the sake of vainglory, but for the exuding of manly sweat. Nor are we to struggle with cunning and showiness, but in a stand-up wrestling bout, by disentangling of neck, hands, and sides. For such a struggle with graceful strength is more becoming and manly, being undertaken for the sake of serviceable and profitable health. But let those others, who profess the practice of illiberal postures in gymnastics, be dismissed. We must always aim at moderation. For as it is best that labour should precede food, so to labour above measure is both very bad, very exhausting, and apt to make us ill. Neither, then, should we be idle altogether, nor completely fatigued. For similarly to what we have laid down with respect to food, are we to do everywhere and with everything. Our mode of life is not to accustom us to voluptuousness and licentiousness, nor to the

---

[1] Gen. xxix. 9. [2] Ibid. [3] Φενίνδα or φενίς.
[4] The text has ἤλθιν. The true reading, doubtless, is ἤληθεν. That Pittacus exercised himself thus, is stated by Isidore of Pelusium, Diogenes, Laertius, Plutarch.
[5] Gen. xxx. 37. Not poplar, as in A. V.

opposite extreme, but to the medium between these, that which is harmonious and temperate, and free of either evil, luxury and parsimony. And now, as we have also previously remarked, attending to one's own wants is an exercise free of pride,—as, for example, putting on one's own shoes, washing one's own feet, and also rubbing one's self when anointed with oil. To render one who has rubbed you the same service in return, is an exercise of reciprocal justice; and to sleep beside a sick friend, help the infirm, and supply him who is in want, are proper exercises. "And Abraham," it is said, "served up for three, dinner under a tree, and waited on them as they ate."[1] The same with fishing, as in the case of Peter, if we have leisure from necessary instructions in the Word. But that is the better sport which the Lord assigned to the disciple, when He taught him to "catch men" as fishes in the water.

[1] Gen. xviii. 8.

CHAPTER XI.

A COMPENDIOUS VIEW OF THE CHRISTIAN LIFE.

WHEREFORE the wearing of gold and the use of softer clothing is not to be entirely prohibited. But irrational impulses must be curbed, lest, carrying us away through excessive relaxation, they impel us to voluptuousness. For luxury, that has dashed on to surfeit, is prone to kick up its heels and toss its mane, and shake off the charioteer, the Instructor; who, pulling back the reins from far, leads and drives to salvation the human horse—that is, the irrational part of the soul—which is wildly bent on pleasures, and vicious appetites, and precious stones, and gold, and variety of dress, and other luxuries.

Above all, we are to keep in mind what was spoken sacredly: "Having your conversation honest among the Gentiles; that, whereas they speak against you as evil-doers, they may, by the good works which they behold, glorify God."[1]

Clothes.

The Instructor permits us, then, to use simple clothing, and of a white colour, as we said before. So that, accommodating ourselves not to variegated art, but to nature as it is produced, and pushing away whatever is deceptive and belies the truth, we may embrace the uniformity and simplicity of the truth.

Sophocles, reproaching a youth, says:

"Decked in women's clothes."

For, as in the case of the soldier; the sailor, and the ruler, so also the proper dress of the temperate man is what is

[1] 1 Pet. ii. 12.

plain, becoming, and clean. Whence also in the law, the law enacted by Moses about leprosy rejects what has many colours and spots, like the various scales of the snake. He therefore wishes man, no longer decking himself gaudily in a variety of colours, but white all over from the crown of the head to the sole of the foot, to be clean; so that, by a transition from the body, we may lay aside the varied and versatile passions of the man, and love the unvaried, and unambiguous, and simple colour of truth. And he who also in this emulates Moses—Plato best of all—approves of that texture on which not more than a chaste woman's work has been employed. And white colours well become gravity. And elsewhere he says, "Nor apply dyes or weaving, except for warlike decorations."[1]

To men of peace and of light, therefore, white is appropriate. As, then, signs, which are very closely allied to causes, by their presence indicate, or rather demonstrate, the existence of the result; as smoke is the sign of fire, and a good complexion and a regular pulse of health; so also clothing of this description shows the character of our habits. Temperance is pure and simple; since purity is a habit which ensures pure conduct unmixed with what is base. Simplicity is a habit which does away with superfluities.

Substantial clothing also, and chiefly what is unfulled, protects the heat which is in the body; not that the clothing has heat in itself, but that it turns back the heat issuing from the body, and refuses it a passage. And whatever heat falls upon it, it absorbs and retains, and being warmed by it, warms in turn the body. And for this reason it is chiefly to be worn in winter.

It also (temperance) is contented. And contentment is a habit which dispenses with superfluities, and, that there may be no failure, is receptive of what suffices for the healthful and blessed life according to the Word.[2]

[1] Plato's words are: "The web is not to be more than a woman's work for a month. White colour is peculiarly becoming for the gods in other things, but especially in cloth. Dyes are not to be applied, except for warlike decorations."—PLATO, *De Legibus*, xii. 992.

[2] Κατὰ Λόγον. The reading in the text is κατάλογον.

Let the woman wear a plain and becoming dress, but softer than what is suitable for a man, yet not quite immodest or entirely gone in luxury. And let the garments be suited to age, person, figure, nature, pursuits. For the divine apostle most beautifully counsels us "to put on Jesus Christ, and make no provision for the lusts of the flesh."[1]

Ear-rings.

The Word prohibits us from doing violence to nature by boring the lobes of the ears. For why not the nose too?—so that, what was spoken, may be fulfilled: "As an ear-ring in a swine's nose, so is beauty to a woman without discretion."[2] For, in a word, if one thinks himself made beautiful by gold, he is inferior to gold; and he that is inferior to gold is not lord of it. But to confess one's self less ornamental than the Lydian ore, how monstrous! As, then, the gold is polluted by the dirtiness of the sow, which stirs up the mire with her snout, so those women that are luxurious to excess in their wantonness, elated by wealth, dishonour by the stains of amatory indulgences what is the true beauty.

Finger-rings.

The Word, then, permits them a finger-ring of gold. Nor is this for ornament, but for sealing things which are worth keeping safe in the house, in the exercise of their charge of housekeeping.

For if all were well trained, there would be no need of seals, if servants and masters were equally honest. But since want of training produces an inclination to dishonesty, we require seals.

But there are circumstances in which this strictness may be relaxed. For allowance must sometimes be made in favour of those women who have not been fortunate[3] in falling in with chaste husbands, and adorn themselves in order to please their husbands. But let desire for the admiration of their husbands alone be proposed as their aim. I would not have

---

[1] Rom. xiii. 14.   [2] Prov. xi. 22.
[3] Εὐτυχούσαις, for which the text has ἐντυχούσαις.

them to devote themselves to personal display, but to attract their husbands by chaste love for them—a powerful and legitimate charm. But since they wish their wives to be unhappy in mind, let the latter, if they would be chaste, make it their aim to allay by degrees the irrational impulses and passions of their husbands. And they are to be gently drawn to simplicity, by gradually accustoming them to sobriety. For decency is not produced by the imposition of what is burdensome, but by the abstraction of excess. For women's articles of luxury are to be prohibited, as things of swift wing producing unstable follies and empty delights; by which, elated and furnished with wings, they often fly away from the marriage bonds. Wherefore also women ought to dress neatly, and bind themselves around with the band of chaste modesty, lest through giddiness they slip away from the truth. It is right, then, for men to repose confidence in their wives, and commit the charge of the household to them, as they are given to be their helpers in this.

And if it is necessary for us, while engaged in public business, or discharging other avocations in the country, and often away from our wives, to seal anything for the sake of safety, He (the Word) allows us a signet for this purpose only. Other finger-rings are to be cast off, since, according to the Scripture, "instruction is a golden ornament for a wise man."[1]

But women who wear gold seem to me to be afraid, lest, if one strip them of their jewellery, they should be taken for servants, without their ornaments. But the nobility of truth, discovered in the native beauty which has its seat in the soul, judges the slave not by buying and selling, but by a servile disposition. And it is incumbent on us not to seem, but to be free, trained by God, adopted by God.

Wherefore we must adopt a mode of standing and motion, and a step, and dress, and in a word, a mode of life, in all respects as worthy as possible of freemen. But men are not to wear the ring on the joint; for this is feminine; but to place it on the little finger at its root. For so the hand will

[1] Ecclus. xxi. 24.

be freest for work, in whatever we need it; and the signet will not very easily fall off, being guarded by the large knot of the joint.

And let our seals be either a dove, or a fish, or a ship scudding before the wind, or a musical lyre, which Polycrates used, or a ship's anchor, which Seleucus got engraved as a device; and if there be one fishing, he will remember the apostle, and the children drawn out of the water. For we are not to delineate the faces of idols, we who are prohibited to cleave to them; nor a sword, nor a bow, following as we do, peace; nor drinking-cups, being temperate.

Many of the licentious have their lovers[1] engraved,[2] or their mistresses, as if they wished to make it impossible ever to forget their amatory indulgences, by being perpetually put in mind of their licentiousness.

The Hair.

About the hair, the following seems right. Let the head of men be shaven, unless it has curly hair. But let the chin have the hair. But let not twisted locks hang far down from the head, gliding into womanish ringlets. For an ample beard suffices for men. And if one, too, shave a part of his beard, it must not be made entirely bare, for this is a disgraceful sight. The shaving of the chin to the skin is reprehensible, approaching to plucking out the hair and smoothing. For instance, thus the Psalmist, delighted with the hair of the beard, says, "As the ointment that descends on the beard, the beard of Aaron."[3]

Having celebrated the beauty of the beard by a repetition, he made the face to shine with the ointment of the Lord.

Since cropping is to be adopted not for the sake of elegance, but on account of the necessity of the case; the hair of the head, that it may not grow so long as to come down and interfere with the eyes, and that of the moustache similarly,

---

[1] Masculine.

[2] γεγλυμμένους, written on the margin of Reg. for γεγυμνωμένους (naked) of the text.

[3] Ps. cxxxiii. 2.

which is dirtied in eating, is to be cut round, not by the razor, for that were ungenteel, but by a pair of cropping scissors. But the hair on the chin is not to be disturbed, as it gives no trouble, and lends to the face dignity and paternal terror.

Moreover, the shape instructs many not to sin, because it renders detection easy. To those who do [not][1] wish to sin openly, a habit that will escape observation and is not conspicuous is most agreeable, which, when assumed, will allow them to transgress without detection; so that, being undistinguishable from others, they may fearlessly go their length in sinning.[2] A cropped head not only shows a man to be grave, but renders the cranium less liable to injury, by accustoming it to the presence of both cold and heat; and it averts the mischiefs arising from these, which the hair absorbs into itself like a sponge, and so inflicts on the brain constant mischief from the moisture.

It is enough for women to protect[3] their locks, and bind up their hair simply along the neck with a plain hair-pin, nourishing chaste locks with simple care to true beauty. For meretricious plaiting of the hair, and putting it up in tresses, contribute to make them look ugly, cutting the hair and plucking off it those treacherous braidings; on account of which they do not touch their head, being afraid of disordering their hair. Sleep, too, comes on, not without fear lest they pull down without knowing the shape of the braid.

But additions of other people's hair are entirely to be rejected, and it is a most sacrilegious thing for spurious hair to shade the head, covering the skull with dead locks. For on whom does the presbyter lay his hand? Whom does he bless? Not the woman decked out, but another's hair, and through them another head. And if "the man is head of the woman, and God of the man,"[4] how is it not impious

---

[1] "Not" does not occur in the MSS.

[2] For διδοικότες, the conjectural emendation διδυκότες has been adopted.

[3] φυλάσσειν, Sylburg and Bod. Reg., agrees better than μαλάσσειν with the context.

[4] 1 Cor. xi. 3. Nov. reads "Christ," as in St. Paul, instead of "God."

that they should fall into double sins? For they deceive the men by the excessive quantity of their hair; and shame the Lord as far as in them lies, by adorning themselves meretriciously, in order to dissemble the truth. And they defame the head, which is truly beautiful.

Consequently neither is the hair to be dyed, nor grey hair to have its colour changed. For neither are we allowed to diversify our dress. And above all, old age, which conciliates trust, is not to be concealed. But God's mark of honour is to be shown in the light of day, to win the reverence of the young. For sometimes, when they have been behaving shamefully, the appearance of hoary hairs, arriving like an instructor, has changed them to sobriety, and paralysed juvenile lust with the splendour of the sight.

Painting the Face.

Nor are the women to smear their faces with the ensnaring devices of wily cunning. But let us show to them the decoration of sobriety. For, in the first place, the best beauty is that which is spiritual, as we have often pointed out. For when the soul is adorned by the Holy Spirit, and inspired with the radiant charms which proceed from Him, —righteousness, wisdom, fortitude, temperance, love of the good, modesty, than which no more blooming colour was ever seen,—then let corporeal beauty be cultivated too, symmetry of limbs and members, with a fair complexion. The adornment of health is here in place, through which the transition of the artificial image to the truth, in accordance with the form which has been given by God, is effected. But temperance in drinks, and moderation in articles of food, are effectual in producing beauty according to nature; for not only does the body maintain its health from these, but they also make beauty to appear. For from what is fiery arises a gleam and sparkle; and from moisture, brightness and grace; and from dryness, strength and firmness; and from what is aërial, free-breathing and equipoise; from which this well-proportioned and beautiful image of the Word is adorned. Beauty is the free flower of health; for the latter is produced within the body; while the former, blossoming out from the body, exhibits manifest beauty of complexion. Accordingly, these most decorous and healthful practices, by exercising the body, produce true and lasting beauty, the heat attracting to itself all the moisture and cold spirit. Heat, when agitated by moving causes, is a thing which attracts to itself; and when it does attract, it gently exhales through the flesh itself, when warmed, the abundance of food, with some moisture, but with excess of heat. Wherefore also the first food is carried off. But when the body is not moved, the food consumed does not adhere, but falls away, as the loaf from a cold oven, either entire, or leaving only the lower part. Accordingly, urine and dung are in excess in the case of those who do not throw off the excrementitious matters by the rubbings necessitated by exercise. And other superfluous matters abound in their case too, and also perspiration, as the food is not assimilated by the body, but is flowing out to waste. Thence also lusts are excited, the redundance flowing to the organs of generation by commensurate motions. Wherefore this redundance ought to be liquefied and dispersed for digestion, by which beauty acquires its ruddy hue. But it is monstrous for those who are made in "the image and likeness of God," to dishonour the archetype by assuming a foreign ornament, preferring the mischievous contrivance of man to the divine creation.

The Instructor orders them to go forth "in becoming apparel, and adorn themselves with shamefacedness and sobriety,"[1] "subject to their own husbands; that, if any obey not the word, they may without the word be won by the conversation of the wives; while they behold," he says, "your chaste conversation. Whose adorning, let it not be that outward adorning of plaiting the hair, and of wearing of gold, or of putting on of apparel; but let it be the hidden man of the heart, in that which is not corruptible, even the ornament of a meek and quiet spirit, which is in the sight of God of great price."[2]

For the labour of their own hands, above all, adds genuine

[1] 1 Tim. ii. 9.   [2] 1 Pet. iii. 1–4.

beauty to women, exercising their bodies and adorning themselves by their own exertions; not bringing unornamental ornament wrought by others, which is vulgar and meretricious, but that of every good woman, supplied and woven by her own hands whenever she most requires. For it is never suitable for women whose lives are framed according to God, to appear arrayed in things bought from the market, but in their own home-made work. For a most beautiful thing is a thrifty wife, who clothes both herself and her husband with fair array of her own working;[1] in which all are glad—the children on account of their mother, the husband on account of his wife, she on their account, and all in God.

In brief, "A store of excellence is a woman of worth, who eateth not the bread of idleness; and the laws of mercy are on her tongue; who openeth her mouth wisely and rightly; whose children rise up and call her blessed," as the sacred Word says by Solomon: "Her husband also, and he praiseth her. For a pious woman is blessed; and let her praise the fear of the Lord."[2]

And again, "A virtuous woman is a crown to her husband."[3] They must, as far as possible, correct their gestures, looks, steps, and speech. For they must not do as some, who, imitating the acting of comedy, and practising the mincing motions of dancers, conduct themselves in society as if on the stage, with voluptuous movements, and gliding steps, and affected voices, casting languishing glances round, tricked out with the bait of pleasure. "For honey drops from the lips of a woman who is an harlot; who, speaking to please, lubricates thy throat. But at last thou wilt find it bitterer than bile, and sharper than a two-edged sword. For the feet of folly lead those who practise it to hell after death."[4]

The noble Samson was overcome by the harlot, and by another woman was shorn of his manhood. But Joseph was not thus beguiled by another woman. The Egyptian harlot

---

[1] In reference to Prov. xxxi. 22.
[2] Prov. xxxi. 26, 27, 28, 30, quoted from memory, and with variety of reading.
[3] Prov. xii. 4.   [4] Prov. v. 3-5, Septuagint.

was conquered. And chastity,[1] assuming to itself bonds, appears superior to dissolute licence. Most excellent is what has been said:

> "In fine, I know not how
> To whisper, nor effeminately,
> To walk about with my neck awry,
> As I see others—lechers there
> In numbers in the city, with hair plucked out."[2]

But feminine motions, dissoluteness, and luxury, are to be entirely prohibited. For voluptuousness of motion in walking, "and a mincing gait," as Anacreon says, are altogether meretricious.

"As seems to me," says the comedy, "it is time[3] to abandon meretricious steps and luxury." And the steps of harlotry lean not to the truth; for they approach not the paths of life. Her tracks are dangerous, and not easily known.[4] The eyes especially are to be sparingly used, since it is better to slip with the feet than with the eyes.[5] Accordingly, the Lord very summarily cures this malady: "If thine eye offend thee, cut it out,"[6] He says, dragging lust up from the foundation. But languishing looks, and ogling, which is to wink with the eyes, is nothing else than to commit adultery with the eyes, lust skirmishing through them. For of the whole body, the eyes are first destroyed. "The eye contemplating beautiful objects (καλά), gladdens the heart;" that is, the eye which has learned rightly (καλῶς) to see, gladdens. "Winking with the eye, with guile, heaps woes on men."[7] Such they introduce the effeminate Sardanapalus, king of the Assyrians, sitting on a couch with his

---

[1] We have read from Nov. σωφροσύνη for σωφροσύνης.

[2] From some comic poet.

[3] Nov. reads ὥραν ἀπολείπει. In the translation the conjecture ὥρα ἀπολείπειν is adopted.

[4] An adaptation of Prov. v. 5, 6.

[5] An imitation of Zeno's saying, "It is better to slip with the feet than the tongue."

[6] Quoting from memory, he has substituted ἔκκοψον for ἔξελε (Matt. v. 29).

[7] Prov. x. 10.

legs up, fumbling at his purple robe, and casting up the whites of his eyes. Women that follow such practices, by their looks offer themselves for prostitution. "For the light of the body is the eye," says the Scripture, by which the interior illuminated by the shining light appears. Fornication in a woman is in the raising of the eyes.[1]

"Mortify therefore your members which are upon the earth; fornication, uncleanness, inordinate affection, and concupiscence, and covetousness, which is idolatry: for which things' sake cometh the wrath of God upon the children of disobedience,"[2] cries the apostle.

But we enkindle the passions, and are not ashamed.

Some of these women eating mastich, going about, show their teeth to those that come near. And others, as if they had not fingers, give themselves airs, scratching their heads with pins; and these made either of tortoise or ivory, or some other dead creature they procure at much pains. And others, as if they had certain efflorescences, in order to appear comely in the eyes of spectators, stain their faces by adorning them with gay-coloured unguents. Such a one is called by Solomon "a foolish and bold woman," who "knows not shame. She sits at the door of her house, conspicuously in a seat, calling to all that pass by the way, who go right on their ways;" by her style and whole life manifestly saying, "Who among you is very silly? let him turn to me." And those devoid of wisdom she exhorts, saying, "Touch sweetly secret bread, and sweet stolen water;" meaning by this, clandestine love (from this point the Bœotian Pindar, coming to our help, says, "The clandestine pursuit of love is something sweet"). But the miserable man "knoweth not that the sons of earth perish beside her, and that she tends to the level of hell." But says the Instructor: "Hie away, and tarry not in the place; nor fix thine eye on her: for thus shalt thou pass over a strange water, and cross to Acheron."[3] Wherefore thus saith the Lord by Isaiah, "Because the daughters of Sion walk with lofty neck, and with winkings of the eyes, and sweeping their garments as they walk, and playing with their feet; the

[1] Ecclus. xxvi. 12.   [2] Col. iii. 5, 6.   [3] Prov. ix. 13-18.

Lord shall humble the daughters of Sion, and will uncover their form"[1]—their deformed form. I deem it wrong that servant girls, who follow women of high rank, should either speak or act unbecomingly to them. But I think it right that they should be corrected by their mistresses. With very sharp censure, accordingly, the comic poet Philemon says: "You may follow at the back of a pretty servant girl, seen behind a gentlewoman; and any one from the Platæicum may follow close, and ogle her." For the wantonness of the servant recoils on the mistress; allowing those who attempt to take lesser liberties not to be afraid to advance to greater; since the mistress, by allowing improprieties, shows that she does not disapprove of them. And not to be angry at those who act wantonly, is a clear proof of a disposition inclining to the like. "For like mistress like wench,"[2] as they say in the proverb.

Walking.

Also we must abandon a furious mode of walking, and choose a grave and leisurely, but not a lingering step.

Nor is one to swagger in the ways, nor throw back his head to look at those he meets, if they look at him, as if he were strutting on the stage, and pointed at with the finger. Nor, when pushing up hill, are they to be shoved up by their domestics, as we see those that are more luxurious, who appear strong, but are enfeebled by effeminacy of soul.

A true gentleman must have no mark of effeminacy visible on his face, or any other part of his body. Let no blot on his manliness, then, be ever found either in his movements or habits. Nor is a man in health to use his servants as horses to bear him. For as it is enjoined on them, "to be subject to their masters with all fear, not only to the good and gentle, but also to the froward,"[3] as Peter says; so fairness, and

---

[1] τὸ ἄσχημον σχῆμα (Isa. iii. 16, 17), Sept.
[2] ἁ κύων, catella. The literal English rendering is coarser and more opprobrious than the original, which Helen applies to herself (*Iliad*, vi. 344, v. 356).
[3] 1 Pet. ii. 18.

forbearance, and kindness, are what well becomes the masters. For he says: "Finally, be ye all of one mind, having compassion one of another; love as brethren, be pitiful, be humble," and so forth, "that ye may inherit a blessing,"[1] excellent and desirable.

The model Maiden.

Zeno the Cittiæan thought fit to represent the image of a young maid, and executed the statue thus: "Let her face be clean, her eyebrows not let down, nor her eyelids open nor turned back. Let her neck not be stretched back, nor the members of her body be loose. But let the parts that hang from the body look as if they were well strung; let there be the keenness of a well-regulated mind[2] for discourse, and retention of what has been rightly spoken; and let her attitudes and movements give no ground of hope to the licentious; but let there be the bloom of modesty, and an expression of firmness. But far from her be the wearisome trouble that comes from the shops of perfumers, and goldsmiths, and dealers in wool, and that which comes from the other shops where women, meretriciously dressed, pass whole days as if sitting in the stews."

Amusements and Associates.

And let not men, therefore, spend their time in barbers' shops and taverns, babbling nonsense; and let them give up hunting for the women who sit near,[3] and ceaselessly talking slander against many to raise a laugh.

The game of dice[4] is to be prohibited, and the pursuit of gain, especially by dicing,[5] which many keenly follow.

---

[1] 1 Pet. iii. 8. Clement has substituted ταπεινόφρονες for φιλόφρονες (courteous).

[2] This passage has been variously amended and translated. The reading of the text has been adhered to, but ὀρθίνου has been coupled with what follows.

[3] Sylburg suggests παριούσας (passing by) instead of παριζούσας.

[4] κύβος, a die marked on all the six sides.

[5] διὰ τῶν ἀστραγάλων. The ἀστράγαλοι were dice marked on four sides only. Clemens seems to use these terms here indifferently.

Such things the prodigality of luxury invents for the idle. For the cause is idleness, and a love[1] for frivolities apart from the truth. For it is not possible otherwise to obtain enjoyment without injury; and each man's preference of a mode of life is a counterpart of his disposition.

But, as appears, only intercourse with good men benefits; on the other hand, the all-wise Instructor, by the mouth of Moses, recognising companionship with bad men as swinish, forbade the ancient people to partake of swine; to point out that those who call on God ought not to mingle with unclean men, who, like swine, delight in corporeal pleasures, in impure food, and in itching with filthy pruriency after the mischievous delights of lewdness.

Further, He says: "Thou art not to eat a kite or swift-winged ravenous bird, or an eagle,"[2] meaning: Thou shalt not come near men who gain their living by rapine. And other things also are exhibited figuratively.

With whom, then, are we to associate? With the righteous, He says again, speaking figuratively; for everything "which parts the hoof and chews the cud is clean." For the parting of the hoof indicates the equilibrium of righteousness, and ruminating points to the proper food of righteousness, the word, which enters from without, like food, by instruction, but is recalled from the mind, as from the stomach, to rational recollection. And the spiritual man, having the word in his mouth, ruminates the spiritual food; and righteousness parts the hoof rightly, because it sanctifies us in this life, and sends us on our way to the world to come.

Public Spectacles.

The Instructor will not then bring us to public spectacles; nor inappropriately might one call the racecourse and the theatre "the seat of plagues;"[3] for there is evil counsel as against the Just One,[4] and therefore the assembly against Him is execrated. These assemblies, indeed, are full of

[1] Lowth's conjecture of ἔρως instead of ἰσῶ has been adopted.
[2] Lev. xi. 13, 14; Deut. xiv. 12.   [3] Ps. i. 1, Septuagint.
[4] Acts iii. 14.

confusion[1] and iniquity; and these pretexts for assembling are the cause of disorder—men and women assembling promiscuously for the sight of one another. In this respect the assembly has already shown itself bad: for when the eye is lascivious,[2] the desires grow warm; and the eyes that are accustomed to look impudently at one's neighbours during the leisure granted to them, inflame the amatory desires. Let spectacles, therefore, and plays that are full of scurrility and of abundant gossip, be forbidden. For what base action is it that is not exhibited in the theatres? And what shameless saying is it that is not brought forward by the buffoons? And those who enjoy the evil that is in them, stamp the clear images of it at home. And, on the other hand, those that are proof against these things, and unimpressible, will never make a stumble in regard to luxurious pleasures.

For if people shall say that they betake themselves to the spectacles as a pastime for recreation, I should say that the cities which make a serious business of pastime are not wise; for cruel contests for glory which have been so fatal are not sport. No more is senseless expenditure of money, nor are the riots that are occasioned by them sport. And ease of mind is not to be purchased by zealous pursuit of frivolities, for no one who has his senses will ever prefer what is pleasant to what is good.

Religion in Ordinary Life.

But it is said we do not all philosophize. Do we not all, then, follow after life? What sayest thou? How hast thou believed? How, pray, dost thou love God and thy neighbour, if thou dost not philosophize? And how dost thou love thyself, if thou dost not love life? It is said, I have not learned letters; but if thou hast not learned to read, thou canst not excuse thyself in the case of hearing, for it is not taught. And faith is the possession not of the wise according to the world,

---

[1] ἀναμιξίας adopted instead of the reading ἀμιξίας, which is plainly wrong.

[2] λιχνευούσης on the authority of the Pal. MS. Nov. Reg. Bod.

but of those according to God; and it is taught without letters; and its handbook, at once rude and divine, is called love—a spiritual book. It is in your power to listen to divine wisdom, ay, and to frame your life in accordance with it. Nay, you are not prohibited from conducting affairs in the world decorously according to God. Let not him who sells or buys aught name two prices for what he buys or sells; but stating the net price, and studying to speak the truth, if he get not his price, he gets the truth, and is rich in the possession of rectitude. But, above all, let an oath on account of what is sold be far from you; and let swearing, too, on account of other things be banished.

And in this way let those who frequent the market-place and the shop philosophize. "For thou shalt not take the name of the Lord thy God in vain: for the Lord will not hold him guiltless that taketh His name in vain."[1]

But those who act contrary to these things—the avaricious, the liars, the hypocrites, those who make merchandise of the truth—the Lord cast out of His Father's court,[2] not willing that the holy house of God should be the house of unrighteous traffic either in words or in material things.

Going to Church.

Woman and man are to go to church decently attired, with natural step, embracing silence, possessing unfeigned love, pure in body, pure in heart, fit to pray to God. Let the woman observe this, further. Let her be entirely covered, unless she happen to be at home. For that style of dress is grave, and protects from being gazed at. And she will never fall, who puts before her eyes modesty, and her shawl; nor will she invite another to fall into sin by uncovering her face. For this is the wish of the Word, since it is becoming for her to pray veiled.[3]

They say that the wife of Æneas, through excess of pro-

---

[1] Ex. xx. 7.

[2] In allusion to the cleansing of the temple (John ii. 13-17; Matt. xxi. 12, 13; Luke xix. 45, 46).

[3] 1 Cor. xi. 5.

priety, did not, even in her terror at the capture of Troy, uncover herself; but, though fleeing from the conflagration, remained veiled.

Out of Church.

Such ought those who are consecrated to Christ appear, and frame themselves in their whole life, as they fashion themselves in the church for the sake of gravity; and to be, not to seem such—so meek, so pious, so loving. But now I know not how people change their fashions and manners with the place. As they say that polypi, assimilated to the rocks to which they adhere, are in colour such as they; so, laying aside the inspiration of the assembly, after their departure from it, they become like others with whom they associate. Nay, in laying aside the artificial mask of solemnity, they are proved to be what they secretly were. After having paid reverence to the discourse about God, they leave within [the church] what they have heard. And outside they foolishly amuse themselves with impious playing, and amatory quavering, occupied with flute-playing, and dancing, and intoxication, and all kinds of trash. They who sing thus, and sing in response, are those who before hymned immortality,—found at last wicked and wickedly singing this most pernicious palinode, "Let us eat and drink, for to-morrow we die." But not to-morrow in truth, but already, are these dead to God; burying their dead,[1] that is, sinking themselves down to death. The apostle very firmly assails them: "Be not deceived; neither adulterers, nor effeminate, nor abusers of themselves with mankind, nor thieves, nor covetous, nor drunkards, nor railers," and whatever else he adds to these, "shall inherit the kingdom of God."[2]

Love and the Kiss of Charity.

And if we are called to the kingdom of God, let us walk worthy of the kingdom, loving God and our neighbour. But love is not tested by a kiss, but by kindly feeling. But there are those, that do nothing but make the churches resound

[1] Matt. viii. 22. [2] 1 Cor. vi. 9, 10.

with a kiss, not having love itself within. For this very thing, the shameless use of the kiss, which ought to be mystic, occasions foul suspicions and evil reports. The apostle calls the kiss holy.[1]

When the kingdom is worthily tasted, we dispense the affection of the soul by a chaste and closed mouth, by which chiefly gentle manners are expressed.

But there is another unholy kiss, full of poison, counterfeiting sanctity. Do you not know that spiders, merely by touching the mouth, afflict men with pain? And often kisses inject the poison of licentiousness. It is then very manifest to us, that a kiss is not love. For the love meant is the love of God. "And this is the love of God," says John, "that we keep His commandments;"[2] not that we stroke each other on the mouth. "And His commandments are not grievous." But salutations of beloved ones in the ways, full as they are of foolish boldness, are characteristic of those who wish to be conspicuous to those without, and have not the least particle of grace. For if it is proper mystically "in the closet" to pray to God, it will follow that we are also to greet mystically our neighbour, whom we are commanded to love second similarly to God, within doors, "redeeming the time." "For we are the salt of the earth."[3] "Whosoever shall bless his friend early in the morning with a loud voice, it shall be regarded not to differ from cursing."[4]

The Government of the Eyes.

But, above all, it seems right that we turn away from the sight of women. For it is sin not only to touch, but to look; and he who is rightly trained must especially avoid them. "Let thine eyes look straight, and thine eyelids wink right."[5] For while it is possible for one who looks to remain stedfast; yet care must be taken against falling. For it is possible for one who looks to slip; but it is impossible for one, who looks not, to lust. For it is not enough for the chaste to be pure; but they must give all diligence, to be beyond the range

[1] Rom. xvi. 16. [2] 1 John iv. 7. [3] Matt. v. 13.
[4] Prov. xxvii. 14. [5] Prov. iv. 25.

of censure, shutting out all ground of suspicion, in order to the consummation of chastity; so that we may not only be faithful, but appear worthy of trust. For this is also consequently to be guarded against, as the apostle says, "that no man should blame us; providing things honourable, not only in the sight of the Lord, but also in the sight of men."[1] "But turn away thine eye from a graceful woman, and contemplate not another's beauty," says the Scripture.[2] And if you inquire the reason, it will further tell you, "For by the beauty of woman many have gone astray, and at it affection blazes up like fire;"[3] the affection which arises from the fire which we call love, leading to the fire which will never cease in consequence of sin.

[1] 2 Cor. viii. 20, 21.   [2] Ecclus. ix. 8.   [3] Ecclus. ix. 8.

CHAPTER XII.

CONTINUATION: WITH TEXTS FROM SCRIPTURE.

I WOULD counsel the married never to kiss their wives in the presence of their domestics. For Aristotle does not allow people to laugh to their slaves. And by no means must a wife be seen saluted in their presence. It is moreover better that, beginning at home with marriage, we should exhibit propriety in it. For it is the greatest bond of chastity, breathing forth pure pleasure. Very admirably the tragedy says:

> "Well! well! ladies, how is it, then, that among men,
> Not gold, not empire, or luxury of wealth,
> Conferred to such an extent signal delights,
> As the right and virtuous disposition
> Of a man of worth and a dutiful wife?"

Such injunctions of righteousness uttered by those who are conversant with worldly wisdom are not to be refused. Knowing, then, the duty of each, "pass the time of your sojourning here in fear: forasmuch as ye know that ye were not redeemed with corruptible things, such as silver or gold, from your vain conversation received by tradition from your fathers; but with the precious blood of Christ, as of a lamb without blemish and without spot."[1] "For," says Peter, "the time past of our life may suffice us to have wrought the will of the Gentiles, when we walked in lasciviousness, lusts, excess of wine, revellings, banquetings, and abominable idolatries."[2] We have as a limit the cross of the Lord, by which we are fenced and hedged about from our former sins. Therefore, being regenerated, let us fix our-

[1] 1 Pet. i. 17-19.   [2] 1 Pet. iv. 3.

selves to it in truth, and return to sobriety, and sanctify ourselves; "for the eyes of the Lord are on the righteous, and His ears are open to their prayer; but the face of the Lord is against them that do evil." "And who is he that will harm us, if we be followers of that which is good?"[1]— "us" for "you." But the best training is good order, which is perfect decorum, and stable and orderly power, which in action maintains consistence in what it does. If these things have been adduced by me with too great asperity, in order to effect the salvation which follows from your correction; they have been spoken also, says the Instructor, by me: "Since he who reproves with boldness is a peacemaker."[2] And if ye hear me, ye shall be saved. And if ye attend not to what is spoken, it is not my concern. And yet it is my concern thus: "For he desires the repentance rather than the death of a sinner."[3] "If ye shall hear me, ye shall eat the good of the land," the Instructor again says, calling by the appellation "the good of the land," beauty, wealth, health, strength, sustenance. For those things which are really good, are what "neither ear hath heard, nor hath ever entered into the heart"[4] respecting Him who is really King, and the realities truly good which await us. For He is the giver and the guard of good things. And with respect to their participation, He applies the same names of things in this world, the Word thus training in God the feebleness of men from sensible things to understanding.

What has to be observed at home, and how our life is to be regulated, the Instructor has abundantly declared. And the things which He is wont to say to children by the way, while He conducts them to the Master, these He suggests, and adduces the Scriptures themselves in a compendious form, setting forth bare injunctions, accommodating them to the period of guidance, and assigning the interpretation of them to the Master. For the intention of His law is to dissipate fear, emancipating free-will in order to faith. "Hear," He says, "O child," who art rightly instructed, the principal

[1] Ps. xxxiii. 16, 17; 1 Pet. iii. 13.   [2] Prov. x. 10, Sept.
[3] Ezek. xviii. 23.   [4] 1 Cor. ii. 9.

points of salvation. For I will disclose my ways, and lay before thee good commandments; by which thou wilt reach salvation. And I lead thee by the way of salvation. Depart from the paths of deceit.

"For the Lord knoweth the way of the righteous, and the way of the ungodly shall perish."[1] "Follow, therefore, O son, the good way which I shall describe, lending to me attentive ears." "And I will give to thee the treasures of darkness, hidden and unseen"[2] by the nations, but seen by us. And the treasures of wisdom are unfailing, in admiration of which the apostle says, "O the depth of the riches and the wisdom!"[3] And by one God are many treasures dispensed; some disclosed by the law, others by the prophets; some to the divine mouth, and others to the heptad of the spirit singing accordant. And the Lord being one, is the same Instructor by all these. Here is then a comprehensive precept, and an exhortation of life, all-embracing: "As ye would that men should do unto you, do ye likewise to them."[4] We may comprehend the commandments in two, as the Lord says, "Thou shalt love the Lord thy God with all thy heart, with all thy soul, and with all thy strength; and thy neighbour as thyself." Then from these He infers, "on this hang the law and the prophets."[5] Further, to him that asked, "What good thing shall I do, that I may inherit eternal life?" He answered, "Thou knowest the commandments?" And on him replying Yea, He said, "This do, and thou shalt be saved." Especially conspicuous is the love of the Instructor set forth in various salutary commandments, in order that the discovery may be readier, from the abundance and arrangement of the Scriptures. We have the Decalogue given by Moses, which, indicating by an elementary principle, simple and of one kind, defines the designation of sins in a way conducive to salvation: "Thou shalt not commit adultery. Thou shalt not worship idols. Thou shalt not corrupt boys. Thou shalt not steal. Thou shalt not bear false witness. Honour thy father and thy mother."[6] And so forth. These things are to

---

[1] Ps. i. 6.   [2] Isa. xlv. 3.   [3] Rom. xi. 33.
[4] Luke vi. 31.   [5] Matt. xxii. 37, 39, 40.   [6] Ex. xx.; Deut. v.

be observed, and whatever else is commanded in reading the Bible. And He enjoins on us by Isaiah: "Wash you, and make you clean. Put away iniquities from your souls before mine eyes. Learn to do well. Seek judgment. Deliver the wronged. Judge for the orphan, and justify the widow. And come, and let us reason together, saith the Lord."[1] And we shall find many examples also in other places,—as, for instance, respecting prayer: "Good works are an acceptable prayer to the Lord," says the Scripture.[2] And the manner of prayer is described. "If thou seest," it is said, "the naked, cover him; and thou shalt not overlook those who belong to thy seed. Then shall thy light spring forth early, and thy healing shall spring up quickly; and thy righteousness shall go before thee, and the glory of God shall encompass thee." What, then, is the fruit of such prayer? "Then shalt thou call, and God will hear thee; whilst thou art yet speaking, He will say, I am here."[3]

In regard to fasting it is said, "Wherefore do ye fast to me? saith the Lord. Is it such a fast that I have chosen, even a day for a man to humble his soul? Thou shalt not bend thy neck like a circle, and spread sackcloth and ashes under thee. Not thus shall ye call it an acceptable fast."

What means a fast, then? "Lo, this is the fast which I have chosen, saith the Lord. Loose every band of wickedness. Dissolve the knots of oppressive contracts. Let the oppressed go free, and tear every unjust bond. Break thy bread to the hungry; and lead the houseless poor into thy house. If thou see the naked, cover him."[4] About sacrifices too: "To what purpose is the multitude of your sacrifices to me? saith the Lord. I am full of burnt-offerings and of rams; and the fat of lambs, and the blood of bulls and kids I do not wish; nor that ye should come to appear before me. Who hath required this at your hands? You shall no more tread my court. If ye bring fine flour, the vain oblation is an abomination to me. Your new moons and your sabbaths I cannot away with."[5] How, then, shall I sacrifice to the

---

[1] Isa. i. 16, 17, 18.   [2] Where, no one knows.
[3] Isa. lviii. 7, 8, 9.   [4] Isa. i. 7, 11, 13.   [5] Isa. i. 11-13.

Lord? "The sacrifice of the Lord is," He says, "a broken heart."¹ How, then, shall I crown myself, or anoint with ointment, or offer incense to the Lord? "An odour of a sweet fragrance," it is said,² "is the heart that glorifies Him who made it." These are the crowns and sacrifices, aromatic odours, and flowers of God.

Further, in respect to forbearance. "If thy brother," it is said, "sin against thee, rebuke him; and if he repent, forgive him. If he sin against thee seven times in a day, and turn to thee the seventh time, and say, I repent, forgive him."³ Also to the soldiers, by John, He commands, "to be content with their wages only;" and to the publicans, "to exact no more than is appointed." To the judges He says, "Thou shalt not show partiality in judgment. For gifts blind the eyes of those who see, and corrupt just words. Rescue the wronged."

And to householders: "A possession which is acquired with iniquity becomes less."⁴

Also of "love." "Love," He says, "covers a multitude of sins."⁵

And of civil government: "Render to Cæsar the things which are Cæsar's; and unto God the things which are God's."⁶

Of swearing and the remembrance of injuries: "Did I command your fathers, when they went out of Egypt, to offer burnt-offerings and sacrifices? But I commanded them, Let none of you bear malice in his heart against his neighbour, or love a false oath."⁷

The liars and the proud, too, He threatens; the former thus: "Woe to them that call bitter sweet, and sweet bitter;" and the latter: "Woe unto them that are wise in their own eyes, and prudent in their own sight."⁸ "For he that humbleth himself shall be exalted, and he that exalteth himself shall be humbled."⁹

---

¹ Ps. li. 19. ² Not in Scripture. ⁵ Luke xvii. 3, 4.
⁴ Prov. xiii. 11. ⁵ 1 Pet. iv. 8.
⁶ Matt. xxii. 21; Mark xii. 17; Luke xx. 28.
⁷ In Jer. vii. 22, 23, and Zech. viii. we find the substance of what Clement gives here.
⁸ Isa. v. 20, 21. ⁹ Luke xiv 11, xviii. 14.

And "the merciful" He blesses, "for they shall obtain mercy." Wisdom pronounces anger a wretched thing, because "it will destroy the wise."[1] And now He bids us "love our enemies, bless them that curse us, and pray for them that despitefully use us." And He says: "If any one strike thee on the one cheek, turn to him the other also; and if any one take away thy coat, hinder him not from taking thy cloak also."[2]

Of faith He says: "Whatsoever ye shall ask in prayer, believing, ye shall receive."[3] "To the unbelieving nothing is trustworthy," according to Pindar.

Domestics, too, are to be treated like ourselves; for they are human beings, as we are. For God is the same to free and bond, if you consider.

Such of our brethren as transgress, we must not punish, but rebuke. "For he that spareth the rod hateth his son."[4]

Further, He banishes utterly love of glory, saying, "Woe to you, Pharisees! for ye love the chief seat in the synagogues, and greetings in the markets."[5] But He welcomes the repentance of the sinner—loving repentance—which follows sins. For this Word of whom we speak alone is sinless. For to sin is natural and common to all. But to return [to God] after sinning is characteristic not of any man, but only of a man of worth.

Respecting liberality He said: "Come to me, ye blessed, inherit the kingdom prepared for you from the foundation of the world: for I was an hungry, and ye gave me meat; I was thirsty, and ye gave me drink; I was a stranger, and ye took me in; naked, and ye clothed me; sick, and ye visited me; in prison, and ye came unto me." And when have we done any of these things to the Lord?

The Instructor Himself will say again, loving to refer to Himself the kindness of the brethren, "Inasmuch as ye have done it to these least, ye have done it to me. And these shall go away into everlasting life."[6]

Such are the laws of the Word, the consolatory words not

---

[1] Prov. xvi. Sept.
[2] Matt. v. 40; Luke vi. 27-29.
[3] Matt. xxi. 22.
[4] Prov. xiii. 24.
[5] Luke xi. 43.
[6] Matt. xxv. 34-36, 40, 46.

on tables of stone which were written by the finger of the Lord, but inscribed on men's hearts, on which alone they can remain imperishable. Wherefore the tablets of those who had hearts of stone are broken, that the faith of the children may be impressed on softened hearts.

However, both the laws served the Word for the instruction of humanity, both that given by Moses and that by the apostles. What, therefore, is the nature of the training by the apostles, appears to me to require to be treated of. Under this head, I, or rather the Instructor by me,[1] will recount; and I shall again set before you the precepts themselves, as it were in the germ.

"Putting away lying, speak every man truth with his neighbour: for we are members one of another. Let not the sun go down upon your wrath; neither give place to the devil. Let him that stole steal no more: but rather let him labour, working with his hands the thing which is good, that he may have to give to him that needeth. Let all bitterness, and wrath, and anger, and clamour, and evil-speaking, be put away from you, with all malice: and be ye kind one to another, tender-hearted, forgiving one another, as God in Christ hath forgiven you. Be therefore wise,[2] followers of God, as dear children; and walk in love, as Christ also hath loved us. Let wives be subject to their own husbands, as to the Lord. And let husbands love their wives, as Christ also hath loved the church." Let those who are yoked together love one another "as their own bodies." "Children, be obedient to your parents. Parents, provoke not your children to wrath; but bring them up in the nurture and admonition of the Lord. Servants, be obedient to those that are your masters according to the flesh, with fear and trembling, in the singleness of your hearts, as unto Christ; with good-will from the soul doing service. And, ye masters, treat your servants well, forbearing threatening: knowing that both their and your Lord is in heaven; and there is no respect of persons with Him."[3]

---

[1] δι' ἐμαυτοῦ. The reading here adopted is found in Bod. and Reg.
[2] φρόνιμοι, not found in Eph. v. 1.
[3] Eph. iv. 25-29, v. 1, 2, 22, 25, vi. 1, 4-9.

"If we live in the Spirit, let us walk in the Spirit. Let us not be desirous of vainglory, provoking one another, envying one another. Bear ye one another's burdens, and so fulfil the law of Christ. Be not deceived; God is not mocked. Let us not be weary in well-doing: for in due time we shall reap, if we faint not."[1]

"Be at peace among yourselves. Now we admonish you, brethren, warn them who are unruly, comfort the feeble-minded, support the weak, be patient toward all men. See that none render evil for evil to any man. Quench not the Spirit. Despise not prophesyings. Prove all things: hold fast that which is good. Abstain from every form of evil."[2]

"Continue in prayer, watching thereunto with thanksgiving. Walk in wisdom towards them that are without, redeeming the time. Let your speech be always with grace, seasoned with salt, that ye may know how ye ought to answer every man."[3]

"Nourish yourselves up in the words of faith. Exercise yourselves unto godliness: for bodily exercise profiteth little; but godliness is profitable for all things, having the promise of the life which now is, and that which is to come."[4]

"Let those who have faithful masters not despise them, because they are brethren; but rather do them service, because they are faithful."[5]

"He that giveth, let him do it with simplicity; he that ruleth, with diligence; he that showeth mercy, with cheerfulness. Let love be without dissimulation. Abhor that which is evil; cleave to that which is good. Be kindly affectioned one to another with brotherly love, in honour preferring one another. Not slothful in business; fervent in spirit, serving the Lord. Rejoicing in hope; patient in tribulation; continuing instant in prayer. Given to hospitality; communicating to the necessities of the saints."

Such are a few injunctions out of many, for the sake of example, which the Instructor, running over the divine Scrip-

[1] Gal. v. 25, 26, vi. 2, 7, 9.
[2] 1 Thess. v. 13-15, 19-22.
[3] Col. iv. 2, 5, 6.
[4] 1 Tim. iv. 6-8.
[5] 1 Tim. vi. 2.

tures, sets before His children ; by which, so to speak, vice is cut up by the roots, and iniquity is circumscribed.

Innumerable commands such as these are written in the holy Bible appertaining to chosen persons, some to presbyters, some to bishops, some to deacons, others to widows, of whom we shall have another opportunity of speaking. Many things spoken in enigmas, many in parables, may benefit such as fall in with them. But it is not my province, says the Instructor, to teach these any longer. But we need a Teacher of the exposition of those sacred words, to whom we must direct our steps.

And now, in truth, it is time for me to cease from my instruction, and for you to listen to the Teacher.[1] And He, receiving you who have been trained up in excellent discipline, will teach you the oracles. To noble purpose has the church sung, and the Bridegroom also, the alone Teacher, the good Counsel, of the good Father, the true Wisdom, the Sanctuary of knowledge. "And He is the propitiation for our sins," as John says ; Jesus, who heals both our body and soul—which are the proper man. "And not for our sins only, but also for the whole world. And by this we know that we know Him, if we keep His commandments. He that saith, I know Him, and keepeth not His commandments, is a liar ; and the truth is not in Him. But whoso keepeth His word, in him verily is the love of God perfected. Hereby know we that we are in Him. He that saith he abideth in Him, ought himself to walk even as He also walked."[2] O nurslings of His blessed training! let us complete the fair face of the church; and let us run as children to our good mother. And if we become listeners to the Word, let us glorify the blessed dispensation by which man is trained and sanctified as a child of God, and has his conversation in heaven, being trained from earth, and there receives the Father, whom he learns to know on earth. The Word both does and teaches all things, and trains in all things.

[1] That is, he who undertakes the instruction of those that are full-grown, as Clemens does in the *Stromata*.
[2] 1 John ii. 2-6.

A horse is guided by a bit, and a bull is guided by a yoke, and a wild beast is caught in a noose. But man is transformed by the Word, by whom wild beasts are tamed, and fishes caught, and birds drawn down. He it is, in truth, who fashions the bit for the horse, the yoke for the bull, the noose for the wild beast, the rod for the fish, the snare for the bird. He both manages the state and tills the ground; commands, and helps, and creates the universe.

"There were figured earth, and sky, and sea,
The ever-circling sun, and full-orbed moon,
And all the signs that crown the vault of heaven."[1]

O divine works! O divine commands! "Let this water undulate within itself; let this fire restrain its wrath; let this air wander into ether; and this earth be consolidated, and acquire motion! When I want to form man, I want matter, and have matter in the elements. I dwell with what I have formed. If you know me, the fire will be your slave."

Such is the Word, such is the Instructor, the Creator of the world and of man: and of Himself, now the world's Instructor, by whose command we and the universe subsist, and await judgment. "For it is not he who brings a stealthy vocal word to men," as Bacchylidis says, "who shall be the Word of Wisdom;" but "the blameless, the pure, and faultless sons of God," according to Paul, "in the midst of a crooked and perverse generation, to shine as lights in the world."[2]

All that remains therefore now, in such a celebration of the Word as this, is that we address to the Word our prayer.

[1] *Iliad*, xviii. 483-485; spoken of Vulcan making the shield of Achilles.
[2] Phil. ii. 15.

PRAYER TO THE PÆDAGOGUS.

Be gracious, O Instructor, to us Thy children, Father, Charioteer of Israel, Son and Father, both in One, O Lord. Grant to us who obey Thy precepts, that we may perfect the likeness of the image, and with all our power know Him who is the good God and not a harsh judge. And do Thou Thyself cause that all of us who have our conversation in Thy peace, who have been translated into Thy commonwealth, having sailed tranquilly over the billows of sin, may be wafted in calm by Thy Holy Spirit, by the ineffable wisdom, by night and day to the perfect day; and giving thanks may praise, and praising thank the Alone Father and Son, Son and Father, the Son, Instructor and Teacher, with the Holy Spirit, all in One, in whom is all, for whom all is One, for whom is eternity, whose members we all are, whose glory the æons[1] are; for the All-good, All-lovely, All-wise, All-just One. To whom be glory both now and for ever. Amen.

And since the Instructor, by translating us into His church, has united us to Himself, the teaching and all-surveying Word, it were right that, having got to this point, we should offer to the Lord the reward of due thanksgiving—praise suitable to His fair instruction.

[1] Αἰῶνες, "celestial spirits and angels."—GRABE, in a note on Bull's *Defence of the Nicene Creed.*

A HYMN TO CHRIST THE SAVIOUR.

COMPOSED BY ST. CLEMENT.[1]

BRIDLE of colts untamed,
    Over our wills presiding;
Wing of unwandering birds,
    Our flight securely guiding.
Rudder of youth unbending,
    Firm against adverse shock;
Shepherd, with wisdom tending
    Lambs of the royal flock:
Thy simple children bring
In one, that they may sing
In solemn lays
Their hymns of praise
With guileless lips to Christ their King.

King of saints, almighty Word
Of the Father highest Lord;
Wisdom's head and chief;
Assuagement of all grief;
Lord of all time and space,
Jesus, Saviour of our race;

---

[1] The translator has done what he could to render this hymn literally. He has been obliged, however, to add somewhat to it in the way of expansion, for otherwise it would have been impossible to secure anything approaching the flow of English versification. The original is in many parts a mere string of epithets, which no ingenuity could render in rhymed verse without some additions.

Shepherd, who dost us keep;
  Husbandman, who tillest,
Bit to restrain us, Rudder
  To guide us as Thou willest;
Of the all-holy flock celestial wing;
Fisher of men, whom Thou to life dost bring;
  From evil sea of sin,
    And from the billowy strife,
  Gathering pure fishes in,
    Caught with sweet bait of life:
Lead us, Shepherd of the sheep,
  Reason-gifted, holy One;
King of youths, whom Thou dost keep,
  So that they pollution shun:
Steps of Christ, celestial Way;
  Word eternal, Age unending;
Life that never can decay;
  Fount of mercy, virtue-sending;
Life august of those who raise
Unto God their hymn of praise,
                  Jesus Christ!

Nourished by the milk of heaven,
To our tender palates given;
Milk of wisdom from the breast
Of that bride of grace exprest;
By a dewy spirit filled
From fair Reason's breast distilled;
Let us sucklings join to raise
With pure lips our hymns of praise
As our grateful offering,
Clean and pure, to Christ our King.
Let us, with hearts undefiled,
Celebrate the mighty Child.
We, Christ-born, the choir of peace;
  We, the people of His love,
Let us sing, nor ever cease,
  To the God of peace above.

We subjoin the following literal translation of the foregoing hymn:—

Bridle of untamed colts, Wing of unwandering birds, sure Helm of babes,[1] Shepherd of royal lambs, assemble Thy simple children to praise holily, to hymn guilelessly with innocent mouths, Christ the guide of children. O King of saints, all-subduing Word of the most high Father, Ruler of wisdom, Support of sorrows, that rejoicest in the ages,[2] Jesus, Saviour of the human race, Shepherd, Husbandman, Helm, Bridle, Heavenly Wing of the all-holy flock, Fisher of men who are saved, catching the chaste fishes with sweet life from the hateful wave of a sea of vices,—Guide [us], Shepherd of rational sheep; guide unharmed children, O holy King,[3] O footsteps of Christ, O heavenly way, perennial Word, immeasurable Age, Eternal Light, Fount of mercy, performer of virtue; noble [is the] life of those who hymn God, O Christ Jesus, heavenly milk of the sweet breasts of the graces of the Bride, pressed out of Thy wisdom. Babes nourished with tender mouths, filled with the dewy spirit of the rational pap, let us sing together simple praises, true hymns to Christ [our] King, holy fee for the teaching of life; let us sing in simplicity the powerful Child. O choir of peace, the Christ-begotten, O chaste people, let us sing together[4] the God of peace.

[1] Or, "ships:" πηῶν, instead of πητίων, has been suggested as better sense and better metre.

[2] Or, "rejoicing in eternity."

[3] By altering the punctuation, we can translate thus: "Guide, O holy King, Thy children safely along the footsteps of Christ."

[4] The word used here is ψάλωμεν, originally signifying, "Let us celebrate on a stringed instrument." Whether it is so used here or not, may be matter of dispute.

TO THE PÆDAGOGUS.

Teacher, to Thee a chaplet I present,
Woven of words culled from the spotless mead,
Where Thou dost feed Thy flocks; like to the bee,
That skilful worker, which from many a flower
Gathers its treasures, that she may convey
A luscious offering to the master's hand.
Though but the least, I am Thy servant still,
(Seemly is praise to Thee for Thy behests).
O King, great Giver of good gifts to men,
Lord of the good, Father, of all the Maker,
Who heaven and heaven's adornment, by Thy word
Divine fitly disposed, alone didst make;
Who broughtest forth the sunshine and the day;
Who didst appoint their courses to the stars,
And how the earth and sea their place should keep;
And when the seasons, in their circling course,
Winter and summer, spring and autumn, each
Should come, according to well-ordered plan;
Out of a confused heap who didst create
This ordered sphere, and from the shapeless mass
Of matter didst the universe adorn;—
Grant to me life, and be that life well spent,
Thy grace enjoying; let me act and speak
In all things as Thy Holy Scriptures teach;
Thee and Thy co-eternal Word, All-wise,
From Thee proceeding, ever may I praise;
Give me nor poverty nor wealth, but what is meet,
Father, in life, and then life's happy close.

THE MISCELLANIES; OR, STROMATA.

THE MISCELLANIES.

BOOK I.

CHAPTER I.

PREFACE—THE AUTHOR'S OBJECT—THE UTILITY OF WRITTEN COMPOSITIONS.

[*Wants the beginning*] . . . . that you may read them under your hand, and may be able to preserve them. Whether written compositions are not to be left behind at all; or if they are, by whom? And if the former, what need there is for written compositions? and if the latter, is the composition of them to be assigned to earnest men, or the opposite? It were certainly ridiculous for one to disapprove of the writing of earnest men, and approve of those, who are not such, engaging in the work of composition. Theopompus and Timæus, who composed fables and slanders, and Epicurus the leader of atheism, and Hipponax and Archilochus, are to be allowed to write in their own shameful manner. But he who proclaims the truth is to be prevented from leaving behind him what is to benefit posterity. It is a good thing, I reckon, to leave to posterity good children. This is the case with children of our bodies. But words are the progeny of the soul. Hence we call those who have instructed us, fathers. Wisdom is a communicative and philanthropic thing. Accordingly, Solomon says, "My son, if thou receive the saying of my commandment, and hide it with thee, thine ear shall hear wisdom."[1] He points out that the word that is

[1] Prov. ii. 1, 2.

sown is hidden in the soul of the learner, as in the earth, and this is spiritual planting. Wherefore also he adds, "And thou shalt apply thine heart to understanding, and apply it for the admonition of thy son." For soul, methinks, joined with soul, and spirit with spirit, in the sowing of the word, will make that which is sown grow and germinate. And every one who is instructed, is in respect of subjection the son of his instructor. "Son," says he, "forget not my laws."[1]

And if knowledge belong not to all (set an ass to the lyre, as the proverb goes), yet written compositions are for the many. "Swine, for instance, delight in dirt more than in clean water." "Wherefore," says the Lord, "I speak to them in parables : because seeing, they see not; and hearing, they hear not, and do not understand;"[2] not as if the Lord caused the ignorance : for it were impious to think so. But He prophetically exposed this ignorance, that existed in them, and intimated that they would not understand the things spoken. And now the Saviour shows Himself, out of His abundance, dispensing goods to His servants according to the ability of the recipient, that they may augment them by exercising activity, and then returning to reckon with them; when, approving of those that had increased His money, those faithful in little, and commanding them to have the charge over many things, He bade them enter into the joy of the Lord. But to him who had hid the money, entrusted to him to be given out at interest, and had given it back as he had received it, without increase, He said, "Thou wicked and slothful servant, thou oughtest to have given my money to the bankers, and at my coming I should have received mine own." Wherefore the useless servant "shall be cast into outer darkness."[3] "Thou, therefore, be strong," says Paul, " in the grace that is in Christ Jesus. And the things which thou hast heard of me among many witnesses, the same commit thou to faithful men, who shall be able to teach others also."[4] And again : "Study to show thyself ap-

---

[1] Prov. iii. 1.   [2] Matt. xiii. 13.
[3] Matt. xviii. 32 ; Luke xix. 22 ; Matt. xxv. 30.
[4] 2 Tim. ii. 1, 2.

proved unto God, a workman that needeth not to be ashamed, rightly dividing the word of truth."

If, then, both proclaim the Word—the one by writing, the other by speech—are not both then to be approved, making, as they do, faith active by love? It is by one's own fault that he does not choose what is best; God is free of blame. As to the point in hand, it is the business of some to lay out the word at interest, and of others to test it, and either choose it or not. And the judgment is determined within themselves. But there is that species of knowledge which is characteristic of the herald, and that which is, as it were, characteristic of a messenger, and it is serviceable in whatever way it operates, both by the hand and tongue. "For he that soweth to the Spirit, shall of the Spirit reap life everlasting. And let us not be weary in well-doing."[1] On him who by Divine Providence meets in with it, it confers the very highest advantages,—the beginning of faith, readiness for adopting a right mode of life, the impulse towards the truth, a movement of inquiry, a trace of knowledge; in a word, it gives the means of salvation. And those who have been rightly reared in the words of truth, and received provision for eternal life, wing their way to heaven. Most admirably, therefore, the apostle says, "In everything approving ourselves as the servants of God; as poor, and yet making many rich; as having nothing, yet possessing all things. Our mouth is opened to you."[2] "I charge thee," he says, writing to Timothy, "before God, and Christ Jesus, and the elect angels, that thou observe these things, without preferring one before another, doing nothing by partiality."[3]

Both must therefore test themselves: the one, if he is qualified to speak and leave behind him written records; the other, if he is in a right state to hear and read: as also some in the dispensation of the Eucharist, according to custom, enjoin that each one of the people individually should take his part. One's own conscience is best for choosing accurately or shunning. And its firm foundation is a right life, with suitable instruction. But the imitation of those who

[1] Gal. vi. 8, 9.   [2] 2 Cor. vi. 4, 10, 11.   [3] 1 Tim. v. 21.

have already been tested, and who have led correct lives, is most excellent for the understanding and practice of the commandments. "So that whosoever shall eat the bread and drink the cup of the Lord unworthily, shall be guilty of the body and blood of the Lord. But let a man examine himself, and so let him eat of the bread and drink of the cup."[1] It therefore follows, that every one of those who undertake to promote the good of their neighbours, ought to consider whether he has betaken himself to teaching rashly and out of rivalry to any; if his communication of the word is out of vainglory; if the only reward he reaps is the salvation of those who hear, and if he speaks not in order to win favour: if so, he who speaks by writings escapes the reproach of mercenary motives. "For neither at any time used we flattering words, as ye know," says the apostle, "nor a cloak of covetousness. God is witness. Nor of men sought we glory, neither of you, nor yet of others, when we might have been burdensome as the apostles of Christ. But we were gentle among you, even as a nurse cherisheth her children."[2]

In the same way, therefore, those who take part in the divine words, ought to guard against betaking themselves to this, as they would to the buildings of cities, to examine them out of curiosity; that they do not come to the task for the sake of receiving worldly things, having ascertained that they who are consecrated to Christ are given to communicate the necessaries of life. But let such be dismissed as hypocrites. But if any one wishes not to seem, but to be righteous, to him it belongs to know the things which are best. If, then, "the harvest is plenteous, but the labourers few," it is incumbent on us "to pray" that there may be as great abundance of labourers as possible.[3]

But the husbandry is twofold,—the one unwritten, and the other written. And in whatever way the Lord's labourer sow the good wheat, and grow and reap the ears, he shall appear a truly divine husbandman. "Labour," says the Lord, "not for the meat which perisheth, but for that which

---

[1] 1 Cor. xi. 27, 28.   [2] 1 Thess. ii. 5, 6, 7.
[3] Matt. ix. 37, 38; Luke x. 2.

endureth to everlasting life."[1] And nutriment is received both by bread and by words. And truly "blessed are the peace-makers,"[2] who instructing those who are at war in their life and errors here, lead them back to the peace which is in the Word, and nourish for the life which is according to God, by the distribution of the bread, those "that hunger after righteousness." For each soul has its own proper nutriment; some growing by knowledge and science, and others feeding on the Hellenic philosophy, the whole of which, like nuts, is not eatable. "And he that planteth and he that watereth," "being ministers" of Him "that gives the increase, are one" in the ministry. "But every one shall receive his own reward, according to his own work. For we are God's husbandmen, God's husbandry. Ye are God's building,"[3] according to the apostle. Wherefore the hearers are not permitted to apply the test of comparison. Nor is the word, given for investigation, to be committed to those who have been reared in the arts of all kinds of words, and in the power of inflated attempts at proof; whose minds are already pre-occupied, and have not been previously emptied. But whoever chooses to banquet on faith, is stedfast for the reception of the divine words, having acquired already faith as a power of judging, according to reason. Hence ensues to him persuasion in abundance. And this was the meaning of that saying of prophecy, "If ye believe not, neither shall ye understand."[4] "As, then, we have opportunity, let us do good to all, especially to the household of faith."[5] And let each of these, according to the blessed David, sing, giving thanks. "Thou shalt sprinkle me with hyssop, and I shall be cleansed. Thou shalt wash me, and I shall be whiter than the snow. Thou shalt make me to hear gladness and joy, and the bones which have been humbled shall rejoice. Turn Thy face from my sins. Blot out mine iniquities. Create in me a clean heart, O God, and renew a right spirit in my inward parts. Cast me not away from Thy face, and take not Thy Holy Spirit from me. Restore to me the joy of Thy salvation, and establish me with Thy princely spirit."[6]

[1] John vi. 27. [2] Matt. vi. 9. [3] 1 Cor. iii. 8, 9.
[4] Isa. vii. 9. [5] Gal. vi. 10. [6] Ps. li. 9-14.

He who addresses those who are present before him, both tests them by time, and judges by his judgment, and from the others distinguishes him who can hear; watching the words, the manners, the habits, the life, the motions, the attitudes, the look, the voice; the road, the rock, the beaten path, the fruitful land, the wooded region, the fertile and fair and cultivated spot, that is able to multiply the seed. But he that speaks through books, consecrates himself before God, crying in writing thus: Not for gain, not for vainglory, not to be vanquished by partiality, nor enslaved by fear, nor elated by pleasure; but only to reap the salvation of those who read, which he does not at present participate in, but awaiting in expectation the recompense which will certainly be rendered by Him, who has promised to bestow on the labourers the reward that is meet. But he who is enrolled in the number of men[1] ought not to desire recompense. For he that vaunts his good services, receives glory as his reward. And he who does any duty for the sake of recompense, is he not held fast in the custom of the world, either as one who has done well, hastening to receive a reward, or as an evildoer avoiding retribution? We must, as far as we can, imitate the Lord. And he will do so, who complies with the will of God, receiving freely, giving freely, and receiving as a worthy reward the citizenship itself. "The hire of an harlot shall not come into the sanctuary," it is said: accordingly it was forbidden to bring to the altar the price of a dog. And in whomsoever the eye of the soul has been blinded by ill-nurture and teaching, let him advance to the true light, to the truth, which shows by writing the things that are unwritten. "Ye that thirst, go to the waters,"[2] says Esaias. And "drink water from thine own vessels,"[3] Solomon exhorts. Accordingly in "The Laws," the philosopher who learned from the Hebrews, Plato, commands husbandmen not to irrigate or take water from others, until they have first dug down in their own ground to what is called the virgin soil, and found it dry. For it is right to supply want, but it is not well to support laziness. For Pythagoras said that, "although it be

---

[1] *i.e.* perfect men.   [2] Isa. lv. 1.   [3] Prov. v. 15.

agreeable to reason to take a share of a burden, it is not a duty to take it away."

Now the Scripture kindles the living spark of the soul, and directs the eye suitably for contemplation; perchance inserting something, as the husbandman when he ingrafts, but, according to the opinion of the divine apostle, exciting what is in the soul. "For there are certainly among us many weak and sickly, and many sleep. But if we judge ourselves, we shall not be judged."[1] Now this work of mine in writing is not artfully constructed for display; but my memoranda are stored up against old age, as a remedy against forgetfulness, truly an image and outline of those vigorous and animated discourses which I was privileged to hear, and of blessed and truly remarkable men.

Of these the one, in Greece, an Ionic;[2] the other in Magna Græcia: the first of these from Cœle-Syria, the second from Egypt, and others in the East. The one was born in the land of Assyria, and the other a Hebrew in Palestine.

When I came upon the last[3] (he was the first in power), having tracked him out concealed in Egypt, I found rest. He, the true, the Sicilian bee, gathering the spoil of the flowers of the prophetic and apostolic meadow, engendered in the souls of his hearers a deathless element of knowledge.

Well, they preserving the tradition of the blessed doctrine derived directly from the holy apostles, Peter, James, John, and Paul, the son receiving it from the father (but few were like the fathers), came by God's will to us also to deposit those ancestral and apostolic seeds. And well I know that they will exult; I do not mean delighted with this tribute, but solely on account of the preservation of the truth, according as they delivered it. For such a sketch as this, will, I think, be agreeable to a soul desirous of preserving from escape the blessed tradition. "In a man who loves wisdom the Father will be glad."[4] Wells, when

[1] 1 Cor. xi. 31, 32. "You" is the reading of New Testament.
[2] The first probably Tatian, the second Theodotus.
[3] Most likely Pantænus, master of the catechetical school in Alexandria, and the teacher of Clement.
[4] Prov. xxix. 3.

pumped out, yield purer water; and that of which no one partakes, turns to putrefaction. Use keeps steel brighter, but disuse produces rust in it. For, in a word, exercise produces a healthy condition both in souls and bodies. "No one lighteth a candle, and putteth it under a bushel, but upon a candlestick, that it may give light to those who are regarded worthy of the feast."[1] For what is the use of wisdom, if it makes not him who can hear it wise? For still the Saviour saves, " and always works, as He sees the Father."[2] For by teaching, one learns more; and in speaking, one is often a hearer along with his audience. For the teacher of him who speaks and of him who hears is one—who waters both the mind and the word. Thus the Lord did not hinder from doing good while keeping the Sabbath; but allowed us to communicate of those divine mysteries, and of that holy light, to those who are able to receive them. He did not certainly disclose to the many what did not belong to the many; but to the few to whom He knew that they belonged, who were capable of receiving and being moulded according to them. But secret things are entrusted to speech, not to writing, as is the case with God.

And if one say that it is written, "There is nothing secret which shall not be revealed, nor hidden which shall not be disclosed,"[3] let him also hear from us, that to him who hears secretly, even what is secret shall be manifested. This is what was predicted by this oracle. And to him who is able secretly to observe what is delivered to him, that which is veiled shall be disclosed as truth; and what is hidden to the many, shall appear manifest to the few. For why do not all know the truth? why is not righteousness loved, if righteousness belongs to all? But the mysteries are delivered mystically, that what is spoken may be in the mouth of the speaker; rather not in his voice, but in his understanding. " God gave to the church, some apostles, and some prophets, and some evangelists, and some pastors and teachers, for the

---

[1] Matt. v. 15; Mark iv. 21.
[2] John v. 17, 19.
[3] Luke viii. 16, xi. 33.

perfecting of the saints, for the work of the ministry, for the edifying of the body of Christ."[1]

The writing of these memoranda of mine, I well know, is weak when compared with that spirit, full of grace, which I was privileged to hear. But it will be an image to recall the archetype to him who was struck with the Thyrsus. For "speak," it is said, "to a wise man, and he will grow wiser; and to him that hath, and there shall be added to him." And we profess not to explain secret things sufficiently—far from it—but only to recall them to memory, whether we have forgot aught, or whether for the purpose of not forgetting. Many things, I well know, have escaped us, through length of time, that have dropped away unwritten. Whence, to aid the weakness of my memory, and provide for myself a salutary help to my recollection in a systematic arrangement of chapters, I necessarily make use of this form. There are then some things of which we have no recollection; for the power that was in the blessed men was great. There are also some things which remained unnoted long, which have now escaped; and others which are effaced, having faded away in the mind itself, since such a task is not easy to those not experienced; these I revive in my commentaries. Some things I purposely omit, in the exercise of a wise selection, afraid to write what I guarded against speaking: not grudging—for that were wrong—but fearing for my readers, lest they should stumble by taking them in a wrong sense; and, as the proverb says, we should be found "reaching a sword to a child." For it is impossible that what has been written should not escape, although remaining unpublished by me. But being always revolved, using the one only voice, that of writing, they answer nothing to him that makes inquiries beyond what is written; for they require of necessity the aid of some one, either of him who wrote, or of some one else who has walked in his footsteps. Some things my treatise will hint; on some it will linger; some it will merely mention. It will try to speak imperceptibly, to exhibit secretly, and to demonstrate silently. The dogmas taught by remark-

[1] Eph. iv. 11, 12.

able sects will be adduced; and to these will be opposed all that ought to be premised in accordance with the profoundest contemplation of the knowledge, which, as we proceed to the renowned and venerable canon of tradition, from the creation of the world, will advance to our view; setting before us what according to natural contemplation necessarily has to be treated of beforehand, and clearing off what stands in the way of this arrangement. So that we may have our ears ready for the reception of the tradition of true knowledge; the soil being previously cleared of the thorns and of every weed by the husbandman, in order to the planting of the vine. For there is a contest, and the prelude to the contest; and there are some mysteries before other mysteries.

Our book will not shrink from making use of what is best in philosophy and other preparatory instruction. "For not only for the Hebrews and those that are under the law," according to the apostle, "is it right to become a Jew, but also a Greek for the sake of the Greeks, that we may gain all."[1] Also in the Epistle to the Colossians he writes, "Admonishing every man, and teaching every man in all wisdom, that we may present every man perfect in Christ."[2] The nicety of speculation, too, suits the sketch presented in my commentaries. In this respect the resources of learning are like a relish mixed with the food of an athlete, who is not indulging in luxury, but entertains a noble desire for distinction.

By music we harmoniously relax the excessive tension of gravity. And as those who wish to address the people, do so often by the herald, that what is said may be better heard; so also in this case. For we have the word, that was spoken to many, before the common tradition. Wherefore we must set forth the opinions and utterances which cried individually to them, by which those who hear shall more readily turn.

And, in truth, to speak briefly: Among many small pearls there is the one; and in a great take of fish there is the beauty-fish; and by time and toil truth will gleam forth, if a good helper is at hand. For most benefits are supplied, from God, through men. All of us who make use of our

[1] 1 Cor. ix. 20, 21.   [2] Col. i. 28.

eyes see what is presented before them. But some look at objects for one reason, others for another. For instance, the cook and the shepherd do not survey the sheep similarly: for the one examines it if it be fat; the other watches to see if it be of good breed. Let a man milk the sheep's milk if he need sustenance: let him shear the wool if he need clothing. And in this way let me produce the fruit of Greek erudition.

For I do not imagine that any composition can be so fortunate as that no one will speak against it. But that is to be regarded as in accordance with reason, which nobody speaks against, with reason. And that course of action and choice is to be approved, not which is faultless, but which no one rationally finds fault with. For it does not follow, that if a man accomplishes anything not purposely, he does it through force of circumstances. But he will do it, managing it by wisdom divinely given, and in accommodation to circumstances. For it is not he who, has virtue, that needs the way to virtue, any more than he, that is strong, needs recovery. For, like farmers who irrigate the land beforehand, so we also water with the liquid stream of Greek learning what in it is earthy; so that it may receive the spiritual seed cast into it, and may be capable of easily nourishing it. The *Stromata* will contain the truth mixed up in the dogmas of philosophy, or rather covered over and hidden, as the edible part of the nut in the shell. For, in my opinion, it is fitting that the seeds of truth be kept for the husbandmen of faith, and no others. I am not oblivious of what is babbled by some, who in their ignorance are frightened at every noise, and say that we ought to occupy ourselves with what is most necessary, and which contains the faith; and that we should pass over what is beyond and superfluous, which wears out and detains us to no purpose, in things which conduce nothing to the great end. Others think that philosophy was introduced into life by an evil influence, for the ruin of men, by an evil inventor. But I shall show, throughout the whole of these *Stromata*, that evil has an evil nature, and can never turn out the producer of aught that is good; indicating that philosophy is in a sense a work of Divine Providence.

CHAPTER II.

OBJECTION TO THE NUMBER OF EXTRACTS FROM PHILO-
SOPHICAL WRITINGS IN THESE BOOKS ANTICIPATED
AND ANSWERED.

IN reference to these commentaries, which contain as the exigencies of the case demand, the Hellenic opinions, I say thus much to those who are fond of finding fault. First, even if philosophy were useless, if the demonstration of its uselessness does good, it is yet useful. Then those cannot condemn the Greeks, who have only a mere hearsay knowledge of their opinions, and have not entered into a minute investigation in each department, in order to acquaintance with them. For the refutation, which is based on experience, is entirely trustworthy. For the knowledge of what is condemned is found the most complete demonstration. Many things, then, though not contributing to the final result, equip the artist. And otherwise erudition commends him, who sets forth the most essential doctrines so as to produce persuasion in his hearers, engendering admiration in those who are taught, and leads them to the truth. And such persuasion is convincing, by which those that love learning admit the truth; so that philosophy does not ruin life by being the originator of false practices and base deeds, although some have calumniated it, though it be the clear image of truth, a divine gift to the Greeks; nor does it drag us away from the faith, as if we were bewitched by some delusive art, but rather, so to speak, by the use of an ampler circuit, obtains a common exercise demonstrative of the faith. Further, the juxtaposition of doctrines, by comparison, saves the truth, from which follows knowledge.

Philosophy came into existence, not on its own account, but for the advantages reaped by us from knowledge, we receiving a firm persuasion of true perception, through the knowledge of things comprehended by the mind. For I do not mention that the *Stromata*, forming a body of varied erudition, wish artfully to conceal the seeds of knowledge. As, then, he who is fond of hunting captures the game after seeking, tracking, scenting, hunting it down with dogs; so truth, when sought and got with toil, appears a delicious[1] thing. Why, then, you will ask, did you think it fit that such an arrangement should be adopted in your memoranda? Because there is great danger in divulging the secret of the true philosophy to those, whose delight it is unsparingly to speak against everything, not justly; and who shout forth all kinds of names and words indecorously, deceiving themselves and beguiling those who adhere to them. " For the Hebrews seek signs," as the apostle says, " and the Greeks seek after wisdom."[2]

[1] Adopting the emendation γλυκύ τι instead of γλυκύτητι.
[2] 1 Cor. i. 22.

CHAPTER III.

AGAINST THE SOPHISTS.

THERE is a great crowd of this description: some of them, enslaved to pleasures and willing to disbelieve, laugh at the truth which is worthy of all reverence, making sport of its barbarousness. Some others, exalting themselves, endeavour to discover calumnious objections to our words, furnishing captious questions, hunters out of paltry sayings, practisers of miserable artifices, wranglers, dealers in knotty points, as that Abderite says:

"For mortals' tongues are glib, and on them are many speeches;
And a wide range for words of all sorts in this place and that."

And—

"Of whatever sort the word you have spoken, of the same sort you must hear."

Inflated with this art of theirs, the wretched Sophists, babbling away in their own jargon; toiling their whole life about the division of names and the nature of the composition and conjunction of sentences, show themselves greater chatterers than turtle-doves; scratching and tickling, not in a manly way, in my opinion, the ears of those who wish to be tickled.

"A river of silly words—not a dropping;"

just as in old shoes, when all the rest is worn and is falling to pieces, and the tongue alone remains. The Athenian Solon most excellently enlarges, and writes:

"Look to the tongue, and to the words of the glozing man,
But you look on no work that has been done;
But each one of you walks in the steps of a fox,
And in all of you is an empty mind."

This, I think, is signified by the utterance of the Saviour,

"'The foxes have holes, but the Son of man hath not where to lay His head."[1] For on the believer alone, who is separated entirely from the rest, who by the Scripture are called wild beasts, rests the head of the universe, the kind and gentle Word, "who taketh the wise in their own craftiness. For the Lord knoweth the thoughts of the wise, that they are vain;"[2] the Scripture calling those the wise (σοφοὺς) who are skilled in words and arts, sophists (σοφιστὰς). Whence the Greeks also applied the denominative appellation of wise and sophists (σοφοὶ, σοφισταί) to those who were versed in anything. Cratinus accordingly, having in the *Archilochii* enumerated the poets, said:

"Such a hive of sophists have ye examined."

And similarly Iophon, the comic poet, in *Flute-playing Satyrs*, says:

"For there entered
A band of sophists, all equipped."

Of these and the like, who devote their attention to empty words, the divine Scripture most excellently says, "I will destroy the wisdom of the wise, and bring to nothing the understanding of the prudent."[3]

[1] Matt. viii. 20; Luke ix. 58.
[2] Job v. 13; 1 Cor. iii. 19, 20; Ps. xciv. 11.
[3] Isa. xxix. 14; 1 Cor. i. 19.

CHAPTER IV.

HUMAN ARTS AS WELL AS DIVINE KNOWLEDGE PROCEED FROM GOD.

OMER calls an artificer wise; and of Margites, if that is his work, he thus writes:

"Him, then, the gods made neither a delver nor a ploughman,
Nor in any other respect wise; but he missed every art."

Hesiod further said the musician Linus was "skilled in all manner of wisdom;" and does not hesitate to call a mariner wise, seeing he writes:

"Having no wisdom in navigation."

And Daniel the prophet says, "The mystery which the king asks, it is not in the power of the wise, the Magi, the diviners, the Gazarenes, to tell the king; but it is God in heaven who revealeth it."[1]

Here he terms the Babylonians wise. And that Scripture calls every secular science or art by the one name wisdom (there are other arts and sciences invented over and above by human reason), and that artistic and skilful invention is from God, will be clear if we adduce the following statement: "And the Lord spake to Moses, See, I have called Bezaleel, the son of Uri, the son of Or, of the tribe of Judah; and I have filled him with the divine spirit of wisdom, and understanding, and knowledge, to devise and to execute in all manner of work, to work gold, and silver, and brass, and blue, and purple, and scarlet, and in working stone work, and in the art of working wood," and even to "all works."[2] And then He adds the general reason, "And to every understanding heart I have given understanding;"[3] that is, to every one capable of acquiring it by pains and exercise.

[1] Dan. ii. 27, 28. [2] Ex. xxxi. 2-5. [3] Ex. xxxi. 6.

And again, it is written expressly in the name of the Lord: "And speak thou to all that are wise in mind, whom I have filled with the spirit of perception."[1] Those who are wise in mind have a certain attribute of nature peculiar to themselves; and they who have shown themselves capable, receive from the Supreme Wisdom a spirit of perception in double measure. For those who practise the common arts, are in what pertains to the senses highly gifted: in hearing, he who is commonly called a musician; in touch, he who moulds clay; in voice the singer, in smell the perfumer, in sight the engraver of devices on seals. Those also that are occupied in instruction, train the sensibility according to which the poets are susceptible to the influence of measure; the sophists apprehend expression; the dialecticians, syllogisms; and the philosophers are capable of the contemplation of which themselves are the objects. For sensibility finds and invents; since it persuasively exhorts to application. And practice will increase the application which has knowledge for its end. With reason, therefore, the apostle has called the wisdom of God "manifold," and which has manifested its power "in many departments and in many modes"[2]—by art, by knowledge, by faith, by prophecy—for our benefit. "For all wisdom is from the Lord, and is with Him for ever," as says the Wisdom of Jesus.[3]

"For if thou call on wisdom and knowledge with a loud voice, and seek it as treasures of silver, and eagerly track it out, thou shalt understand godliness and find divine knowledge."[4] The prophet says this in contradiction to the knowledge according to philosophy, which teaches us to investigate in a magnanimous and noble manner, for our progress in piety. He opposes, therefore, to it the knowledge which is occupied with piety, when referring to knowledge, when he speaks as follows: "For God gives wisdom out of His own mouth, and knowledge along with understanding, and treasures up help for the righteous." For to those who have been justified by philosophy, the knowledge which leads to piety is laid up as a help.

[1] Ex. xxviii. 3.
[2] Eph. iii. 10; Heb. i. 1.
[3] Ecclus. i. 1.
[4] Prov. ii. 3–5.

CHAPTER V.

PHILOSOPHY THE HANDMAID OF THEOLOGY

ACCORDINGLY, before the advent of the Lord, philosophy was necessary to the Greeks for righteousness. And now it becomes conducive to piety; being a kind of preparatory training to those who attain to faith through demonstration. "For thy foot," it is said, "will not stumble, if thou refer what is good, whether belonging to the Greeks or to us, to Providence."[1] For God is the cause of all good things; but of some primarily, as of the Old and the New Testament; and of others by consequence, as philosophy. Perchance, too, philosophy was given to the Greeks directly and primarily, till the Lord should call the Greeks. For this was a schoolmaster to bring "the Hellenic mind," as the law, the Hebrews, "to Christ."[2] Philosophy, therefore, was a preparation, paving the way for him who is perfected in Christ.

"Now," says Solomon, "defend wisdom, and it will exalt thee, and it will shield thee with a crown of pleasure."[3] For when thou hast strengthened wisdom with a cope by philosophy, and with right expenditure, thou wilt preserve it unassailable by sophists. The way of truth is therefore one. But into it, as into a perennial river, streams flow from all sides. It has been therefore said by inspiration: "Hear, my son, and receive my words; that thine may be the many ways of life. For I teach thee the ways of wisdom; that the fountains fail thee not,"[4] which gush forth from the earth itself. Not only did He enumerate several ways of salvation for any one righteous man, but He added many other ways of

[1] Prov. iii. 23. [2] Gal. iii. 24.
[3] Prov. iv. 8, 9. [4] Prov. iv. 10, 11, 21.

many righteous, speaking thus: "The paths of the righteous shine like the light."[1] The commandments and the modes of preparatory training are to be regarded as the ways and appliances of life.

"Jerusalem, Jerusalem, how often would I have gathered thy children, as a hen her chickens!"[2] And Jerusalem is, when interpreted, "a vision of peace." He therefore shows prophetically, that those who peacefully contemplate sacred things are in manifold ways trained to their calling. What then? He "would," and could not. How often, and where? Twice; by the prophets, and by the advent. The expression, then, "how often," shows wisdom to be manifold; and in every mode of quantity and quality, it by all means saves some, both in time and in eternity. "For the Spirit of the Lord fills the earth." And if any should violently say that the reference is to the Hellenic culture, when it is said, "Give not heed to an evil woman; for honey drops from the lips of a harlot," let him hear what follows: "who lubricates thy throat for the time." But philosophy does not flatter. Who, then, does He allude to as having committed fornication? He adds expressly, "For the feet of folly lead those who use her, after death, to Hades. But her steps are not supported." Therefore remove thy way far from silly pleasure. "Stand not at the doors of her house, that thou yield not thy life to others." And He testifies, "Then shalt thou repent in old age, when the flesh of thy body is consumed." For this is the end of foolish pleasure. Such, indeed, is the case. And when He says, "Be not much with a strange woman,"[3] He admonishes us to use indeed, but not to linger and spend time with, secular culture. For what was bestowed on each generation advantageously, and at seasonable times, is a preliminary training for the word of the Lord. "For already some men, ensnared by the charms of handmaidens, have despised their consort philosophy, and have grown old, some of them in music, some in

---

[1] Prov. iv. 18.
[2] Matt. xxiii. 37; Luke xiii. 34.
[3] Prov. v. 2, 3, 5, 8, 9, 11, 20.

geometry, others in grammar, the most in rhetoric."[1] "But as the encyclical branches of study contribute to philosophy, which is their mistress; so also philosophy itself co-operates for the acquisition of wisdom. For philosophy is the study of wisdom, and wisdom is the knowledge of things divine and human; and their causes." Wisdom is therefore queen of philosophy, as philosophy is of preparatory culture. For if philosophy "professes control of the tongue, and the belly, and the parts below the belly, it is to be chosen on its own account. But it appears more worthy of respect and pre-eminence, if cultivated for the honour and knowledge of God."[2] And Scripture will afford a testimony to what has been said in what follows. Sarah was at one time barren, being Abraham's wife. Sarah having no child, assigned her maid, by name Hagar, the Egyptian, to Abraham, in order to get children. Wisdom, therefore, who dwells with the man of faith (and Abraham was reckoned faithful and righteous), was still barren and without child in that generation, not having brought forth to Abraham aught allied to virtue. And she, as was proper, thought that he, being now in the time of progress, should have intercourse with secular culture first (by Egyptian the world is designated figuratively); and afterwards should approach to her according to divine providence, and beget Isaac.[3]

And Philo interprets Hagar to mean "sojourning."[4] For it is said in connection with this, "Be not much with a strange woman."[5] Sarah he interprets to mean "my princedom." He, then, who has received previous training is at liberty to approach to wisdom, which is supreme, from which grows up the race of Israel. These things show that that wisdom can be acquired through instruction, to which Abra-

[1] Philo Judæus, *On seeking Instruction*, 435. See Bohn's translation, ii. 173.
[2] Quoted from Philo with some alterations. See Bohn's translation, vol. ii. p. 173.
[3] See Philo, *Meeting to seek Instruction*, Bohn's translation, vol. ii. 160.
[4] Bohn's trans. vol. ii. 161.
[5] Prov. v. 20. Philo, *On meeting to seek Knowledge*, near beginning.

ham attained, passing from the contemplation of heavenly things to the faith and righteousness which are according to God. And Isaac is shown to mean "self-taught;" wherefore also he is discovered to be a type of Christ. He was the husband of one wife Rebecca, which they translate "Patience." And Jacob is said to have consorted with several, his name being interpreted "Exerciser." And exercises are engaged in by means of many and various dogmas. Whence, also, he who is really "endowed with the power of seeing" is called Israel,[1] having much experience, and being fit for exercise.

Something else may also have been shown by the three patriarchs, namely, that the sure seal of knowledge is composed of nature, of education, and exercise.

You may have also another image of what has been said, in Thamar sitting by the way and presenting the appearance of a harlot, on whom the studious Judas (whose name is interpreted "powerful"), who left nothing unexamined and uninvestigated, looked; and turned aside to her, preserving his profession towards God. Wherefore also, when Sarah was jealous at Hagar being preferred to her, Abraham, as choosing only what was profitable in secular philosophy, said, "Behold, thy maid is in thine hands: deal with her as it pleases thee;"[2] manifestly meaning, "I embrace secular culture as youthful, and a handmaid; but thy knowledge I honour and reverence as true wife." And Sarah afflicted her; which is equivalent to corrected and admonished her. It has therefore been well said, "My son, despise not thou the correction of God; nor faint when thou art rebuked of Him. For whom the Lord loveth He chasteneth, and scourgeth every son whom He receiveth."[3] And the foresaid Scriptures, when examined in other places, will be seen to exhibit other mysteries. We merely therefore assert here, that philosophy is characterized by investigation into truth and the nature of things (this is the truth of which the Lord Himself said, "I

---

[1] Philo, in the book above cited, interprets "Israel," "seeing God." From this book all the instances and etymologies occurring here are taken.
[2] Gen. xvi. 6.   [3] Prov. iii. 11, 12; Heb. xii. 5, 6.

am the truth "[1]); and that, again, the preparatory training for rest in Christ exercises the mind, rouses the intelligence, and begets an inquiring shrewdness, by means of the true philosophy, which the initiated possess, having found it, or rather received it, from the truth itself.

[1] John xiv. 6.

CHAPTER VI.

THE BENEFIT OF CULTURE.

THE readiness acquired by previous training conduces much to the perception of such things as are requisite; but those things which can be perceived only by mind are the special exercise for the mind. And their nature is triple according as we consider their quantity, their magnitude, and what can be predicated of them. For the discourse which consists of demonstrations, implants in the spirit of him who follows it, clear faith; so that he cannot conceive of that which is demonstrated being different; and so it does not allow us to succumb to those who assail us by fraud. In such studies, therefore, the soul is purged from sensible things, and is excited, so as to be able to see truth distinctly. For nutriment, and the training which is maintained gentle, make noble natures; and noble natures, when they have received such training, become still better than before both in other respects, but especially in productiveness, as is the case with the other creatures. Wherefore it is said, "Go to the ant, thou sluggard, and become wiser than it, which provideth much and varied food in the harvest against the inclemency of winter."[1] Or go to the bee, and learn how laborious she is; for she, feeding on the whole meadow, produces one honey-comb. And if "thou prayest in the closet," as the Lord taught, "to worship in spirit,"[2] thy management will no longer be solely occupied about the house, but also about the soul, what must be bestowed on it, and how, and how much; and what must be laid aside and treasured up in

[1] Prov. vi. 6, 8.   [2] Matt. vi. 6; John iv. 23.

it; and when it ought to be produced, and to whom. For it is not by nature, but by learning, that people become noble and good, as people also become physicians and pilots. We all in common, for example, see the vine and the horse. But the husbandman will know if the vine be good or bad at fruit-bearing; and the horseman will easily distinguish between the spiritless and the swift animal. And that some are naturally predisposed to virtue above others, certain pursuits of those, who are so naturally predisposed above others, show. But that perfection in virtue is not the exclusive property of those, whose natures are better, is proved, since also those who by nature are ill-disposed towards virtue, in obtaining suitable training, for the most part attain to excellence; and, on the other hand, those whose natural dispositions are apt, become evil through neglect.

Again, God has created us naturally social and just; whence justice must not be said to take its rise from implantation alone. But the good imparted by creation is to be conceived of as excited by the commandment; the soul being trained to be willing to select what is noblest.

But as we say that a man can be a believer without learning, so also we assert that it is impossible for a man without learning to comprehend the things which are declared in the faith. But to adopt what is well said, and not to adopt the reverse, is caused not simply by faith, but by faith combined with knowledge. But if ignorance is want of training and of instruction, then teaching produces knowledge of divine and human things. But just as it is possible to live rightly in penury of this world's good things, so also in abundance. And we avow, that at once with more ease and more speed will one attain to virtue through previous training. But it is not such as to be unattainable without it; but it is attainable only when they have learned, and have had their senses exercised.[1] "For hatred," says Solomon, "raises strife, but instruction guardeth the ways of life;"[2] in such a way that we are not deceived nor deluded by those who are practised in base arts for the injury of

---

[1] Heb. v. 14.   [2] Prov. x. 12, 17.

those who hear. "But instruction wanders reproachless,"[1] it is said. We must be conversant with the art of reasoning, for the purpose of confuting the deceitful opinions of the sophists. Well and felicitously, therefore, does Anaxarchus write in his book respecting "kingly rule:" "Erudition benefits greatly, and hurts greatly him who possesses it; it helps him who is worthy, and injures him who utters readily every word, and before the whole people. It is necessary to know the measure of time. For this is the end of wisdom. And those who sing at the doors, even if they sing skilfully, are not reckoned wise, but have the reputation of folly." And Hesiod:

"Of the Muses, who make a man loquacious, divine, vocal."

For him who is fluent in words he calls loquacious; and him who is clever, vocal; and "divine," him who is skilled, a philosopher, and acquainted with the truth.

[1] Prov. x. 19.

CHAPTER VII.

THE ECLECTIC PHILOSOPHY PAVES THE WAY FOR DIVINE VIRTUE.

THE Greek preparatory culture, therefore, with philosophy itself, is shown to have come down from God to men, not with a definite direction, but in the way in which showers fall down on the good land, and on the dunghill, and on the houses. And similarly both the grass and the wheat sprout; and the figs and any other reckless trees grow on sepulchres. And things that grow, appear as a type of truths. For they enjoy the same influence of the rain. But they have not the same grace as those which spring up in rich soil, inasmuch as they are withered or plucked up. And here we are aided by the parable of the sower, which the Lord interpreted. For the husbandman of the soil which is among men is one; He who from the beginning, from the foundation of the world, sowed nutritious seeds; He who in each age rained down the Lord, the Word. But the times and places which received [such gifts], created the differences which exist. Further, the husbandman sows not only wheat (of which there are many varieties), but also other seeds—barley, and beans, and peas, and vetches, and vegetable and flower seeds. And to the same husbandry belongs both planting and the operations necessary in the nurseries, and gardens, and orchards, and the planting and rearing of all sorts of trees.

In like manner, not only the care of sheep, but the care of herds, and breeding of horses, and dogs, and bee-craft, all arts, and to speak comprehensively, the care of flocks and the rearing of animals, differ from each other more or less, but are all useful for life. And philosophy—I do not mean the Stoic, or the Platonic, or the Epicurean, or the Aristotelian, but whatever has been well said by each of those sects, which teach righteousness along with a science pervaded by piety, —this eclectic whole I call philosophy. But such conclusions of human reasonings, as men have cut away and falsified, I would never call divine.

And now we must look also at this, that if ever those who know not how to do well, live well;[1] for they have lighted on well-doing. Some, too, have aimed well at the word of truth through understanding. "But Abraham was not justified by works, but by faith."[2] It is therefore of no advantage to them after the end of life, even if they do good works now, if they have not faith. Wherefore also the Scriptures were translated into the language of the Greeks, in order that they might never be able to allege the excuse of ignorance, inasmuch as they are able to hear also what we have in our hands, if they only wish. One speaks in one way of the truth, in another way the truth interprets itself. The guessing at truth is one thing, and truth itself is another. Resemblance is one thing, the thing itself is another. And the one results from learning and practice, the other from power and faith. For the teaching of piety is a gift, but faith is grace. "For by doing the will of God we know the will of God."[3] "Open, then," says the Scripture, "the gates of righteousness; and I will enter in, and confess to the Lord."[4] But the paths to righteousness (since God saves in many ways, for He is good) are many and various, and lead to the Lord's way and gate. And if you ask the royal and true entrance, you will hear, "This is the gate of the Lord, the righteous shall enter in by it."[5] While there are many gates open, that in righteousness is in Christ, by which all the blessed enter, and direct their steps in the sanctity of knowledge. Now Clemens, in his Epistle to the Corinthians, while expounding the differences of those who are approved according to the church, says expressly, "One may be a believer; one may be powerful in uttering knowledge; one may be wise in discriminating between words; one may be terrible in deeds."

[1] Something seems wanting to complete the sense.
[2] Rom. iv. [3] John vii. 17. [4] Ps. cxviii. 19. [5] Ps. cxviii. 20.

CHAPTER VIII.

THE SOPHISTICAL ARTS USELESS.

BUT the art of sophistry, which the Greeks cultivated, is a fantastic power, which makes false opinions like true by means of words. For it produces rhetoric in order to persuasion, and disputation for wrangling. These arts, therefore, if not conjoined with philosophy, will be injurious to every one. For Plato openly called sophistry "an evil art." And Aristotle, following him, demonstrates it to be a dishonest art, which abstracts in a specious manner the whole business of wisdom, and professes a wisdom which it has not studied. To speak briefly, as the beginning of rhetoric is the probable, and an attempted proof[1] the process, and the end persuasion, so the beginning of disputation is what is matter of opinion, and the process a contest, and the end victory. For in the same manner, also, the beginning of sophistry is the apparent, and the process twofold; one of rhetoric, continuous and exhaustive; and the other of logic, and is interrogatory. And its end is admiration. The dialectic in vogue in the schools, on the other hand, is the exercise of a philosopher in matters of opinion, for the sake of the faculty of disputation. But truth is not in these at all. With reason, therefore, the noble apostle, depreciating these superfluous arts occupied about words, says, "If any man do not give heed to wholesome words, but is puffed up by a kind of teaching, knowing nothing, but doting (νοσῶν) about questions and strifes of words, whereof cometh contention, envy, railings, evil surmisings, perverse disputings of men of corrupt minds, destitute of the truth."[2]

[1] ἐπιχείρημα.   [2] 1 Tim. vi. 3-5.

You see how he is moved against them, calling their art of logic—on which, those to whom this garrulous mischievous art is dear, whether Greeks or barbarians, plume themselves—a disease (νόσος). Very beautifully, therefore, the tragic poet Euripides says in the *Phœnissœ*,

> "But a wrongful speech
> Is diseased in itself, and needs skilful medicines."[1]

For the saving Word is called "wholesome," He being the truth; and what is wholesome (healthful) remains ever deathless. But separation from what is healthful and divine is impiety, and a deadly malady. These are rapacious wolves hid in sheep-skins, men-stealers, and glozing soul-seducers, stealing secretly, but proved to be robbers; striving by fraud and force to catch us who are unsophisticated and have less power of speech.

> "Often a man, impeded through want of words, carries less weight
> In expressing what is right, than the man of eloquence.
> But now in fluent mouths the weightiest truths
> They disguise, so that they do not seem what they ought to seem,"

says the tragedy. Such are these wranglers, whether they follow the sects, or practise miserable dialectic arts. These are they that "stretch the warp and weave nothing," says the Scripture;[2] prosecuting a bootless task, which the apostle has called "cunning craftiness of men, whereby they lie in wait to deceive."[3] "For there are," he says, "many unruly and vain talkers and deceivers."[4] Wherefore it was not said to all, "Ye are the salt of the earth."[5] For there are some even of the hearers of the word who are like the fishes of the sea, which, reared from their birth in brine, yet need salt to dress them for food. Accordingly I wholly approve of the tragedy, when it says:

> "O son, false words can be well spoken,
> And truth may be vanquished by beauty of words.
> But this is not what is most correct, but nature and what is right;
> He who practises eloquence is indeed wise,
> But I consider deeds always better than words."

---

[1] *Phœnissœ*, 474, 475. [2] Where, nobody knows. [3] Eph. iv. 14.
[4] Tit. i. 10. [5] Matt. v. 13.

We must not, then, aspire to please the multitude. For we do not practise what will please them, but what we know is remote from their disposition. "Let us not be desirous of vainglory," says the apostle, "provoking one another, envying one another."[1]

Thus the truth-loving Plato says, as if divinely inspired, "Since I am such as to obey nothing but the word, which, after reflection, appears to me the best."[2]

Accordingly he charges those who credit opinions without intelligence and knowledge, with abandoning right and sound reason unwarrantably, and believing him who is a partner in falsehood. For to cheat one's self of the truth is bad; but to speak the truth, and to hold as our opinions positive realities, is good.

Men are deprived of what is good unwillingly. Nevertheless they are deprived either by being deceived or beguiled, or by being compelled and not believing. He who believes not, has already made himself a willing captive; and he who changes his persuasion is cozened, while he forgets that time imperceptibly takes away some things, and reason others. And after an opinion has been entertained, pain and anguish, and on the other hand contentiousness and anger, compel. Above all, men are beguiled who are either bewitched by pleasure or terrified by fear. And all these are voluntary changes, but by none of these will knowledge ever be attained.

[1] Gal. v. 26.   [2] Plato, *Crito*, 34.

CHAPTER IX.

HUMAN KNOWLEDGE NECESSARY FOR THE UNDERSTANDING OF THE SCRIPTURES.

SOME, who think themselves naturally gifted, do not wish to touch either philosophy or logic; nay more, they do not wish to learn natural science. They demand bare faith alone, as if they wished, without bestowing any care on the vine, straightway to gather clusters from the first. Now the Lord is figuratively described as the vine, from which, with pains and the art of husbandry, according to the word, the fruit is to be gathered.

We must lop, dig, bind, and perform the other operations. The pruning-knife, I should think, and the pick-axe, and the other agricultural implements, are necessary for the culture of the vine, so that it may produce eatable fruit. And as in husbandry, so also in medicine: he has learned to purpose, who has practised the various lessons, so as to be able to cultivate and to heal. So also here, I call him truly learned who brings everything to bear on the truth; so that, from geometry, and music, and grammar, and philosophy itself, culling what is useful, he guards the faith against assault. Now, as was said, the athlete is despised who is not furnished for the contest. For instance, too, we praise the experienced helmsman who "has seen the cities of many men," and the physician who has had large experience; thus also some describe the empiric.[1] And he who brings everything to bear on a right life, procuring examples from the Greeks and barbarians, this man is an experienced searcher after truth, and in reality a man of much counsel, like the touchstone (that is, the Lydian), which is believed to possess the

[1] The empirics were a class of physicians who held practice to be the one thing essential.

power of distinguishing the spurious from the genuine gold. And our much-knowing gnostic can distinguish sophistry from philosophy, the art of decoration from gymnastics, cookery from physic, and rhetoric from dialectics, and the other sects which are according to the barbarian philosophy, from the truth itself. And how necessary is it for him who desires to be partaker of the power of God, to treat of intellectual subjects by philosophising! And how serviceable is it to distinguish expressions which are ambiguous, and which in the Testaments are used synonymously! For the Lord, at the time of His temptation, skilfully matched the devil by an ambiguous expression. And I do not yet, in this connection, see how in the world the inventor of philosophy and dialectics, as some suppose, is seduced through being deceived by the form of speech which consists in ambiguity. And if the prophets and apostles knew not the arts by which the exercises of philosophy are exhibited, yet the mind of the prophetic and instructive spirit, uttered secretly, because all have not an intelligent ear, demands skilful modes of teaching in order to clear exposition. For the prophets and disciples of the Spirit knew infallibly their mind. For they knew it by faith, in a way which others could not easily, as the Spirit has said. But it is not possible for those who have not learned to receive it thus. "Write," it is said, "the commandments doubly, in counsel and knowledge, that thou mayest answer the words of truth to them who send unto thee."[1] What, then, is the knowledge of answering? or what that of asking? It is dialectics. What then? Is not speaking our business, and does not action proceed from the Word? For if we act not for the Word, we shall act against reason. But a rational work is accomplished through God. "And nothing," it is said, "was made without Him"—the Word of God.[2]

And did not the Lord make all things by the Word? Even the beasts work, driven by compelling fear. And do not those who are called orthodox apply themselves to good works, knowing not what they do?

[1] Prov. xxii. 20, 21. The Septuagint and Hebrew both differ from the reading here.   [2] John i. 3.

CHAPTER X.

TO ACT WELL OF GREATER CONSEQUENCE THAN TO SPEAK WELL.

WHEREFORE the Saviour, taking the bread, first spake and blessed. Then breaking the bread, He presented it, that we might eat it, according to reason, and that knowing the Scriptures we might walk obediently. And as those whose speech is evil are no better than those whose practice is evil (for calumny is the servant of the sword, and evil-speaking inflicts pain; and from these proceed disasters in life, such being the effects of evil speech); so also those who are given to good speech are near neighbours to those who accomplish good deeds. Accordingly discourse refreshes the soul and entices it to nobleness; and happy is he who has the use of both his hands. Neither, therefore, is he who can act well to be vilified by him who is able to speak well; nor is he who is able to speak well to be disparaged by him who is capable of acting well. But let each do that for which he is naturally fitted. What the one exhibits as actually done, the other speaks, preparing, as it were, the way for well-doing, and leading the hearers to the practice of good. For there is a saving word, as there is a saving work. Righteousness, accordingly, is not constituted without discourse. And as the receiving of good is abolished if we abolish the doing of good; so obedience and faith are abolished when neither the command, nor one to expound the command, is taken along with us. But now we are benefited mutually and reciprocally by words and deeds; but we must repudiate entirely the art of wrangling and sophistry, since these sentences of the sophists not only bewitch and beguile the many, but sometimes by violence win a Cadmian victory.[1] For true above all is that psalm, "The just shall live to the end, for he shall not see corruption, when he beholds the wise dying."[2] And whom does he call wise? Hear from the Wisdom of Jesus: "Wisdom is not the knowledge of evil."[3] Such he calls what the arts of speaking and of discussing have invented. "Thou shalt therefore seek wisdom among the wicked, and shalt not find it."[4] And if you inquire again of what sort this is, you are told, "The mouth of the righteous man will distil wisdom."[5] And similarly with truth, the art of sophistry is called wisdom.

But it is my purpose, as I reckon, and not without reason, to live according to the Word, and to understand what is revealed; but never affecting eloquence, to be content merely with indicating my meaning. And by what term that which I wish to present is shown, I care not. For I well know that to be saved, and to aid those who desire to be saved, is the best thing, and not to compose paltry sentences like gewgaws. "And if," says the Pythagorean in the *Politicus* of Plato, "you guard against solicitude about terms, you will be richer in wisdom against old age."[6] And in the *Theætetus* you will find again, "And carelessness about names, and expressions, and the want of nice scrutiny, is not vulgar and illiberal for the most part, but rather the reverse of this, and is sometimes necessary."[7] This the Scripture has expressed with the greatest possible brevity, when it said, "Be not occupied much about words." For expression is like the dress on the body. The matter is the flesh and sinews. We must not therefore care more for the dress than the safety of the body. For not only a simple mode of life, but also a style of speech devoid of superfluity and nicety, must be cultivated by him who has adopted the true life, if we are to abandon luxury as treacherous and profligate, as the ancient Lacedæmonians ab-

---

[1] A victory disastrous to the victor and the vanquished.
[2] Ps. xlix. 9, 10, Sept.
[3] Ecclus. xix. 22.
[4] Prov. xiv. 6.
[5] Prov. x. 31.
[6] Plato's *Politicus*, p. 261.
[7] Plato's *Theætetus*, p. 184 c.

jured ointment and purple, deeming and calling them rightly treacherous garments and treacherous unguents; since neither is that mode of preparing food right where there is more of seasoning than of nutriment; nor is that style of speech elegant which can please rather than benefit the hearers. Pythagoras exhorts us to consider the Muses more pleasant than the Sirens, teaching us to cultivate wisdom apart from pleasure, and exposing the other mode of attracting the soul as deceptive. For sailing past the Sirens one man has sufficient strength, and for answering the Sphinx another one, or, if you please, not even one.[1] We ought never, then, out of desire for vainglory, to make broad the phylacteries. It suffices the gnostic[2] if only one hearer is found for him. You may hear therefore Pindar the Bœotian, who writes, "Divulge not before all the ancient speech. The way of silence is sometimes the surest. And the mightiest word is a spur to the fight." Accordingly, the blessed apostle very appropriately and urgently exhorts us "not to strive about words to no profit, but to the subverting of the hearers, but to shun profane and vain babblings, for they increase unto more ungodliness, and their word will eat as doth a canker."[3]

[1] The story of Œdipus being a myth.
[2] The possessor of true divine knowledge.   [3] 2 Tim. ii. 14, 16, 17.

CHAPTER XI.

WHAT IS THE PHILOSOPHY WHICH THE APOSTLE BIDS US SHUN?

THIS, then, "the wisdom of the world is foolishness with God," and of those who are "the wise the Lord knoweth their thoughts that they are vain:"[1] Let no man therefore glory on account of pre-eminence in human thought. For it is written well in Jeremiah, "Let not the wise man glory in his wisdom, and let not the mighty man glory in his might, and let not the rich man glory in his riches: but let him that glorieth glory in this, that he understandeth and knoweth that I am the Lord, that executeth mercy and judgment and righteousness upon the earth: for in these things is my delight, saith the Lord."[2] "That we should trust not in ourselves, but in God who raiseth the dead," says the apostle, "who delivered us from so great a death, that our faith should not stand in the wisdom of men, but in the power of God." "For the spiritual man judgeth all things, but he himself is judged of no man."[3] I hear also those words of his, "And these things I say, lest any man should beguile you with enticing words, or one should enter in to spoil you."[4] And again, "Beware lest any man spoil you through philosophy and vain deceit, after the tradition of men, after the rudiments of the world, and not after Christ;"[5] branding not all philosophy, but the Epicurean, which Paul mentions in the Acts of the Apostles,[6] which abolishes providence and deifies pleasure, and

---

[1] 1 Cor. iii. 19, 20.
[2] Jer. ix. 23, 24.
[3] 2 Cor. i. 9, 10; 1 Cor. ii. 5, 15.
[4] Col. ii. 4, 8.
[5] Col. ii. 8.
[6] Acts xvii. 18.

whatever other philosophy honours the elements, but places not over them the efficient cause, nor apprehends the Creator.

The Stoics also, whom he mentions too, say not well that the Deity, being a body, pervades the vilest matter. He calls the jugglery of logic "the tradition of men." Wherefore also he adds, "Avoid juvenile [1] questions. For such contentions are puerile." "But virtue is no lover of boys," says the philosopher Plato. And our struggle, according to Gorgias Leontinus, requires two virtues — boldness and wisdom, — boldness to undergo danger, and wisdom to understand the enigma. For the Word, like the Olympian proclamation, calls him who is willing, and crowns him who is able to continue unmoved as far as the truth is concerned. And, in truth, the Word does not wish him who has believed to be idle. For He says, "Seek, and ye shall find."[2] But seeking ends in finding, driving out the empty trifling, and approving of the contemplation which confirms our faith. "And this I say, lest any man beguile you with enticing words,"[3] says the apostle, evidently as having learned to distinguish what was said by him, and as being taught to meet objections. "As ye have therefore received Christ Jesus the Lord, so walk in Him, rooted and built up in Him, and stablished in the faith."[4] Now persuasion is [the means of] being established in the faith. "Beware lest any man spoil you of faith in Christ by philosophy and vain deceit," which does away with providence, "after the tradition of men;" for the philosophy which is in accordance with divine tradition establishes and confirms providence, which, being done away with, the economy of the Saviour appears a myth, while we are influenced "after the elements of the world, and not after Christ."[5] For the teaching which is agreeable to Christ deifies the Creator, and traces providence in particular events, and knows the nature of the elements to be capable of change and production, and teaches that we ought to aim at rising up to the power which assimilates to God, and to prefer the dispensation[6] as holding the first rank and superior to all training.

[1] The apostle says "foolish," 2 Tim. ii. 23.   [2] Matt. vii. 7.
[3] Col. ii. 4.   [4] Col. ii. 6, 7.   [5] Col. ii. 8.   [6] *i.e.* of the gospel.

The elements are worshipped,—the air by Diogenes, the water by Thales, the fire by Hippasus; and by those who suppose atoms to be the first principles of things, arrogating the name of philosophers, being wretched creatures devoted to pleasure. "Wherefore I pray," says the apostle, "that your love may abound yet more and more, in knowledge and in all judgment, that ye may approve things that are excellent."[1] "Since, when we were children," says the same apostle, "we were kept in bondage under the rudiments of the world. And the child, though heir, differeth nothing from a servant, till the time appointed of the father."[2] Philosophers, then, are children, unless they have been made men by Christ. "For if the son of the bond woman shall not be heir with the son of the free,"[3] at least he is the seed of Abraham, though not of promise, receiving what belongs to him by free gift. "But strong meat belongeth to those that are of full age, even those who by reason of use have their senses exercised to discern both good and evil."[4] "For every one that useth milk is unskilful in the word of righteousness; for he is a babe,"[5] and not yet acquainted with the word, according to which he has believed and works, and not able to give a reason in himself. "Prove all things," the apostle says, "and hold fast that which is good,"[6] speaking to spiritual men, who judge what is said according to truth, whether it seems or truly holds by the truth. "He who is not corrected by discipline errs, and stripes and reproofs give the discipline of wisdom," the reproofs manifestly that are with love. "For the right heart seeketh knowledge."[7] "For he that seeketh the Lord shall find knowledge with righteousness; and they who have sought it rightly have found peace."[8] "And I will know," it is said, "not the speech of those which are puffed up, but the power." In rebuke of those who are wise in appearance, and think themselves wise, but are not in reality wise, he writes: "For the kingdom of God is not in

---

[1] Phil. i. 9, 10. [2] Gal. iv. 3, 1, 2. [3] Gen. xxi. 10; Gal. iv. 30.
[4] Heb. v. 14. [5] Heb. v. 13. [6] 1 Thess. v. 21.
[7] Prov. xv. 14.
[8] The substance of these remarks is found in Prov. ii.

word."[1] It is not in that which is not true, but which is only probable according to opinion; but he said "in power," for the truth alone is powerful. And again: "If any man thinketh that he knoweth anything, he knoweth nothing yet as he ought to know." For truth is never mere opinion. But the "supposition of knowledge inflates," and fills with pride; "but charity edifieth," which deals not in supposition, but in truth. Whence it is said, "If any man loves, he is known."[2]

[1] 1 Cor. iv. 19, 20.   [2] 1 Cor. viii. 1, 2, 3.

CHAPTER XII.

THE MYSTERIES OF THE FAITH NOT TO BE DIVULGED TO ALL.

BUT since this tradition is not published alone for him who perceives the magnificence of the word; it is requisite, therefore, to hide in a mystery the wisdom spoken, which the Son of God taught. Now, therefore, Isaiah the prophet has his tongue purified by fire, so that he may be able to tell the vision. And we must purify not the tongue alone, but also the ears, if we attempt to be partakers of the truth.

Such were the impediments in the way of my writing. And even now I fear, as it is said, "to cast the pearls before swine, lest they tread them under foot, and turn and rend us."[1] For it is difficult to exhibit the really pure and transparent words respecting the true light, to swinish and untrained hearers. For scarcely could anything which they could hear be more ludicrous than these to the multitude; nor any subjects on the other hand more admirable or more inspiring to those of noble nature. "But the natural man receiveth not the things of the Spirit of God; for they are foolishness to him."[2] But the wise do not utter with their mouth what they reason in council. "But what ye hear in the ear," says the Lord, "proclaim upon the houses;"[3] bidding them receive the secret traditions of the true knowledge, and expound them aloft and conspicuously; and as we have heard in the ear, so to deliver them to whom it is requisite; but not enjoining us to communicate to all without distinction, what is said to them in parables. But there is only a delineation in the memoranda, which have the truth sowed sparse and broadcast, that it may escape the notice of those who pick up seeds like jackdaws; but when they find a good husbandman, each one of them will germinate and produce corn.

[1] Matt. vii. 6.   [2] 1 Cor. ii. 14.   [3] Matt. x. 27.

CHAPTER XIII.

ALL SECTS OF PHILOSOPHY CONTAIN A GERM OF TRUTH.

SINCE, therefore, truth is one (for falsehood has ten thousand by-paths); just as the Bacchantes tore asunder the limbs of Pentheus, so the sects both of barbarian and Hellenic philosophy have done with truth, and each vaunts as the whole truth the portion which has fallen to its lot. But all, in my opinion, are illuminated by the dawn of Light.[1] Let all, therefore, both Greeks and barbarians, who have aspired after the truth,—both those who possess not a little, and those who have any portion,—produce whatever they have of the word of truth.

Eternity, for instance, presents in an instant the future and the present, also the past of time. But truth, much more powerful than limitless duration, can collect its proper germs, though they have fallen on foreign soil. For we shall find that very many of the dogmas that are held by such sects as have not become utterly senseless, and are not cut out from the order of nature (by cutting off Christ, as the women of the fable dismembered the man),[2] though appearing unlike one another, correspond in their origin and with the truth as a whole. For they coincide in one, either as a part, or a species, or a genus. For instance, though the highest note is different from the lowest note, yet both compose one harmony. And in numbers an even number differs from an odd number; but both suit in arithmetic; as also is the case with figure, the circle, and the triangle, and the square, and whatever figures differ from one another. Also, in the whole universe, all the

[1] Namely Jesus: John viii. 12.
[2] We have adopted the translation of Potter, who supposes a reference to the fate of Pentheus. Perhaps the translation should be: "excluding Christ, as the apartments destined for women exclude the man" [all males].

parts, though differing one from another, preserve their relation to the whole. So, then, the barbarian and Hellenic philosophy has torn off a fragment of eternal truth not from the mythology of Dionysus, but from the theology of the ever-living Word. And He who brings again together the separate fragments, and makes them one, will without peril, be assured, contemplate the perfect Word, the truth. Therefore it is written in Ecclesiastes: "And I added wisdom above all who were before me in Jerusalem; and my heart saw many things; and besides, I knew wisdom and knowledge, parables and understanding. And this also is the choice of the spirit, because in abundance of wisdom is abundance of knowledge."[1] He who is conversant with all kinds of wisdom, will be pre-eminently a gnostic. Now it is written, "Abundance of the knowledge of wisdom will give life to him who is of it."[2] And again, what is said is confirmed more clearly by this saying, "All things are in the sight of those who understand"—all things, both Hellenic and barbarian; but the one or the other is not all. "They are right to those who wish to receive understanding. Choose instruction, and not silver, and knowledge above tested gold," and prefer also sense to pure gold; "for wisdom is better than precious stones, and no precious thing is worth it."[3]

[1] Eccles. i. 16, 17, 18.   [2] Eccles. vii. 13, according to Sept.
[3] Prov. viii. 9, 10, 11.

CHAPTER XIV.

SUCCESSION OF PHILOSOPHERS IN GREECE.

THE Greeks say, that after Orpheus and Linus, and the most ancient of the poets that appeared among them, the seven, called wise, were the first that were admired for their wisdom. Of whom four were of Asia—Thales of Miletus, and Bias of Priene, Pittacus of Mitylene, and Cleobulus of Lindos; and two of Europe, Solon the Athenian, and Chilon the Lacedæmonian; and the seventh, some say, was Periander of Corinth; others, Anacharsis the Scythian; others, Epimenides the Cretan, whom Paul knew as a Greek prophet, whom he mentions in the Epistle to Titus, where he speaks thus: "One of themselves, a prophet of their own, said, *The Cretans are always liars, evil beasts, slow bellies.* And this witness is true."[1] You see how even to the prophets of the Greeks he attributes something of the truth, and is not ashamed, when discoursing for the edification of some and the shaming of others, to make use of Greek poems. Accordingly to the Corinthians (for this is not the only instance), while discoursing on the resurrection of the dead, he makes use of a tragic Iambic line, when he said, "What advantageth it me if the dead are not raised? Let us eat and drink, for to-morrow we die. Be not deceived;

Evil communications corrupt good manners."[2]

Others have enumerated Acusilaus the Argive among the seven wise men; and others, Pherecydes of Syros. And Plato substitutes Myso the Chenian for Periander, whom

[1] Tit. i. 12, 13. [2] 1 Cor. xv. 32, 33.

he deemed unworthy of wisdom, on account of his having reigned as a tyrant. That the wise men among the Greeks flourished after the age of Moses, will, a little after, be shown. But the style of philosophy among them, as Hebraic and enigmatical, is now to be considered. They adopted brevity, as suited for exhortation, and most useful. Even Plato says, that of old this mode was purposely in vogue among all the Greeks, especially the Lacedæmonians and Cretans, who enjoyed the best laws.

The expression, "Know thyself," some supposed to be Chilon's. But Chamæleon, in his book *About the Gods*, ascribes it to Thales; Aristotle to the Pythian. It may be an injunction to the pursuit of knowledge. For it is not possible to know the parts without the essence of the whole; and one must study the genesis of the universe, that thereby we may be able to learn the nature of man. Again, to Chilon the Lacedæmonian they attribute, "Let nothing be too much."[1] Strato, in his book *Of Inventions*, ascribes the apophthegm to Stratodemus of Tegea. Didymus assigns it to Solon; as also to Cleobulus the saying, "A middle course is best." And the expression, "Come under a pledge, and mischief is at hand," Cleomenes says, in his book *Concerning Hesiod*, was uttered before by Homer in the lines:

"Wretched pledges, for the wretched, to be pledged."[2]

The Aristotelians judge it to be Chilon's; but Didymus says the advice was that of Thales. Then, next in order, the saying, "All men are bad," or, "The most of men are bad" (for the same apophthegm is expressed in two ways), Sotades the Byzantian says that it was Bias's. And the aphorism, "Practice conquers everything,"[3] they will have it to be Periander's; and likewise the advice, "Know the opportunity," to have been a saying of Pittacus. Solon made laws for the Athenians, Pittacus for the Mitylenians. And at a late date, Pythagoras, the pupil of Pherecydes, first called himself a philosopher. Accordingly, after the fore-mentioned three men, there were three schools of philosophy, named

---

[1] "Nequid nimis." Μηδὶν ἄγαν.   [2] *Odyss.* ix. 351.
[3] Μελίτη πάντα καθαιρεῖ.

after the places where they lived: the Italic from Pythagoras, the Ionic from Thales, the Eleatic from Xenophanes. Pythagoras was a Samian, the son of Mnesarchus, as Hippobotus says: according to Aristoxenus, in his life of Pythagoras and Aristarchus and Theopompus, he was a Tuscan; and according to Neanthes, a Syrian or a Tyrian. So that Pythagoras was, according to the most, of barbarian extraction. Thales, too, as Leander and Herodotus relate, was a Phœnician; as some suppose, a Milesian. He alone seems to have met the prophets of the Egyptians. But no one is described as his teacher, nor is any one mentioned as the teacher of Pherecydes of Syros, who had Pythagoras as his pupil. But the Italic philosophy, that of Pythagoras, grew old in Metapontum in Italy. Anaximander of Miletus, the son of Praxiades, succeeded Thales; and was himself succeeded by Anaximenes of Miletus, the son of Eurustratus; after whom came Anaxagoras of Clazomenæ, the son of Hegesibulus.[1] He transferred his school from Ionia to Athens. He was succeeded by Archelaus, whose pupil Socrates was.

"From these turned aside, the stone-mason;
Talker about laws; the enchanter of the Greeks,"

says Timon in his *Satirical Poems*, on account of his quitting physics for ethics. Antisthenes, after being a pupil of Socrates, introduced the Cynic philosophy; and Plato withdrew to the Academy. Aristotle, after studying philosophy under Plato, withdrew to the Lyceum, and founded the Peripatetic sect. He was succeeded by Theophrastus, who was succeeded by Strato, and he by Lycon, then Critolaus, and then Diodorus. Speusippus was the successor of Plato; his successor was Xenocrates; and the successor of the latter, Polemo. And the disciples of Polemo were Crates and Crantor, in whom the old Academy founded by Plato ceased. Arcesilaus was the associate of Crantor; from whom, down to Hegesilaus, the Middle Academy flourished. Then Carneades succeeded Hegesilaus, and others came in succession. The disciple of Crates was Zeno of Citium, the founder of the Stoic sect. He was succeeded by Cleanthes; and the

[1] Or Eubulus.

latter by Chrysippus, and others after him. Xenophanes of Colophon was the founder of the Eleatic school, who, Timæus says, lived in the time of Hiero, lord of Sicily, and Epicharmus the poet; and Apollodorus says that he was born in the fortieth Olympiad, and reached to the times of Darius and Cyrus. Parmenides, accordingly, was the disciple of Xenophanes, and Zeno of him; then came Leucippus, and then Democritus. Disciples of Democritus were Protagoras of Abdera, and Metrodorus of Chios, whose pupil was Diogenes of Smyrna; and his again Anaxarchus, and his Pyrrho, and his Nausiphanes. Some say that Epicurus was a scholar of his.

Such, in an epitome, is the succession of the philosophers among the Greeks. The periods of the originators of their philosophy are now to be specified successively, in order that, by comparison, we may show that the Hebrew philosophy was older by many generations.

It has been said of Xenophanes that he was the founder of the Eleatic philosophy. And Eudemus, in the *Astrological Histories*, says that Thales foretold the eclipse of the sun, which took place at the time that the Medians and the Lydians fought, in the reign of Cyaxares the father of Astyages over the Medes, and of Alyattus the son of Crœsus over the Lydians. Herodotus in his first book agrees with him. The date is about the fiftieth Olympiad. Pythagoras is ascertained to have lived in the days of Polycrates the tyrant, about the sixty-second Olympiad. Mnesiphilus is described as a follower of Solon, and was a contemporary of Themistocles. Solon therefore flourished about the forty-sixth Olympiad. For Heraclitus, the son of Bauso, persuaded Melancomas the tyrant to abdicate his sovereignty. He despised the invitation of king Darius to visit the Persians.

CHAPTER XV.

THE GREEK PHILOSOPHY IN GREAT PART DERIVED FROM THE BARBARIANS.

THESE are the times of the oldest wise men and philosophers among the Greeks. And that the most of them were barbarians by extraction, and were trained among barbarians, what need is there to say? Pythagoras is shown to have been either a Tuscan or a Tyrian. And Antisthenes was a Phrygian. And Orpheus was an Odrysian or a Thracian. The most, too, show Homer to have been an Egyptian. Thales was a Phœnician by birth, and was said to have consorted with the prophets of the Egyptians; as also Pythagoras did with the same persons, by whom he was circumcised, that he might enter the adytum and learn from the Egyptians the mystic philosophy. He held converse with the chief of the Chaldeans and the Magi; and he gave a hint of the church, now so called, in the common hall[1] which he maintained.

And Plato does not deny that he procured all that is most excellent in philosophy from the barbarians; and he admits that he came into Egypt. Whence, writing in the *Phædo* that the philosopher can receive aid from all sides, he said: "Great indeed is Greece, O Cebes, in which everywhere there are good men, and many are the races of the barbarians."[2] Thus Plato thinks that some of the barbarians,

---

[1] ὁμακοεῖον.

[2] Greece is ample, O Cebes, in which everywhere there are good men; and many are the races of the barbarians, over all of whom you must search, seeking such a physician, sparing neither money nor pains.—*Phædo*, p. 78 A.

too, are philosophers. But Epicurus, on the other hand, supposes that only Greeks can philosophise. And in the *Symposium*, Plato, lauding the barbarians as practising philosophy with conspicuous excellence,[1] truly says: "And in many other instances both among Greeks and barbarians, whose temples reared for such sons are already numerous." And it is clear that the barbarians signally honoured their lawgivers and teachers, designating them gods. For, according to Plato, "they think that good souls, on quitting the super-celestial region, submit to come to this Tartarus, and assuming a body, share in all the ills which are involved in birth, from their solicitude for the race of men;" and these make laws and publish philosophy, "than which no greater boon ever came from the gods to the race of men, or will come."[2]

And as appears to me, it was in consequence of perceiving the great benefit which is conferred through wise men, that the men themselves were honoured and philosophy cultivated publicly by all the Brahmins, and the Odrysi, and the Getæ. And such were strictly deified by the race of the Egyptians, by the Chaldeans and the Arabians, called the Happy, and those that inhabited Palestine, by not the least portion of the Persian race, and by innumerable other races besides these. And it is well known that Plato is found perpetually celebrating the barbarians, remembering that both himself and Pythagoras learned the most and the noblest of their dogmas among the barbarians. Wherefore he also called the races of the barbarians, "races of barbarian philosophers," recognising, in the Phædrus, the Egyptian king, and shows him to us wiser than Theut, whom he knew to be Hermes. But in the Charmides, it is manifest that he knew certain Thracians who were said to make the soul immortal. And Pythagoras

---

[1] This sense is obtained by the omission of μόνους from the text, which may have crept in in consequence of occurring in the previous text, to make it agree with what Plato says, which is, "And both among Greeks and barbarians, there are many who have shown many and illustrious deeds, generating virtue of every kind, to whom many temples on account of such sons are raised."—*Symp.* p. 209 E.

[2] Plato, *Timæus*, p. 47 A.

is reported to have been a disciple of Sonches the Egyptian arch-prophet; and Plato, of Sechnuphis of Heliopolis; and Eudoxus, of Cnidius of Konuphis, who was also an Egyptian. And in his book, *On the Soul*,[1] Plato again manifestly recognises prophecy, when he introduces a prophet announcing the word of Lachesis, uttering predictions to the souls whose destiny is being fixed. And in the *Timæus* he introduces Solon, the very wise, learning from the barbarian. The substance of the declaration is to the following effect: "O Solon, Solon, you Greeks are always children. And no Greek is an old man. For you have no learning that is hoary with age."[2]

Democritus appropriated the Babylonian ethic discourses, for he is said to have combined with his own compositions a translation of the column of Acicarus.[3] And you may find the distinction notified by him when he writes, "Thus says Democritus." About himself, too, where, pluming himself on his erudition, he says, "I have roamed over the most ground of any man of my time, investigating the most remote parts. I have seen the most skies and lands, and I have heard of learned men in very great numbers. And in composition no one has surpassed me; in demonstration, not even those among the Egyptians who are called Arpenodaptæ, with all of whom I lived in exile up to eighty years." For he went to Babylon, and Persis, and Egypt, to learn from the Magi and the priests.

Zoroaster the Magus, Pythagoras showed to be a Persian. Of the secret books of this man, those who follow the heresy of Prodicus boast to be in possession. Alexander, in his book *On the Pythagorean Symbols*, relates that Pythagoras was a pupil of Nazaratus the Assyrian[4] (some think that he is Ezekiel; but he is not, as will afterwards be shown), and will

---

[1] A mistake of Clement for *The Republic*. [2] *Timæus*, p. 22 B.
[3] About which the learned have tortured themselves greatly. The reference is doubtless here to some pillar inscribed with what was deemed a writing of importance. But as to Acicarus nothing is known.
[4] Otherwise Zaratus, or Zabratus, or Zaras, who, Huet says, was Zoroaster.

have it that, in addition to these, Pythagoras was a hearer of the Galatæ and the Brahmins. Clearchus the Peripatetic says that he knew a Jew who associated with Aristotle. Heraclitus says that, not humanly, but rather by God's aid, the Sibyl spoke.[1] They say, accordingly, that at Delphi a stone was shown beside the oracle, on which, it is said, sat the first Sibyl, who came from Helicon, and had been reared by the Muses. But some say that she came from Milea, being the daughter of Lamia of Sidon.[2] And Serapion, in his epic verses, says that the Sibyl, even when dead, ceased not from divination. And he writes that, what proceeded from her into the air after her death, was what gave oracular utterances in voices and omens; and on her body being changed into earth, and the grass as natural growing out of it, whatever beasts happening to be in that place fed on it exhibited to men an accurate knowledge of futurity by their entrails. He thinks also, that the face seen in the moon is her soul. So much for the Sibyl.

Numa the king of the Romans was a Pythagorean, and aided by the precepts of Moses, prohibited from making an image of God in human form, and of the shape of a living creature. Accordingly, during the first hundred and seventy years, though building temples, they made no cast or graven image. For Numa secretly showed them that the Best of Beings could not be apprehended except by the mind alone. Thus philosophy, a thing of the highest utility, flourished in antiquity among the barbarians, shedding its light over the nations. And afterwards it came to Greece. First in its ranks were the prophets of the Egyptians; and the Chaldeans among the Assyrians; and the Druids among the Gauls; and the Samanæans among the Bactrians; and the philosophers of the Celts; and the Magi of the Persians, who foretold the Saviour's birth, and came into the land of Judæa guided by a star. The Indian gymnosophists are also in the number, and the other barbarian philosophers. And of these there

---

[1] Adopting Lowth's emendation, Σιβύλλην φάναι.

[2] Or, according to the reading in Pausanias, and the statement of Plutarch, "who was the daughter of Poseidon."

are two classes, some of them called Sarmanæ,[1] and others Brahmins. And those of the Sarmanæ who are called Hylobii[2] neither inhabit cities, nor have roofs over them, but are clothed in the bark of trees, feed on nuts, and drink water in their hands. Like those called Encratites in the present day, they know not marriage nor begetting of children.

Some, too, of the Indians obey the precepts of Buddha;[3] whom, on account of his extraordinary sanctity, they have raised to divine honours.

Anacharsis was a Scythian, and is recorded to have excelled many philosophers among the Greeks. And the Hyperboreans, Hellanicus relates, dwelt beyond the Riphæan mountains, and inculcated justice, not eating flesh, but using nuts. Those who are sixty years old they take without the gates, and do away with. There are also among the Germans those called holy women, who, by inspecting the whirlpools of rivers and the eddies, and observing the noises of streams, presage and predict future events.[4] These did not allow the men to fight against Cæsar till the new moon shone.

Of all these, by far the oldest is the Jewish race; and that their philosophy committed to writing has the precedence of philosophy among the Greeks, the Pythagorean Philo[5] shows at large; and, besides him, Aristobulus the Peripatetic, and several others, not to waste time, in going over them by name. Very clearly the author Megasthenes, the contemporary of Seleucus Nicanor, writes as follows in the third of his books, *On Indian Affairs:* "All that was said about nature by the ancients is said also by those who philosophise beyond Greece: some things by the Brahmins among the Indians, and others by those called Jews in Syria." Some more fabulously say that certain of those called the Idæan

---

[1] Or Samanæi.
[2] Altered for 'Αλλόβιοι in accordance with the note of Montacutius, who cites Strabo as an authority for the existence of a sect of Indian sages called Hylobii, ὑλόβιοι—Silvicolæ.
[3] Βούττα.   [4] Cæsar, *Gallic War*, book i. chap. 50.
[5] Sozomen also calls Philo a Pythagorean.

Dactyli were the first wise men; to whom are attributed the invention of what are called the "Ephesian letters," and of numbers in music. For which reason dactyls in music received their name. And the Idæan Dactyli were Phrygians and barbarians. Herodotus relates that Hercules, having grown a sage and a student of physics, received from the barbarian Atlas, the Phrygian, the columns of the universe; the fable meaning that he received by instruction the knowledge of the heavenly bodies. And Hermippus of Berytus calls Charon the Centaur wise; about whom, he that wrote *The Battle of the Titans* says, "that he first led the race of mortals to righteousness, by teaching them the solemnity of the oath, and propitiatory sacrifices and the figures of Olympus." By him Achilles, who fought at Troy, was taught. And Hippo, the daughter of the Centaur, who dwelt with Æolus, taught him her father's science, the knowledge of physics. Euripides also testifies of Hippo as follows:

"Who first, by oracles, presaged,
And by the rising stars, events divine."

By this Æolus, Ulysses was received as a guest after the taking of Troy. Mark the epochs by comparison with the age of Moses, and with the high antiquity of the philosophy promulgated by him.

CHAPTER XVI.

THAT THE INVENTORS OF OTHER ARTS WERE MOSTLY BARBARIANS.

AND barbarians were inventors not only of philosophy, but almost of every art. The Egyptians were the first to introduce astrology among men. Similarly also the Chaldeans. The Egyptians first showed how to burn lamps, and divided the year into twelve months, prohibited intercourse with women in the temples, and enacted that no one should enter the temples from a woman without bathing. Again, they were the inventors of geometry. There are some who say that the Carians invented prognostication by the stars. The Phrygians were the first who attended to the flight of birds. And the Tuscans, neighbours of Italy, were adepts at the art of the Haruspex. The Isaurians and the Arabians invented augury, as the Telmesians divination by dreams. The Etruscans invented the trumpet, and the Phrygians the flute. For Olympus and Marsyas were Phrygians. And Cadmus, the inventor of letters among the Greeks, as Euphorus says, was a Phœnician; whence also Herodotus writes that they were called Phœnician letters. And they say that the Phœnicians and the Syrians first invented letters; and that Apis, an aboriginal inhabitant of Egypt, invented the healing art before Io came into Egypt. But afterwards they say that Asclepius improved the art. Atlas the Libyan was the first who built a ship and navigated the sea. Kelmis and Damnaneus, Idæan Dactyli, first discovered iron in Cyprus. Another Idæan discovered the tempering of brass; according to Hesiod, a Scythian. The Thracians first invented what is called a scimitar (ἅρπη),—it is a curved sword,—and were the first to use shields on horseback. Similarly also the Illyrians invented the shield (πέλτη). Besides, they say that the Tuscans invented the art of moulding clay; and that Itanus (he was a Samnite) first fashioned the oblong shield (θυρεός). Cadmus the Phœnician invented stonecutting, and discovered the gold mines on the Pangæan mountain. Further, another nation, the Cappadocians, first invented the instrument called the nabla,[1] and the Assyrians in the same way the dichord. The Carthaginians were the first that constructed a trireme; and it was built by Bosporus, an aboriginal.[2] Medea, the daughter of Æetas, a Colchian, first invented the dyeing of hair. Besides, the Noropes (they are a Pæonian race, and are now called the Norici) worked copper, and were the first that purified iron. Amycus the king of the Bebryci was the first inventor of boxing-gloves.[3] In music, Olympus the Mysian practised the Lydian harmony; and the people called Troglodytes invented the sambuca,[4] a musical instrument. It is said that the crooked pipe was invented by Satyrus the Phrygian; likewise also diatonic harmony by Hyagnis, a Phrygian too; and notes by Olympus, a Phrygian; as also the Phrygian harmony, and the half-Phrygian and the half-Lydian, by Marsyas, who belonged to the same region as those mentioned above. And the Doric was invented by Thamyris the Thracian. We have heard that the Persians were the first who fashioned the chariot, and bed, and footstool; and the Sidonians the first to construct a trireme. The Sicilians, close to Italy, were the first inventors of the phorminx, which is not much inferior to the lyre. And they invented castanets. In the time of Semiramis queen of the Assyrians,[5]

[1] νάβλα and ναύλα; Lat. *nablium*; doubtless the Hebrew נֶבֶל (psaltery, A.V.), described by Josephus as a lyre or harp of twelve strings (in Ps. xxxiv. it is said ten), and played with the fingers. Jerome says it was triangular in shape.

[2] αὐτόχθων, Eusebius. The text has αὐτοσχέδιον, off-hand.

[3] Literally, fist-straps, the cæstus of the boxers.

[4] σαμβύκη, a triangular lyre with four strings.

[5] "King of the Egyptians" in the MSS. of Clement. The correction is made from Eusebius, who extracts the passage.

they relate that linen garments were invented. And Hellanicus says that Atossa queen of the Persians was the first who composed a letter. These things are reported by Scamo of Mitylene, Theophrastus of Ephesus, Cydippus of Mantinea, also Antiphanes, Aristodemus, and Aristotle; and besides these, Philostephanus, and also Strato the Peripatetic, in his books *Concerning Inventions*. I have added a few details from them, in order to confirm the inventive and practically useful genius of the barbarians, by whom the Greeks profited in their studies. And if any one objects to the barbarous language, Anacharsis says, "All the Greeks speak Scythian to me." It was he who was held in admiration by the Greeks, who said, " My covering is a cloak; my supper, milk and cheese." You see that the barbarian philosophy professes deeds, not words. The apostle thus speaks: "So likewise ye, except ye utter by the tongue a word easy to be understood, how shall ye know what is spoken? for ye shall speak into the air. There are, it may be, so many kind of voices in the world, and none of them is without signification. Therefore if I know not the meaning of the voice, I shall be unto him that speaketh a barbarian, and he that speaketh shall be a barbarian unto me." And, "Let him that speaketh in an unknown tongue pray that he may interpret."[1]

Nay more, it was late before the teaching and writing of discourses reached Greece. Alcmæon, the son of Perithus, of Crotona, first composed a treatise on nature. And it is related that Anaxagoras of Clazomenæ, the son of Hegesibulus, first published a book in writing. The first to adapt music to poetical compositions was Terpander of Antissa; and he set the laws of the Lacedæmonians to music. Lasus of Hermione invented the dithyramb; Stesichorus of Himera, the hymn; Alcman the Spartan, the choral song; Anacreon of Teos, love songs; Pindar the Theban, the dance accompanied with song. Timotheus of Miletus was the first to execute those musical compositions called νόμοι on the lyre, with dancing. Moreover, the iambus was invented by Ar-

[1] 1 Cor. xiv. 9, 10, 11, 13.

chilochus of Paros, and the choliambus by Hipponax of Ephesus. Tragedy owed its origin to Thespis the Athenian, and comedy to Susarion of Icaria. Their dates are handed down by the grammarians. But it were tedious to specify them accurately: presently, however, Dionysus, on whose account the Dionysian spectacles are celebrated, will be shown to be later than Moses. They say that Antiphon of Rhamnusium, the son of Sophilus, first invented scholastic discourses and rhetorical figures, and was the first who pled causes for a fee, and wrote a forensic speech for delivery,[1] as Diodorus says. And Apollodorus of Cuma first assumed the name of critic, and was called a grammarian. Some say it was Eratosthenes of Cyrene who was first so called, since he published two books which he entitled *Grammatica*. The first who was called a grammarian, as we now use the term, was Praxiphanes, the son of Disnysophenes of Mitylene. Zeleucus the Locrian was reported to have been the first to have framed laws (in writing). Others say that it was Menos the son of Zeus, in the time of Lynceus. He comes after Danaus, in the eleventh generation from Inachus and Moses; as we shall show a little further on. And Lycurgus, who lived many years after the taking of Troy, legislated for the Lacedæmonians a hundred and fifty years before the Olympiads. We have spoken before of the age of Solon. Draco (he was a legislator too) is discovered to have lived about the three hundred and ninth Olympiad. Antilochus, again, who wrote of the learned men from the age of Pythagoras to the death of Epicurus, which took place in the tenth day of the month Gamelion, makes up altogether three hundred and twelve years. Moreover, some say that Phanothea, the wife of Icarius, invented the heroic hexameter; others Themis, one of the Titanides. Didymus, however, in his work *On the Pythagorean Philosophy*, relates that Theano of Crotona was the first woman who cultivated philosophy and composed poems. The Hellenic philosophy then, accord-

[1] By one or other of the parties in the case, it being a practice of advocates in ancient times to compose speeches which the litigants delivered.

ing to some, apprehended the truth accidentally, dimly, partially; as others will have it, was set a-going by the devil. Several suppose that certain powers, descending from heaven, inspired the whole of philosophy. But if the Hellenic philosophy comprehends not the whole extent of the truth, and besides is destitute of strength to perform the commandments of the Lord, yet it prepares the way for the truly royal teaching; training in some way or other, and moulding the character, and fitting him who believes in Providence for the reception of the truth.

CHAPTER XVII.

ON THE SAYING OF THE SAVIOUR, "ALL THAT CAME BEFORE ME WERE THIEVES AND ROBBERS."[1]

BUT, say they, it is written, "All who were before the Lord's advent are thieves and robbers." All, then, who are in the Word (for it is these that were previous to the incarnation of the Word) are understood generally. But the prophets, being sent and inspired by the Lord, were not thieves, but servants. The Scripture accordingly says, "Wisdom sent her servants, inviting with loud proclamation to a goblet of wine."[2]

But philosophy, it is said, was not sent by the Lord, but came stolen, or given by a thief. It was then some power or angel that had learned something of the truth, but abode not in it, that inspired and taught these things, not without the Lord's knowledge, who knew before the constitution of each essence the issues of futurity, but without His prohibition.

For the theft which reached men then, had some advantage; not that he who perpetrated the theft had utility in his eye, but Providence directed the issue of the audacious deed to utility. I know that many are perpetually assailing us with the allegation, that not to prevent a thing happening, is to be the cause of it happening. For they say, that the man who does not take precaution against a theft, or does not prevent it, is the cause of it: as he is the cause of the conflagration who has not quenched it at the beginning; and the master of the vessel who does not reef the sail, is the cause of the shipwreck. Certainly those who are the causes of such events are punished by the law. For to him who had

[1] John x. 8. [2] Prov. ix. 3.

power to prevent, attaches the blame of what happens. We say to them, that causation is seen in doing, working, acting; but the not preventing is in this respect inoperative. Further, causation attaches to activity; as in the case of the shipbuilder in relation to the origin of the vessel, and the builder in relation to the construction of the house. But that which does not prevent is separated from what takes place. Wherefore the effect will be accomplished; because that which could have prevented neither acts nor prevents. For what activity does that which prevents not exert? Now their assertion is reduced to absurdity, if they shall say that the cause of the wound is not the dart, but the shield, which did not prevent the dart from passing through; and if they blame not the thief, but the man who did not prevent the theft. Let them then say, that it was not Hector that burned the ships of the Greeks, but Achilles; because, having the power to prevent Hector, he did not prevent him; but out of anger (and it depended on himself to be angry or not) did not keep back the fire, and was a concurring cause. Now the devil, being possessed of free-will, was able both to repent and to steal; and it was he who was the author of the theft, not the Lord, who did not prevent him. But neither was the gift hurtful, so as to require that prevention should intervene.

But if strict accuracy must be employed in dealing with them, let them know, that that which does not prevent what we assert to have taken place in the theft, is not a cause at all; but that what prevents is involved in the accusation of being a cause. For he that protects with a shield is the cause of him whom he protects not being wounded; preventing him, as he does, from being wounded. For the demon of Socrates was a cause, not by not preventing, but by exhorting, even if (strictly speaking) he did not exhort. And neither praises nor censures, neither rewards nor punishments, are right, when the soul has not the power of inclination and disinclination, but evil is involuntary. Whence he who prevents is a cause; while he who prevents not judges justly the soul's choice. So in no respect is God the author of evil. But since free choice and inclination originate sins, and a mistaken judgment sometimes prevails, from which, since it is ignorance and stupidity, we do not take pains to recede, punishments are rightly inflicted. For to take fever is involuntary; but when one takes fever through his own fault, from excess, we blame him. Inasmuch, then, as evil is involuntary,—for no one prefers evil as evil; but induced by the pleasure that is in it, and imagining it good, considers it desirable;—such being the case, to free ourselves from ignorance, and from evil and voluptuous choice, and above all, to withhold our assent from those delusive phantasies, depends on ourselves. The devil is called "thief and robber;" having mixed false prophets with the prophets, as tares with the wheat. "All, then, that came before the Lord, were thieves and robbers;" not absolutely all men, but all the false prophets, and all who were not properly sent by Him. For the false prophets possessed the prophetic name dishonestly, being prophets, but prophets of the liar. For the Lord says, "Ye are of your father the devil; and the lusts of your father ye will do. He was a murderer from the beginning, and abode not in the truth, because there is no truth in him. When he speaketh a lie, he speaketh of his own; for he is a liar, and the father of it."[1]

But among the lies, the false prophets also told some true things. And in reality they prophesied "in an ecstasy," as the servants of the apostate. And the Shepherd, the angel of repentance, says to Hermas, of the false prophet: "For he speaks some truths. For the devil fills him with his own spirit, if perchance he may be able to cast down any one from what is right." All things, therefore, are dispensed from heaven for good, "that by the church may be made known the manifold wisdom of God, according to the eternal foreknowledge,[2] which He purposed in Christ."[3] Nothing withstands God: nothing opposes Him: seeing He is Lord and omnipotent. Further, the counsels and activities of those who have rebelled, being partial, proceed from a bad

[1] John viii. 44. [2] Clement reads πρόγνωσιν for πρόθεσιν.
[3] Eph. iii. 10, 11.

disposition, as bodily diseases from a bad constitution, but are guided by universal Providence to a salutary issue, even though the cause be productive of disease. It is accordingly the greatest achievement of divine Providence, not to allow the evil, which has sprung from voluntary apostasy, to remain useless, and for no good, and not to become in all respects injurious. For it is the work of the divine wisdom, and excellence, and power, not alone to do good (for this is, so to speak, the nature of God, as it is of fire to warm and of light to illumine), but especially to ensure that what happens through the evils hatched by any, may come to a good and useful issue, and to use to advantage those things which appear to be evils, as also the testimony which accrues from temptation.

There is then in philosophy, though stolen as the fire by Prometheus, a slender spark, capable of being fanned into flame, a trace of wisdom and an impulse from God. Well, be it so that "the thieves and robbers" are the philosophers among the Greeks, who from the Hebrew prophets before the coming of the Lord received fragments of the truth, not with full knowledge, and claimed these as their own teachings, disguising some points, treating others sophistically by their ingenuity, and discovering other things, for perchance they had "the spirit of perception."[1] Aristotle, too, assented to Scripture, and declared sophistry to have stolen wisdom, as we intimated before. And the apostle says, "Which things we speak, not in the words which man's wisdom teacheth, but which the Holy Ghost teacheth."[2] For of the prophets it is said, "We have all received of His fulness,"[3] that is, of Christ's. So that the prophets are not thieves. "And my doctrine is not mine," saith the Lord, "but the Father's which sent me." And of those who steal He says: "But he that speaketh of himself, seeketh his own glory."[4] Such are the Greeks, "lovers of their own selves, and boasters."[5] Scripture, when it speaks of these as wise, does not brand those who are really wise, but those who are wise in appearance.

[1] Ex. xxviii. 3.   [2] 1 Cor. ii. 13.   [3] John i. 16.
[4] John vii. 16, 18.   [5] 2 Tim. iii. 2.

CHAPTER XVIII.

HE ILLUSTRATES THE APOSTLE'S SAYING, "I WILL DESTROY THE WISDOM OF THE WISE."

AND of such it is said, "I will destroy the wisdom of the wise: I will bring to nothing the understanding of the prudent." The apostle accordingly adds, " Where is the wise ? Where is the scribe ? Where is the disputer of this world?" setting in contradistinction to the scribes, the disputers[1] of this world, the philosophers of the Gentiles. " Hath not God made foolish the wisdom of the world?"[2] which is equivalent to, showed it to be foolish, and not true, as they thought. And if you ask the cause of their seeming wisdom, he will say, " because of the blindness of their heart ;" since " in the wisdom of God," that is, as proclaimed by the prophets, " the world knew not," in the wisdom " which spake by the prophets," " Him,"[3] that is, God,—" it pleased God by the foolishness of preaching"— what seemed to the Greeks foolishness—" to save them that believe. For the Jews require signs," in order to faith; " and the Greeks seek after wisdom," plainly those reasonings styled "irresistible," and those others, namely, syllogisms. " But we preach Jesus Christ crucified; to the Jews a stumbling-block," because, though knowing prophecy, they did not believe the event: " to the Greeks, foolishness ;" for those who in their own estimation are wise, consider it fabulous that the Son of God should speak by man and that God should have a Son, and especially that that Son should have suffered. Whence their preconceived idea inclines them to disbelieve. For the advent of the Saviour did not make people foolish,

[1] Or, "inquirers."   [2] 1 Cor. i. 19, 20.
[3] 1 Cor. i. 21-24 ; where the reading is Θεόν, not Αὐτόν.

and hard of heart, and unbelieving, but made them understanding, amenable to persuasion, and believing. But those that would not believe, by separating themselves from the voluntary adherence of those who obeyed, were proved to be without understanding, unbelievers and fools. " But to them who are called, both Jews and Greeks, Christ is the power of God, and the wisdom of God." Should we not understand (as is better) the words rendered, " Hath not God made foolish the wisdom of the world?" negatively: "God hath not made foolish the wisdom of the world?"—so that the cause of their hardness of heart may not appear to have proceeded from God, " making foolish the wisdom of the world." For on all accounts, being wise, they incur greater blame in not believing the proclamation. For the preference and choice of truth is voluntary. But that declaration, " I will destroy the wisdom of the wise," declares Him to have sent forth light, by bringing forth in opposition the despised and contemned barbarian philosophy; as the lamp, when shone upon by the sun, is said to be extinguished, on account of its not then exerting the same power. All having been therefore called, those who are willing to obey have been named " called." For there is no unrighteousness with God. Those of either race who have believed, are " a peculiar people."[1] And in the Acts of the Apostles you will find this, word for word, " Those then who received his word were baptized;"[2] but those who would not obey kept themselves aloof. To these prophecy says, " If ye be willing and hear me, ye shall eat the good things of the land;"[3] proving that choice or refusal depends on ourselves. The apostle designates the doctrine which is according to the Lord, " the wisdom of God," in order to show that the true philosophy has been communicated by the Son. Further, he, who has a show of wisdom, has certain exhortations enjoined on him by the apostle: " That ye put on the new man, which after God is renewed in righteousness and true holiness. Wherefore, putting away lying, speak every man truth. Neither give place to the devil. Let him that stole, steal no more; but

[1] Tit. ii. 14.   [2] Acts ii. 41.   [3] Isa. i. 19.

rather let him labour, working that which is good" (and to work is to labour in seeking the truth; for it is accompanied with rational well-doing), "that ye may have to give to him that has need,"[1] both of worldly wealth and of divine wisdom. For he wishes both that the word be taught, and that the money be put into the bank, accurately tested, to accumulate interest. Whence he adds, "Let no corrupt communication proceed out of your mouth,"—that is " corrupt communication" which proceeds out of conceit,—"but that which is good for the use of edifying, that it may minister grace to the hearers." And the word of the good God must needs be good. And how is it possible that he who saves shall not be good?

[1] Eph. iv. 24, 25, 27-29.

CHAPTER XIX.

THAT THE PHILOSOPHERS HAVE ATTAINED TO SOME PORTION OF TRUTH.

SINCE, then, the Greeks are testified to have laid down some true opinions, we may from this point take a glance at the testimonies. Paul, in the Acts of the Apostles, is recorded to have said to the Areopagites, "I perceive that ye are more than ordinarily religious. For as I passed by, and beheld your devotions, I found an altar with the inscription, To The Unknown God. Whom therefore ye ignorantly worship, Him declare I unto you. God, that made the world and all things therein, seeing that He is Lord of heaven and earth, dwelleth not in temples made with hands; neither is worshipped with men's hands, as though He needed anything, seeing He giveth to all life, and breath, and all things; and hath made of one blood all nations of men to dwell on all the face of the earth, and hath determined the times before appointed, and the bounds of their habitation; that they should seek God, if haply they might feel after Him, and find Him; though He be not far from every one of us: for in Him we live, and move, and have our being; as certain also of your own poets have said, For we also are His offspring."[1] Whence it is evident that the apostle, by availing himself of poetical examples from the *Phenomena* of Aratus, approves of what had been well spoken by the Greeks; and intimates that, by the unknown God, God the Creator was in a roundabout way worshipped by the Greeks; but that it was necessary by positive knowledge to apprehend and learn Him by the Son.

[1] Acts xvii. 22-28.

"Wherefore, then, I send thee to the Gentiles," it is said, "to open their eyes, and to turn them from darkness to light, and from the power of Satan unto God; that they may receive forgiveness of sins, and inheritance among them that are sanctified by faith which is in me."[1] Such, then, are the eyes of the blind which are opened. The knowledge of the Father by the Son is the comprehension of the "Greek circumlocution;"[2] and to turn from the power of Satan is to change from sin, through which bondage was produced. We do not, indeed, receive absolutely all philosophy, but that of which Socrates speaks in Plato. "For there are (as they say) in the mysteries many bearers of the thyrsus, but few bacchanals;" meaning, "that many are called, but few chosen." He accordingly plainly adds: "These, in my opinion, are none else than those who have philosophized right; to belong to whose number, I myself have left nothing undone in life, as far as I could, but have endeavoured in every way. Whether we have endeavoured rightly and achieved aught, we shall know when we have gone there, if God will, a little afterwards." Does he not then seem to declare from the Hebrew Scriptures the righteous man's hope, through faith, after death? And in *Demodocus*[3] (if that is really the work of Plato): "And do not imagine that I call it philosophizing to spend life pottering about the arts, or learning many things, but something different; since I, at least, would consider this a disgrace." For he knew, I reckon, "that the knowledge of many things does not educate the mind,"[4] according to Heraclitus. And in the fifth book of the *Republic*, he says, "'Shall we then call all these, and the others which study such things, and those who apply themselves to the meaner arts, philosophers?'

[1] Acts xxvi. 17, 18.   [2] Viz., "The Unknown God."
[3] There is no such utterance in the *Demodocus*. But in the *Amatores*, Basle Edition, p. 237, Plato says: "But it is not so, my friend; nor is it philosophizing to occupy oneself in the arts, nor lead a life of bustling meddling activity, nor to learn many things: but it is something else. Since I, at least, would reckon this a reproach; and that those who devote themselves to the arts ought to be called mechanics."
[4] According to the emendation of Menagius: "ὡς ἄρα ἡ πολυμάθεια νόον οὐχὶ διδάσκει."

'By no means,' I said, 'but like philosophers.' 'And whom,' said he, 'do you call true?' 'Those,' said I, 'who delight in the contemplation of truth. For philosophy is not in geometry, with its postulates and hypotheses; nor in music, which is conjectural; nor in astronomy, crammed full of physical, fluid, and probable causes. But the knowledge of the good and truth itself are requisite,—what is good being one thing, and the ways to the good another.'"[1] So that he does not allow that the curriculum of training suffices for the good, but co-operates in rousing and training the soul to intellectual objects. Whether, then, they say that the Greeks gave forth some utterances of the true philosophy by accident, it is the accident of a divine administration (for no one will, for the sake of the present argument with us, deify chance); or by good fortune, good fortune is not unforeseen. Or were one, on the other hand, to say that the Greeks possessed a natural conception of these things, we know the one Creator of nature; just as we also call righteousness natural; or that they had a common intellect, let us reflect who is its father, and what righteousness is in the mental economy. For were one to name "prediction,"[2] and assign as its cause "combined utterance,"[3] he specifies forms of prophecy. Further, others will have it that some truths were uttered by the philosophers, in appearance.

The divine apostle writes accordingly respecting us: "For now we see as through a glass;"[4] knowing ourselves in it by reflection, and simultaneously contemplating, as we can, the efficient cause, from that, which, in us, is divine. For it is said, "Having seen thy brother, thou hast seen thy God:" methinks that now the Saviour God is declared to us. But after the laying aside of the flesh, "face to face,"—then definitely and comprehensively, when the heart becomes pure. And by reflection and direct vision, those among the Greeks who have philosophized accurately, see God. For such, through our weakness, are our true views, as images are seen

[1] Adopting the emendations, δεῖ ἐπιστήμης instead of δι' ἐπιστήμης, and τἀγαθῶν for τἀγαθοῦ, omitting ὥσπερ.
[2] προαναφώνησις.   [3] συνεκφώνησις.   [4] 1 Cor. xiii. 12.

in the water, and as we see things through pellucid and transparent bodies. Excellently therefore Solomon says: "He who soweth righteousness, worketh faith."[1] "And there are those who, sowing their own, make increase."[2] And again: "Take care of the verdure on the plain, and thou shalt cut grass and gather ripe hay, that thou mayest have sheep for clothing."[3] You see how care must be taken for external clothing and for keeping. "And thou shalt intelligently know the souls of thy flock."[4] "For when the Gentiles, which have not the law, do by nature the things contained in the law, these, having not the law, are a law unto themselves; uncircumcision observing the precepts of the law,"[5] according to the apostle, both before the law and before the advent. As if making comparison of those addicted to philosophy with those called heretics, the Word most clearly says: "Better is a friend that is near, than a brother that dwelleth afar off."[6] "And he who relies on falsehoods, feeds on the winds, and pursues winged birds."[7] I do not think that philosophy directly declares the Word, although in many instances philosophy attempts and persuasively teaches us probable arguments; but it assails the sects. Accordingly it is added: "For he hath forsaken the ways of his own vineyard, and wandered in the tracks of his own husbandry." Such are the sects which deserted the primitive church. Now he who has fallen into heresy passes through an arid wilderness, abandoning the only true God, destitute of God, seeking waterless water, reaching an uninhabited and thirsty land, collecting sterility with his hands. And those destitute of prudence, that is, those involved in heresies, "I enjoin," remarks Wisdom, saying, " Touch sweetly stolen bread and the sweet water of theft;"[8] the Scripture manifestly applying the terms bread and water to nothing else but to those heresies, which employ bread and water in the oblation, not according to the rule of the church. For there are those who celebrate the Eucharist with mere water. "But begone, stay not in her

[1] Prov. xi. 21. [2] Prov. xi. 24. [3] Prov. xxvii. 25, 26.
[4] Prov. xxvii. 23. [5] Rom. ii. 14, 16. [6] Prov. xxvii. 10.
[7] Prov. ix. 12. [8] Prov. ix. 17.

place." It is the synagogue, not the church, that is called by the equivocal name, place. Then He subjoins: "For so shalt thou pass through the water of another;" reckoning heretical baptism not proper and true water. "And thou shalt pass over another's river," that rushes along and sweeps down to the sea; into which he is cast who, having diverged from the stability which is according to truth, rushes back into the heathenish and tumultuous waves of life.

CHAPTER XX.

IN WHAT RESPECT PHILOSOPHY CONTRIBUTES TO THE COMPREHENSION OF DIVINE TRUTH.

AS many men drawing down the ship, cannot be called many causes, but one cause consisting of many;—for each individual by himself is not the cause of the ship being drawn, but along with the rest;—so also philosophy, being the search for truth, contributes to the comprehension of truth; not as being the cause of comprehension, but a cause along with other things, and co-operator; perhaps also a joint cause. And as the several virtues are causes of the happiness of one individual; and as both the sun, and the fire, and the bath, and clothing are of one getting warm: so while truth is one, many things contribute to its investigation. But its discovery is by the Son. If then we consider, virtue is, in power, one. But it is the case, that when exhibited in some things, it is called prudence, in others temperance, and in others manliness or righteousness. By the same analogy, while truth is one, in geometry there is the truth of geometry; in music, that of music; and in the right philosophy, there will be Hellenic truth. But that is the only authentic truth, unassailable, in which we are instructed by the Son of God. In the same way we say, that the drachma being one and the same, when given to the shipmaster, is called the fare; to the tax-gatherer, tax; to the landlord, rent; to the teacher, fees; to the seller, an earnest. And each, whether it be virtue or truth, called by the same name, is the cause of its own peculiar effect alone; and from the blending of them arises a happy life. For we are not made happy by names alone, when we say that a good life is happiness, and that the man who is adorned in his soul with virtue is happy. But if philosophy contributes remotely to the discovery of truth, by reaching, by diverse essays, after the knowledge which touches close on the truth, the knowledge possessed by us, it aids him who aims at grasping it, in accordance with the Word, to apprehend knowledge. But the Hellenic truth is distinct from that held by us (although it has got the same name), both in respect of extent of knowledge, certainty of demonstration, divine power, and the like. For we are taught of God, being instructed in the truly "sacred letters"[1] by the Son of God. Whence those, to whom we refer, influence souls not in the way we do, but by different teaching. And if, for the sake of those who are fond of fault-finding, we must draw a distinction, by saying that philosophy is a concurrent and co-operating cause of true apprehension, being the search for truth, then we shall avow it to be a preparatory training for the enlightened man (τοῦ γνωστικοῦ); not assigning as the cause that which is but the joint-cause; nor as the upholding cause, what is merely co-operative; nor giving to philosophy the place of a *sine quâ non*. Since almost all of us, without training in arts and sciences, and the Hellenic philosophy, and some even without learning at all, through the influence of a philosophy divine and barbarous, and by power, have through faith received the word concerning God, trained by self-operating wisdom. But that which acts in conjunction with something else, being of itself incapable of operating by itself, we describe as co-operating and concausing, and say that it becomes a cause only in virtue of its being a joint-cause, and receives the name of cause only in respect of its concurring with something else, but that it cannot by itself produce the right effect.

Although at one time philosophy justified the Greeks, not conducting then to that entire righteousness to which it is ascertained to co-operate, as the first and second flight of steps

[1] ἱερὰ γράμματα (2 Tim. iii. 15), translated in A. V. "sacred scriptures;" also in contradistinction to the so-called sacred letters of the Egyptians, Chaldeans, etc.

help you in your ascent to the upper room, and the grammarian helps the philosopher. Not as if by its abstraction, the perfect Word would be rendered incomplete, or truth perish; since also sight, and hearing, and the voice contribute to truth, but it is the mind which is the appropriate faculty for knowing it. But of those things which co-operate, some contribute a greater amount of power; some, a less. Perspicuity accordingly aids in the communication of truth, and logic in preventing us from falling under the heresies by which we are assailed. But the teaching, which is according to the Saviour, is complete in itself and without defect, being "the power and wisdom of God;"[1] and the Hellenic philosophy does not, by its approach, make the truth more powerful; but rendering powerless the assault of sophistry against it, and frustrating the treacherous plots laid against the truth, is said to be the proper "fence and wall of the vineyard." And the truth which is according to faith is as necessary for life as bread; while the preparatory discipline is like sauce and sweetmeats. "At the end of the dinner, the dessert is pleasant," according to the Theban Pindar. And the Scripture has expressly said, "The innocent will become wiser by understanding, and the wise will receive knowledge."[2] "And he that speaketh of himself," saith the Lord, "seeketh his own glory; but He that seeketh His glory that sent Him is true, and there is no unrighteousness in Him."[3] On the other hand, therefore, he who appropriates what belongs to the barbarians, and vaunts it is his own, does wrong, increasing his own glory, and falsifying the truth. It is such an one that is by Scripture called a "thief." It is therefore said, "Son, be not a liar; for falsehood leads to theft." Nevertheless the thief possesses really, what he has possessed himself of dishonestly, whether it be gold, or silver, or speech, or dogma. The ideas, then, which they have stolen, and which are partially true, they know by conjecture and necessary logical deduction: on becoming disciples, therefore, they will know them with intelligent apprehension.

[1] 1 Cor. i. 24.   [2] Prov. xxi. 11.   [3] John vii. 18.

CHAPTER XXI.

THE JEWISH INSTITUTIONS AND LAWS OF FAR HIGHER ANTIQUITY THAN THE PHILOSOPHY OF THE GREEKS.

N the plagiarizing of the dogmas of the philosophers from the Hebrews, we shall treat a little afterwards. But first, as due order demands, we must now speak of the epoch of Moses, by which the philosophy of the Hebrews will be demonstrated beyond all contradiction to be the most ancient of all wisdom. This has been discussed with accuracy by Tatian in his book *To the Greeks,* and by Casian in the first book of his *Exegetics.* Nevertheless our commentary demands that we too should run over what has been said on the point. Apion, then, the grammarian, surnamed Pleistonices, in the fourth book of *The Egyptian Histories,* although of so hostile a disposition towards the Hebrews, being by race an Egyptian, as to compose a work against the Jews, when referring to Amosis king of the Egyptians, and his exploits, adduces, as a witness, Ptolemy of Mendes. And his remarks are to the following effect: Amosis, who lived in the time of the Argive Inachus, overthrew Athyria, as Ptolemy of Mendes relates in his *Chronology.* Now this Ptolemy was a priest; and setting forth the deeds of the Egyptian kings in three entire books, he says, that the exodus of the Jews from Egypt, under the conduct of Moses, took place while Amosis was king of Egypt. Whence it is seen that Moses flourished in the time of Inachus. And of the Hellenic states, the most ancient is the Argolic, I mean that which took its rise from Inachus, as Dionysius of Halicarnassus teaches in his *Times.* And younger by forty generations than it was Attica, founded by

Cecrops, who was an aboriginal of double race, as Tatian expressly says; and Arcadia, founded by Pelasgus, younger too by nine generations; and he, too, is said to have been an aboriginal. And more recent than this last by fifty-two generations, was Pthiotis, founded by Deucalion. And from the time of Inachus to the Trojan war twenty generations or more are reckoned; let us say, four hundred years and more. And if Ctesias says that the Assyrian power is many years older than the Greek, the exodus of Moses from Egypt will appear to have taken place in the forty-second year of the Assyrian empire,[1] in the thirty-second year of the reign of Belochus, in the time of Amosis the Egyptian, and of Inachus the Argive. And in Greece, in the time of Phoroneus, who succeeded Inachus, the flood of Ogyges occurred; and monarchy subsisted in Sicyon first in the person of Ægialeus, then of Europs, then of Telches; in Crete, in the person of Cres. For Acusilaus says that Phoroneus was the first man. Whence, too, the author of *Phoronis* said that he was "the father of mortal men." Thence Plato in the *Timæus*, following Acusilaus, writes: "And wishing to draw them out into a discussion respecting antiquities, he[2] said that he ventured to speak of the most remote antiquities of this city[3] respecting Phoroneus, called the first man, and Niobe, and what happened after the deluge." And in the time of Phorbus lived Actæus, from whom is derived Actaia, Attica; and in the time of Triopas lived Prometheus, and Atlas, and Epimetheus, and Cecrops of double race, and Ino. And in the time of Crotopus occurred the burning of Phaethon, and the deluge[4] of Deucalion; and in the time of Sthenelus, the reign of Amphictyon, and the arrival of Danaus in the Peloponnesus; and under Dardanus happened the building of Dardania, whom, says Homer,

"First cloud-compelling Zeus begat,"—

---

[1] The deficiencies of the text in this place have been supplied from Eusebius' *Chronicles*.

[2] *i.e.* Solon, in his conversation with the Egyptian priests.

[3] πόλις, "city," is not in Plato.

[4] ἐπομβρία.

and the transmigration from Crete into Phœnicia. And in the time of Lynceus took place the abduction of Proserpine, and the dedication of the sacred enclosure in Eleusis, and the husbandry of Triptolemus, and the arrival of Cadmus in Thebes, and the reign of Minos. And in the time of Prœtus the war of Eumolpus with the Athenians took place; and in the time of Acrisius, the removal of Pelops from Phrygia, the arrival of Ion at Athens; and the second Cecrops appeared, and the exploits of Perseus and Dionysus took place, and Orpheus and Musæus lived. And in the eighteenth year of the reign of Agamemnon, Troy was taken, in the first year of the reign of Demophon the son of Theseus at Athens, on the twelfth day of the month Thargelion, as Dionysius the Argive says; but Ægias and Dercylus, in the third book, say that it was on the eighth day of the last division of the month Panemus; Hellanicus says that it was on the twelfth of the month Thargelion; and some of the authors of the *Attica* say that it was on the eighth of the last division of the month in the last year of Menestheus, at full moon.

"It was midnight,"

says the author of the *Little Iliad*,

"And the moon shone clear."

Others say, it took place on the same day of Scirophorion. But Theseus, the rival of Hercules, is older by a generation than the Trojan war. Accordingly Tlepolemus, a son of Hercules, is mentioned by Homer, as having served at Troy.

Moses, then, is shown to have preceded the deification of Dionysus six hundred and four years, if he was deified in the thirty-second year of the reign of Perseus, as Apollodorus says in his *Chronology*. From Bacchus to Hercules and the chiefs that sailed with Jason in the ship Argo, are comprised sixty-three years. Æsculapius and the Dioscuri sailed with them, as Apollonius Rhodius testifies in his *Argonautics*. And from the reign of Hercules, in Argos, to the deification of Hercules and of Æsculapius, are comprised thirty-eight years, according to Apollodorus the chronologist; from this to the deification of Castor and Pollux, fifty-three years. And at this time

Troy was taken. And if we may believe the poet Hesiod, let us hear him:

> "Then to Jove, Maia, Atlas' daughter, bore renowned Hermes,
> Herald of the immortals, having ascended the sacred couch.
> And Semele, the daughter of Cadmus, too, bore an illustrious son,
> Dionysus, the joy-inspiring, when she mingled with him in love."

Cadmus, the father of Semele, came to Thebes in the time of Lynceus, and was the inventor of the Greek letters. Triopas was a cotemporary of Isis, in the seventh generation from Inachus. And Isis, who is the same as Io, is so called, it is said, from her going (ἰέναι) roaming over the whole earth. Her, Istrus, in his work on the migration of the Egyptians, calls the daughter of Prometheus. Prometheus lived in the time of Triopas, in the seventh generation after Moses. So that Moses appears to have flourished even before the birth of men, according to the chronology of the Greeks. Leon, who treated of the Egyptian divinities, says that Isis by the Greeks was called Ceres, who lived in the time of Lynceus, in the eleventh generation after Moses. And Apis the king of Argos built Memphis, as Aristippus says in the first book of the *Arcadica*. And Aristeas the Argive says that he was named Serapis, and that it is he that the Egyptians worship. And Nymphodorus of Amphipolis, in the third book of the *Institutions of Asia*, says that the bull Apis, dead and laid in a coffin (σορός), was deposited in the temple of the god (δαίμονος) there worshipped, and thence was called Soroapis, and afterwards Serapis by the custom of the natives. And Apis is third after Inachus. Further, Latona lived in the time of Tityus. "For he dragged Latona, the radiant consort of Zeus." Now Tityus was contemporary with Tantalus. Rightly, therefore, the Bœotian Pindar writes, "And in time was Apollo born;" and no wonder when he is found along with Hercules, serving Admetus "for a long year." Zethus and Amphion, the inventors of music, lived about the age of Cadmus. And should one assert that Phemonoe was the first who sang oracles in verse to Acrisius, let him know that twenty-seven years after Phemonoe, lived Orpheus, and Musæus, and

Linus the teacher of Hercules. And Homer and Hesiod are much more recent than the Trojan war; and after them the legislators among the Greeks are far more recent, Lycurgus and Solon, and the seven wise men, and Pherecydes of Syros, and Pythagoras the great, who lived later, about the Olympiads, as we have shown. We have also demonstrated Moses to be more ancient, not only than those called poets and wise men among the Greeks, but than the most of their deities. Nor he alone, but the Sibyl also is more ancient than Orpheus. For it is said, that respecting her appellation and her oracular utterances there are several accounts; that being a Phrygian, she was called Artemis; and that on her arrival at Delphi, she sang—

"O Delphians, ministers of far-darting Apollo,
I come to declare the mind of Ægis-bearing Zeus,
Enraged as I am at my own brother Apollo."

There is another also, an Erythræan, called Herophile. These are mentioned by Heraclides of Pontus in his work *On Oracles*. I pass over the Egyptian Sibyl, and the Italian, who inhabited the Carmentale in Rome, whose son was Evander, who built the temple of Pan in Rome, called the Lupercal.

It is worth our while, having reached this point, to examine the dates of the other prophets among the Hebrews who succeeded Moses. After the close of Moses' life, Joshua succeeded to the leadership of the people, and he, after warring for sixty-five years, rested in the good land other five-and-twenty. As the book of Joshua relates, the above mentioned man was the successor of Moses twenty-seven years. Then the Hebrews having sinned, were delivered to Chusachar[1] king of Mesopotamia for eight years, as the book of Judges mentions. But having afterwards besought the Lord, they receive for leader Gothoniel,[2] the younger brother of Caleb, of the tribe of Judah, who, having slain the king of Mesopotamia, ruled over the people forty years in succession. And having again sinned, they were delivered into the hands of Æglom[3] king of the Moabites for eighteen years. But on their repentance, Aod,[4] a man who had equal use of both hands, of the tribe

[1] Chushan-rishathaim; Judg. iii. 8.   [2] Othniel.   [3] Eglon.   [4] Ehud.

of Ephraim, was their leader for eighty years. It was he that despatched Æglom. On the death of Aod, and on their sinning again, they were delivered into the hand of Jabim[1] king of Canaan twenty years. After him Deborah the wife of Lapidoth, of the tribe of Ephraim, prophesied; and Ozias the son of Rhiesu was high priest. At her instance Barak the son of Bener,[2] of the tribe of Naphtali, commanding the army, having joined battle with Sisera, Jabim's commander-in-chief, conquered him. And after that Deborah ruled, judging the people forty years. On her death, the people having again sinned, were delivered into the hands of the Midianites seven years. After these events, Gideon, of the tribe of Manasseh, the son of Joas, having fought with his three hundred men, and killed a hundred and twenty thousand, ruled forty years; after whom the son of Ahimelech, three years. He was succeeded by Boleas, the son of Bedan, the son of Charran,[3] of the tribe of Ephraim, who ruled twenty-three years. After whom, the people having sinned again, were delivered to the Ammonites eighteen years; and on their repentance were commanded by Jephtha the Gileadite, of the tribe of Manasseh; and he ruled six years. After whom, Abatthan[4] of Bethlehem, of the tribe of Juda, ruled seven years. Then Ebron[5] the Zebulonite, eight years. Then Eglom of Ephraim, eight years. Some add to the seven years of Abatthan the eight of Ebrom.[6] And after him, the people having again transgressed, came under the power of the foreigners, the Philistines, for forty years. But on their returning [to God], they were led by Samson, of the tribe of Dan, who conquered the foreigners in battle. He ruled twenty years. And after him, there being no governor, Eli the priest judged the people for forty years. He was succeeded by Samuel the

---

[1] Jabin.   [2] Abinoam; Judg. iv. 6.
[3] Sic. Θωλιᾶς may be the right reading instead of Βωλιᾶς. But Judg. x. 1 says Tola, the son of Puah, the son of Dodo.
[4] Ibzan, A.V., Judg. xii. 8; 'Αβαισσάν, *Septuagint*. According to Judg. xii. 11, Elon the Zebulonite succeeded Ibzan.
[5] Not mentioned in Scripture.   [6] Sic.

prophet; contemporaneously with whom Saul reigned, who held sway for twenty-seven years. He anointed David. Samuel died two years before Saul, while Abimelech was high priest. He anointed Saul as king, who was the first that bore regal sway over Israel after the judges; the whole duration of whom, down to Saul, was four hundred and sixty-three years and seven months.

Then in the first book of Kings there are twenty years of Saul, during which he reigned after he was renovated. And after the death of Saul, David the son of Jesse, of the tribe of Judah, reigned next in Hebron, forty years, as is contained in the second book of Kings. And Abiathar the son of Abimelech, of the kindred of Eli, was high priest. In his time Gad and Nathan prophesied. From Joshua the son of Nun, then, till David received the kingdom, there intervene, according to some, four hundred and fifty years. But, as the chronology set forth shows, five hundred and twenty-three years and seven months are comprehended till the death of David.

And after this Solomon the son of David reigned forty years. Under him Nathan continued to prophesy, who also exhorted him respecting the building of the temple. Achias of Shilo also prophesied. And both the kings, David and Solomon, were prophets. And Sadoc the high priest was the first who ministered in the temple which Solomon built, being the eighth from Aaron, the first high priest. From Moses, then, to the age of Solomon, as some say, are five hundred and ninety-five years, and as others, five hundred and seventy-six.

And if you count, along with the four hundred and fifty years from Joshua to David, the forty years of the rule of Moses, and the other eighty years of Moses' life previous to the exodus of the Hebrews from Egypt, you will make up the sum in all of six hundred and ten years. But our chronology will run more correctly, if to the five hundred and twenty-three years and seven months till the death of David, you add the hundred and twenty years of Moses and the forty years of Solomon. For you will make up in all, down to the death of Solomon, six hundred and eighty-three years and seven months.

Hiram gave his daughter to Solomon about the time of the arrival of Menelaus in Phenicia, after the capture of Troy, as is said by Menander of Pergamus, and Lætus in *The Phenicia*. And after Solomon, Roboam his son reigned for seventeen years; and Abimelech the son of Sadoc was high priest. In his reign, the kingdom being divided, Jeroboam, of the tribe of Ephraim, the servant of Solomon, reigned in Samaria; and Achias the Shilonite continued to prophesy; also Samæas the son of Amame, and he who came from Judah to Jeroboam,[1] and prophesied against the altar. After him his son Abijam, twenty-three years; and likewise his son Asaman.[2] The last, in his old age, was diseased in his feet; and in his reign prophesied Jehu the son of Ananias.

After him Jehosaphat his son reigned twenty-five years.[3] In his reign prophesied Elias the Thesbite, and Michæas the son of Jebla, and Abdias the son of Ananias. And in the time of Michæas there was also the false prophet Zedekias, the son of Chonaan. These were followed by the reign of Joram the son of Jehosaphat, for eight years; during whose time prophesied Elias; and after Elias, Elisæus the son of Saphat. In his reign the people in Samaria ate doves' dung and their own children. The period of Jehosaphat extends from the close of the third book of Kings to the fourth. And in the reign of Joram, Elias was translated, and Elisæus the son of Saphat commenced prophesying, and prophesied for six years, being forty years old.

Then Ochozias reigned a year. In his time Elisæus continued to prophesy, and along with him Adadonæus.[4] After him the mother of Ozias,[5] Gotholia,[6] reigned eight[7] years,

[1] See 1 Kings xiii. 1, 2. The text has ἐπὶ 'Ροβοάμ, which, if retained, must be translated, "in the reign of Roboam." But Jeroboam was probably the original reading.

[2] Asa. [3] So Lowth corrects the text, which has five.

[4] Supposed to be "son of Oded" or "Adad," *i.e.* Azarias.

[5] *i.e.* of Ochozias. [6] Athalia.

[7] She was slain in the seventh year of her reign.

having slain the children of her brother.[1] For she was of the family of Ahab. But the sister of Ozias, Josabæa, stole Joas the son of Ozias, and invested him afterwards with the kingdom. And in the time of this Gotholia, Elisæus was still prophesying. And after her reigned, as I said before, Joash, rescued by Josabæa the wife of Jodæ the high priest, and lived in all forty years.

There are comprised, then, from Solomon to the death of Elisæus the prophet, as some say, one hundred and five years; according to others, one hundred and two; and, as the chronology before us shows, from the reign of Solomon an hundred and eighty-one.

Now from the Trojan war to the birth of Homer, according to Philochorus, a hundred and eighty years elapsed; and he was posterior to the Ionic migration. But Aristarchus, in the *Archilochian Memoirs*, says that he lived during the Ionic migration, which took place a hundred and twenty years after the siege of Troy. But Apollodorus alleges it was an hundred and twenty years after the Ionic migration, while Agesilaus son of Doryssæus was king of the Lacedæmonians: so that he brings Lycurgus the legislator, while still a young man, near him. Euthymenes, in the *Chronicles*, says that he flourished contemporaneously with Hesiod, in the time of Acastus, and was born in Chios, about the four hundredth year after the capture of Troy. And Archimachus, in the third book of his *Eubœan History*, is of this opinion. So that both he and Hesiod were later than Elisæus the prophet. And if you choose to follow the grammarian Crates, and say that Homer was born about the time of the expedition of the Heraclidæ, eighty years after the taking of Troy, he will be found to be later again than Solomon, in whose days occurred the arrival of Menelaus in Phenicia, as was said above. Eratosthenes says that Homer's age was two hundred years after the capture of Troy. Further, Theopompus, in the forty-third book of the *Philippics*, relates that Homer was born five hundred years after the war at Troy.

[1] Not of her brother, but of her son Ahaziah, all of whom she slew except Joash.

And Euphorion, in his book about the *Aleuades*, maintains that he was born in the time of Gyges, who began to reign in the eighteenth Olympiad, who, also he says, was the first that was called tyrant (τύραννος). Sosibius Lacon, again, in his *Record of Dates*, brings Homer down to the eighth year of the reign of Charillus the son of Polydectus. Charillus reigned for sixty-four years, after whom the son of Nicander reigned thirty-nine years. In his thirty-fourth year it is said that the first Olympiad was instituted; so that Homer was ninety years before the introduction of the Olympic games.

After Joas, Amasias his son reigned as his successor thirty-nine years. He in like manner was succeeded by his son Ozias, who reigned for fifty-two years, and died a leper. And in his time prophesied Amos, and Isaiah his son,[1] and Hosea the son of Beeri, and Jonas the son of Amathi, who was of Geth-chober, who preached to the Ninevites, and passed through the whale's belly.

Then Jonathan the son of Ozias reigned for sixteen years. In his time Esaias still prophesied, and Hosea, and Michæas the Morasthite, and Joel the son of Bethuel.

Next in succession was his son Ahaz, who reigned for sixteen years. In his time, in the fifteenth year, Israel was carried away to Babylon. And Salmanasar the king of the Assyrians carried away the people of Samaria into the country of the Medes and to Babylon.

Again Ahaz was succeeded by Osee,[2] who reigned for eight years. Then followed Hezekiah, for twenty-nine years. For his sanctity, when he had approached his end, God, by Isaiah, allowed him to live for other fifteen years, giving as a sign the going back of the sun. Up to his times Esaias, Hosea, and Micah continued prophesying.

And these are said to have lived after the age of Lycurgus,

---

[1] Clement is wrong in asserting that Amos the prophet was the father of Isaiah. The names are written differently in Hebrew, though the same in Greek.

[2] By a strange mistake Hosea king of Israel is reckoned among the kings of Judah.

the legislator of the Lacedæmonians. For Dieuchidas, in the fourth book of the *Megarics*, places the era of Lycurgus about the two hundred and ninetieth year after the capture of Troy.

And Esaias is still seen prophesying in the two hundredth year after the reign of Solomon, in whose time Menelaus was proved to have come to Phenicia; and along with Esaias, Michaiah, and Hosea, and Joel the son of Bethuel.

After Hezekiah, his son Manasses reigned for fifty-five years. Then his son Amos for two years. After him reigned his son Josias, distinguished for his observance of the law, for thirty-one years. He "laid the carcases of men upon the carcases of the idols," as is written in the book of Leviticus.[1] In his reign, in the eighteenth year, the passover was celebrated, not having been kept from the days of Samuel in the intervening period.[2] Then Chelkias the priest, the father of the prophet Jeremiah, having fallen in with the book of the law, that had been laid up in the temple, read it and died.[3] And in his days Olda[4] prophesied, and Sophonias,[5] and Jeremiah. And in the days of Jeremiah was Ananias the son of Azor,[6] the false prophet. He[7] having disobeyed Jeremiah the prophet, was slain by Pharaoh Necho king of Egypt at the river Euphrates, having encountered the latter, who was marching on the Assyrians.

Josiah was succeeded by Jechoniah, called also Joachas,[8] his son, who reigned three months and ten days. Necho king of Egypt bound him and led him to Egypt, after making his brother Joachim king in his stead, who continued his tributary for eleven years. After him his namesake[9] Joakim reigned for three months. Then Zedekiah reigned for eleven years; and up to his time Jeremiah continued to prophesy. Along with him Ezekiel[10] the son of Buzi, and

[1] Lev. xxvi. 30.   [2] 2 Kings xxiii. 22.   [3] 2 Kings xxii. 8.
[4] Huldah.   [5] Zephaniah.
[6] ὁ 'Ιωσίου, the reading of the text, is probably corrupt.   [7] Josias.
[8] ὁ καὶ 'Ιωάχας, instead of which the text has καὶ 'Ιωάχας.
[9] The names, however, were not the same. The name of the latter was Jehoiachin. The former in Hebrew is written יהויקים, the latter יהויכין. By copyists they were often confounded, as here by Clement.
[10] Lowth supplies 'Ιεζεκιὴλ, which is wanting in the text.

Urias[1] the son of Samæus, and Ambacum[2] prophesied. Here end the Hebrew kings.

There are then from the birth of Moses till this captivity nine hundred and seventy-two years; but according to strict chronological accuracy, one thousand and eighty-five, six months, ten days. From the reign of David to the captivity by the Chaldeans, four hundred and fifty-two years and six months; but as the accuracy we have observed in reference to dates makes out, four hundred and eighty-two and six months ten days.

And in the twelfth year of the reign of Zedekiah, forty years before the supremacy of the Persians, Nebuchodonosor made war against the Phœnicians and the Jews, as Berosus asserts in his *Chaldæan Histories*. And Joabas,[3] writing about the Assyrians, acknowledges that he had received the history from Berosus, and testifies to his accuracy. Nebuchodonosor, therefore, having put out the eyes of Zedekiah, took him away to Babylon, and transported the whole people (the captivity lasted seventy years), with the exception of a few who fled to Egypt.

Jeremiah and Ambacum were still prophesying in the time of Zedekiah. In the fifth year of his reign Ezekiel prophesied at Babylon; after him Nahum, then Daniel. After him, again, Haggai and Zechariah prophesied in the time of Darius the First for two years; and then the angel among the twelve.[4] After Haggai and Zechariah, Nehemiah, the chief cup-bearer of Artaxerxes, the son of Acheli the Israelite, built the city of Jerusalem and restored the temple. During the captivity lived Esther and Mordecai, whose book is still extant, as also that of the Maccabees. During this captivity Mishael, Ananias, and Azarias, refusing to worship the image, and being thrown into a furnace of fire, were saved by the appearance of an angel. At that time, on account of the serpent,[5] Daniel was thrown into the den of lions; but being

---

[1] He was a contemporary of Jeremiah, but was killed before the time of Zedekiah by Joachin. Jer. xxvi. 20.

[2] Habakkuk. [3] Juba. [4] Malachi, my angel or messenger.

[5] On account of killing the serpent, as is related in the apocryphal book, "Bel and the Dragon, or Serpent."

preserved through the providence of God by Ambacub, he is restored on the seventh day. At this period, too, occurred the sign of Jona; and Tobias, through the assistance of the angel Raphael, married Sarah, the demon having killed her seven first suitors; and after the marriage of Tobias, his father Tobit recovered his sight. At that time Zorobabel, having by his wisdom overcome his opponents, and obtained leave from Darius for the rebuilding of Jerusalem, returned with Esdras to his native land; and by him the redemption of the people and the revisal and restoration of the inspired oracles were effected; and the passover of deliverance celebrated, and marriage with aliens dissolved.

Cyrus had, by proclamation, previously enjoined the restoration of the Hebrews. And his promise being accomplished in the time of Darius, the feast of the dedication was held, as also the feast of tabernacles.

There were in all, taking in the duration of the captivity down to the restoration of the people, from the birth of Moses, one thousand one hundred and fifty-five years, six months, and ten days; and from the reign of David, according to some, four hundred and fifty-two; more correctly, five hundred and seventy-two years, six months, and ten days.

From the captivity at Babylon, which took place in the time of Jeremiah the prophet, was fulfilled what was spoken by Daniel the prophet as follows: "Seventy weeks are determined upon thy people, and upon thy holy city, to finish the transgression, and to seal sins, and to wipe out and make reconciliation for iniquity, and to bring in everlasting righteousness, and to seal the vision and the prophet, and to anoint the Holy of Holies. Know therefore, and understand, that from the going forth of the word commanding an answer to be given, and Jerusalem to be built, to Christ the Prince, are seven weeks and sixty-two weeks; and the street shall be again built, and the wall; and the times shall be expended. And after the sixty-two weeks the anointing shall be overthrown, and judgment shall not be in him; and he shall destroy the city and the sanctuary along with the coming Prince. And they shall be destroyed in a flood, and to the end of the war shall be cut off by desolations. And he shall confirm the covenant with many for one week; and in the middle of the week the sacrifice and oblation shall be taken away; and in the holy place shall be the abomination of desolations, and until the consummation of time shall the consummation be assigned for desolation. And in the midst of the week shall he make the incense of sacrifice cease, and of the wing of destruction, even till the consummation, like the destruction of the oblation."[1] That the temple accordingly was built in seven weeks, is evident; for it is written in Esdras. And thus Christ became King of the Jews, reigning in Jerusalem in the fulfilment of the seven weeks. And in the sixty and two weeks the whole of Judæa was quiet, and without wars. And Christ our Lord, "the Holy of Holies," having come and fulfilled the vision and the prophecy, was anointed in His flesh by the Holy Spirit of His Father. In those "sixty and two weeks," as the prophet said, and "in the one week," was He Lord. The half of the week Nero held sway, and in the holy city Jerusalem placed the abomination; and in the half of the week he was taken away, and Otho, and Galba, and Vitellius. And Vespasian rose to the supreme power, and destroyed Jerusalem, and desolated the holy place. And that such are the facts of the case, is clear to him that is able to understand, as the prophet said.

On the completion, then, of the eleventh year, in the beginning of the following, in the reign of Joachim, occurred the carrying away captive to Babylon by Nabuchodonosor the king, in the seventh year of his reign over the Assyrians, in the second year of the reign of Vaphres over the Egyptians, in the archonship of Philip at Athens, in the first year of the forty-eighth Olympiad. The captivity lasted for seventy years, and ended in the second year of Darius Hystaspes, who had become king of the Persians, Assyrians, and Egyptians; in whose reign, as I said above, Haggai and Zechariah and the angel of the twelve prophesied. And the high priest was Joshua the son of Josedec. And in the

[1] Dan. ix. 24–27.

second year of the reign of Darius, who, Herodotus says, destroyed the power of the Magi, Zorobabel the son of Salathiel was despatched to raise and adorn the temple at Jerusalem.

The times of the Persians are accordingly summed up thus: Cyrus reigned thirty years; Cambyses, nineteen; Darius, forty-six; Xerxes, twenty-six; Artaxerxes, forty-one; Darius, eight; Artaxerxes, forty-two; Ochus or Arses, three. The sum total of the years of the Persian monarchy is two hundred and thirty-five years.

Alexander of Macedon, having despatched this Darius, during this period, began to reign. Similarly, therefore, the times of the Macedonian kings are thus computed: Alexander, eighteen years; Ptolemy the son of Lagus, forty years; Ptolemy Philadelphus, twenty-seven years; then Euergetes, five-and-twenty years; then Philopator, seventeen years; then Epiphanes, four-and-twenty years; he was succeeded by Philometer, who reigned five-and-thirty years; after him Physcon, twenty-nine years; then Lathurus, thirty-six years; then he that was surnamed Dionysus, twenty-nine years; and last Cleopatra reigned twenty-two years. And after her was the reign of the Cappadocians for eighteen days.

Accordingly the period embraced by the Macedonian kings is, in all, three hundred and twelve years and eighteen days.

Therefore those who prophesied in the time of Darius Hystaspes, about the second year of his reign,—Haggai, and Zechariah, and the angel of the twelve, who prophesied about the first year of the forty-eighth Olympiad,—are demonstrated to be older than Pythagoras, who is said to have lived in the sixty-second Olympiad, and than Thales, the oldest of the wise men of the Greeks, who lived about the fiftieth Olympiad. Those wise men that are classed with Thales were then contemporaneous, as Andron says in the *Tripos*. For Heraclitus being posterior to Pythagoras, mentions him in his book. Whence indisputably the first Olympiad, which was demonstrated to be four hundred and seven years later than the Trojan war, is found to be prior to the age of the above-mentioned prophets, together with those called the seven wise men. Accordingly it is easy to perceive that Solomon, who lived in the time of Menelaus (who was during the Trojan war), was earlier by many years than the wise men among the Greeks. And how many years Moses preceded him we showed, in what we said above. And Alexander, surnamed Polyhistor, in his work on the Jews, has transcribed some letters of Solomon to Vaphres king of Egypt, and to the king of the Phenicians at Tyre, and theirs to Solomon; in which it is shown that Vaphres sent eighty thousand Egyptian men to him for the building of the temple, and the other as many, along with a Tyrian artificer, the son of a Jewish mother, of the tribe of Dan,[1] as is there written, of the name of Hyperon.[2] Further, Onomacritus the Athenian, who is said to have been the author of the poems ascribed to Orpheus, is ascertained to have lived in the reign of the Pisistratidæ, about the fiftieth Olympiad. And Orpheus, who sailed with Hercules, was the pupil of Musæus. Amphion precedes the Trojan war by two generations. And Demodocus and Phemius were posterior to the capture of Troy; for they were famed for playing on the lyre, the former among the Phæacians, and the latter among the suitors. And the *Oracles* ascribed to Musæus are said to be the production of Onomacritus, and the *Crateres* of Orpheus the production of Zopyrus of Heraclea, and *The Descent to Hades* that of Prodicus of Samos. Ion of Chios relates in the *Triagmi*,[3] that Pythagoras ascribed certain works [of his own] to Orpheus. Epigenes, in his book respecting *The Poetry attributed to Orpheus*, says that *The Descent to Hades* and the *Sacred Discourse* were the production of Cecrops the Pythagorean; and the *Peplus* and the *Physics* of Brontinus. Some also make Terpander out ancient. Hellanicus, accordingly, relates that he lived in the time of Midas: but Phanias, who places Lesches the Lesbian

---

[1] The text has David.

[2] Hiram or Huram was his name (1 Kings vii. 13, 40). Clement seems to have mistaken the words ὑπὲρ ὧν occurring in the epistle referred to for a proper name.

[3] Such, according to Harpocration, was the title of this work. In the text it is called Τριγράμμοι. Suidas calls it Τριασμαί.

before Terpander, makes Terpander younger than Archilochus, and relates that Lesches contended with Arctinus, and gained the victory. Xanthus the Lydian says that he lived about the eighteenth Olympiad; as also Dionysius says that Thasus was built about the fifteenth Olympiad: so that it is clear that Archilochus[1] was already known after the twentieth Olympiad. He accordingly relates the destruction of Magnetes as having recently taken place. Simonides is assigned to the time of Archilochus. Callinus is not much older; for Archilochus refers to Magnetes as destroyed, while the latter refers to it as flourishing. Eumelus of Corinth being older, is said to have met Archias, who founded Syracuse.

We were induced to mention these things, because the poets of the epic cycle are placed amongst those of most remote antiquity. Already, too, among the Greeks, many diviners are said to have made their appearance, as the Bacides, one a Bœotian, the other an Arcadian, who uttered many predictions to many. By the counsel of Amphiletus the Athenian,[2] who showed the time for the onset, Pisistratus, too, strengthened his government. For we may pass over in silence Cometes of Crete, Cinyras of Cyprus, Admetus the Thessalian, Aristæas the Cyrenian, Amphiaraus the Athenian, Timoxeus[3] the Corcyræan, Demænetus the Phocian, Epigenes the Thespian, Nicias the Carystian, Aristo the Thessalian, Dionysius the Carthaginian, Cleophon the Corinthian, Hippo the daughter of Chiro, and Bœo, and Manto, and the host of Sibyls, the Samian, the Colophonian, the Cumæan, the Erythræan, the Pythian,[4] the Taraxandrian, the Macetian, the Thessalian, and the Thesprotian. And Calchas again, and Mopsus, who lived during the Trojan war. Mopsus, however, was older, having sailed

---

[1] The passage seems incomplete. The bearing of the date of the building of Thasos on the determination of the age of Archilochus, may be, that it was built by Telesiclus his son.

[2] Called so because he sojourned at Athens. His birthplace was Acarnania.

[3] Another reading is Τιμόθεος; Sylburgius conjectures Τιμόξενος.

[4] The text has Φυτώ, which Sylburgius conjectures has been changed from Πυθώ.

along with the Argonauts. And it is said that Battus the Cyrenian composed what is called *the Divination* of Mopsus. Dorotheus in the first *Pandect* relates that Mopsus was the disciple of Alcyon and Corone. And Pythagoras the Great always applied his mind to prognostication, and Abaris the Hyperborean, and Aristæas the Proconnesian, and Epimenides the Cretan, who came to Sparta, and Zoroaster the Mede, and Empedocles of Agrigentum, and Phormion the Lacedæmonian; Polyaratus, too, of Thasus, and Empedotimus of Syracuse; and in addition to these, Socrates the Athenian in particular. "For," he says in the *Theages*, "I am attended by a supernatural intimation, which has been assigned me from a child by divine appointment. This is a voice which, when it comes, prevents what I am about to do, but exhorts never."[1] And Execestus, the tyrant of the Phocians, wore two enchanted rings, and by the sound which they uttered one against the other determined the proper times for actions. But he died, nevertheless, treacherously murdered, although warned beforehand by the sound, as Aristotle says in the *Polity of the Phocians*.

Of those, too, who at one time lived as men among the Egyptians, but were constituted gods by human opinion, were Hermes the Theban, and Asclepius of Memphis; Tireseus and Manto, again, at Thebes, as Euripides says. Helenus, too, and Laocoon, and Œnone, and Crenus in Ilium. For Crenus, one of the Heraclidæ, is said to have been a noted prophet. Another was Jamus in Elis, from whom came the Jamidæ; and Polyidus at Argos and Megara, who is mentioned by the tragedy. Why enumerate Telemus, who, being a prophet of the Cyclops, predicted to Polyphemus the events of Ulysses' wandering; or Onomacritus at Athens; or Amphiaraus, who campaigned with the seven at Thebes, and is reported to be a generation older than the capture of Troy; or Theoclymenus in Cephalonia, or Telmisus in Caria, or Galeus in Sicily?

There are others, too, besides these: Idmon, who was with the Argonauts, Phemonoe of Delphi, Mopsus the son of

[1] Plato's *Theages*, p. 93.

Apollo and Manto in Pamphylia, and Amphilochus the son of Amphiaraus in Cilicia, Alcmæon among the Acarnanians, Anias in Delos, Aristander of Telmessus, who was along with Alexander. Philochorus also relates in the first book of the work, *On Divination*, that Orpheus was a seer. And Theopompus, and Ephorus, and Timæus, write of a seer called Orthagoras; as the Samian Pythocles in the fourth book of *The Italics* writes of Caius Julius Nepos.

But some of these "thieves and robbers," as the Scripture says, predicted for the most part from observation and probabilities, as physicians and soothsayers judge from natural signs; and others were excited by demons, or were disturbed by waters, and fumigations, and air of a peculiar kind. But among the Hebrews the prophets were moved by the power and inspiration of God. Before the law, Adam spoke prophetically in respect to the woman, and the naming of the creatures; Noah preached repentance; Abraham, Isaac, and Jacob gave many clear utterances respecting future and present things. Contemporaneous with the law, Moses and Aaron; and after these prophesied Jesus the son of Nave, Samuel, Gad, Nathan, Achias, Samæas, Jehu, Elias, Michæas, Abdiu, Elisæus, Abbadonai, Amos, Esaias, Osee, Jonas, Joel, Jeremias, Sophonias the son of Buzi, Ezekiel, Urias, Ambacum, Naum, Daniel, Misael, who wrote the syllogisms, Aggai, Zacharias, and the angel among the twelve. These are, in all, five-and-thirty prophets. And of women (for these too prophesied), Sara, and Rebecca, and Mariam, and Debbora, and Olda.

Then within the same period John prophesied till the baptism of salvation; and after the birth of Christ, Anna and Simeon. For Zacharias, John's father, is said in the Gospels to have prophesied before his son. Let us then draw up the chronology of the Greeks from Moses.

From the birth of Moses to the exodus of the Jews from Egypt, eighty years; and the period down to his death, other forty years. The exodus took place in the time of Inachus, before the wandering of Sothis,[1] Moses having gone forth from

[1] *i.e.* of Io, the daughter of Inachus.

Egypt three hundred and forty-five years before. From the rule of Moses, and from Inachus to the flood of Deucalion, I mean the second inundation, and to the conflagration of Phaethon, which events happened in the time of Crotopus, forty generations are enumerated (three generations being reckoned for a century). From the flood to the conflagration of Ida, and the discovery of iron, and the Idæan Dactyls, are seventy-three years, according to Thrasyllus; and from the conflagration of Ida to the rape of Ganymede, sixty-five years. From this to the expedition of Perseus, when Glaucus established the Isthmian games in honour of Melicerta, fifteen years; and from the expedition of Perseus to the building of Troy, thirty-four years. From this to the voyage of the Argo, sixty-four years. From this to Theseus and the Minotaur, thirty-two years; then to the seven at Thebes, ten years. And to the Olympic contest, which Hercules instituted in honour of Pelops, three years; and to the expedition of the Amazons against Athens, and the rape of Helen by Theseus, nine years. From this to the deification of Hercules, eleven years; then to the rape of Helen by Alexander, four years. From the taking of Troy to the descent of Æneas and the founding of Lavinium, ten years; and to the government of Ascanius, eight years; and to the descent of the Heraclidæ, sixty-one years; and to the Olympiad of Iphitus, three hundred and thirty-eight years. Eratosthenes thus sets down the dates: " From the capture of Troy to the descent of the Heraclidæ, eighty years. From this to the founding of Ionia, sixty years; and the period following to the protectorate of Lycurgus, a hundred and fifty-nine years; and to the first year of the first Olympiad, a hundred and eight years. From which Olympiad to the invasion of Xerxes, two hundred and ninety-seven years; from which to the beginning of the Peloponnesian war, forty-eight years; and to its close, and the defeat of the Athenians,-twenty-seven years; and to the battle at Leuctra, thirty-four years; after which to the death of Philip, thirty-five years. And after this to the decease of Alexander, twelve years."

Again, from the first Olympiad, some say, to the building of Rome, are comprehended twenty-four years; and after this to the expulsion of the kings,[1] when consuls were created, about two hundred and forty-three years. And from the taking of Babylon to the death of Alexander, a hundred and eighty-six years. From this to the victory of Augustus, when Antony killed himself at Alexandria, two hundred and ninety-four years, when Augustus was made consul for the fourth time. And from this time to the games which Domitian instituted at Rome, are a hundred and fourteen years; and from the first games to the death of Commodus, a hundred and eleven years.

There are some that from Cecrops to Alexander of Macedon reckon a thousand eight hundred and twenty-eight years; and from Demophon, a thousand two hundred and fifty; and from the taking of Troy to the expedition of the Heraclidæ, a hundred and twenty or a hundred and eighty years. From this to the archonship of Evænetus at Athens, in whose time Alexander is said to have marched into Asia, according to Phanias, are seven hundred and fifty years; according to Ephorus, seven hundred and thirty-five; according to Timæus and Clitarchus, eight hundred and twenty; according to Eratosthenes, seven hundred and seventy-four. As also Duris, from the taking of Troy to the march of Alexander into Asia, a thousand years; and from that to the archonship of Hegesias, in whose time Alexander died, eleven years. From this date to the reign of Germanicus Claudius Cæsar, three hundred and sixty-five years. From which time the years summed up to the death of Commodus are manifest.

After the Grecian period, and in accordance with the dates, as computed by the barbarians, very large intervals are to be assigned.

From Adam to the deluge are comprised two thousand one hundred and forty-eight years, four days. From Shem to

[1] For Βαβυλῶνος, βασιλίων has been substituted. In an old chronologist, as quoted by Clement elsewhere, the latter occurs; and the date of the expulsion of the kings harmonizes with the number of years here given, which that of the destruction of Babylon does not.

Abraham, a thousand two hundred and fifty years. From Isaac to the division of the land, six hundred and sixteen years. Then from the judges to Samuel, four hundred and sixty-three years, seven months. And after the judges there were five hundred and seventy-two years, six months, ten days of kings.

After which periods, there were two hundred and thirty-five years of the Persian monarchy. Then of the Macedonian, till the death of Antony, three hundred and twelve years and eighteen days. After which time, the empire of the Romans, till the death of Commodus, lasted for two hundred and twenty-two years.

Then, from the seventy years' captivity, and the restoration of the people into their own land to the captivity in the time of Vespasian, are comprised four hundred and ten years. Finally, from Vespasian to the death of Commodus, there are ascertained to be one hundred and twenty-one years, six months, and twenty-four days.

Demetrius, in his book, *On the Kings in Judæa*, says that the tribes of Juda, Benjamin, and Levi were not taken captive by Sennacherim; but that there were from this captivity to the last, which Nabuchodonosor made out of Jerusalem, a hundred and twenty-eight years and six months; and from the time that the ten tribes were carried captive from Samaria till Ptolemy the Fourth, were five hundred and seventy-three years, nine months; and from the time that the captivity from Jerusalem took place, three hundred and thirty-eight years and three months.

Philo himself set down the kings differently from Demetrius.

Besides, Eupolemus, in a similar work, says that all the years from Adam to the fifth year of Ptolemy Demetrius, who reigned twelve years in Egypt, when added, amount to five thousand a hundred and forty-nine; and from the time that Moses brought out the Jews from Egypt to the above-mentioned date, there are, in all, two thousand five hundred and eighty years. And from this time till the consulship in Rome of Caius Domitian and Casian, a hundred and twenty years are computed.

Euphorus and many other historians say that there are seventy-five nations and tongues, in consequence of hearing the statement made by Moses: "All the souls that sprang from Jacob, which went down into Egypt, were seventy-five."[1] According to the true reckoning, there appear to be seventy-two generic dialects, as our Scriptures hand down. The rest of the vulgar tongues are formed by the blending of two, or three, or more dialects. A dialect is a mode of speech which exhibits a character peculiar to a locality, or a mode of speech which exhibits a character peculiar or common to a race. The Greeks say, that among them are five dialects —the Attic, Ionic, Doric, Æolic, and the fifth the Common; and that the languages of the barbarians, which are innumerable, are not called dialects, but tongues.

Plato attributes a dialect also to the gods, forming this conjecture mainly from dreams and oracles, and especially from demoniacs, who do not speak their own language or dialect, but that of the demons who have taken possession of them. He thinks also that the irrational creatures have dialects, which those that belong to the same genus understand. Accordingly, when an elephant falls into the mud and bellows out, any other one that is at hand, on seeing what has happened, shortly turns, and brings with him a herd of elephants, and saves the one that has fallen in. It is said also in Libya, that a scorpion, if it does not succeed in stinging a man, goes away and returns with several more; and that, hanging on one to the other like a chain, they make in this way the attempt to succeed in their cunning design.

The irrational creatures do not make use of an obscure intimation, or hint their meaning by assuming a particular attitude, but, as I think, by a dialect of their own. And some others say, that if a fish which has been taken escape by breaking the line, no fish of the same kind will be caught in the same place that day. But the first and generic barbarous dialects have terms by nature, since also men confess that prayers uttered in a barbarian tongue are more powerful. And Plato, in the *Cratylus*, when wishing to interpret πῦρ

[1] Gen. xlvi. 27.

(*fire*), says that it is a barbaric term. He testifies, accordingly, that the Phrygians use this term with a slight deviation.

And nothing, in my opinion, after these details, need stand in the way of stating the periods of the Roman emperors, in order to the demonstration of the Saviour's birth. Augustus, forty-three years; Tiberius, twenty-two years; Caius, four years; Claudius, fourteen years; Nero, fourteen years; Galba, one year; Vespasian, ten years; Titus, three years; Domitian, fifteen years; Nerva, one year; Trajan, nineteen years; Adrian, twenty-one years; Antoninus, twenty-one years; likewise again, Antoninus and Commodus, thirty-two. In all, from Augustus to Commodus, are two hundred and twenty-two years; and from Adam to the death of Commodus, five thousand seven hundred and eighty-four years, two months, twelve days.

Some set down the dates of the Roman emperors thus:

Caius Julius Cæsar, three years, four months, five days; after him Augustus reigned forty-six years, four months, one day. Then Tiberius, twenty-six years, six months, nineteen days. He was succeeded by Caius Cæsar, who reigned three years, ten months, eight days; and he by Claudius for thirteen years, eight months, twenty-eight days. Nero reigned thirteen years, eight months, twenty-eight days; Galba, seven months and six days; Otho, five months, one day; Vitellius, seven months, one day; Vespasian, eleven years, eleven months, twenty-two days; Titus, two years, two months; Domitian, fifteen years, eight months, five days; Nerva, one year, four months, ten days; Trajan, nineteen years, seven months, ten days; Adrian, twenty years, ten months, twenty-eight days; Antoninus, twenty-two years, three months, and seven days; Marcus Aurelius Antoninus, nineteen years, eleven days; Commodus, twelve years, nine months, fourteen days.

From Julius Cæsar, therefore, to the death of Commodus, are two hundred and thirty-six years, six months. And the whole from Romulus, who founded Rome, till the death of Commodus, amounts to nine hundred and fifty-three years, six months. And our Lord was born in the twenty-eighth year, when first the census was ordered to be taken in the reign of Augustus. And to prove that this is true, it is written in the Gospel by Luke as follows: "And in the fifteenth year, in the reign of Tiberius Cæsar, the word of the Lord came to John, the son of Zacharias." And again in the same book: "And Jesus was coming to His baptism, being about thirty years old,"[1] and so on. And that it was necessary for Him to preach only a year, this also is written: "He hath sent me to proclaim the acceptable year of the Lord."[2] This both the prophet spake, and the gospel. Accordingly, in fifteen years of Tiberius and fifteen years of Augustus; so were completed the thirty years till the time He suffered. And from the time that He suffered till the destruction of Jerusalem are forty-two years and three months; and from the destruction of Jerusalem to the death of Commodus, a hundred and twenty-eight years, ten months, and three days. From the birth of Christ, therefore, to the death of Commodus are, in all, a hundred and ninety-four years, one month, thirteen days. And there are those who have determined not only the year of our Lord's birth, but also the day; and they say that it took place in the twenty-eighth year of Augustus, and in the twenty-fifth day of Pachon. And the followers of Basilides hold the day of his baptism as a festival, spending the night before in readings.

And they say that it was the fifteenth year of Tiberius Cæsar, the fifteenth day of the month Tubi; and some that it was the eleventh of the same month. And treating of His passion, with very great accuracy, some say that it took place in the sixteenth year of Tiberius, on the twenty-fifth of Phamenoth; and others the twenty-fifth of Pharmuthi; and others say that on the nineteenth of Pharmuthi the Saviour suffered. Further, others say that He was born on the twenty-fourth or twenty-fifth of Pharmuthi.

We have still to add to our chronology the following,—I mean the days which Daniel indicates from the desolation of Jerusalem, the seven years and seven months of the reign of Vespasian. For the two years are added to the seventeen months and eighteen days of Otho, and Galba, and Vitellius;

[1] Luke iii. 1, 2, 23.   [2] Isa. lxi. 1, 2.

and the result is three years and six months, which is "the half of the week," as Daniel the prophet said. For he said that there were two thousand three hundred days from the time that the abomination of Nero stood in the holy city, till its destruction. For thus the declaration, which is subjoined, shows: "How long shall be the vision, the sacrifice taken away, the abomination of desolation, which is given, and the power and the holy place shall be trodden under foot? And he said to him, Till the evening and morning, two thousand three hundred days, and the holy place shall be taken away."[1]

These two thousand three hundred days, then, make six years four months, during the half of which Nero held sway, and it was half a week; and for a half, Vespasian with Otho, Galba, and Vitellius reigned. And on this account Daniel says, "Blessed is he that cometh to the thousand three hundred and thirty-five days."[2] For up to these days was war, and after them it ceased. And this number is demonstrated from a subsequent chapter, which is as follows: "And from the time of the change of continuation, and of the giving of the abomination of desolation, there shall be a thousand two hundred and ninety days. Blessed is he that waiteth, and cometh to the thousand three hundred and thirty-five days."[3]

Flavius Josephus the Jew, who composed the history of the Jews, computing the periods, says that from Moses to David were five hundred and eighty-five years; from David to the second year of Vespasian, a thousand one hundred and seventy-nine; then from that to the tenth year of Antoninus, seventy-seven. So that from Moses to the tenth year of Antoninus there are, in all, two thousand one hundred and thirty-three years.

Of others, counting from Inachus and Moses to the death of Commodus, some say there were three thousand one hundred and forty-two years; and others, two thousand eight hundred and thirty-one years.

And in the Gospel according to Matthew, the genealogy which begins with Abraham is continued down to Mary the

[1] Dan. viii. 13, 14.   [2] Dan. xii. 12.   [3] Dan. xii. 11, 12.

mother of the Lord. "For," it is said,[1] "from Abraham to David are fourteen generations; and from David to the carrying away into Babylon are fourteen generations; and from the carrying away into Babylon till Christ are likewise other fourteen generations,"—three mystic intervals completed in six weeks.

[1] Matt. i. 17.

CHAPTER XXII.

ON THE GREEK TRANSLATION OF THE OLD TESTAMENT.

S( ) much for the details respecting dates, as stated variously by many, and as set down by us.

It is said that the Scriptures both of the law and of the prophets were translated from the dialect of the Hebrews into the Greek language in the reign of Ptolemy the son of Lagos, or, according to others, of Ptolemy surnamed Philadelphus; Demetrius Phalereus bringing to this task the greatest earnestness, and employing painstaking accuracy on the materials for the translation. For the Macedonians being still in possession of Asia, and the king being ambitious of adorning the library he had at Alexandria with all writings, desired the people of Jerusalem to translate the prophecies they possessed into the Greek dialect. And they being the subjects of the Macedonians, selected from those of highest character among them seventy elders, versed in the Scriptures, and skilled in the Greek dialect, and sent them to him with the divine books. And each having severally translated each prophetic book, and all the translations being compared together, they agreed both in meaning and expression. For it was the counsel of God carried out for the benefit of Grecian ears. It was not alien to the inspiration of God, who gave the prophecy, also to produce the translation, and make it as it were Greek prophecy. Since the Scriptures having perished in the captivity of Nabuchodonosor, Esdras the Levite, the priest, in the time of Artaxerxes king of the Persians, having become inspired, in the exercise of prophecy restored again the whole of the ancient Scriptures. And Aristobulus, in his first book addressed to Philometor, writes in these words: "And Plato followed the laws given to us, and had manifestly studied all that is said in them." And before Demetrius there had been translated by another, previous to the dominion of Alexander and of the Persians, the account of the departure of our countrymen the Hebrews from Egypt, and the fame of all that happened to them, and their taking possession of the land, and the account of the whole code of laws; so that it is perfectly clear that the above-mentioned philosopher derived a great deal from this source, for he was very learned, as also Pythagoras, who transferred many things from our books to his own system of doctrines. And Numenius, the Pythagorean philosopher, expressly writes: "For what is Plato, but Moses speaking in Attic Greek?" This Moses was a theologian and prophet, and as some say, an interpreter of sacred laws. His family, his deeds, and life, are related by the Scriptures themselves, which are worthy of all credit; but have nevertheless to be stated by us also as well as we can.

CHAPTER XXIII.

THE AGE, BIRTH, AND LIFE OF MOSES.

MOSES, originally of a Chaldean[1] family, was born in Egypt, his ancestors having migrated from Babylon into Egypt on account of a protracted famine. Born in the seventh generation,[2] and having received a royal education, the following are the circumstances of his history. The Hebrews having increased in Egypt to a great multitude, and the king of the country being afraid of insurrection in consequence of their numbers, he ordered all the female children born to the Hebrews to be reared (woman being unfit for war), but the male to be destroyed, being suspicious of stalwart youth. But the child being goodly, his parents nursed him secretly three months, natural affection being too strong for the monarch's cruelty. But at last, dreading lest they should be destroyed along with the child, they made a basket of the papyrus that grew there, put the child in it, and laid it on the banks of the marshy river. The child's sister stood at a distance, and watched what would happen. In this emergency, the king's daughter, who for a long time had not been pregnant, and who longed for a child, came that day to the river to bathe and wash herself; and hearing the child cry, she ordered it to be brought to her; and touched with pity, sought a nurse. At that moment the child's sister ran up, and said that, if she wished, she could procure for her as nurse one of the Hebrew

---

[1] This is the account given by Philo, of whose book on the life of Moses this chapter is an epitome, for the most part in Philo's words.

[2] "He was the seventh in descent from the first, who, being a foreigner, was the founder of the whole Jewish race."—PHILO.

women who had recently had a child. And on her consenting and desiring her to do so, she brought the child's mother to be nurse for a stipulated fee, as if she had been some other person. Thereupon the queen gave the babe the name of Moses, with etymological propriety, from his being drawn out of "the water,"—for the Egyptians call water "mou,"—in which he had been exposed to die. For they call Moses one who "who breathed [on being taken] from the water." It is clear that previously the parents gave a name to the child on his circumcision; and he was called Joachim. And he had a third name in heaven, after his ascension, as the mystics say—Melchi. Having reached the proper age, he was taught arithmetic, geometry, poetry, harmony, and besides, medicine and music, by those that excelled in these arts among the Egyptians; and besides, the philosophy which is conveyed by symbols, which they point out in the hieroglyphical inscriptions. The rest of the usual course of instruction, Greeks taught him in Egypt as a royal child, as Philo says in his life of Moses. He learned, besides, the literature of the Egyptians, and the knowledge of the heavenly bodies from the Chaldeans and the Egyptians; whence in the Acts[1] he is said "to have been instructed in all the wisdom of the Egyptians." And Eupolemus, in his book *On the Kings in Judea*, says that "Moses was the first wise man, and the first that imparted grammar to the Jews, that the Phenicians received it from the Jews, and the Greeks from the Phenicians." And betaking himself to their philosophy, he increased his wisdom, being ardently attached to the training received from his kindred and ancestors, till he struck and slew the Egyptian who wrongfully attacked the Hebrew. And the mystics say that he slew the Egyptian by a word only; as, certainly, Peter in the Acts is related to have slain by speech those who appropriated part of the price of the field, and lied.[3] And so Artapanus, in his work *On the Jews*, relates "that Moses, being shut up in custody by

---

[1] Acts vii. 22.
[2] Adopting the reading φιλοσοφίαν δίξας instead of φύσιν δίξας.
[3] Acts v. 1.

Nechephres,[1] king of the Egyptians, on account of the people demanding to be let go from Egypt, the prison being opened by night, by the interposition of God, went forth, and reaching the palace, stood before the king as he slept, and aroused him; and that the latter, struck with what had taken place, bade Moses tell him the name of the God who had sent him; and that he, bending forward, told him in his ear; and that the king on hearing it fell speechless, but being supported by Moses, revived again." And respecting the education of Moses, we shall find a harmonious account in Ezekiel, the composer of Jewish tragedies in the drama entitled *The Exodus*. He thus writes in the person of Moses:

> " For, seeing our race abundantly increase,
> His treacherous snares King Pharaoh 'gainst us laid,
> And cruelly in brick-kilns some of us,
> And some, in toilsome works of building, plagued.
> And towns and towers by toil of ill-starred men
> He raised. Then to the Hebrew race proclaimed,
> That each male child should in deep-flowing Nile
> Be drowned. My mother bore and hid me then
> Three months (so afterwards she told). Then took,
> And me adorned with fair array, and placed
> On the deep sedgy marsh by Nilus bank,
> While Miriam, my sister, watched afar.
> Then, with her maids, the daughter of the king,
> To bathe her beauty in the cleansing stream,
> Came near, straight saw, and took and raised me up;
> And knew me for a Hebrew. Miriam
> My sister to the princess ran, and said,
> ' Is it thy pleasure, that I haste and find
> A nurse for thee to rear this child
> Among the Hebrew women?' The princess
> Gave assent. The maiden to her mother sped,
> And told, who quick appeared. My own
> Dear mother took me in her arms. Then said
> The daughter of the king: ' Nurse me this child,
> And I will give thee wages.' And my name
> Moses she called, because she drew and saved
> Me from the waters on the river's bank.
> And when the days of childhood had flown by,

---

[1] Or Chenephres.

> My mother brought me to the palace where
> The princess dwelt, after disclosing all
> About my ancestry, and God's great gifts.
> In boyhood's years I royal nurture had,
> And in all princely exercise was trained,
> As if the princess' very son. But when
> The circling days had run their course,
> I left the royal palace."

Then, after relating the combat between the Hebrew and the Egyptian, and the burying of the Egyptian in the sand, he says of the other contest :

> " Why strike one feebler than thyself?
> And he rejoined : Who made thee judge o'er us,
> Or ruler? Wilt thou slay me, as thou didst
> Him yesterday? And I in terror said,
> How is this known?"

Then he fled from Egypt and fed sheep, being thus trained beforehand for pastoral rule. For the shepherd's life is a preparation for sovereignty in the case of him who is destined to rule over the peaceful flock of men, as the chase, for those who are by nature warlike. Thence God brought him to lead the Hebrews. Then the Egyptians, oft admonished, continued unwise; and the Hebrews were spectators of the calamities that others suffered, learning in safety the power of God. And when the Egyptians gave no heed to the effects of that power, through their foolish infatuation disbelieving, then, as is said, " the children knew" what was done; and the Hebrews afterwards going forth, departed carrying much spoil from the Egyptians, not for avarice, as the cavillers say, for God did not persuade them to covet what belonged to others. But, in the first place, they took wages for the services they had rendered the Egyptians all the time; and then in a way recompensed the Egyptians, by afflicting them in requital as avaricious, by the abstraction of the booty, as they had done the Hebrews by enslaving them. Whether, then, as may be alleged is done in war, they thought it proper, in the exercise of the rights of conquerors, to take away the property of their enemies, as those who have gained the day do from those who are worsted (and there was just cause of hostilities. The Hebrews came as suppliants to the Egyptians on account of famine; and they, reducing their guests to slavery, compelled them to serve them after the manner of captives, giving them no recompense); or as in peace, took the spoil as wages against the will of those who for a long period had given them no recompense, but rather had robbed them, [it is all one.]

CHAPTER XXIV.

HOW MOSES DISCHARGED THE PART OF A MILITARY LEADER.

OUR Moses then is a prophet, a legislator, skilled in military tactics and strategy, a politician, a philosopher. And in what sense he was a prophet, shall be by and by told, when we come to treat of prophecy. Tactics belong to military command, and the ability to command an army is among the attributes of kingly rule. Legislation, again, is also one of the functions of the kingly office, as also judicial authority.

Of the kingly office one kind is divine,—that which is according to God and His holy Son, by whom both the good things which are of the earth, and external and perfect felicity too, are supplied. "For," it is said, "seek what is great, and the little things shall be added."[1] And there is a second kind of royalty, inferior to that administration which is purely rational and divine, which brings to the task of government merely the high mettle of the soul; after which fashion Hercules ruled the Argives, and Alexander the Macedonians. The third kind is what aims after one thing—merely to conquer and overturn; but to turn conquest either to a good or a bad purpose, belongs not to such rule. Such was the aim of the Persians in their campaign against Greece. For, on the one hand, fondness for strife is solely the result of passion, and acquires power solely for the sake of domination; while, on the other, the love of good is characteristic of a soul which uses its high spirit for noble ends. The fourth, the worst of all, is the sovereignty which acts according to the promptings of the passions, as that of Sardanapalus, and those who pro-

[1] Not in Scripture. The reference may be to Matt. vi. 33.

pose to themselves as their end the gratification of the passions to the utmost. But the instrument of regal sway—the instrument at once of that which overcomes by virtue, and that which does so by force—is the power of managing (or tact). And it varies according to the nature and the material. In the case of arms and of fighting animals the ordering power is the soul and mind, by means animate and inanimate; and in the case of the passions of the soul, which we master by virtue, reason is the ordering power, by affixing the seal of continence and self-restraint, along with holiness, and sound knowledge with truth, making the result of the whole to terminate in piety towards God. For it is wisdom which regulates in the case of those who so practise virtue; and divine things are ordered by wisdom, and human affairs by politics—all things by the kingly faculty. He is a king, then, who governs according to the laws, and possesses the skill to sway willing subjects. Such is the Lord, who receives all who believe on Him and by Him. For the Father has delivered and subjected all to Christ our King, "that at the name of Jesus every knee may bow, of things in heaven, and things in earth, and things under the earth, and every tongue confess that Jesus Christ is Lord, to the glory of God the Father."[1]

Now, generalship involves three ideas: caution, enterprise, and the union of the two. And each of these consists of three things, acting as they do either by word, or by deeds, or by both together. And all this can be accomplished either by persuasion, or by compulsion, or by inflicting harm in the way of taking vengeance on those who ought to be punished; and this either by doing what is right, or by telling what is untrue, or by telling what is true, or by adopting any of these means conjointly at the same time.

Now, the Greeks had the advantage of receiving from Moses all these, and the knowledge of how to make use of each of them. And, for the sake of example, I shall cite one or two instances of leadership. Moses, on leading the people forth, suspecting that the Egyptians would pursue, left the

[1] Phil. ii. 10, 11.

short and direct route, and turned to the desert, and marched mostly by night. For it was another kind of arrangement by which the Hebrews were trained in the great wilderness, and for a protracted time, to belief in the existence of one God alone, being inured by the wise discipline of endurance to which they were subjected. The strategy of Moses, therefore, shows the necessity of discerning what will be of service before the approach of dangers, and so to encounter them. It turned out precisely as he suspected, for the Egyptians pursued with horses and chariots, but were quickly destroyed by the sea breaking on them and overwhelming them with their horses and chariots, so that not a remnant of them was left. Afterwards the pillar of fire, which accompanied them (for it went before them as a guide), conducted the Hebrews by night through an untrodden region, training and bracing them, by toils and hardships, to manliness and endurance, that after their experience of what appeared formidable difficulties, the benefits of the land, to which from the trackless desert he was conducting them, might become apparent. Furthermore, he put to flight and slew the hostile occupants of the land, falling upon them from a desert and rugged line of march (such was the excellence of his generalship). For the taking of the land of those hostile tribes was a work of skill and strategy.

Perceiving this, Miltiades, the Athenian general, who conquered the Persians in battle at Marathon, imitated it in the following fashion. Marching over a trackless desert, he led on the Athenians by night, and eluded the barbarians that were set to watch him. For Hippias, who had deserted from the Athenians, conducted the barbarians into Attica, and seized and held the points of vantage, in consequence of having a knowledge of the ground. The task was then to elude Hippias. Whence rightly Miltiades, traversing the desert and attacking by night the Persians commanded by Dates, led his soldiers to victory.

But further, when Thrasybulus was bringing back the exiles from Phyla, and wished to elude observation, a pillar became his guide as he marched over a trackless region. To

Thrasybulus by night, the sky being moonless and stormy, a fire appeared leading the way, which, having conducted them safely, left them near Munychia, where is now the altar of the light-bringer (Phosphorus).

From such an instance, therefore, let our accounts become credible to the Greeks, namely, that it was possible for the omnipotent God to make the pillar of fire, which was their guide on their march, go before the Hebrews by night. It is said also in a certain oracle,

"A pillar to the Thebans is joy-inspiring Bacchus,"

from the history of the Hebrews. Also Euripides says, in *Antiope*,

"In the chambers within, the herdsman,
With chaplet of ivy, pillar of the Evœan god."

The pillar indicates that God cannot be portrayed. The pillar of light, too, in addition to its pointing out that God cannot be represented, shows also the stability and the permanent duration of the Deity, and His unchangeable and inexpressible light. Before, then, the invention of the forms of images, the ancients erected pillars, and reverenced them as statues of the Deity. Accordingly, he who composed the *Phoronis* writes,

"Callithoe, key-bearer of the Olympian queen:
Argive Hera, who first with fillets and with fringes
The queen's tall column all around adorned."

Further, the author of *Europia* relates that the statue of Apollo at Delphi was a pillar in these words:

"That to the god first-fruits and tithes we may
On sacred pillars and on lofty column hang."

Apollo, interpreted mystically by "privation of many,"[1] means the one God. Well, then, that fire like a pillar, and the fire in the desert, is the symbol of the holy light which passed through from earth and returned again to heaven, by the wood [of the cross], by which also the gift of intellectual vision was bestowed on us.

[1] ἀ privative, and πολλοί, many.

CHAPTER XXV.

PLATO AN IMITATOR OF MOSES IN FRAMING LAWS.

PLATO the philosopher, aided in legislation by the books of Moses, censured the polity of Minos, and that of Lycurgus, as having bravery alone as their aim; while he praised as more seemly the polity which expresses some one thing, and directs according to one precept. For he says that it becomes us to philosophize with strength, and dignity, and wisdom,—holding unalterably the same opinions about the same things, with reference to the dignity of heaven. Accordingly, therefore, he interprets what is in the law, enjoining us to look to one God and to do justly. Of politics, he says there are two kinds,—the department of law, and that of politics, strictly so called.

And he refers to the Creator, as the Statesman (ὁ πολιτικός) by way of eminence, in his book of this name (ὁ πολιτικός); and those who lead an active and just life, combined with contemplation, he calls statesmen (πολιτικοί). That department of politics which is called "Law," he divides into administrative magnanimity and private good order, which he calls orderliness, and harmony, and sobriety, which are seen when rulers suit their subjects, and subjects are obedient to their rulers; a result which the system of Moses sedulously aims at effecting. Further, that the department of law is founded on generation, that of politics on friendship and consent, Plato, with the aid he received, affirms; and so, coupled with the laws the philosopher in the *Epinomis*, who knew the course of all generation, which takes place by the instrumentality of the planets; and the other philosopher, *Timæus*, who was an astronomer and student of the motions of the stars, and of their sympathy and association with one another, he consequently joined to the "polity" (or "republic"). Then, in my opinion, the end both of the statesman, and of him who lives according to the law, is contemplation. It is necessary, therefore, that public affairs should be rightly managed. But to philosophize is best. For he who is wise will live concentrating all his energies on knowledge, directing his life by good deeds, despising the opposite, and following the pursuits which contribute to truth. And the law is not what is decided by law (for what is seen is not vision), nor every opinion (not certainly what is evil). But law is the opinion which is good, and what is good is that which is true, and what is true is that which finds "true being," and attains to it. "He who is,"[1] says Moses, "sent me." In accordance with which, namely, good opinion, some have called law, right reason, which enjoins what is to be done and forbids what is not to be done.

[1] "I am," A.V.; Ex. iii. 13.

CHAPTER XXVI.

MOSES RIGHTLY CALLED A DIVINE LEGISLATOR, AND, THOUGH INFERIOR TO CHRIST, FAR SUPERIOR TO THE GREAT LEGISLATORS OF THE GREEKS, MINOS AND LYCURGUS.

WHENCE the law was rightly said to have been given by Moses, being a rule of right and wrong; and we may call it with accuracy the divine ordinance ($\theta\epsilon\sigma\mu o\varsigma$[1]), inasmuch as it was given by God through Moses. It accordingly conducts to the divine. Paul says: "The law was instituted because of transgressions, till the seed should come, to whom the promise was made." Then, as if in explanation of his meaning, he adds: "But before faith came, we were kept under the law, shut up," manifestly through fear, in consequence of sins, "unto the faith which should afterwards be revealed; so that the law was a schoolmaster to bring us to Christ, that we should be justified by faith."[2] The true legislator is he who assigns to each department of the soul what is suitable to it and to its operations. Now Moses, to speak comprehensively, was a living law, governed by the benign Word. Accordingly, he furnished a good polity, which is the right discipline of men in social life. He also handled the administration of justice, which is that branch of knowledge which deals with the correction of transgressors in the interests of justice. Co-ordinate with it is the faculty of dealing with punishments, which is a knowledge of the due measure to be observed in punishments. And punishment, in virtue of its being so, is the correction of the soul. In a word, the whole system of Moses is suited for the training of such as are

[1] From the ancient derivation of this word from $\theta\iota o\varsigma$.
[2] Gal. iii. 19, 23, 24.

capable of becoming good and noble men, and for hunting out men like them; and this is the art of command. And that wisdom, which is capable of treating rightly those who have been caught by the Word, is legislative wisdom. For it is the property of this wisdom, being most kingly, to possess and use.

It is the wise man, therefore, alone whom the philosophers proclaim king, legislator, general, just, holy, God-beloved. And if we discover these qualities in Moses, as shown from the Scriptures themselves, we may, with the most assured persuasion, pronounce Moses to be truly wise. As then we say that it belongs to the shepherd's art to care for the sheep; for so "the good shepherd giveth his life for the sheep;"[1] so also we shall say that legislation, inasmuch as it presides over and cares for the flock of men, establishes the virtue of men, by fanning into flame, as far as it can, what good there is in humanity.

And if the flock figuratively spoken of as belonging to the Lord is nothing but a flock of men, then He Himself is the good Shepherd and Lawgiver of the one flock, "of the sheep who hear Him," the one who cares for them, "seeking," and finding by the law and the word, "that which was lost;" since, in truth, the law is spiritual and leads to felicity. For that which has arisen through the Holy Spirit is spiritual. And he is truly a legislator, who not only announces what is good and noble, but understands it. The law of this man who possesses knowledge is the saving precept; or rather, the law is the precept of knowledge. For the Word is "the power and the wisdom of God."[2] Again, the expounder of the laws is the same one by whom the law was given; the first expounder of the divine commands, who unveiled the bosom of the Father, the only-begotten Son.

Then those who obey the law, since they have some knowledge of Him, cannot disbelieve or be ignorant of the truth. But those who disbelieve, and have shown a repugnance to engage in the works of the law, whoever else may, certainly confess their ignorance of the truth.

[1] John x. 11.   [2] 1 Cor. i. 24.

What, then, is the unbelief of the Greeks? Is it not their unwillingness to believe the truth which declares that the law was divinely given by Moses, whilst they honour Moses in their own writers? They relate that Minos received the laws from Zeus in nine years, by frequenting the cave of Zeus; and Plato, and Aristotle, and Ephorus write that Lycurgus was trained in legislation by going constantly to Apollo at Delphi. Chamæleo of Heraclea, in his book *On Drunkenness*, and Aristotle in *The Polity of Locrians*, mention that Zaleucus the Locrian received the laws from Athene.

But those who exalt the credit of Greek legislation, as far as in them lies, by referring it to a divine source, after the model of Mosaic prophecy, are senseless in not owning the truth, and the archetype of what is related among them.

CHAPTER XXVII.

THE LAW, EVEN IN CORRECTING AND PUNISHING, AIMS AT THE GOOD OF MEN.

LET no one, then, run down law, as if, on account of the penalty, it were not beautiful and good. For shall he who drives away bodily disease appear a benefactor; and shall not he who attempts to deliver the soul from iniquity, as much more appear a friend, as the soul is a more precious thing than the body? Besides, for the sake of bodily health we submit to incisions, and cauterizations, and medicinal draughts; and he who administers them is called saviour and healer, even though amputating parts, not from grudge or ill-will towards the patient, but as the principles of the art prescribe, so that the sound parts may not perish along with them, and no one accuses the physician's art of wickedness; and shall we not similarly submit, for the soul's sake, to either banishment, or punishment, or bonds, provided only from unrighteousness we shall attain to righteousness?

For the law, in its solicitude for those who obey, trains up to piety, and prescribes what is to be done, and restrains each one from sins, imposing penalties even on lesser sins.

But when it sees any one in such a condition as to appear incurable, posting to the last stage of wickedness, then in its solicitude for the rest, that they may not be destroyed by it (just as if amputating a part from the whole body), it condemns such an one to death, as the course most conducive to health. "Being judged by the Lord," says the apostle, "we are chastened, that we may not be condemned with the world."[1]

[1] 1 Cor. xi. 32.

For the prophet had said before, "Chastening, the Lord hath chastised me, but hath not given me over unto death."[1] "For in order to teach thee His righteousness," it is said, "He chastised thee and tried thee, and made thee to hunger and thirst in the desert land; that all His statutes and His judgments may be known in thy heart, as I command thee this day; and that thou mayest know in thine heart, that just as if a man were chastising his son, so the Lord our God shall chastise thee."[2]

And to prove that example corrects, he says directly to the purpose: "A clever man, when he seeth the wicked punished, will himself be severely chastised, for the fear of the Lord is the source of wisdom."[3]

But it is the highest and most perfect good, when one is able to lead back any one from the practice of evil to virtue and well-doing, which is the very function of the law. So that, when one falls into any incurable evil,—when taken possession of, for example, by wrong or covetousness,—it will be for his good if he is put to death. For the law is beneficent, being able to make some righteous from unrighteous, if they will only give ear to it, and by releasing others from present evils; for those who have chosen to live temperately and justly, it conducts to immortality. To know the law is characteristic of a good disposition. And again: "Wicked men do not understand the law; but they who seek the Lord shall have understanding in all that is good."[4]

It is essential, certainly, that the providence which manages all, be both supreme and good. For it is the power of both that dispenses salvation—the one correcting by punishment, as supreme, the other showing kindness in the exercise of beneficence, as a benefactor. It is in your power not to be a son of disobedience, but to pass from darkness to life, and lending your ear to wisdom, to be the legal slave of God, in the first instance, and then to become a faithful servant, fearing the Lord God. And if one ascend higher, he is enrolled among the sons.

[1] Ps. cxviii. 18.
[2] Deut. viii. 2, 3, 5, 11.
[3] Prov. xxii. 3, 4.
[4] Prov. xxviii. 5.

But when "charity covers the multitude of sins,"[1] by the consummation of the blessed hope, then may we welcome him as one who has been enriched in love, and received into the elect adoption, which is called the beloved of God, while he chants the prayer, saying, "Let the Lord be my God."

The beneficent action of the law, the apostle showed in the passage relating to the Jews, writing thus: "Behold, thou art called a Jew and restest in the law, and makest thy boast in God, and knowest the will of God, and approvest the things that are more excellent, being instructed out of the law, and art confident that thou thyself art a guide of the blind, a light of them who are in darkness, an instructor of the foolish, a teacher of babes, who hast the form of knowledge and of truth in the law."[2] For it is admitted that such is the power of the law, although those whose conduct is not according to the law, make a false pretence, as if they lived in the law. "Blessed is the man that hath found wisdom, and the mortal who has seen understanding; for out of its mouth," manifestly Wisdom's, "proceeds righteousness, and it bears law and mercy on its tongue."[3] For both the law and the gospel are the energy of one Lord, who is "the power and wisdom of God;" and the terror which the law begets is merciful and in order to salvation. "Let not alms, and faith, and truth fail thee, but hang them around thy neck."[4] In the same way as Paul, prophecy upbraids the people with not understanding the law. "Destruction and misery are in their ways, and the way of peace have they not known."[5] "There is no fear of God before their eyes."[6] "Professing themselves wise, they became fools."[7] "And we know that the law is good, if a man use it lawfully."[8] "Desiring to be teachers of the law, they understand," says the apostle, "neither what they say, nor whereof they affirm."[9] "Now the end of the commandment is charity out of a pure heart, and a good conscience, and faith unfeigned."[10]

---

[1] 1 Pet. iv. 8.
[2] Rom. ii. 17-20.
[3] Prov. iii. 13, 16.
[4] Prov. iii. 3.
[5] Isa. lix. 7, 8; Rom. iii. 16, 17.
[6] Ps. xiii. 3; Rom. iii. 18.
[7] Rom. i. 22.
[8] 1 Tim. i. 8.
[9] 1 Tim. i. 7.
[10] 1 Tim. i. 5.

CHAPTER XXVIII.

THE FOURFOLD DIVISION OF THE MOSAIC LAW.

THE Mosaic philosophy is accordingly divided into four parts,—into the historic, and that which is specially called the legislative, which two properly belong to an ethical treatise; and the third, that which relates to sacrifice, which belongs to physical science; and the fourth, above all, the department of theology, "vision,"[1] which Plato predicates of the truly great mysteries. And this species Aristotle calls metaphysics. Dialectics, according to Plato, is, as he says in *The Statesman*, a science devoted to the discovery of the explanation of things. And it is to be acquired by the wise man, not for the sake of saying or doing aught of what we find among men (as the dialecticians, who occupy themselves in sophistry, do), but to be able to say and do, as far as possible, what is pleasing to God. But the true dialectic, being philosophy mixed with truth, by examining things, and testing forces and powers, gradually ascends in relation to the most excellent essence of all, and essays to go beyond to the God of the universe, professing not the knowledge of mortal affairs, but the science of things divine and heavenly; in accordance with which follows a suitable course of practice with respect to words and deeds, even in human affairs. Rightly, therefore, the Scripture, in its desire to make us such dialecticians, exhorts us: "Be ye skilful money-changers,"[2] rejecting some things, but retaining what is good. For this true dialectic is the science which analyses

---

[1] ἐποπτεία; the third and highest grade of initiation into the mysteries.
[2] A saying not in Scripture; but by several of the ancient fathers attributed to Christ or an apostle.

the objects of thought, and shows abstractly and by itself the individual substratum of existences, or the power of dividing things into genera, which descends to their most special properties, and presents each individual object to be contemplated simply such as it is.

Wherefore it alone conducts to the true wisdom, which is the divine power which deals with the knowledge of entities as entities, which grasps what is perfect, and is freed from all passion; not without the Saviour, who withdraws, by the divine word, the gloom of ignorance arising from evil training, which had overspread the eye of the soul, and bestows the best of gifts,

"That we might well know or God or man."[1]

It is He who truly shows how we are to know ourselves. It is He who reveals the Father of the universe to whom He wills, and as far as human nature can comprehend. "For no man knoweth the Son but the Father, nor the Father but the Son, and he to whom the Son shall reveal Him."[2] Rightly, then, the apostle says that it was by revelation that he knew the mystery: "As I wrote afore in few words, according as ye are able to understand my knowledge in the mystery of Christ."[3] "According as ye are able," he said, since he knew that some had received milk only, and had not yet received meat, nor even milk simply. The sense of the law is to be taken in three ways,[4]—either as exhibiting a symbol, or laying down a precept for right conduct, or as uttering a prophecy. But I well know that it belongs to men [of full age] to distinguish and declare these things. For the whole Scripture is not in its meaning a single Myconos, as the proverbial expression has it; but those who hunt after the connection of the divine teaching, must approach it with the utmost perfection of the logical faculty.

---

[1] "That thou may'st well know whether he be a god or a man."—HOMER.
[2] Matt. xi. 27.   [3] Eph. iii. 3, 4.
[4] The text has τετραχῶς, which is either a mistake for τριχῶς, or belongs to a clause which is wanting. The author asserts the triple sense of Scripture—the mystic, the moral, and the prophetic.

CHAPTER XXIX.

THE GREEKS BUT CHILDREN COMPARED WITH THE HEBREWS.

WHENCE most beautifully the Egyptian priest in Plato said, "O Solon, Solon, you Greeks are always children, not having in your souls a single ancient opinion received through tradition from antiquity. And not one of the Greeks is an old man;" meaning by old, I suppose, those who know what belongs to the more remote antiquity, that is, our literature; and by young, those who treat of what is more recent and made the subject of study by the Greeks,—things of yesterday and of recent date as if they were old and ancient. Wherefore he added, "and no study hoary with time;" for we, in a kind of barbarous way, deal in homely and rugged metaphor. Those, therefore, whose minds are rightly constituted approach the interpretation utterly destitute of artifice. And of the Greeks, he says that their opinions "differ but little from myths." For neither puerile fables nor stories current among children are fit for listening to. And he called the myths themselves "children," as if the progeny of those, wise in their own conceits among the Greeks, who had but little insight; meaning by the "hoary studies" the truth which was possessed by the barbarians, dating from the highest antiquity. To which expression he opposed the phrase "child fable," censuring the mythical character of the attempts of the moderns, as, like children, having nothing of age in them, and affirming both in common—their fables and their speeches—to be puerile.

Divinely, therefore, the power which spoke to Hermas by revelation said, "The visions and revelations are for those who are of double mind, who doubt in their hearts if these things are or are not."

Similarly, also, demonstrations from the resources of erudition, strengthen, confirm, and establish demonstrative reasonings, in so far as men's minds are in a wavering state like young people's. "The good commandment," then, according to the Scripture, "is a lamp, and the law is a light to the path; for instruction corrects the ways of life."[1] "Law is monarch of all, both of mortals and of immortals," says Pindar. I understand, however, by these words, Him who enacted law. And I regard, as spoken of the God of all, the following utterance of Hesiod, though spoken by the poet at random and not with comprehension:

> "For the Saturnian framed for men this law:
> Fishes, and beasts, and winged birds may eat
> Each other, since no rule of right is theirs;
> But Right (by far the best) to men he gave."

Whether, then, it be the law which is connate and natural, or that given afterwards, which is meant, it is certainly of God; and both the law of nature and that of instruction are one. Thus also Plato, in *The Statesman*, says that the lawgiver is one; and in *The Laws*, that he who shall understand music is one; teaching by these words that the Word is one, and God is one. And Moses manifestly calls the Lord a covenant: "Behold I am my Covenant with thee,"[2] having previously told him not to seek the covenant in writing.[3] For it is a covenant which God, the Author of all, makes. For God is called Θεός, from θέσις (placing), and order or arrangement. And in the *Preaching*[4] of Peter you will find the Lord called Law and Word. But at this point, let our first Miscellany[5] of gnostic notes, according to the true philosophy, come to a close.

---

[1] Prov. vi. 23.

[2] Gen. xvii. 4. "As for me, behold, my covenant is with thee."—A.V.

[3] The allusion here is obscure. The suggestion has been made that it is to ver. 2 of the same chapter, which is thus taken to intimate that the covenant would be verbal, not written.

[4] Referring to an apocryphal book so called. [5] Στρωματεύς.

Just published, in demy 8vo, price 10s. 6d.,

ECCE DEUS:

Essays on the Life and Doctrine of Jesus Christ.

With Controversial Notes on 'Ecce Homo.'

'As a whole, it is a brilliant and masterly argument for the proper divinity of our Lord. .... Neither "Ecce Homo" nor any other representative of its class can hold its ground for a moment under the pressure of such a polemic as that of "Ecce Deus."'—*London Quarterly Review.*

'We cannot, as we should enjoy the doing, follow the writer in this brief article through the splendid conceptions which shine along his magnificent book. .... We fancy when a man is able to write a book like this, he must be tolerably indifferent to the words reviewers say about him. We have, however, great pleasure in expressing to him the gratitude we feel for a work of uncommon wealth and richness of spiritual insight, thought, and fervour.'—*Eclectic Review.*

'The author of "Ecce Deus" is a man of the highest intellectual gifts, of good scholarship, and of a pure and reverential spirit. .... He is a man rarely endowed, and we fondly hope that he may be spared to do further service to the cause he so much loves. ...... Finer sentences than those we have quoted, we make bold to say, are not found even in Jeremy Taylor.'—*Edinburgh Daily Review.*

'It is the production of a clever, sincere, religious mind. .... The style is decidedly scholarlike, forcible, and pithy. ...... Thoroughly readable in every page.'—*London Review.*

'The ability of the author is manifest, even in passages to the structure and very conception of which we should object.'—*Journal of Sacred Literature.*

'.... Such, then, is the plan of the author, and he follows it out carefully, learnedly, and piously, and the result is a most suggestive and pleasing book.'—*Clerical Journal.*

'It seems to us undeniable that the abilities of the author of "Ecce Deus" are to be spoken of with respect. There is clear evidence in the book of much earnest thinking, and that of a character which is neither shallow nor cloudy; while the style is clear, forcible, and interesting.'—*Church and State Review.*

'We read the volume to the conclusion, our interest and admiration expanding and deepening as we advanced.'—*Evangelical Repository.*

'The author of "Ecce Deus" has a mind of no common order. ...... He writes with the force, and often with the fire, of sincere conviction.'

EDINBURGH: T. AND T. CLARK.
LONDON: HAMILTON, ADAMS, AND CO.

Works Published by T. & T. Clark,

Just published, in Four Volumes 8vo, price 32s.,

THE
COMPARATIVE GEOGRAPHY OF PALESTINE

AND THE

SINAITIC PENINSULA.

BY PROFESSOR CARL RITTER, OF BERLIN.

Translated and Adapted for the Use of Biblical Students,

By WILLIAM L. GAGE.

'I have always looked on Ritter's *Comparative Geography of Palestine*, comprised in his famous "Erdkunde," as the great classical work on the subject; a clear and full résumé of all that was known of Bible Lands up to the time he wrote; and, as such, indispensable to the student of Bible Geography and History. This translation will open up a flood of knowledge to the English reader, especially as the editor is a man thoroughly imbued with the spirit of this noble-minded and truly Christian author.'—A. KEITH JOHNSTON, Esq., *Geographer in Ordinary to Her Majesty for Scotland.*

'One of the most valuable works on Palestine ever published.'—REV. H. B. TRISTRAM, *Author of 'The Land of Israel.'*

'By far the most important of Messrs. Clark's publications is this very handsome and complete edition of Ritter's *Palestine*. The great Berlin geographer can *never be out of date*; and though he did not live to complete his great work, by availing himself of the discoveries of recent explorers, yet the present editor has to a considerable extent supplied the deficiency; and we may say that, among the voluminous products of the well-known Edinburgh press, few exceed this publication in importance and completeness.'—*Christian Remembrancer, Jan. 1867.*

'To clergymen these volumes will prove not less interesting than instructive and useful. Theological students will find in them the most exhaustive storehouse of facts on the subjects existing in the language, while upon all the moot points of Palestinian and Sinaitic geography they will meet with a condensed summary of all the arguments of every writer of note, from the earliest ages down to the period of the author's death. In a word, these four volumes give the essence of the entire literature of the subject of every age and language. . . . . . The readers of these volumes have every reason to be satisfied with the result. . . . . . But it would be impossible to mention all the good things in these volumes. We must, however, say a few words upon Ritter's magnificent monograph on the situation of Ophir, which we regard as one of the gems of the work. . . . . Ritter's treatment of this apparently hopeless question is a masterpiece of mature scholarship and sound judgment. The whole monograph is a model of its kind. . . . . . What we are now saying of the monograph on the situation of Ophir is, however, applicable to everything our author wrote.'—*Spectator.*

'Mr. Gage has, with a perfect knowledge of the matter in hand, and by the use of a clear and lively style, produced a thoroughly readable book.'—*Daily Review.*

'By the publication of this geography of Palestine, Messrs. Clark have placed within the reach of a large number of students, clerical and lay, an exhaustive and comprehensive work on biblical geography, which will greatly facilitate the study of the sacred writings.'—*Churchman.*

'It is superfluous to commend a work of so peerless a character as this.'—*British Quarterly Review.*

'The translator has fulfilled his task admirably. . . . . . The book is pleasant to read, and will be found very interesting, not only by biblical students, but by the public in general.'—*Evangelical Magazine.*

38, George Street, Edinburgh.

WORKS OF PATRICK FAIRBAIRN, D.D.,
PRINCIPAL AND PROFESSOR OF THEOLOGY IN THE FREE CHURCH COLLEGE, GLASGOW.

In Two Volumes, demy 8vo, price 21s., Fourth Edition,

THE TYPOLOGY OF SCRIPTURE,
VIEWED IN CONNECTION WITH THE WHOLE SERIES OF THE DIVINE DISPENSATIONS.

'One of the most sober, profound, and thorough treatises which we possess on a subject of great importance in its bearing on Christian doctrine.'—*Archdeacon Denison's Church and State Review.*

'As the product of the labours of an original thinker and of a sound theologian, who has at the same time scarcely left unexamined one previous writer on the subject, ancient or modern, this work will be a most valuable accession to the library of the theological student. As a whole, we believe it may, with the strictest truth, be pronounced the best work on the subject that has yet been published.'—*Record.*

'A work fresh and comprehensive, learned and sensible, and full of practical religious feeling.'—*British and Foreign Evangelical Review.*

In demy 8vo, price 10s. 6d., Third Edition,

EZEKIEL, AND THE BOOK OF HIS PROPHECY:
AN EXPOSITION; WITH A NEW TRANSLATION.

In demy 8vo, price 10s. 6d., Second Edition,

PROPHECY,
VIEWED IN ITS DISTINCTIVE NATURE, ITS SPECIAL FUNCTIONS, AND PROPER INTERPRETATION.

'We would express our conviction, that if ever this state of things is to end, and the church is blest with the dawn of a purer and brighter day, it will be through the sober and well-considered efforts of such a man as Dr Fairbairn, and through the general acceptance of some such principles as are laid down for our guidance in this book.'—*Christian Advocate.*

In demy 8vo, price 10s. 6d.,

HERMENEUTICAL MANUAL;
OR, INTRODUCTION TO THE EXEGETICAL STUDY OF THE SCRIPTURES OF THE NEW TESTAMENT.

PART I. Discussion of Facts and Principles bearing on the Language and Interpretation of the New Testament.
PART II. Dissertations on particular subjects connected with the Exegesis of the New Testament.
PART III. On the Use made of Old Testament Scripture in the Writings of the New Testament.

'Dr Fairbairn has precisely the training which would enable him to give a fresh and suggestive book on Hermeneutics. Without going into any tedious detail, it presents the points that are important to a student. There is a breadth of view, a clearness and manliness of thought, and a ripeness of learning, which make the work one of peculiar freshness and interest. I consider it a very valuable addition to every student's library.' —*Rev. Dr Moore, Author of the able Commentary on 'The Prophets of the Restoration.'*

BIBLICAL, THEOLOGICAL AND ECCLESIASTICAL LITERATURE.

ON SALE BY C. J. STEWART,

11, KING WILLIAM STREET, WEST STRAND, LONDON, W.C.

Generally, Books valuable for their subjects, or from circumstances connected with their individual histories; but *particularly*, Holy Scriptures in critical editions of the Original Texts, Polyglots, Ancient Versions, etc.; the best Commentators, ancient and modern, and works in every department of Sacred Criticism; Liturgies, liturgical and ritualistic writers; Church Fathers, Middle-age Authors and Schoolmen; the Reformers and other Divines of the Sixteenth Century; the standard English and Foreign Theologians to the present time; Ecclesiastical Historians of all countries, and Monastic Histories; Illustrations of Antiquities, Ecclesiastical and Civil; Councils, Canon and Civil Law, Ecclesiastical Polity, etc.; Secular History and Antiquities.

Foreign orders promptly executed.

Catalogues issued from time to time, and sent post free.

Libraries purchased, exchanges made, valuation for legacy-duty, etc.

This day, in One Volume, crown 8vo, cloth, price 10s. 6d.,

HISTORY OF RATIONALISM;

Embracing a Survey of Protestant Theology, with an Appendix of Literature.

By JOHN F. HURST, D.D.

Revised and Enlarged from the Third American Edition.

'Rationalism is the most recent but not the least violent and insidious of all the developments of scepticism. We propose to show its historical position, and to present as faithfully as possible its antagonism to evangelical Christianity. . . . We have half conquered an enemy when we have gained a full knowledge of his strength.'—See *Author's Introduction.*

LONDON: TRÜBNER & CO., 60, PATERNOSTER ROW.

THE IMPERIAL BIBLE-DICTIONARY:

HISTORICAL, BIOGRAPHICAL, GEOGRAPHICAL, AND DOCTRINAL.

Including the Natural History, Antiquities, Manners, Customs, Religious Rites and Ceremonies mentioned in the Scriptures, and an Account of the several Books of the Old and New Testaments. By numerous Eminent Writers.

EDITED BY THE REV. PATRICK FAIRBAIRN, D.D.,

AUTHOR OF 'TYPOLOGY OF SCRIPTURE,' ETC.

Illustrated by many Hundred Engravings on Wood and Steel.

In Two Volumes, imperial 8vo, cloth, £3, 12s.

'In some important respects we think this "Dictionary of the Bible" the most satisfactory of any which have been published.'—*Churchman.*

'The matter is of the highest order, the letterpress most beautiful, and the illustrations equal to anything of the sort that has yet appeared.'—*British Standard.*

'In the doctrinal parts of the work a catholic temper is especially visible. . . . . This is one of the very best aids to the study of the Bible, for general purposes, which it has been our good fortune to be able to recommend.'—*Wesleyan Methodist Magazine.*

BLACKIE AND SON,

44, PATERNOSTER ROW, LONDON; GLASGOW, AND EDINBURGH.

The Art Journal Illustrated Catalogue.

PARIS UNIVERSAL EXHIBITION, 1867.

Edited by S. C. HALL, Esq., F.S.A.

DEDICATED, BY GRACIOUS PERMISSION,
TO THE EMPEROR OF THE FRENCH.

Each Part contains about ONE HUNDRED AND TWENTY ENGRAVINGS *of Objects of Art-Manufacture contributed to the Exhibition.*

THIS ILLUSTRATED CATALOGUE will be continued, Monthly, throughout the year 1867, and into part of the year 1868, as a portion of the *Art-Journal*,

Price Two SHILLINGS AND SIXPENCE, Monthly.

The First and Second Parts now ready. May be had of any Bookseller in Great Britain, France, Germany, and America.

LONDON: VIRTUE & CO., 26 IVY LANE, PATERNOSTER ROW, E.C.

JUST PUBLISHED BY J. & C. MOZLEY.

Principles of Religion; or, A Commentary on the Church Catechism. With 6640 Scripture Proofs, and 1007 Passages translated from early Christian Writers. By the Rev. SAMUEL PAGAN, Loverbridge, Bolton. Crown 8vo, cloth, pp. 477, 7s. 6d.
This Manual (with Proofs) treats on most subjects of Doctrine and Practice.

Selection from the Sermons of the late Rev. Samuel Rickards, Rector of Stowlangtoft; formerly Fellow of Oriel College, Oxford. Crown 8vo, cloth, 6s.

Mediæval Preachers and Mediæval Preaching. A Series of Extracts, translated from the Sermons of the Middle Ages, Chronologically arranged, with Notes and an Introduction. By the late Rev. J. M. NEALE, D.D., Warden of Sackville College, East Grinsted. Post 8vo, cloth, 7s.

Sermons, preached in Village Churches. By Wm. Jackson, M.A., Vicar of Heathfield, Sussex. Second Edition. Foolscap 8vo, cloth, 5s.

Sermons in Plain Language, adapted to the Poor. By the Rev. W. H. RIDLEY, M.A., Rector of Hambleden. Fourth Edition. Foolscap 8vo, cloth limp, 2s.; cloth boards, 2s. 6d.

The Monthly Paper of Sunday Teaching. Under the same Editorship as *The Monthly Packet*. Volumes I. to VI. Demy 8vo, cloth, 1s. 6d. each.
'A treasury of biblical information, as well as a storehouse for the teacher of a Bible class or a Sunday school.'—*Literary Churchman.*

LONDON: JOHN AND CHARLES MOZLEY, 6, PATERNOSTER ROW.

Works Published by T. & T. Clark,

JOHN ALBERT BENGEL'S
GNOMON OF THE NEW TESTAMENT.
Now First Translated into English.

WITH ORIGINAL NOTES, EXPLANATORY AND ILLUSTRATIVE.

The Translation is comprised in Five Large Volumes, demy 8vo, of (on an average) fully 550 pages each.

SUBSCRIPTION, 31s. 6d.; *or free by Post*, 35s.

The very large demand for Bengel's Gnomon enables the Publishers still to supply it at the Subscription Price.

The whole work is issued under the Editorship of the Rev. ANDREW R. FAUSSET, M.A., Rector of St Cuthbert's, York, late University and Queen's Scholar, and Senior Classical and Gold Medalist, T.C.D.

'There are few devout students of the Bible who have not long held Bengel in the highest estimation,—nay, revered and loved him. It was not, however, without some apprehension for his reputation with English readers, that we saw the announcement of a translation of his work. We feared that his sentences, terse and condensed as they are, would necessarily lose much of their pointedness and force by being clothed in another garb. But we confess gladly to a surprise at the success the translators have achieved in preserving so much of the spirit of the original. We are bound to say that it is executed in the most scholarlike and able manner. The translation has the merit of being faithful and perspicuous. Its publication will, we are confident, do much to bring back readers to the *devout* study of the Bible, and at the same time prove one of the most valuable of exegetical aids. The "getting up" of these volumes, combined with their marvellous cheapness, cannot fail, we should hope, to command for them a large sale.'—*Eclectic Review.*

In crown 8vo, price 5s.,
THE SINLESSNESS OF JESUS:
AN EVIDENCE FOR CHRISTIANITY.
BY DR C. ULLMANN.

'We warmly recommend this beautiful work as eminently fitted to diffuse, among those who peruse it, a higher appreciation of the sinlessness and moral eminence of Christ.'—*British and Foreign Evangelical Review.*

In demy 8vo, price 9s.,
GERMAN RATIONALISM
IN ITS RISE, PROGRESS, AND DECLINE. A CONTRIBUTION TO THE CHURCH HISTORY OF THE 18TH AND 19TH CENTURIES.
BY DR K. HAGENBACH.

'This is a volume we have long wished to see in our language. Hagenbach is a veteran in this field, and this volume is the ablest, and is likely to be the most useful, of his works.'—*British Quarterly Review.*

'There is not a work more seasonable, not one more likely to be productive of the best effects, not one more entitled to the study and solemn consideration of Christian people.' —*Christian Witness.*

'This volume can hardly be surpassed for the brevity and clearness, and for the skill with which the main points in the great works of the Augustan age of German literature are brought out by way of illustrating their relation, direct or indirect, to Christianity.'— *London Review.*

'A most valuable and attractive volume, and a really useful addition to our too scanty histories of the growth of religious ideas and the progress of thought.'—*Churchman.*

88, George Street, Edinburgh.

In demy 8vo, price 10s. 6d.,

INSPIRATION:
THE INFALLIBLE TRUTH AND DIVINE AUTHORITY OF THE HOLY SCRIPTURES.

BY JAMES BANNERMAN, D.D.,
PROFESSOR OF THEOLOGY, NEW COLLEGE, EDINBURGH.

'It is a volume which we commend earnestly to such of our readers as wish to look at the topic in all its bearings.'—*British Quarterly Review.*

'We look upon it as a most important and valuable contribution to our theological literature; most sound in its principles, and able in its enunciation of them.'—*Church and State Review.*

'We regard the work of Dr Bannerman as one of much merit. It is lucid and instructive, while it defends the more rigid doctrine of Inspiration.'—*Bibliotheca Sacra.*

'We welcome this treatise with peculiar pleasure, as pre-eminently a *book for the times,* possessing just those qualities, and distinguished by just those characteristics, which will make it of essential use in guiding the controversy to a wise and righteous issue. . . . . There is no doubt it is by far the most consistent, clear, well-ordered (with the exceptions noted), comprehensive book on the subject which has yet appeared.'—*Literary Churchman.*

'This volume contains incomparably the most systematic and complete discussion of this great question which has yet appeared. The various topics are treated in a very worthy manner, and most of them with a fulness, accuracy, and satisfactoriness which leave little to be desired, and go far towards raising it to the honourable position of a standard work on the question, or even *the* standard work demanded by the present state of things in the theological world.'—*British and Foreign Evangelical Review.*

In demy 8vo, price 9s.,

THE SCRIPTURE TESTIMONY TO THE HOLY SPIRIT.
BY JAMES MORGAN, D.D.,
BELFAST.

'Controversy and criticism are avoided. Scripture ideas are unfolded in a clear and popular way, so as not only to inform the judgment, but also to purify the heart.'—*Evangelical Magazine.*

'Dr Morgan's book is one of the best works on the subject of the Holy Spirit which has appeared since the days of Dr Owen, and may well become a standard work of reference on our book-shelves.'—*Christian Advocate.*

'It is thorough in its scope, and so exhaustive that there is not a passage of importance which has not come under consideration.'—*Wesleyan Times.*

BY THE SAME AUTHOR.
In demy 8vo, price 9s.,

AN EXPOSITION OF THE FIRST EPISTLE OF ST JOHN.

In Two Volumes, crown 8vo, price 12s.,

BIBLICAL STUDIES ON ST JOHN'S GOSPEL.
BY DR BESSER.

'This book is full of warm and devout exposition. Luther's own rugged words start out, boulder-like, in almost every page.'—*News of the Churches.*

'We now call attention to the great merit of this volume. The character of this commentary is practical and devotional. There are often very exquisite devotional passages, and a vein of earnest piety runs through the whole work. We recommend the book most warmly to all.'—*Literary Churchman.*

'There is a quiet, simple, penetrating good sense in what Dr Besser says, and withal a spirit of truly Christian devoutness, which the reader must feel to be in beautiful accordance with the inspired teachings which awaken it.'—*British Quarterly Review.*

WORKS PUBLISHED BY WILLIAMS AND NORGATE.

THE APOCRYPHAL GOSPELS, and other Documents relating to the History of Christ. Translated from the original in Greek, Latin, Syriac, etc., with Notes, Scriptural References, and Prolegomena. By B. HARRIS COWPER, Editor of 'The Journal of Sacred Literature,' etc. Just published, crown 8vo. Price 7s. 6d.

S. JOHN CHRYSOSTOM ON THE PRIESTHOOD. Newly translated from the Greek, with an Introduction. By B. H. COWPER. Crown 8vo, cloth, red edges. 6s.

'Mr. Cowper has displayed excellent judgment and tact in adhering closely to the text, yet presenting the thought lucidly and forcibly. . . . . . The translator's preface is an altogether admirable introduction to a first perusal of this interesting little treatise.'—*Nonconformist.*

'A careful and scholarlike rendering.'—*John Bull.*

'Mr. Cowper has done his work faithfully and well.'—*Church and State Review.*

CODEX ALEXANDRINUS. Novem Testamentum Graece, ex antiquissimo Codice Alexandrino a C. G. Woide olim descriptum: ad fidem ipsius Codicis denuo accuratius editit B. H. COWPER. 8vo, cloth. 6s.

In this edition is reproduced in modern type the exact text of the celebrated Codex Alexandrinus, without any deviation from the peculiar orthography of the MS. beyond the development of the contractions. In all other respects it will be found to be a faithful and accurate transcript; but, at the same time, in order to present at one view the entire Text of the New Testament, the few passages which are lost from the MS. have been supplied from the text of Mill, due care being taken to enclose such passages in brackets, in order to distinguish them from that which is actually existing in the Codex at the present time.

BENGELII (J. A.) GNOMON NOVI TESTAMENTI in quo ex nativa verborum vi simplicitas, profunditas, concinnitas, salubritas sensuum coelestium indicatur. Edit. III. per filium superstitem E. BENGEL quondam curata quinto recusa adjuvante J. STEUDEL. One vol, royal 8vo, cloth boards, 12s.; or half morocco, 15s.

PROPER NAMES OF THE OLD TESTAMENT, Arranged Alphabetically from the Original Text, with Historical and Geographical Illustrations, for the use of Hebrew Students and Teachers, with an Appendix of the Hebrew and Aramaic Names in the New Testament. 8vo, cloth. 4s. 6d.

THE BOOK OF GENESIS IN HEBREW, with a critically revised Text, various Readings, and Grammatical and Critical Notes, etc. By the Rev. C. H. H. WRIGHT, M.A. 8vo, cloth. 5s.

'The notes are characterized by caution and judgment. . . . . Highly creditable to the learning of the editor; and we think he has conferred a great benefit on Hebrew students by its publication.'—*Literary Churchman.*

THE BOOK OF JONAH, in Four Shemitic Versions, viz. Chaldee, Syriac, Æthiopic, and Arabic, with corresponding Glossaries. By W. WRIGHT, MS. Department, British Museum. 8vo, cloth. 4s.

A GRAMMAR OF THE EGYPTIAN LANGUAGE, as contained in the Coptic, Sahidic, and Bashmuric Dialects; together with Alphabets and Numerals in the Hieroglyphic and Enchorial Characters. By the Rev. HENRY TATTAM, D.D., F.R.S. Second edition, revised and corrected. 8vo, cloth. 9s.

ORTHODOXY, SCRIPTURE, AND REASON. An Examination of some of the Principal Articles of the Creeds of Christendom. By the Rev. WILLIAM KIRKUS, LL.B. Crown 8vo, cloth. 10s. 6d.

'Temperate and well reasoned. . . . . Students of theology will find this volume very worthy of perusal.'—*Spectator.*

'The essays are clever, and often give noble views of Christian truth.'—*Clerical Journal.*

'He writes like a worthy man, genuinely seeking after divine truth. His book may well be studied quite apart from the question of agreement or disagreement with its teachings.'—*Literary Churchman.*

WILLIAMS AND NORGATE,
14, HENRIETTA STREET, COVENT GARDEN, LONDON; and
20, SOUTH FREDERICK STREET, EDINBURGH.

WORKS PUBLISHED BY WILLIAMS AND NORGATE.

AN INTRODUCTION TO THE OLD TESTAMENT, Critical, Historical, and Theological. Containing a discussion of the most important questions belonging to the several Books. By SAMUEL DAVIDSON, D.D., LL.D. 3 vols, 8vo, cloth. 42s.

THE JOURNAL OF SACRED LITERATURE. Edited by B. HARRIS COWPER. New Series. No. I. April 1867.
CONTENTS:—1. The Church and the Working Men.—2. Rites and Ceremonies.—3. The Tripartite Nature of Man.—4. On the Eternity of Future Punishments. By the Rev. C. HOPE ROBERTSON.—5. Mr. Hinton's Metaphysical Views.—6. The Breton Bible. By Dr. TREGELLES.—7. Ritualism. By the Rev. W. KIRKUS.—8. Plea for a Revised Translation of the Scriptures.—9. The Pantheism of Auguste Comte. By J. W. JACKSON, F.A.S.L.—10. The State of Parties in the Church of England. By the Rev. C. A. Row.—11. The Book of Job. A Revised Translation. By the Rev. J. M. RODWELL, M.A.—12. The Liturgy of St. Celestine, Bishop of Rome (Syriac Text). Edited by Dr. W. WRIGHT.—13. Correspondence.—14. Reviews and Notices of Books. Price 5s., Quarterly; Annual Subscription, (prepaid,) 17s., post free.

S. ANSELMI, (Archiepisc. Cantuar.) CUR DEUS HOMO? Libri II. Foolscap 8vo. Cloth 2s.; sewed 1s. 6d.

CONTRIBUTIONS TO THE APOCRYPHAL LITERATURE OF THE NEW TESTAMENT. Collected from Syriac MSS. in the British Museum, and Edited, with an English Translation and Notes, by W. WRIGHT, LL.D., Assistant in the Department of MSS., British Museum. 8vo, cloth. 7s. 6d.

ANCIENT SYRIAC DOCUMENTS, Relative to the Earliest Establishment of Christianity in Edessa and the neighbouring Countries, from the year after our Lord's Ascension to the beginning of the Fourth Century. Discovered, Edited, Translated, and Annotated by W. CURETON, D.D., Canon of Westminster. With a Preface by W. WRIGHT, Ph.D., LL.D. 4to, cloth. 31s. 6d.

COWPER, B. H. SYRIAC GRAMMAR. The Principles of Syriac Grammar. Translated and Abridged from that of Dr. HOFFMAN, with Additions, by B. HARRIS COWPER, Editor of the 'Journal of Sacred Literature,' etc. 8vo, cloth. 7s. 6d.

SYRIAC MISCELLANIES, or Extracts Relating to the First and Second General Councils, and various other Quotations, Theological, Historical, and Classical, Translated from MSS. in the British Museum and Imperial Library of Paris, with Notes. By B. HARRIS COWPER. 8vo, cloth. 3s. 6d.

ANALECTA NICAENA. Fragments Relating to the Council of Nice. The Syriac Text from an ancient MS. in the British Museum, with a Translation, Notes, etc. By B. HARRIS COWPER. 4to. 5s.

MAR JACOB (Bp. of Edessa) SCHOLIA ON PASSAGES OF THE OLD TESTAMENT. Now first edited in the original Syriac, with an English Translation and Notes, by the Rev. G. PHILLIPS, D.D., President of Queen's College, Cambridge. 8vo, cloth. 5s.

ON THE INSPIRATION OF THE SCRIPTURES. Showing the Testimony which they themselves bear as to their own Inspiration. By JAMES STARK, M.D., F.R.S.E., Author of 'The Westminster Confession of Faith critically compared with the Holy Scriptures,' etc. Crown 8vo, cloth. 3s. 6d.

THE REVELATION OF JOHN. Edited in Greek, with a new English Version and a Statement of the chief Authorities and Various Readings. By WILLIAM KELLY, Author of 'Lectures on the Book of Revelation,' 'Lectures introductory to the Study of the Gospels,' etc. 8vo. 4s. 6d.

THE LEGENDS AND THEORIES OF THE BUDDHISTS, compared with History and Science. With Introductory Notices of the Life and System of Gotama Buddha. By R. SPENCE HARDY, Hon. M.R.A.S., Author of 'Eastern Monachism,' 'A Manual of Buddhism,' etc. Crown 8vo, cloth. 7s. 6d.
'No missionary in any part of the world where the tenets of Buddhism are held in reverence ought to be without this volume. But it will attract others besides missionaries to India and the bordering states; the student of history and of the aberrations of the human mind will find much to interest, and will be improved by the researches of the writer.'—*Churchman.*

WILLIAMS AND NORGATE,
14, HENRIETTA STREET, COVENT GARDEN, LONDON; and
20, SOUTH FREDERICK STREET, EDINBURGH.

Works Published by T. & T. Clark.

WORKS OF JOHN CALVIN,

IN 51 VOLUMES, DEMY 8vo.

Messrs CLARK beg respectfully to announce that the whole STOCK and COPYRIGHTS of the WORKS OF CALVIN, published by the Calvin Translation Society, are now their property, and that this valuable Series will be issued by them on the following very favourable terms:—

1. Complete Sets in 51 Volumes, Nine Guineas. (Original Subscription price about £13.) The 'LETTERS,' edited by Dr BONNET, 2 vols., 10s. 6d. additional.
2. Complete Sets of Commentaries, 45 vols., £7, 17s. 6d.
3. A *Selection* of SIX VOLUMES (or more at the same proportion) for 21s., with the exception of the INSTITUTES, 3 vols.
4. Any Separate Volume (except INSTITUTES), 6s.

The Contents of the Series are as follow:—

Institutes of the Christian Religion, 3 vols.
Tracts on the Reformation, 3 vols.
Commentary on Genesis, 2 vols.
Harmony of the last Four Books of the Pentateuch, 4 vols.
Commentary on Joshua, 1 vol.
    „ on the Psalms, 5 vols.
    „ on Isaiah, 4 vols.
    „ on Jeremiah and Lamentations, 5 vols.
    „ on Ezekiel, 2 vols.
    „ on Daniel, 2 vols.
    „ on Hosea, 1 vol.
    „ on Joel, Amos, and Obadiah, 1 vol.
    „ on Jonah, Micah, and Nahum, 1 vol.
    „ on Habakkuk, Zephaniah, and Haggai, 1 vol.
Commentary on Zechariah and Malachi, 1 vol.
Harmony of the Synoptical Evangelists, 3 vols.
Commentary on John's Gospel, 2 vols.
    „ on Acts of the Apostles, 2 vols.
    „ on Romans, 1 vol.
    „ on Corinthians, 2 vols.
    „ on Galatians and Ephesians, 1 vol.
    „ on Philippians, Colossians, and Thessalonians, 1 vol.
    „ on Timothy, Titus, and Philemon, 1 vol.
    „ on Hebrews, 1 vol.
    „ on Peter, John, James, and Jude, 1 vol.

In Two Volumes, 8vo, price 14s. (1300 pages),

THE INSTITUTES OF THE CHRISTIAN RELIGION.

By JOHN CALVIN.

TRANSLATED BY HENRY BEVERIDGE.

This translation of Calvin's Institutes was originally executed for the Calvin Translation Society, and is universally acknowledged to be the best English version of the work. The Publishers have reprinted it in an elegant form, and have at the same time fixed a price so low as to bring it within the reach of all.

In One Volume, 8vo, price 8s. 6d.,

CALVIN:

HIS LIFE, LABOURS, AND WRITINGS.

BY FELIX BUNGENER,

AUTHOR OF THE 'HISTORY OF THE COUNCIL OF TRENT,' ETC.

'M. Bungener's French vivacity has admirably combined with critical care and with admiring reverence, to furnish what we venture to think the best portrait of Calvin hitherto drawn. He tells us all that we need to know; and instead of overlaying his work with minute details and needless disquisitions, he simply presents the disencumbered features, and preserves the true proportions of the great Reformer's character. We heartily commend the work.'—*Patriot.*

'Few will sit down to this volume without resolving to read it to the close.'—*Clerical Journal.*

38, George Street, Edinburgh.

WORKS BY DR E. W. HENGSTENBERG.

In Two Volumes, 8vo, price 21s.,

COMMENTARY ON THE GOSPEL OF ST JOHN.

'The author has brought to bear upon his work all the resources of his long experience, his rare mental powers, his great learning, and his deep religiousness.'—*Journal of Sacred Literature.*

'We can have little hesitation in saying that the student is scarcely likely to find any other helps in reading this priceless and precious Gospel so useful as this.'—*Eclectic Review.*

'The peculiarity of this Commentary is a thorough persuasive and striking appeal, not only to Old Testament doctrine and prophecy, but also to Old Testament phraseology in the elucidation of the text; and for this the venerable author's studies have rendered him singularly competent.'

In Four Volumes, price £2, 2s., Second Edition,

CHRISTOLOGY OF THE OLD TESTAMENT,
AND A COMMENTARY ON THE MESSIANIC PREDICTIONS.

'A noble specimen of exegetical theology and critical analysis.'—*Clerical Journal.*

'The well-matured production of a great and learned man. It is thoroughly ripe in the spirit of Christian philosophy and true biblical scholarship.'—*Homilist.*

In Three Volumes, 8vo, price 33s.,

COMMENTARY ON THE PSALMS.

'We have met with no commentator who displays higher powers or sounder qualifications; and we feel persuaded, to quote the words of a very competent judge with reference to his work on the Prophecies of Daniel, that "it will leave nothing to desire."'—*Churchman's Monthly Review.*

In One Volume, 8vo, price 9s.,

COMMENTARY ON THE BOOK OF ECCLESIASTES.
TO WHICH ARE APPENDED
TREATISES ON THE SONG OF SOLOMON; ON THE BOOK OF JOB; ON THE PROPHET ISAIAH; ON THE SACRIFICES OF HOLY SCRIPTURE; AND ON THE JEWS AND THE CHRISTIAN CHURCH.

'A Commentary on this difficult book by one who has so long and so successfully devoted himself to biblical subjects, will awaken new interest in its study. As an exposition of the language and the general current of the writer's views, the work is full and rich.'—*Bibliotheca Sacra.*

In 8vo, price 7s. 6d.,

EGYPT AND THE BOOKS OF MOSES;
OR, THE BOOKS OF MOSES ILLUSTRATED BY THE MONUMENTS OF EGYPT.

In 8vo, price 12s.,

DISSERTATIONS ON THE GENUINENESS OF DANIEL AND THE INTEGRITY OF ZECHARIAH.
WITH A DISSERTATION ON THE HISTORY AND PROPHECIES OF BALAAM.

NEW WORKS

PUBLISHED BY

J. T. HAYES, LYALL PLACE, EATON SQUARE.

Price 13s. 6d.; by post 14s. 6d.,
THE VOLUME OF THE 'UNION REVIEW' FOR 1866.
A MAGAZINE OF LITERATURE AND ART,

Faithfully representing the 'Catholic' and 'Re-union' Schools in the Church of England; to which, however, Anglicans, Greeks, and Roman Catholics are constant Contributors.

(Published in Bi-Monthly Numbers, 2s. each. Yearly Subscription, 13s., including Postage.)

Price 5s.; by post, 5s. 4d.,
THE SECOND SERIES OF
SERMONS ON THE 'RE-UNION OF CHRISTENDOM.'
BY
MEMBERS OF THE ENGLISH, ROMAN, AND GREEK CHURCHES.

Price 7s.; by post 7s. 5d.,
SANCTA CLARA ON THE THIRTY-NINE ARTICLES.
REPRINTED FROM THE EDITION IN LATIN OF 1646.

With a Translation, together with Expositions and Comments in English from the Theological Problems and Propositions of the same Writer, and with Additional Notes and References.

EDITED BY THE
REV. F. G. LEE, D.C.L.,
Chaplain to the Earl of Morton.

Also, uniform with the above, 7s.; by post, 7s. 5d.,
THE LITURGY OF THE CHURCH OF SARUM.
TRANSLATED FROM THE LATIN, AND WITH AN INTRODUCTION AND EXPLANATORY NOTES.

BY CHARLES WALKER.

Price 3s. 6d.; by post, 3s. 9d.,
THE BIBLE AND ITS INTERPRETERS.
I. THE POPULAR THEORY.
II. THE ROMAN THEORY.   III. THE LITERARY THEORY.   IV. THE TRUTH.

BY W. J. IRONS, D.D.,
Prebendary of St. Paul's.

THE LAST TWO WORKS OF THE LATE REV. J. M. NEALE, D.D.

Price 2s. 6d.; by post, 2s. 9d.,
ORIGINAL SEQUENCES,
HYMNS, AND OTHER ECCLESIASTICAL VERSES;
WITH PROLOGUE IN 'MEMORY OF JOHN KEBLE.'

Also, 1s.; by post, 1s. 2d.,
STABAT MATER SPECIOSA:
'FULL OF BEAUTY STOOD THE MOTHER.'

NEW WORKS

PUBLISHED BY

J. T. HAYES, LYALL PLACE, EATON SQUARE.

Now ready. Price 6s.; by post, 6s. 4d.,

SERMONS ON THE SONG OF SONGS, Preached in the Oratory of St. Margaret's, East Grinsted. By the Rev. JOHN MASON NEALE, D.D., Founder and first Chaplain of the Sisterhood.

'It may be mentioned that in this volume there are ten Sermons which were not published in the first edition, the greater part of which were preached since the others were printed; some only a short time before the Author's decease.

When the first edition of these Sermons was published, now nearly ten years ago, it seems not unlikely that the Author withheld his name from a fear that the great cause of Sisterhoods, which he had so dearly at heart, might be compromised by any exception that might be taken to the words of one who had been called to take his stand "through evil report and good report" in the fore-ranks of the great Church movement. But whatever the reason may have been, it had, in his opinion, been removed, for he was preparing a new Edition with his name affixed, when he was seized with the painful illness, by means of which, after five months' severe suffering, it pleased his heavenly Father to call him to Himself.

These Sermons will be found of deep interest, not only as showing the varied learning of the writer, blended with a singular earnestness and gentleness of heart, all his own; but also as affording a fair example of what he believed to be the fit training and guidance for a Sisterhood, whose chief object was nursing the sick poor in their own homes. . . . . The mystical interpretation of Holy Scripture, whereby a celestial glory might be thrown on the common things of every-day life, he also deemed a true way of brightening the road to the heavenly country. And that GOD was pleased to bless his efforts, he humbly but thankfully acknowledged. What a joy to him to remember the *three* Sisters at St. Margaret's ten years before, and then to think of the *more than forty* who, in his last illness, were gathered under its different roofs!'—*Preface.*

SERMON HELP.

Now ready, the Second Edition, 8s., by Post 8s. 2d., of

THE MORAL CONCORDANCES OF ST. ANTHONY OF PADUA. Translated, verified, and adapted to modern use. By the late Rev. J. M. NEALE; with Additions from the '*Promptuarium Morale Sacræ*' of Thomas Hibernicus, an Irish Franciscan of the 14th Century. With new Preface by the Rev. Dr. LITTLEDALE.

'Is a really edited as well as translated republication of a long-forgotten attempt, made about six centuries since, to accomplish a very useful work—viz. a Concordance of Scripture texts according to identity of sense, and not of words. St. Anthony's book refers to practical topics principally, and *contains the pith of more skeleton sermons within some hundred pages, than are contained in the score of volumes which compose Mr. Simeon's* Horæ Homileticæ, *or in similar modern publications.*'—*Guardian.*

'A second edition of the late Dr. Neale's *Moral Concordance of St. Anthony of Padua* has just appeared, revised and slightly augmented from another mediæval arrangement of texts. The new issue is given to the world by Dr. Littledale. The book is one of singular utility to those who desire to penetrate into the mystical sense of Holy Scripture; and the additional matter on this subject, in Dr. Neale's few words of new preface, will be read with interest. The additional texts, dealing only with Saints' Days, are to be found, distinguished by italics, in the last seven pages of the book. They are often very beautiful. Here, for example, is one for the Martyrdom of St. Lawrence: "Take away the dross from the silver, and there shall come forth a vessel for the finer" (Prov. xxv. 4). We trust that these Concordances may obtain wide circulation amongst preachers.'—*Church Times.*

RITUALISM—THE QUESTION OF THE DAY.

Now ready. Price 4s.; by post, 4s. 3d.,

THE RITUAL 'REASON WHY:' Being an Explanation of some Four Hundred and Fifty Points of Ritual.

'An extremely valuable work. Its object is to give a concise *rationale* of Ceremonial worship. It is, in fact, a complete handbook of Ritualism. A copious index in no small degree adds to the value of the work. Woodcuts are freely used, illustrating the various vestments and furniture appertaining to public worship.'—*Church Times.*

'Is a manual of the *rationale* of Symbolism and Ceremonialism, and Liturgicism, got together by Mr. Walker with very great pains and assiduity.'—*Christian Remembrancer.*

Works Published by T. & T. Clark.

In demy 8vo, price 10s. 6d.,
A CRITICAL AND EXEGETICAL
COMMENTARY ON THE BOOK OF GENESIS.
WITH A NEW TRANSLATION.
BY JAMES G. MURPHY, LL.D., T.C.D.

'Dr Murphy has conferred a great service on a difficult department of scriptural learning.'—*Clerical Journal.*
'A work of most massive scholarship, abounding in rich and noble thought, and remarkably fresh and suggestive.'—*Evangelical Magazine.*
'This is emphatically a great work; the subject is great, and so is the management.'—*Christian Witness.*

BY THE SAME AUTHOR.
In demy 8vo, price 9s.,
A CRITICAL AND EXEGETICAL
COMMENTARY ON THE BOOK OF EXODUS.

In demy 8vo, price 10s. 6d.,
THE EARLY SCOTTISH CHURCH:
THE ECCLESIASTICAL HISTORY OF SCOTLAND FROM THE FIRST TO THE MIDDLE OF THE TWELFTH CENTURY.
BY THOMAS M'LAUCHLAN, LL.D., F.S.A.S.

'The author has given it an air of thoroughness and originality, which will justify its claim to a permanent place in literature. We do not now undertake to analyse the work, but we are able to bear witness to its genuine character.'—*Journal of Sacred Literature.*
'To those who delight to trace in the distant past the germs of the present, "The Early Scottish Church" will afford gratification and instruction.'—*Reader.*
'We regard the work before us as the most important contribution which has been made for many years towards the illustration of Early Scottish Church History.'—*United Presbyterian Magazine.*
'An able, honest work, conscientiously executed, after extensive reading, with a thorough knowledge of the ancient language and history of Scotland.'—*Inverness Courier.*
'A work marked by sound judgment, great candour, and extensive reading.'—*Nonconformist.*

In Two Volumes, demy 8vo, price 21s.,
A HISTORY OF CHRISTIAN DOCTRINE.
BY WILLIAM G. SHEDD, D.D.,
PROFESSOR OF THEOLOGY, UNION COLLEGE, NEW YORK.

'The high reputation of Dr Shedd will be increased by this remarkable work. The style is lucid and penetrating. No one can master these volumes without being quickened and strengthened.'—*American Theological Review.*
'We do not hesitate to pronounce the work a great improvement on anything we have had before. To the young student it will be valuable as a guide to his critical reading, and to the literary man it will be indispensable as a book of reference.'—*Bibliotheca Sacra.*
'We hail the appearance of the volumes as being much wanted at the present time in our own country.'—*Clerical Journal.*

In foolscap 8vo, price 5s.,
THE PARABLES OF CHRIST ILLUSTRATED & EXPOUNDED.
BY DR F. G. LISCO.

88, George Street, Edinburgh.

WORKS BY THE LATE WILLIAM CUNNINGHAM, D.D.,
PRINCIPAL AND PROFESSOR OF CHURCH HISTORY, NEW COLLEGE, EDINBURGH.
COMPLETE IN FOUR VOLUMES 8VO, PRICE £2, 2s.

In Two Volumes, demy 8vo, price 21s., Second Edition,

HISTORICAL THEOLOGY:
A REVIEW OF THE PRINCIPAL DOCTRINAL DISCUSSIONS IN THE CHRISTIAN CHURCH SINCE THE APOSTOLIC AGE.

Chapter 1. The Church; 2. The Council of Jerusalem; 3. The Apostles' Creed; 4. The Apostolical Fathers; 5. Heresies of the Apostolical Age; 6. The Fathers of the Second and Third Centuries, 7. The Church of the Second and Third Centuries; 8. The Constitution of the Church; 9. The Doctrine of the Trinity; 10. The Person of Christ; 11. The Pelagian Controversy; 12. Worship of Saints and Images; 13. The Civil and Ecclesiastical Authorities; 14. The Scholastic Theology; 15. The Canon Law; 16. Witnesses for the Truth during Middle Ages; 17. The Church at the Reformation; 18. The Council of Trent; 19. The Doctrine of the Fall; 20. Doctrine of the Will; 21. Justification; 22. The Sacramental Principle; 23. The Socinian Controversy; 24. Doctrine of the Atonement; 25. The Arminian Controversy; 26. Church Government; 27. The Erastian Controversy.

In demy 8vo (624 pages), price 10s. 6d., Second Edition,

THE REFORMERS AND THE THEOLOGY OF THE REFORMATION.

Chapter 1. Leaders of the Reformation; 2. Luther; 3. The Reformers and the Doctrine of Assurance; 4. Melancthon and the Theology of the Church of England; 5. Zwingle and the Doctrine of the Sacraments; 6. John Calvin; 7. Calvin and Beza; 8. Calvinism and Arminianism; 9. Calvinism and the Doctrine of Philosophical Necessity; 10. Calvinism and its Practical Application; 11. The Reformers and the Lessons from their History.

'This volume is a most magnificent vindication of the Reformation, in both its men and its doctrines, suited to the present time and to the present state of the controversy.' —*Witness.*

In One Volume, demy 8vo, price 10s. 6d.,

DISCUSSIONS ON CHURCH PRINCIPLES:
POPISH, ERASTIAN, AND PRESBYTERIAN.

Chapter 1. The Errors of Romanism; 2. Romanist Theory of Development; 3. The Temporal Sovereignty of the Pope; 4. The Temporal Supremacy of the Pope; 5. The Liberties of the Gallican Church; 6. Royal Supremacy in Church of England; 7. Relation between Church and State; 8. The Westminster Confession on Relation between Church and State; 9. Church Power; 10. Principles of the Free Church; 11. The Rights of the Christian People; 12. The Principle of Non-Intrusion; 13. Patronage and Popular Election.

In Two Volumes, demy 8vo, price 21s.,

INTRODUCTION TO THE PENTATEUCH:
AN INQUIRY, CRITICAL AND DOCTRINAL, INTO THE GENUINENESS, AUTHORITY, AND DESIGN OF THE MOSAIC WRITINGS.
BY REV. D. MACDONALD.

'The object of this work is very opportune at the present time. It contains a full review of the evidences, external and internal, for the genuineness, authenticity, and divine character of the Pentateuch. While it gives full space and weight to the purely critical and historical portions of the inquiry, its special attention is devoted to the certainly more profound and more conclusive considerations derived from the connection between the Pentateuch and the great scheme of revelation, of which it forms the basis; and this portion of the work is that upon which the author lays most stress. We entirely agree with him in his view of its importance. The work is singularly complete also in its view of the literature of the subject, as well as in the outline of its plan.'—*Guardian.*

STANDARD THEOLOGICAL WORKS.

Joseph Addison Alexander, D.D.

THE GOSPEL ACCORDING TO ST. MATTHEW EXPLAINED. Post 8vo, 5s., cloth.

THE GOSPEL ACCORDING TO ST. MARK EXPLAINED. Post 8vo, 7s. 6d.

THE ACTS OF THE APOSTLES EXPLAINED. Two Volumes, post 8vo, 15s.

The Rev. Edward Williams, D.D.

THE WORKS OF THE REV. EDWARD WILLIAMS, D.D. Edited by EVAN THOMAS. Four Volumes, post 8vo, 27s.

Archdeacon Pratt.

ECLECTIC NOTES; or, Notes of Discussions at Meetings of the Eclectic Society, London, during the Years 1798–1814. New Edition. 8vo, 10s. 6d.

Charles Hodge, D.D.

A COMMENTARY ON ST. PAUL'S EPISTLE TO THE EPHESIANS. Crown 8vo, 3s. 6d.

A COMMENTARY ON THE FIRST EPISTLE TO THE CORINTHIANS. Post 8vo, 5s.

A COMMENTARY ON THE SECOND EPISTLE TO THE CORINTHIANS. Post 8vo, 5s.

Rev. Thomas West.

TEN YEARS IN SOUTH-CENTRAL POLYNESIA: Being Reminiscences of a Personal Mission to the Friendly Islands and their Dependencies. 8vo, 12s., cloth.

Rev. A. A. Bonar.

A COMMENTARY ON LEVITICUS, EXPOSITORY AND PRACTICAL, 8vo, 8s. 6d.

CHRIST AND HIS CHURCH IN THE BOOK OF PSALMS. Demy 8vo, 10s. 6d.

Rev. A. Moody Stuart.

CAPERNAUM, AS THE SPHERE OF CHRIST'S MIRACLES AND MINISTRY, FROM ITS FIRST LOVE TO ITS GREAT DECLENSION. Crown 8vo, 5s.

THE SONG OF SONGS: A Practical Exposition of the Song of Solomon. With Critical Notes. 8vo, 12s.

Rev. Horatius Bonar, D.D.

PROPHETICAL LANDMARKS: Containing Data for helping to Determine the Question of Christ's Pre-Millenial Advent. Crown 8vo, 5s.

CATECHISMS OF THE SCOTTISH REFORMATION. With Preface and Notes. Crown 8vo, 6s.

LONDON: JAMES NISBET & CO., 21, BERNERS STREET, W.

Published Monthly, price Three Shillings and Sixpence,

THE BRITISH AND FOREIGN EVANGELICAL REVIEW.

CONTENTS of No. LX., for APRIL 1867.

1. The Divine and Human Natures in Christ.
2. The Liberal Theology.
3. The Sensational Philosophy—Mr. J. S. Mill's Theory of Mind.
4. Renan's History of the Apostles.
5. The Organized Structure of the New Testament.
6. Trials of Irving and Campbell of Row.
7. Cyclopædia Literature.
8. Interpretation of the Psalms.
9. The Antiquity of Man.
10. General Literature.
11. Foreign Literature.
12. Critical Notices.

THIS long-established Review is conducted on the principles by which it has been characterized since its commencement. The theological sentiments of the Editor and his Contributors are substantially those expressed in the Scottish Confession of Faith, and are sufficiently indicated by the term 'Evangelical.' Indebted, almost equally, to writers in all the three kingdoms, it cannot be fairly charged with national or party bias, and may be considered as reflecting the sentiments of all who love the blessed Evangel of Jesus Christ. To speak the truth in love,—to meet error in the varied phases which it has assumed in modern times,—to handle the religious questions now agitating the public mind,—to mark the progress of science in its relations to revealed truth, —to canvass the merits of important and interesting publications as they appear, —such are the main objects of this Periodical. In the treatment of these topics the most earnest exertions have been made to blend the thorough and scientific discussion demanded by the student of theology, with the popular and literary element so essential to render any periodical of the kind readable and attractive in our day.

An interesting feature of this *Review* is the attention devoted to the Religious Literature of France, Germany, and America. It is arranged that each Number shall contain a Compend of American Journals, and an Analysis of important German or other foreign works, embodying their substance, and accompanied with extracts and annotations. With these advantages, and aided by a competent staff of home contributors and foreign correspondents, it is confidently hoped that the *British and Foreign Evangelical Review* will retain the estimation in which it has ever been held by the religious public, and that its circulation will be still more widely extended.

LONDON: JAMES NISBET & CO., 21, BERNERS STREET, W.

Works Published by T. & T. Clark.

In Five Volumes, demy 8vo, £2, 12s. 6d.,
HISTORY OF THE DEVELOPMENT OF THE DOCTRINE OF THE PERSON OF CHRIST.

By Dr J. A. DORNER,
PROFESSOR OF THEOLOGY, GÖTTINGEN.

TO WHICH IS ADDED, A
HISTORICAL AND CRITICAL REVIEW OF THE CONTROVERSIES ON THE SUBJECT WHICH HAVE BEEN AGITATED IN BRITAIN SINCE THE MIDDLE OF THE SEVENTEENTH CENTURY TO THE PRESENT TIME.

By the Rev. Dr FAIRBAIRN, Author of 'The Typology of Scripture,' etc.

'We earnestly recommend this most valuable and important work to the attention of all theological students. So great a mass of learning and thought so ably set forth, has never before been presented to English readers, at least on this subject.'—*Journal of Sacred Literature.*

In crown 8vo, price 7s. 6d.,
THE PROPHECIES OF DANIEL AND THE REVELATION OF ST JOHN IN THEIR MUTUAL RELATION.

By Professor AUBERLEN.

'One of the latest contributions to the study of Apocalyptic prophecy. It is one of a very high order, and which must command attention. The author appears to us to possess, in no ordinary degree, those faculties of head and heart so absolutely necessary for the prosecution of this most difficult branch of sacred exegesis.'—*Ecclesiastic.*

In demy 8vo, price 10s. 6d.,
COMMENTARY ON THE PENTATEUCH.

By OTTO VON GERLACH.

'This work possesses a high character among the Evangelical parties in Germany. It is decidedly orthodox and conservative in its statements; and its spirit and its publication here will confer a great service on sacred literature.'—*Clerical Journal.*

WORKS BY PROFESSOR THOLUCK.

In 8vo, price 10s. 6d.,
COMMENTARY ON THE SERMON ON THE MOUNT.

'Its learning is exhaustive, it avoids no difficulties, and in its exegesis it seizes always the kernel of a passage, and thoroughly and soundly builds up a fair and complete exposition.'—*London Guardian.*

In One Volume, price 9s.,
COMMENTARY ON THE GOSPEL OF ST JOHN.

In crown 8vo, price 5s., Second Edition,
LIGHT FROM THE CROSS.
SERMONS ON THE PASSION OF OUR LORD.

'With no ordinary confidence and pleasure we commend these most noble, solemnizing, and touching discourses.'—*British and Foreign Evangelical Review.*

38, George Street, Edinburgh.

In Eight Volumes, demy 8vo, £4, 4s.,

THE WORDS OF THE LORD JESUS.
BY RUDOLPH STIER, D.D.,
DOCTOR OF THEOLOGY, AND SUPERINTENDENT OF SCHKEUDITZ.

'We know no work that contains, within anything like the same compass, so many pregnant instances of what true genius under chastened submission to the control of a sound philology, and gratefully accepting the seasonable and suitable helps of a wholesome erudition, is capable of doing in the spiritual exegesis of the sacred volume. Every page is fretted and studded with lines and forms of the most alluring beauty. At every step the reader is constrained to pause and ponder, lest he should overlook one or other of the many precious blossoms that, in the most dazzling profusion, are scattered around his path. We venture to predict that his "Words of Jesus" are destined to produce a great and happy revolution in the interpretation of the New Testament in this country.' —*British and Foreign Evangelical Review.*

'One of the most precious books for the spiritual interpretation of the Gospels.'—*Archdeacon Hare.*

'Dr Stier brings to the exposition of our Lord's discourses sound learning, a vigorous understanding, and a quick discernment; but what is better, he brings also a devout mind, and a habit of thought spiritual and deferential to the truth.'—*Evangelical Christendom.*

BY THE SAME AUTHOR.
In One Volume, demy 8vo, 10s. 6d.,

THE WORDS OF THE RISEN SAVIOUR,
AND
COMMENTARY ON THE EPISTLE OF ST JAMES.

'This volume is in all respects alike remarkable and valuable. We are unable to name any exposition so novel, so striking, so instructive, and so edifying. It cannot fail to bring forward those portions of Scripture—portions of infinite moment—which have hitherto, in a great degree, been neglected. The exposition is everywhere most excellent, and adapted to be helpful to the public instructor as well as to the private student. . . The latter half of this volume consists of thirty-two discourses expounding the Epistle of James. By these sermons we set great store. Nothing can be more full, clear, scriptural, and practical.'—*Christian Witness.*

In One Thick Volume, 12s., Fifth Edition,

A GRAMMAR OF THE NEW TESTAMENT DICTION.
INTENDED AS AN INTRODUCTION TO THE CRITICAL STUDY OF THE GREEK NEW TESTAMENT.
BY DR G. B. WINER.

Extract from letter from the late Archdeacon HARDWICK, *Christian Advocate:*—
'It is a subject of sincere pleasure to all critics of the sacred text that this elaborate and exhaustive treatise is at length in a fair way of becoming familiar to England as it has long been to Germany. I have great pleasure in commending it to my divinity class.'

'This is the standard classical work on the Grammar of the New Testament, and it is of course indispensable to every one who would prosecute intelligently the critical study of the most important portion of the inspired record. It is a great service to render such a work accessible to the English reader.'—*British and Foreign Evangelical Review.*

'We gladly welcome the appearance of Winer's great work in an English translation, and most strongly recommend it to all who wish to attain to a sound and accurate knowledge of the language of the New Testament. We need not say it is *the* Grammar of the New Testament. It is not only superior to all others, but so superior as to be by common consent the one work of reference on the subject. No other could be mentioned with it.' —*Literary Churchman.*

WORKS FOR MINISTERS AND STUDENTS.

The Christian Year-Book; containing a Summary of Christian Work, and the Results of Missionary Effort throughout the World. Price 4s., watered cloth.

The First Volume of the Pulpit Analyst. Elegantly bound in cloth, price 7s. 6d. Also published Monthly, price 6d.

'It is impossible to conceive how any preacher can read it habitually without feeling his mind strengthened, his thought stimulated, and his efficiency in his work promoted.'—*Morning Star*.

Idolatries, Old and New: their Cause and Cure. By J. Baldwin Brown, B.A., Author of 'The Home Life,' etc. Crown 8vo, 5s., cloth.

BY THE SAME AUTHOR,

1. *The Divine Life in Man. Second Edition.* 7s. 6d.
2. *The Divine Treatment of Sin. Crown 8vo, 5s., cloth.*
3. *The Divine Mystery of Peace. Crown 8vo, 3s., cloth.*
4. *The Doctrine of the Divine Fatherhood in relation to the Atonement.* Cloth limp, 1s. 6d.

Ecclesiastical History; from the Opening of the Long Parliament to the Death of Oliver Cromwell. By JOHN STOUGHTON, Author of 'Church and State Two Hundred Years Ago.' In 2 vols. 8vo, price 28s., cloth.

'We hail the publication of these volumes as a valuable contribution to the history of a grand period of our English annals. The matter is thoroughly digested and clearly unfolded. Presented in a clear and well-wrought style by one who is master of his subject, it holds the reader with unfailing interest.'—*London Quarterly Review*.

Memorials of the Clayton Family; with Unpublished Letters of the Countess of Huntingdon, Lady Glenorchy, Rev. John Newton, etc. etc. By the Rev. THOMAS AVELING, Kingsland. In one vol. 8vo, with Portraits, cloth, price 12s.

Jesus Christ: His Times, Life, and Work. By E. de Pressensé, D.D. 8vo, 14s., cloth.

'He has written on the greatest of all subjects, and has written with a simplicity of intention to instruct, with a ripeness of ability, and learning, and Christian wisdom, and a largeness of apprehension well worthy to be devoted to the illustration of so great and sacred a theme.'—*Contemporary Review*.

'M. de Pressensé's work is characterized by the learning, patience, brilliance, and insight which have given him so high a place among the literary men of Europe.'—*British Quarterly Review*.

Discourses delivered on Special Occasions. By R. W. Dale, M.A. Crown 8vo, 6s., cloth.

'In Mr. Dale's 'Discourses on Special Occasions' we have some of the finest specimens of modern preaching.'—*Contemporary Review*.

'It is long since we read sermons more full of stimulating thought, of catholic sympathies, of manly and noble eloquence.'—*British Quarterly Review*.

The Jewish Temple and the Christian Church. By the same Author. A Series of Discourses on the Epistle to the Hebrews. Crown 8vo, 7s. 6d., cloth.

Symbols of Christ. By Charles Stanford. Crown 8vo, 7s., cloth.

'Mr. Stanford has an order of mind, and has acquired habits of study, eminently adapting him to be a teacher of wise and thoughtful men.'—*Evangelical Magazine*.

Central Truths. By the same Author. Second Edition, in small crown 8vo, 3s. 6d., cloth.

'A brief and sound view of evangelical truth, in attractive language. The style possesses the uncommon charm of being at once rich and clear.'—*Record*.

Instrumental Strength. By the same Author. Thoughts for Students and Pastors. 1s., cloth.

Money: a Popular Exposition in Rough Notes. With Remarks on Stewardship and Systematic Beneficence. By Rev. THOMAS BINNEY. Third Edition, crown 8vo, 5s., cloth.

'Mr. Binney has here dealt with a great practical subject, and has treated it in his usual clear, masterly, and suggestive style.'—*British Quarterly Review*.

The Practical Power of Faith. By the same Author. Crown 8vo, 5s., cloth.

LONDON: JACKSON, WALFORD, & HODDER, 27, PATERNOSTER ROW.

Demy 8vo, cloth antique, 10s. 6d.,

SERMONS, PRAYERS, AND PULPIT ADDRESSES.

By ALEXANDER HENDERSON.

DELIVERED IN ST. ANDREWS AND LEUCHARS IN THE YEAR 1638.

Edited by the Rev. R. THOMSON MARTIN, Wishaw.

EDINBURGH: JOHN MACLAREN.
London: HAMILTON, ADAMS, AND CO., and SIMPKIN, MARSHALL, AND CO.

In 2 vols., crown 8vo, cloth, price 12s.,

THE WORKS OF THE REV. JOHN MACLAURIN.

Edited by W. H. GOOLD, D.D., Edinburgh.

'We heartily commend this new and complete edition of Maclaurin's works, and hope it will find a place in every theological library.'—*North British Review.*

EDINBURGH: JOHN MACLAREN.
London: HAMILTON, ADAMS, AND CO., and SIMPKIN, MARSHALL, AND CO.

In crown octavo, price 6s.,

THE REDEEMER:

DISCOURSES BY E. DE PRESSENSÉ, D.D.

WITH INTRODUCTION BY W. LINDSAY ALEXANDER, D.D.

'The whole volume is marked by a rare richness of thought and illustration, and by a high and fervid eloquence.'—*Evangelical Magazine.*

'De Pressensé stands forth as one of the most zealous, fearless, and eloquent defenders of evangelical truth and the claims of the Bible. A man of high culture and large intellectual resources, gifted with remarkable powers of clear, pointed, and eloquent discourse, he has ever shown himself ready to consecrate his best energies to the defence and propagation of the Gospel of Christ.'—*Dr Lindsay Alexander.*

BY THE SAME AUTHOR.

In demy 8vo, price 7s. 6d.,

THE RELIGIONS BEFORE CHRIST:

BEING AN INTRODUCTION TO THE HISTORY OF THE FIRST THREE CENTURIES OF THE CHURCH.

'Stamped with the true genius of a historian, and imbued with the devoutness of a Christian.'—*Patriot.*

In Two Volumes, demy octavo, price 21s.,

MEDIATORIAL SOVEREIGNTY:

THE MYSTERY OF CHRIST AND THE REVELATION OF THE OLD AND NEW TESTAMENTS.

BY GEORGE STEWARD.

'A large and exhaustive work, with great fulness of argument.'—*Christian Remembrancer.*

'Certainly one of the books of the age,—we might say of the century. Anything more massive, comprehensive, and thoroughly theological we cannot name. The author has achieved a noble triumph on behalf of the cause he loves.'—*Christian Witness.*

EDINBURGH: T. AND T. CLARK, 38, GEORGE STREET.

Works Published by T. & T. Clark, Edinburgh.

In demy 8vo, price 10s. 6d., Second Edition,

THE GOSPEL HISTORY:

A COMPENDIUM OF CRITICAL INVESTIGATIONS IN SUPPORT OF THE HISTORICAL CHARACTER OF THE FOUR GOSPELS.

BY DR J. H. A. EBRARD,
PROFESSOR OF THEOLOGY IN THE UNIVERSITY OF ERLANGEN.

'Nothing could have been more opportune than the republication in English of this admirable work. It has long been highly valued in Germany, and has done most effective service against the many assailants of the Gospels in that country. . . . . . . We are heartily glad that such a thorough and comprehensive work on the vital subject of the Gospels should at this moment have been presented to the British public, and we anticipate much good from it, in view of the attacks which have already been made, and which will doubtless for a time be continued, on the inestimably precious records of our Saviour's life.'—*British and Foreign Evangelical Review.*

'Executed with the hand of a master; Ebrard is on countless matters of detail, as well as principle, invaluable. Let our University students acquaint themselves with such a work as this, and they will find their own way safely to the rest of our Gospel literature.' —*Literary Churchman.*

BY THE SAME AUTHOR.
In demy 8vo, price 10s. 6d.,

COMMENTARY ON THE EPISTLE TO THE HEBREWS.

In demy 8vo, price 10s. 6d.,

COMMENTARY ON THE EPISTLES OF ST JOHN.

'Dr Ebrard is one of the finest of German evangelical scholars in the department of philology and criticism. He has comprehensiveness of intellect, and is eminent for spiritual insight and theological depth.'—*Nonconformist.*

In Three Volumes, demy 8vo, price 31s. 6d.,

BIBLICAL COMMENTARY ON THE PENTATEUCH.

BY PROFESSORS KEIL AND DELITZSCH.

'There is a life in the criticisms, a happy realizing power in the words, which will make this work most acceptable. The Commentary, while it is verbal and critical, has also the faculty of gathering up and generalizing the lesson and the story, which will add immensely to its value. It aims to be an exegetical handbook, by which some fuller understanding of the Old Testament economy of salvation may be obtained from a study in the light of the New Testament teachings.'—*Eclectic Review.*

'We can safely recommend this work to the clergy and others who desire to study the Bible as the *Word of God*.'—*Scottish Guardian.*

BY THE SAME AUTHORS.
In 8vo, price 10s. 6d.,

Biblical Commentary on Joshua, Judges, and Ruth.

In Two Volumes, 8vo, price 21s.,

REFORMERS BEFORE THE REFORMATION.

PRINCIPALLY IN GERMANY AND THE NETHERLANDS.

BY DR CARL ULLMANN.

'Beyond doubt one of the finest ornaments of the recent theology of Germany, and a masterpiece of historical research and composition, as profound as it is clear.'—*Dr Schaff.*

www.ingramcontent.com/pod-product-compliance
Lightning Source LLC
Chambersburg PA
CBHW020832020526
44114CB00040B/594